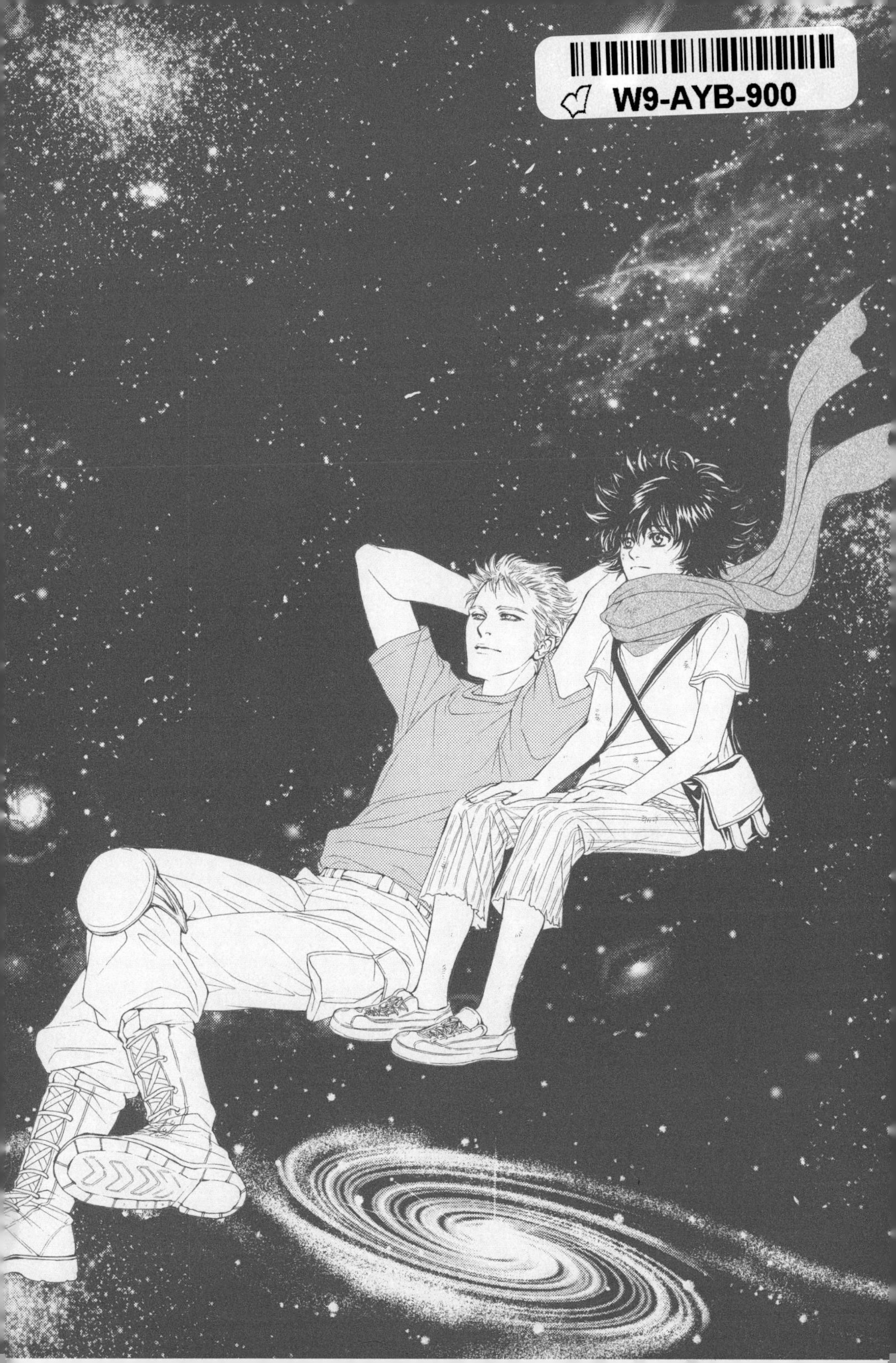

One thousand and one nights

vol. 7

Han SeungHee
Jeon JinSeok

Yen Press

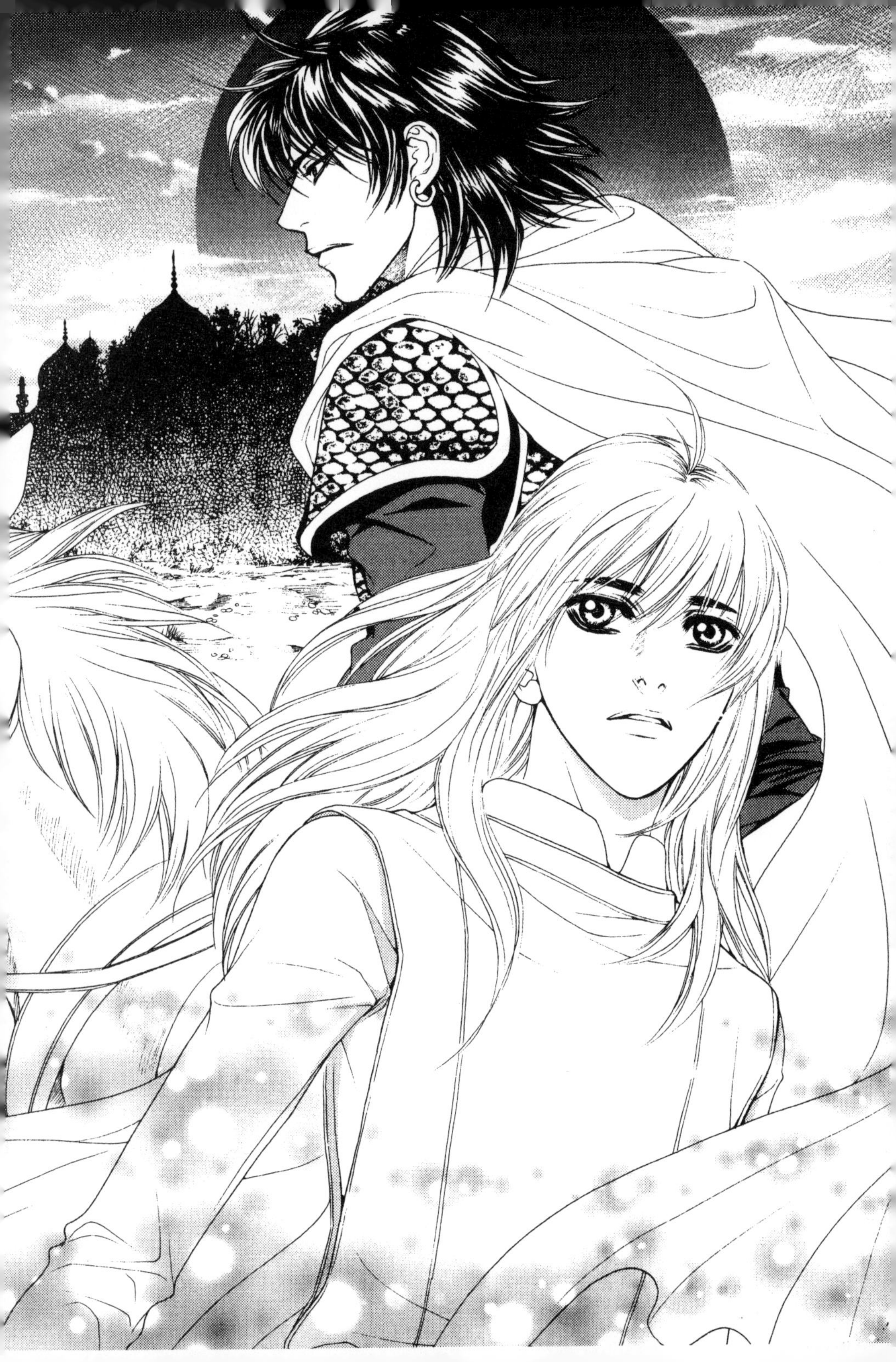

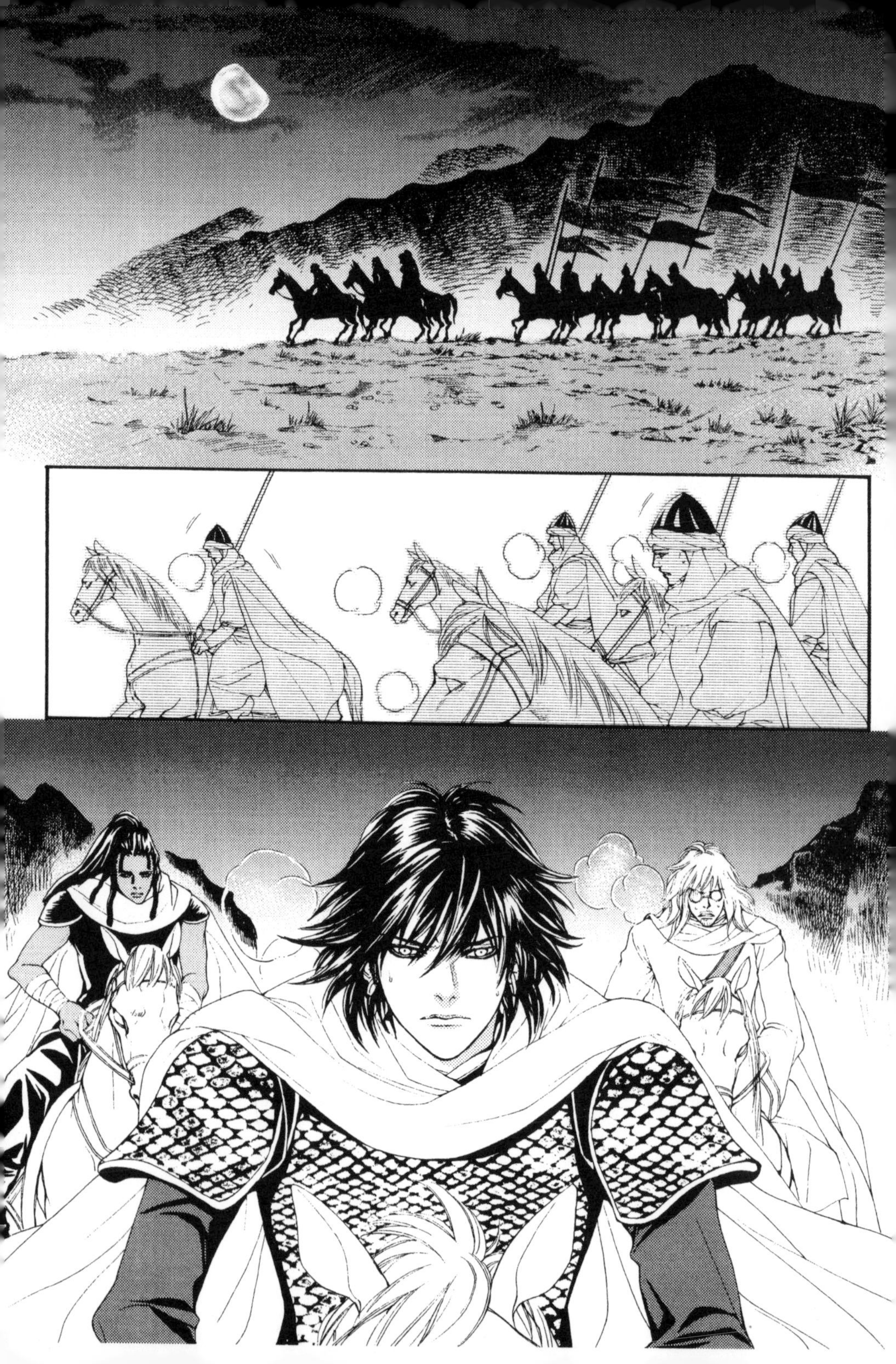

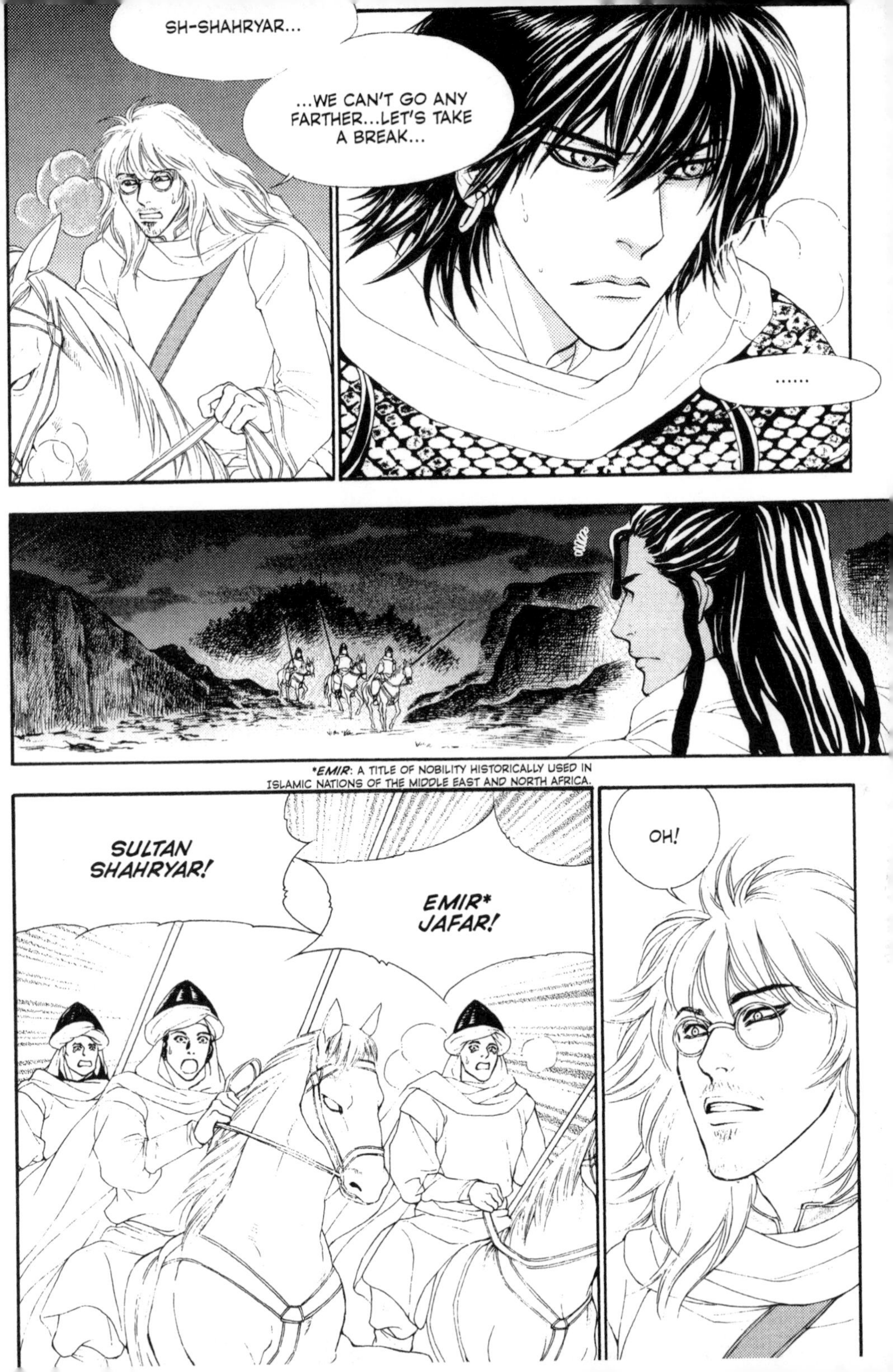
SH-SHAHRYAR...
...WE CAN'T GO ANY FARTHER...LET'S TAKE A BREAK...
......
SULTAN SHAHRYAR!
EMIR* JAFAR!
OH!

*EMIR: A TITLE OF NOBILITY HISTORICALLY USED IN ISLAMIC NATIONS OF THE MIDDLE EAST AND NORTH AFRICA.

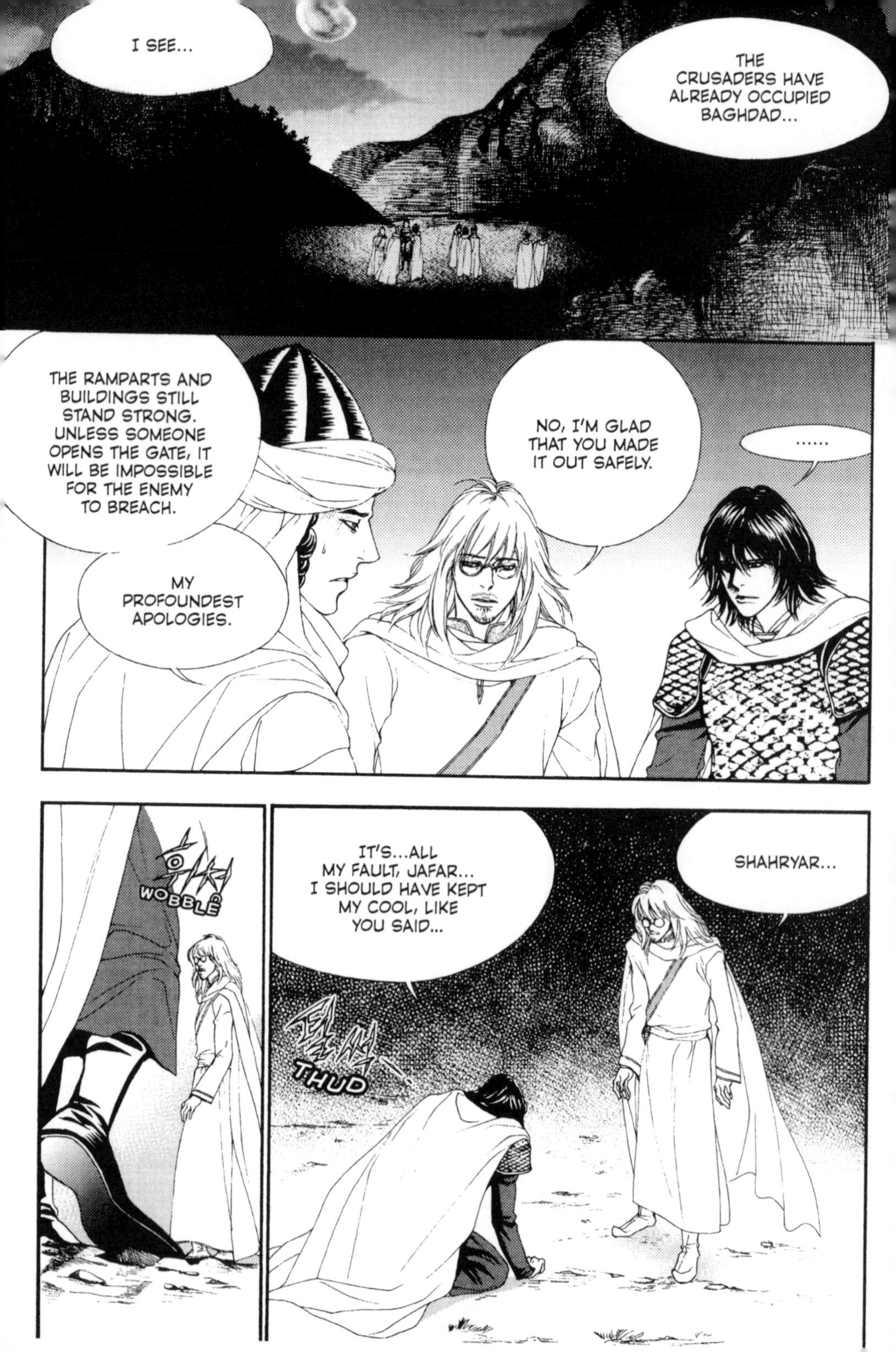
I SEE...
THE CRUSADERS HAVE ALREADY OCCUPIED BAGHDAD...
THE RAMPARTS AND BUILDINGS STILL STAND STRONG. UNLESS SOMEONE OPENS THE GATE, IT WILL BE IMPOSSIBLE FOR THE ENEMY TO BREACH.
MY PROFOUNDEST APOLOGIES.
NO, I'M GLAD THAT YOU MADE IT OUT SAFELY.
......
WOBBLE
IT'S...ALL MY FAULT, JAFAR... I SHOULD HAVE KEPT MY COOL, LIKE YOU SAID...
SHAHRYAR...
THUD

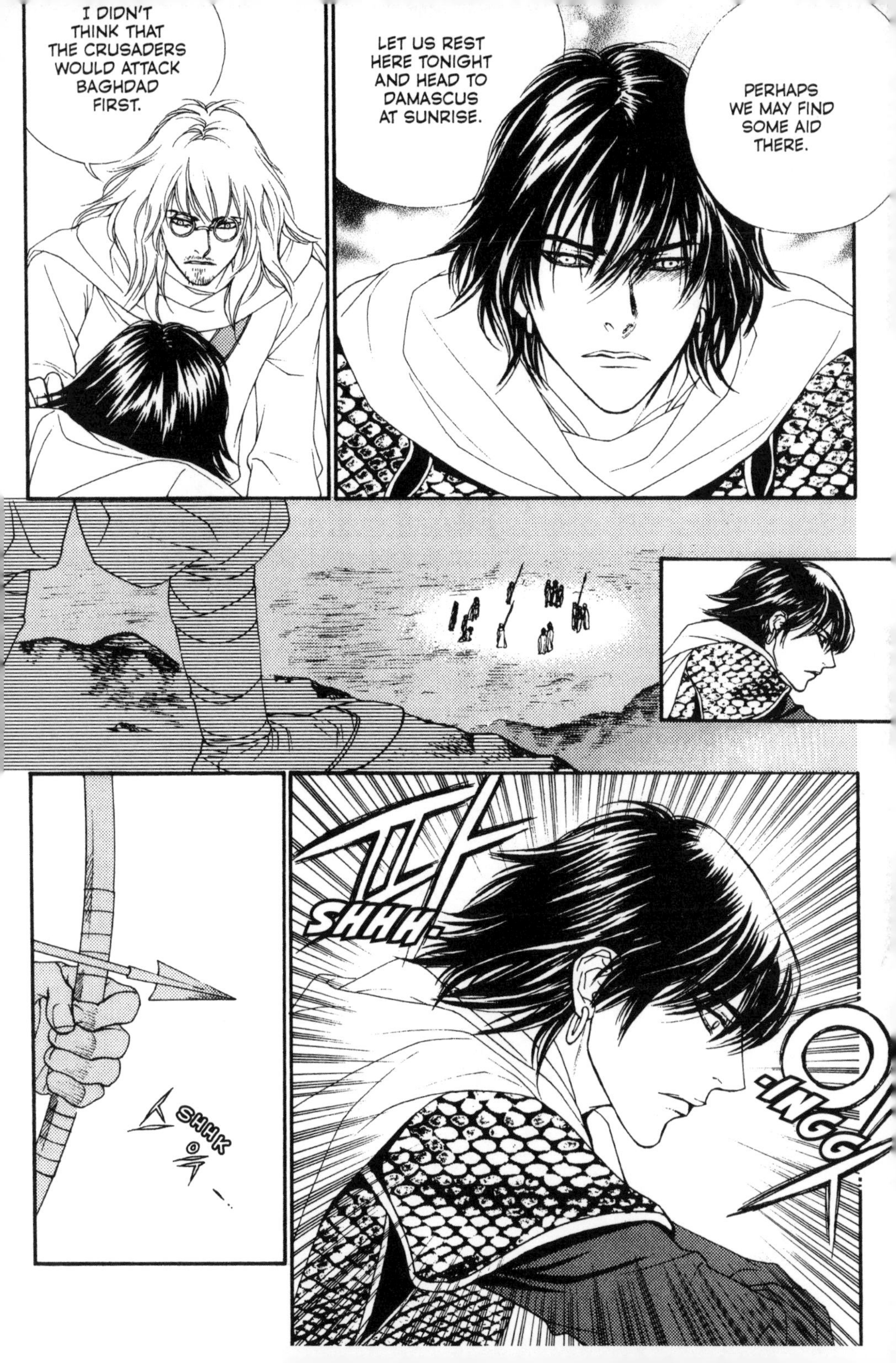
I DIDN'T THINK THAT THE CRUSADERS WOULD ATTACK BAGHDAD FIRST.
LET US REST HERE TONIGHT AND HEAD TO DAMASCUS AT SUNRISE.
PERHAPS WE MAY FIND SOME AID THERE.
SHHH.
SHHK
-INGG

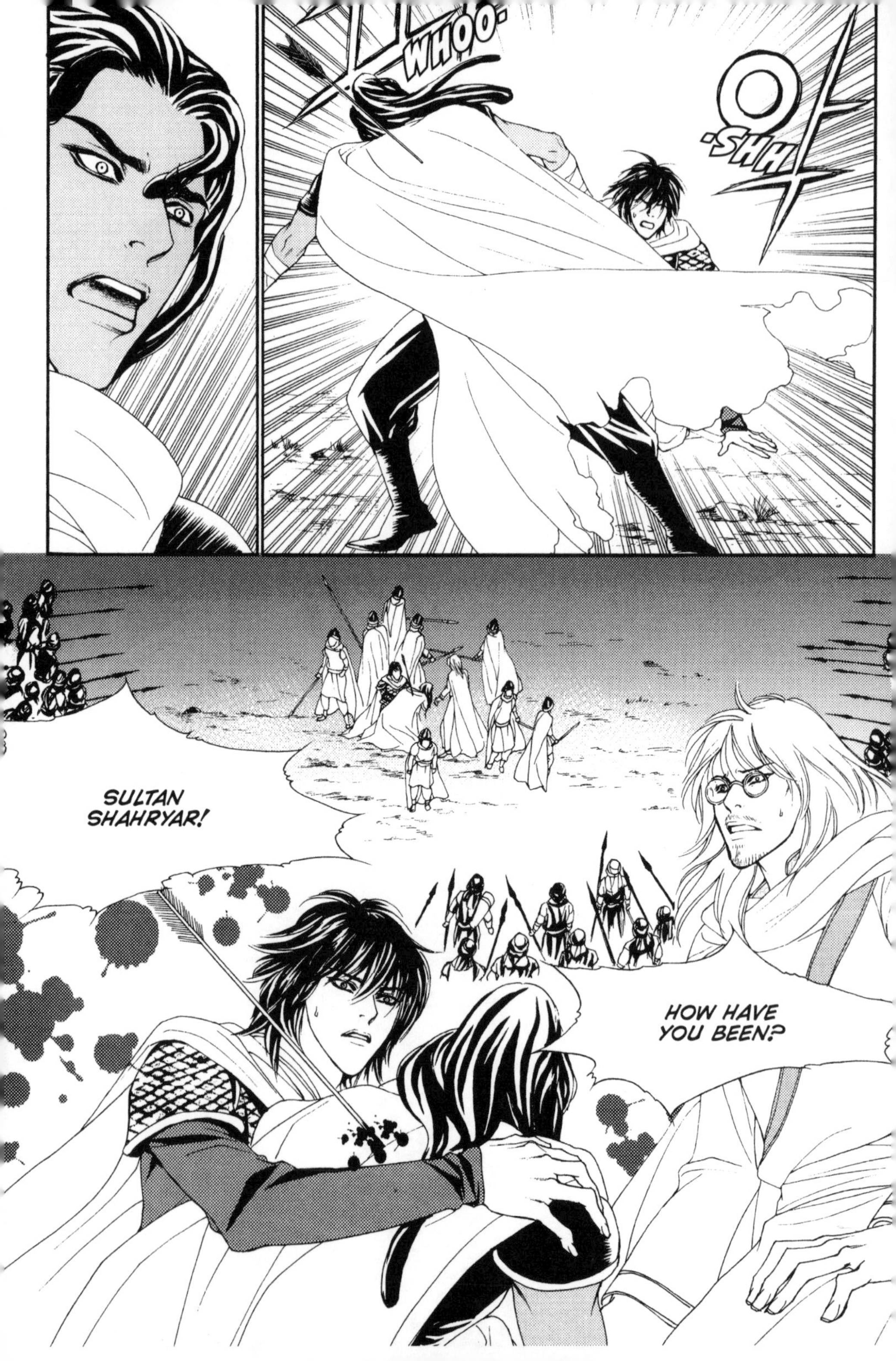
WHOO-
O
-SHH
SULTAN
SHAHRYAR!
HOW HAVE
YOU BEEN?

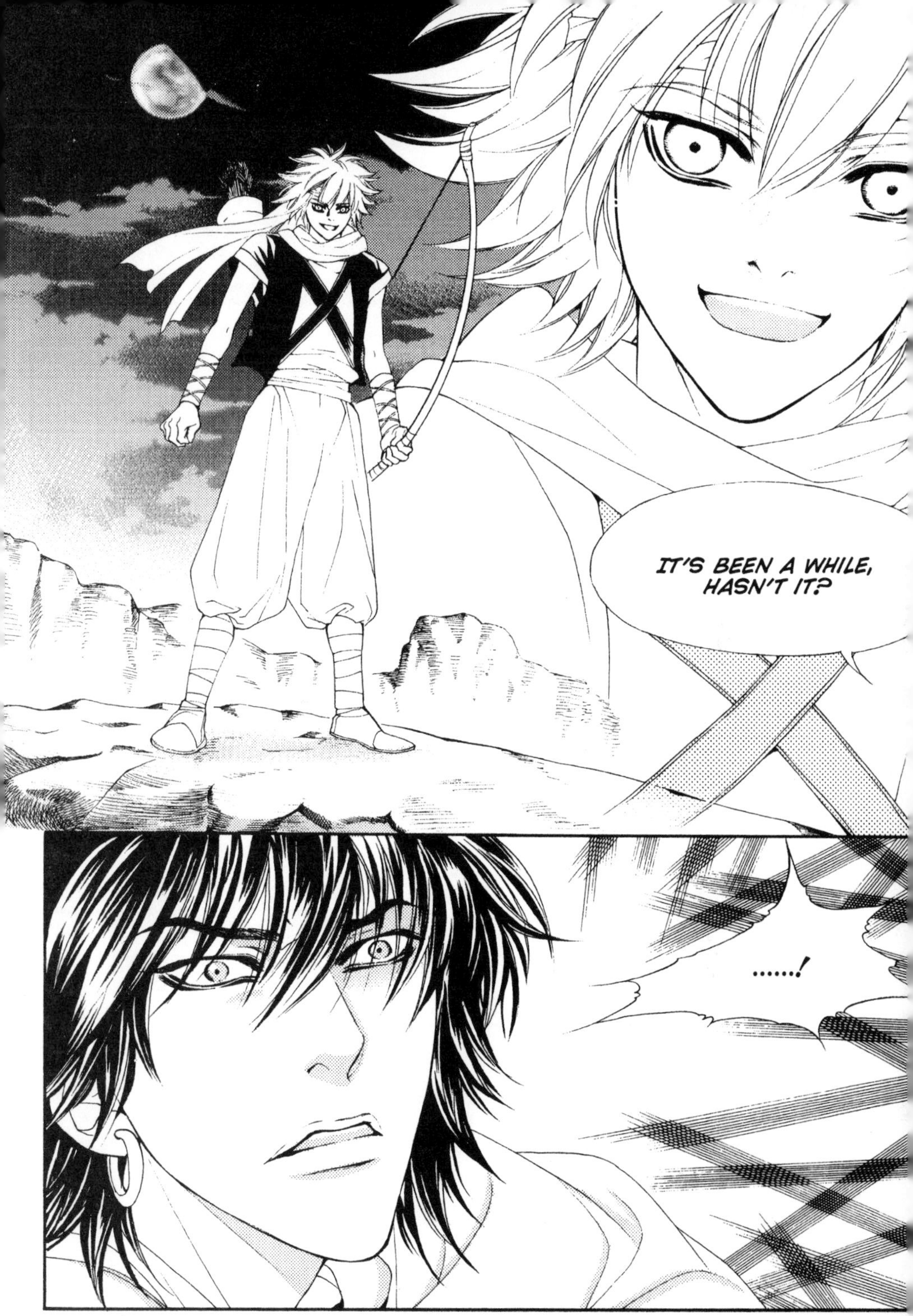
IT'S BEEN A WHILE, HASN'T IT?
......!

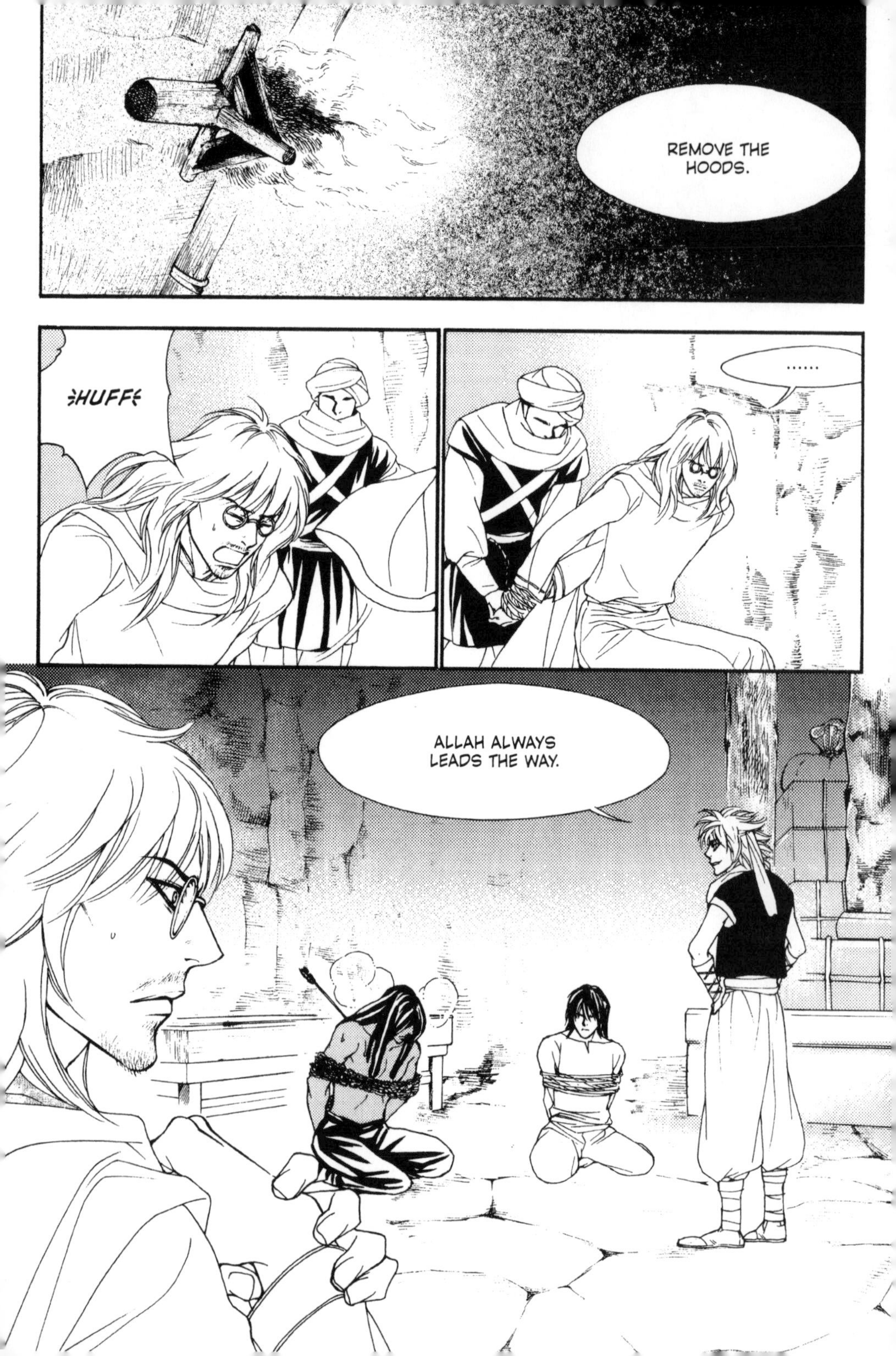
REMOVE THE HOODS.
HUFF
......
ALLAH ALWAYS LEADS THE WAY.

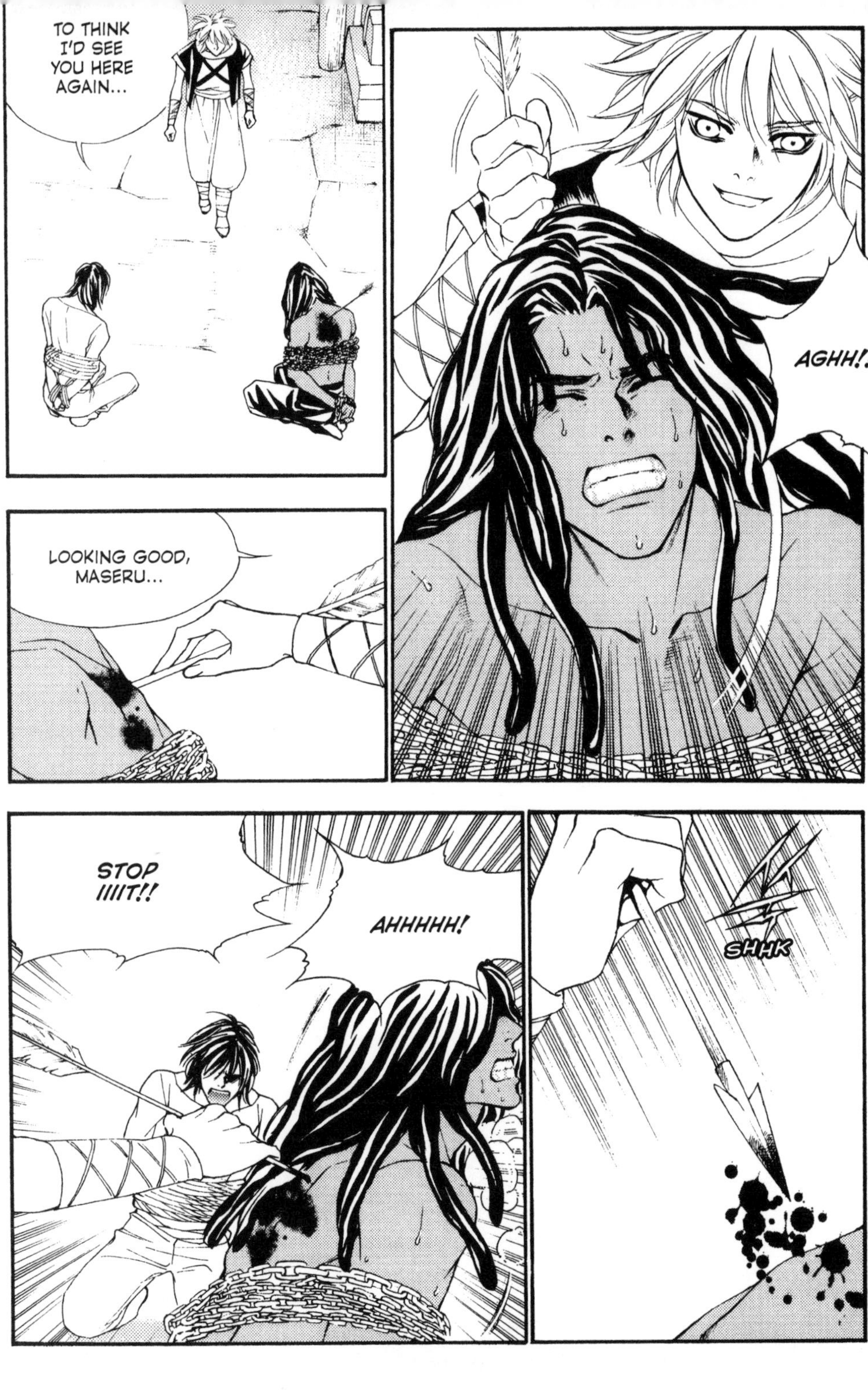
TO THINK I'D SEE YOU HERE AGAIN...
LOOKING GOOD, MASERU...
AGHH!!
STOP IIIIT!!
AHHHHH!
SHHK

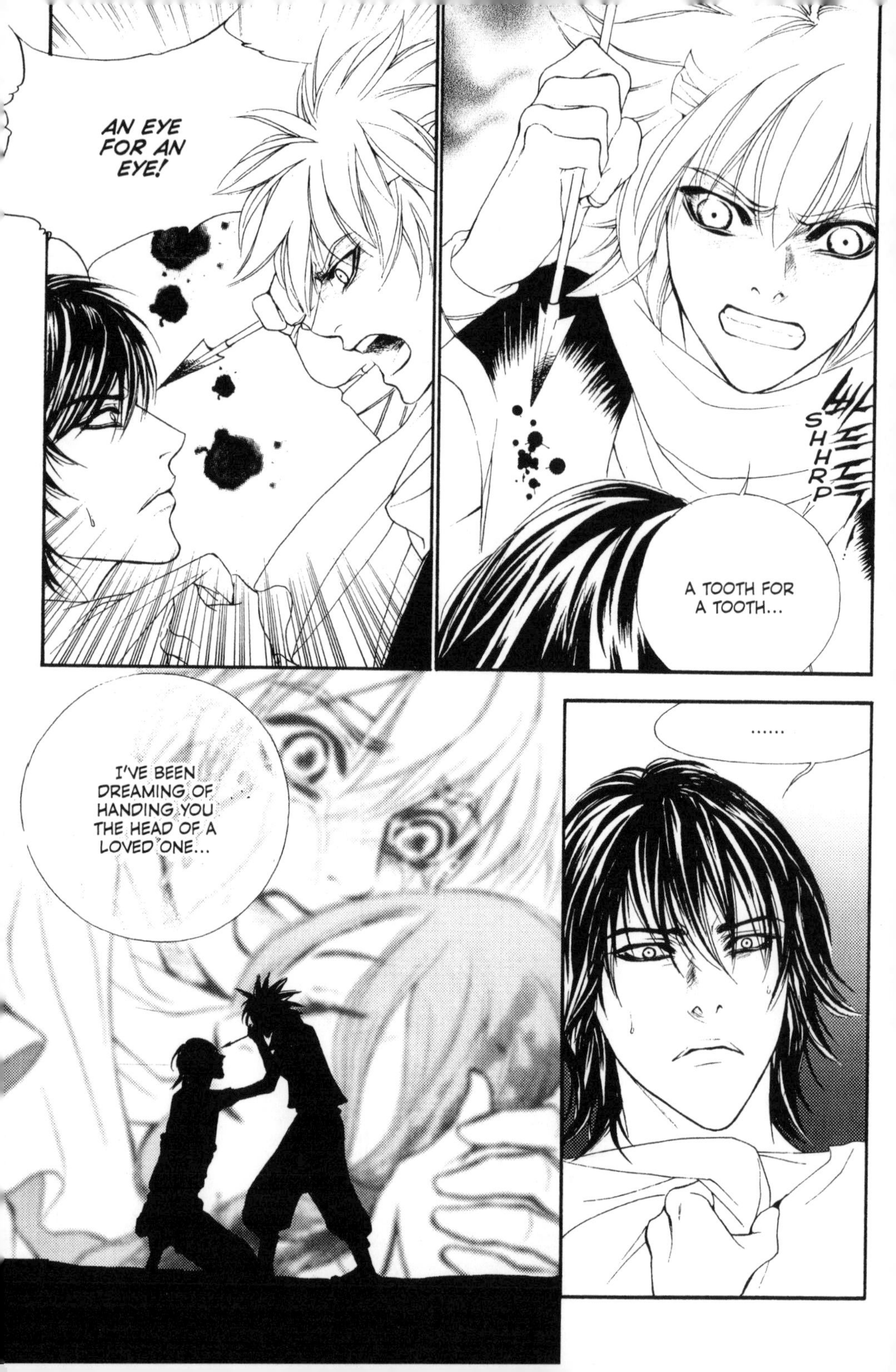
AN EYE FOR AN EYE!
SHHRP
A TOOTH FOR A TOOTH...
I'VE BEEN DREAMING OF HANDING YOU THE HEAD OF A LOVED ONE...
......

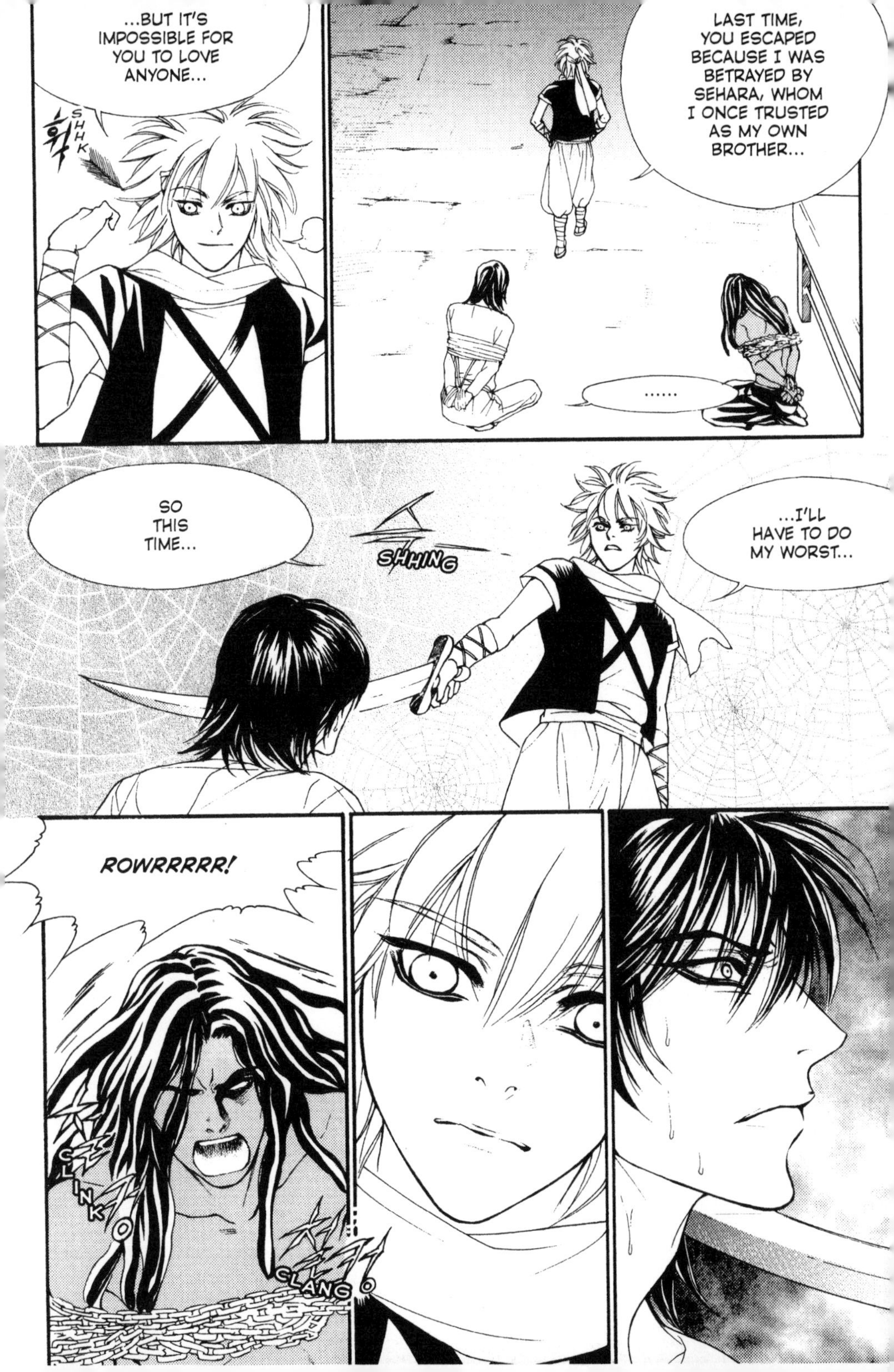
...BUT IT'S IMPOSSIBLE FOR YOU TO LOVE ANYONE...
SHHK
LAST TIME, YOU ESCAPED BECAUSE I WAS BETRAYED BY SEHARA, WHOM I ONCE TRUSTED AS MY OWN BROTHER...
......
SO THIS TIME...
SHHING
...I'LL HAVE TO DO MY WORST...
ROWRRRRR!
CLINK
CLANG

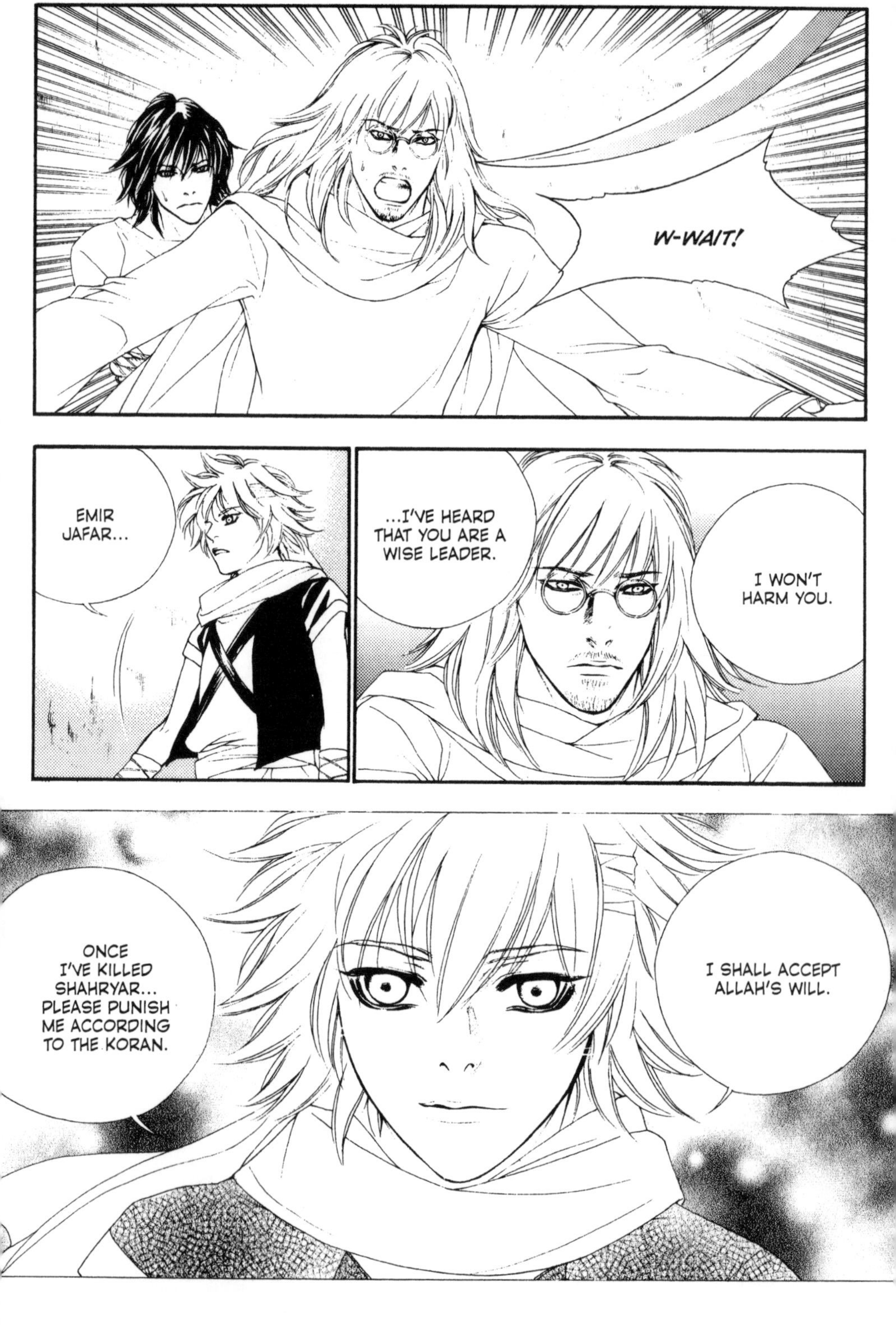
W-WAIT!
EMIR JAFAR...
...I'VE HEARD THAT YOU ARE A WISE LEADER.
I WON'T HARM YOU.
ONCE I'VE KILLED SHAHRYAR... PLEASE PUNISH ME ACCORDING TO THE KORAN.
I SHALL ACCEPT ALLAH'S WILL.

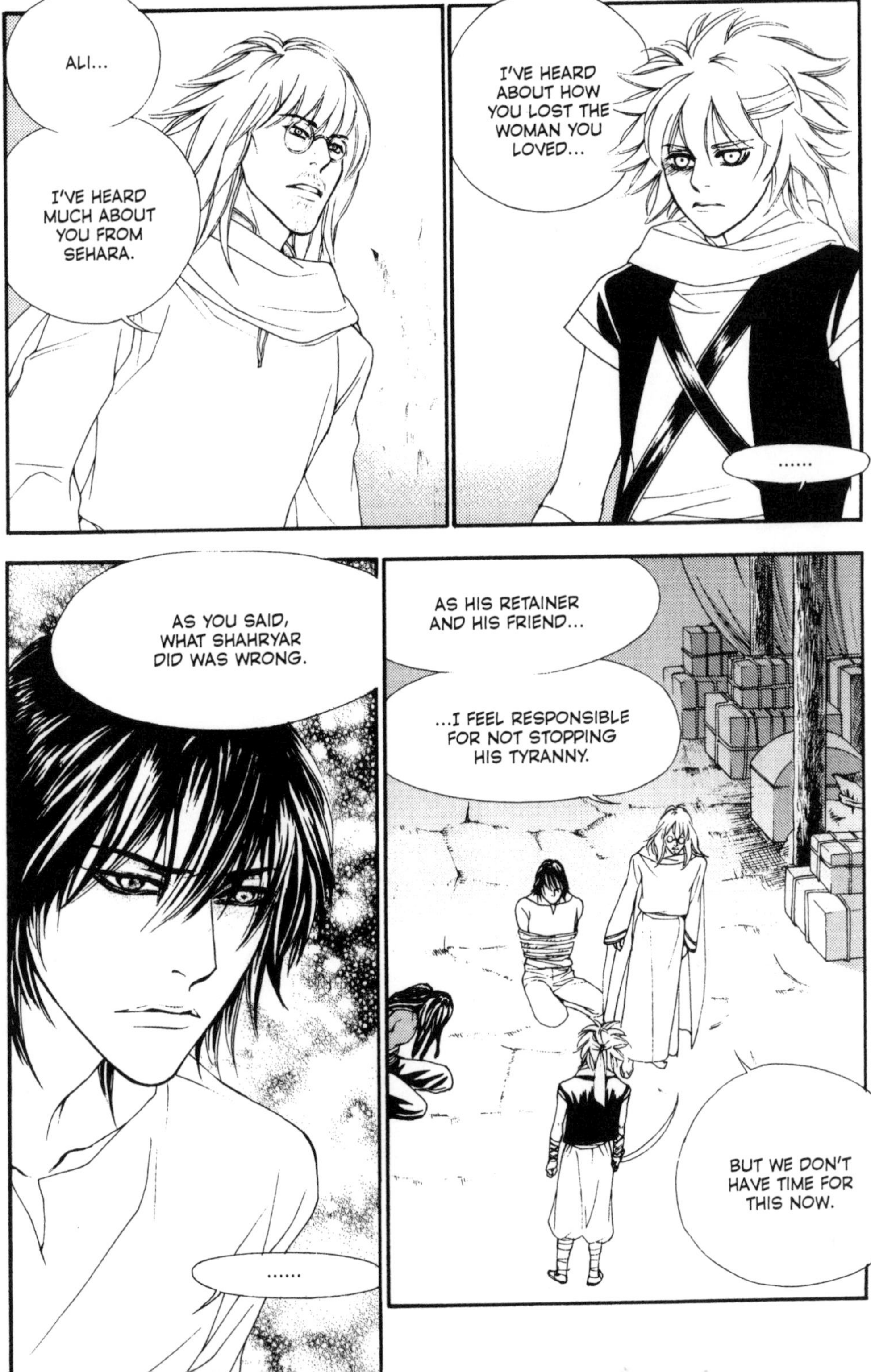
ALI...
I'VE HEARD MUCH ABOUT YOU FROM SEHARA.
I'VE HEARD ABOUT HOW YOU LOST THE WOMAN YOU LOVED...
......
AS YOU SAID, WHAT SHAHRYAR DID WAS WRONG.
......
AS HIS RETAINER AND HIS FRIEND...
...I FEEL RESPONSIBLE FOR NOT STOPPING HIS TYRANNY.
BUT WE DON'T HAVE TIME FOR THIS NOW.

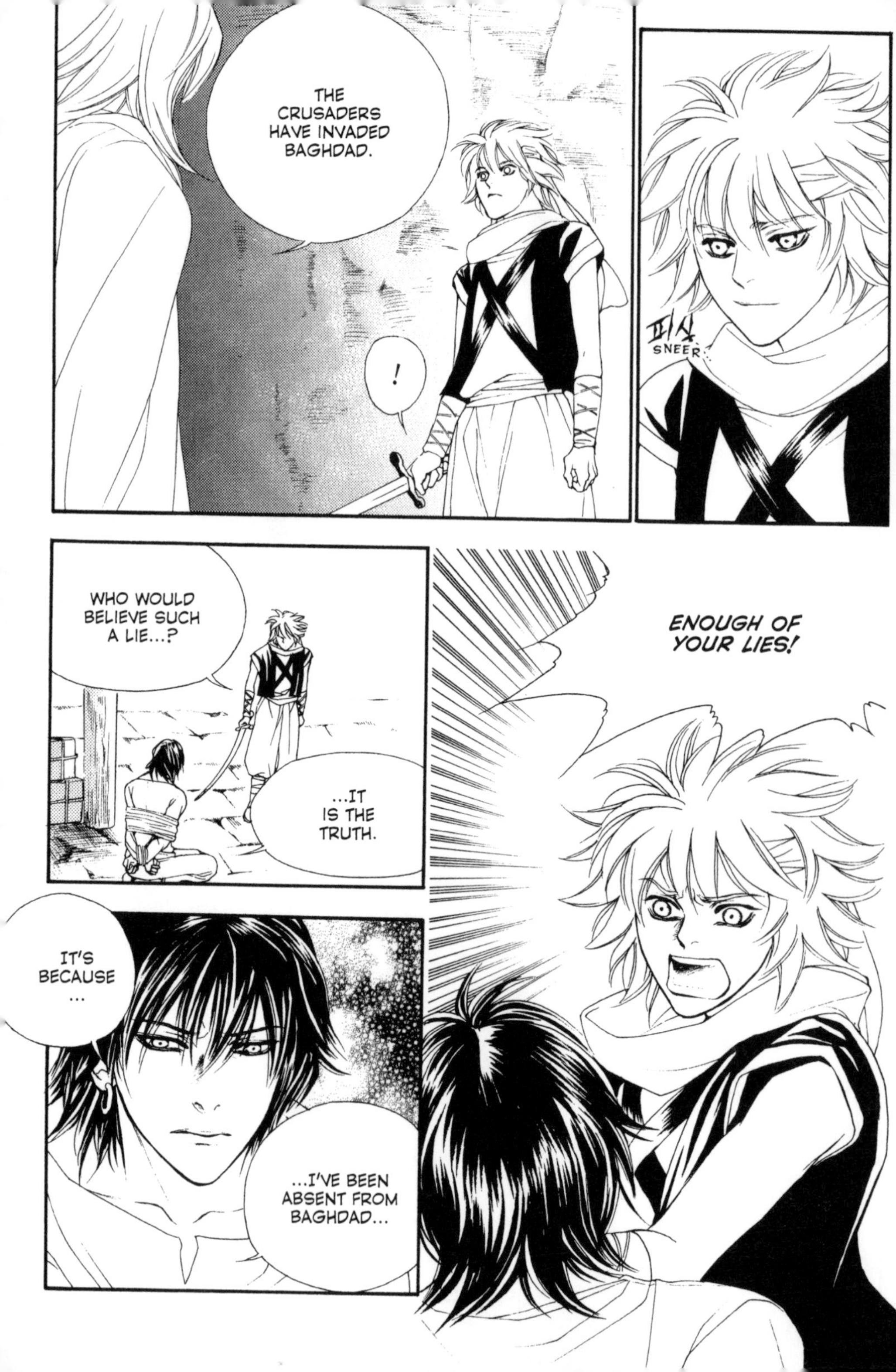
THE CRUSADERS HAVE INVADED BAGHDAD.
!
피식
SNEER...
WHO WOULD BELIEVE SUCH A LIE...?
...IT IS THE TRUTH.
IT'S BECAUSE ...
...I'VE BEEN ABSENT FROM BAGHDAD...
ENOUGH OF YOUR LIES!

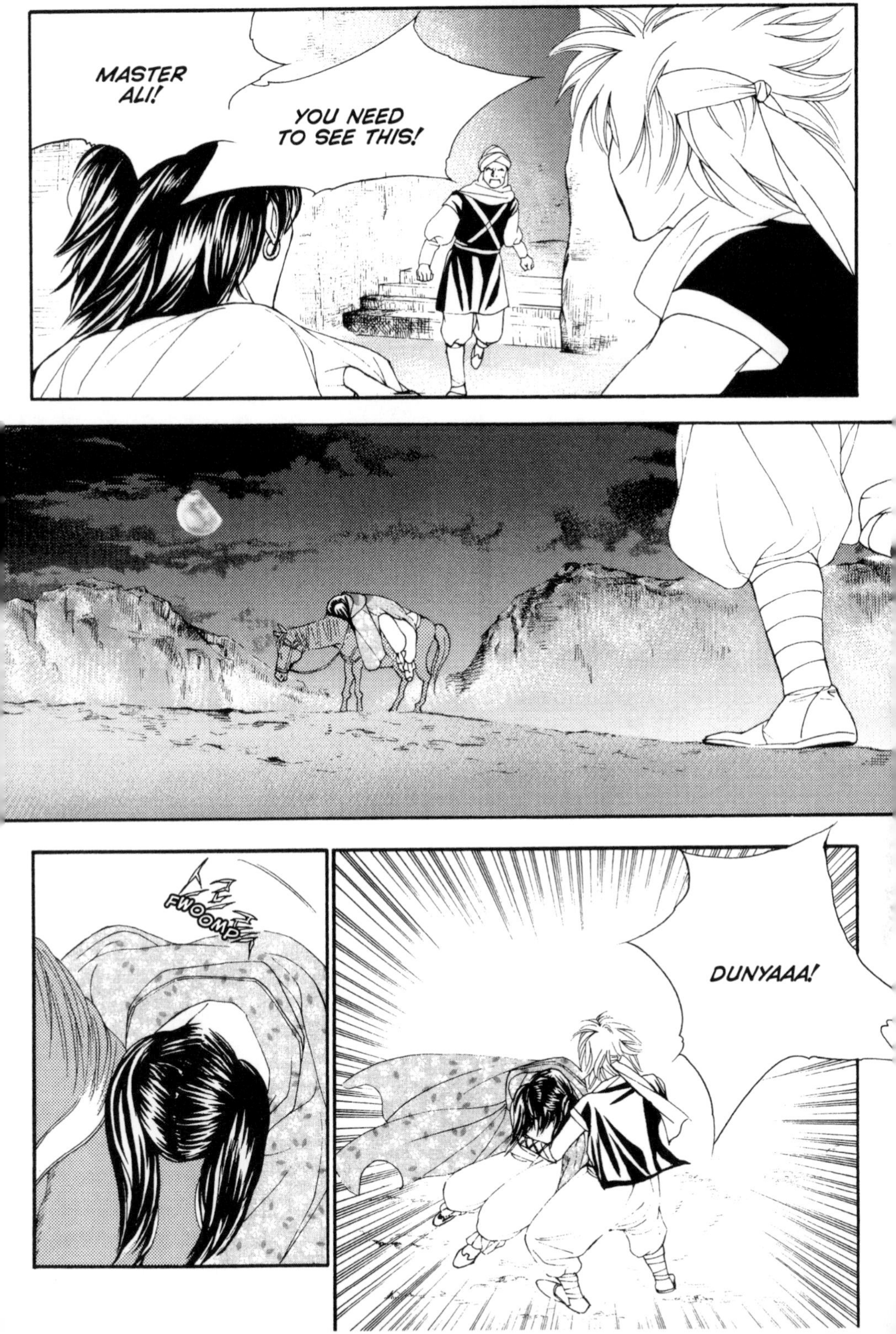
MASTER ALI!
YOU NEED TO SEE THIS!
FWOOMP
DUNYAAA!

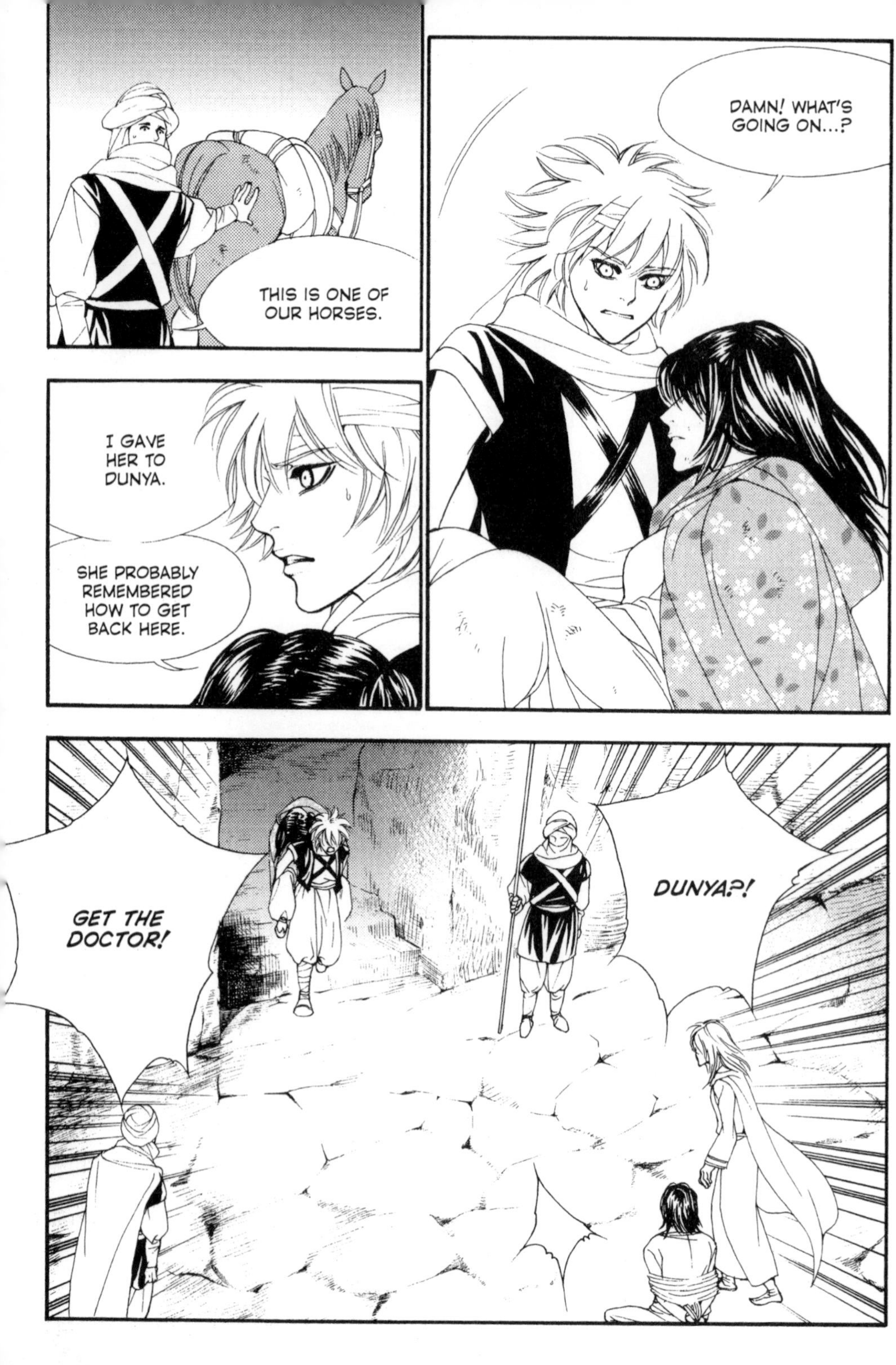
THIS IS ONE OF OUR HORSES.
I GAVE HER TO DUNYA.
SHE PROBABLY REMEMBERED HOW TO GET BACK HERE.
DAMN! WHAT'S GOING ON...?
GET THE DOCTOR!
DUNYA?!

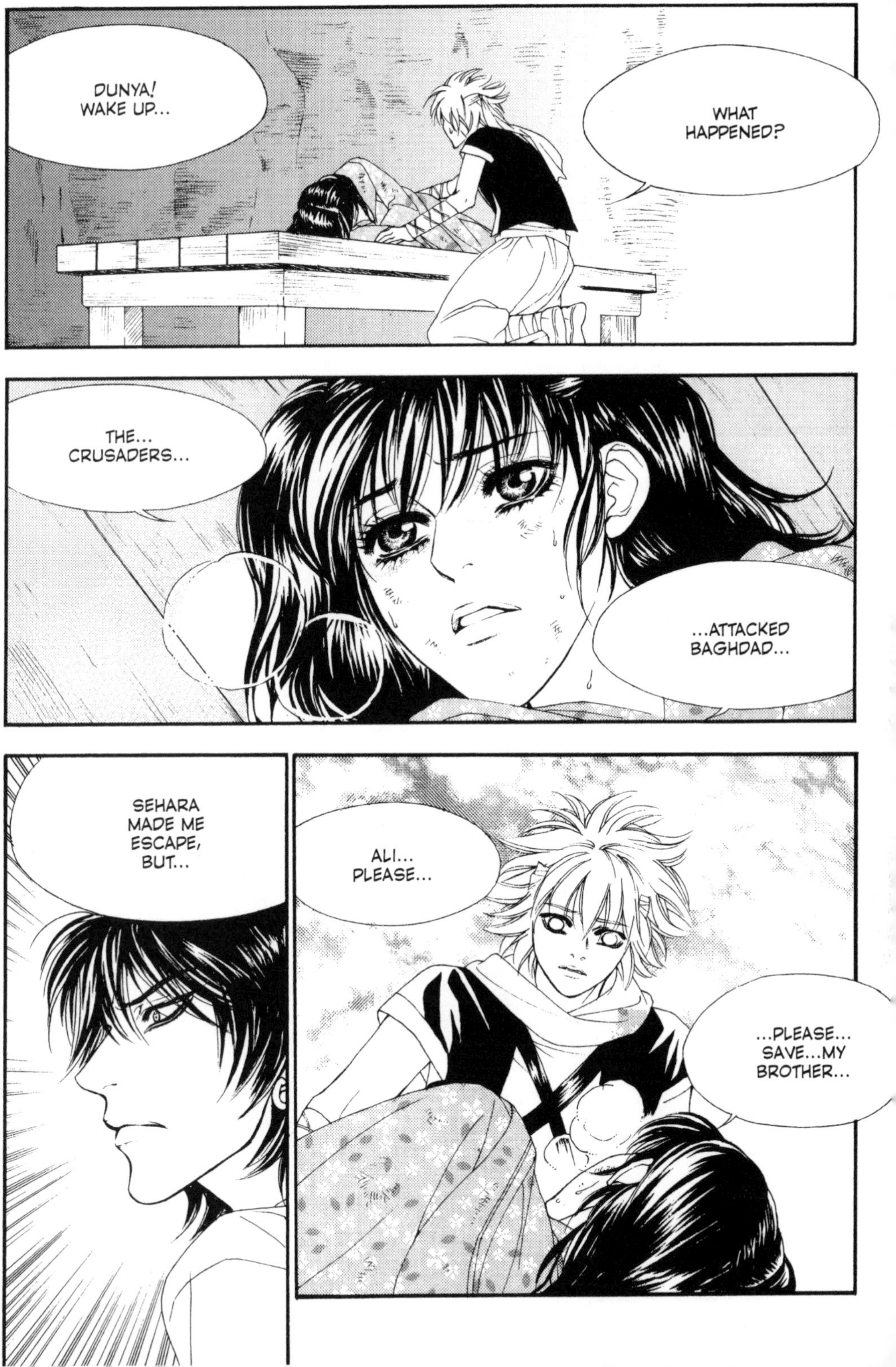
DUNYA! WAKE UP...
WHAT HAPPENED?
THE... CRUSADERS...
...ATTACKED BAGHDAD...
SEHARA MADE ME ESCAPE, BUT...
ALI... PLEASE...
...PLEASE... SAVE...MY BROTHER...

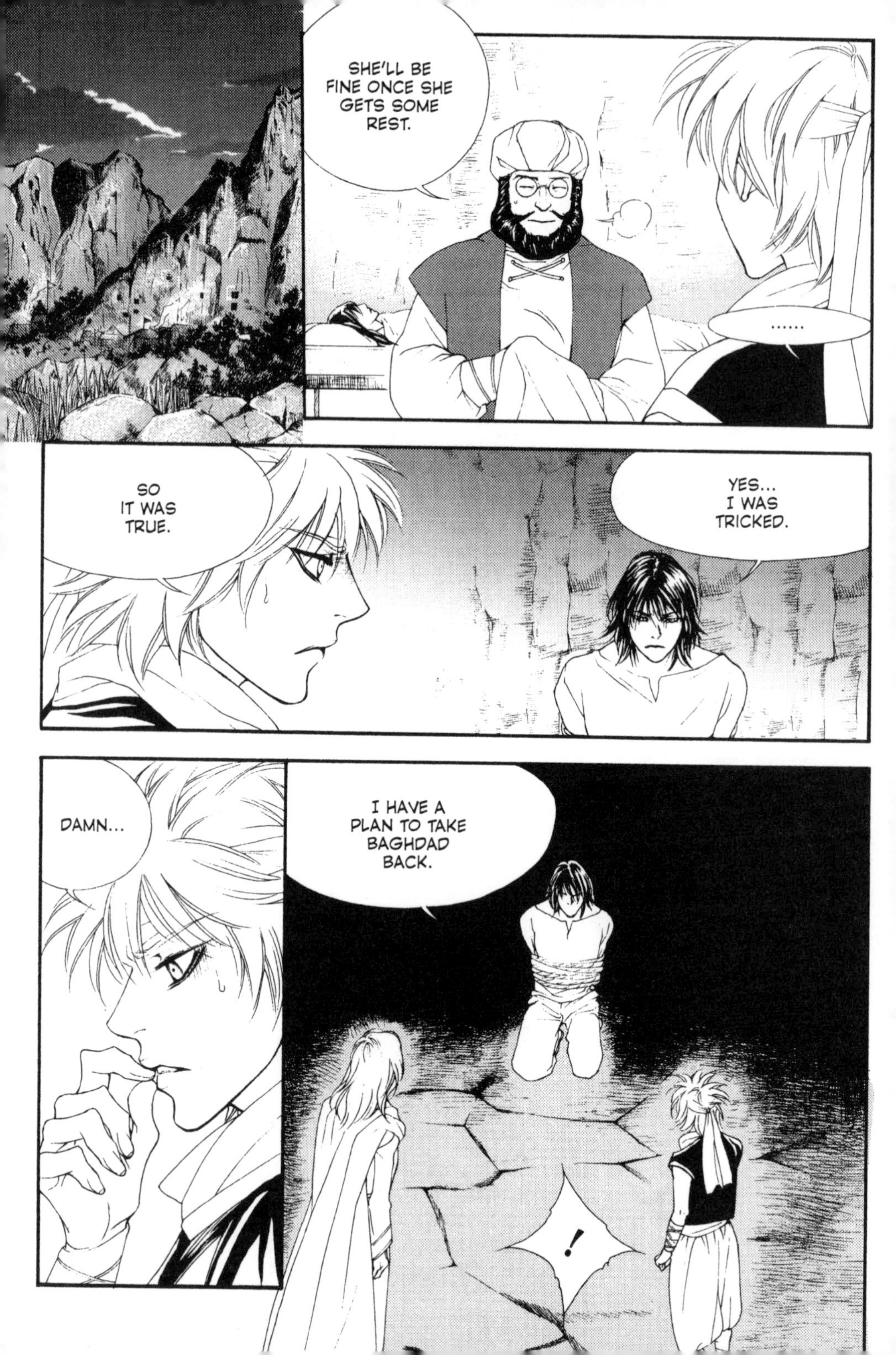
SHE'LL BE FINE ONCE SHE GETS SOME REST.
......
SO IT WAS TRUE.
YES... I WAS TRICKED.
DAMN...
I HAVE A PLAN TO TAKE BAGHDAD BACK.
!

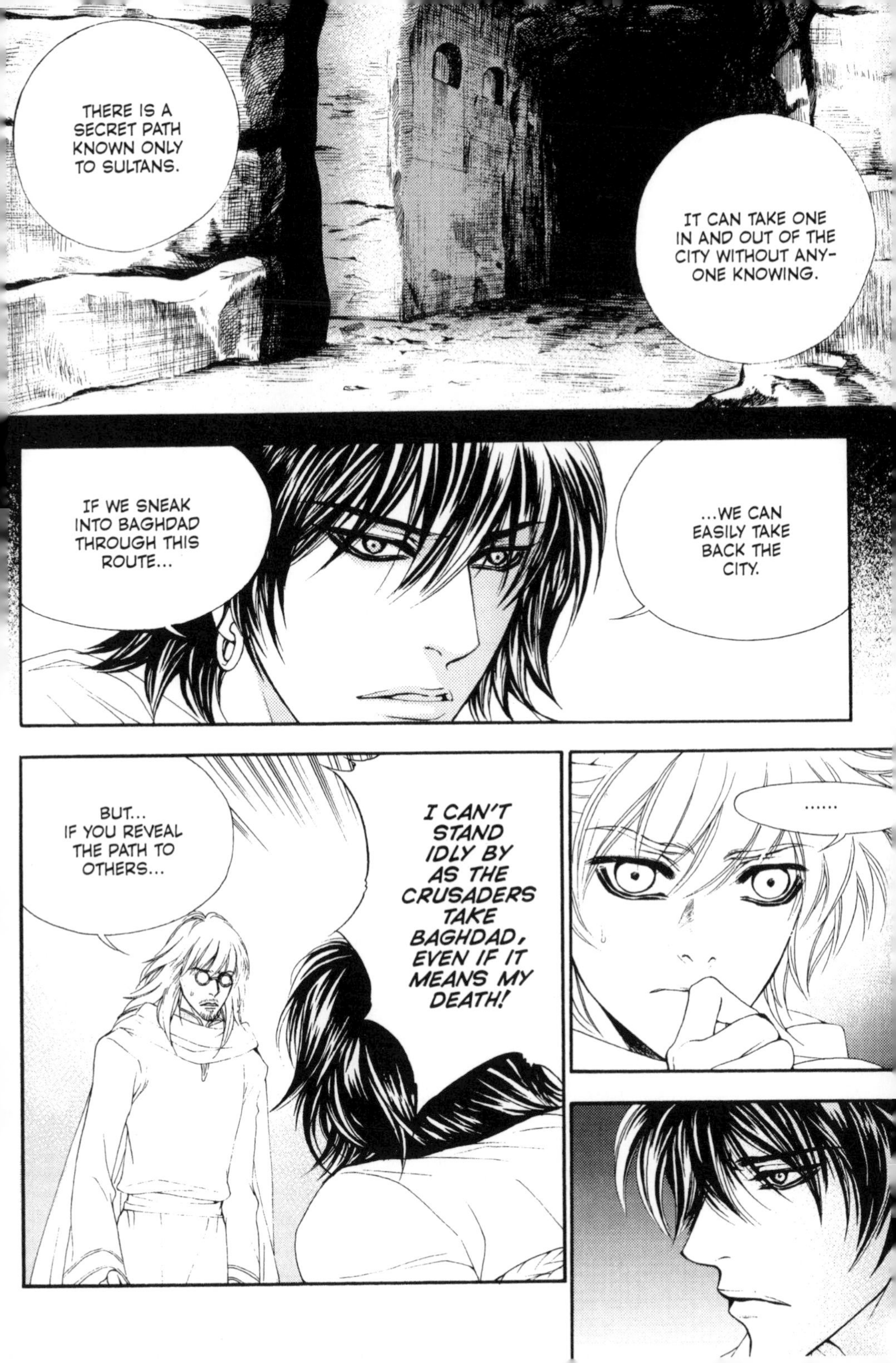
THERE IS A SECRET PATH KNOWN ONLY TO SULTANS.
IT CAN TAKE ONE IN AND OUT OF THE CITY WITHOUT ANY-ONE KNOWING.
IF WE SNEAK INTO BAGHDAD THROUGH THIS ROUTE...
...WE CAN EASILY TAKE BACK THE CITY.
BUT... IF YOU REVEAL THE PATH TO OTHERS...
I CAN'T STAND IDLY BY AS THE CRUSADERS TAKE BAGHDAD, EVEN IF IT MEANS MY DEATH!
......

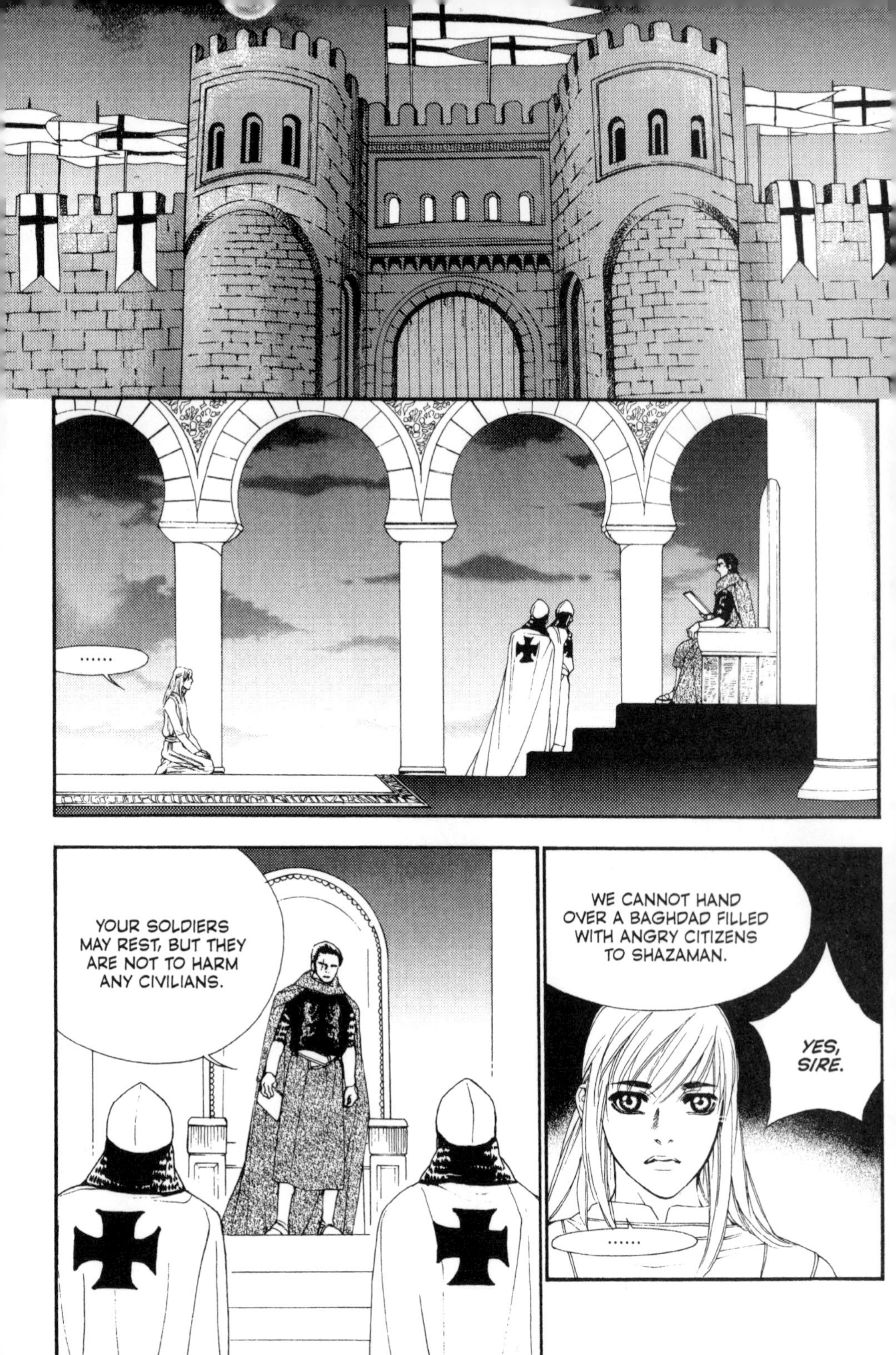
......
YOUR SOLDIERS MAY REST, BUT THEY ARE NOT TO HARM ANY CIVILIANS.
WE CANNOT HAND OVER A BAGHDAD FILLED WITH ANGRY CITIZENS TO SHAZAMAN.
YES, SIRE.
......

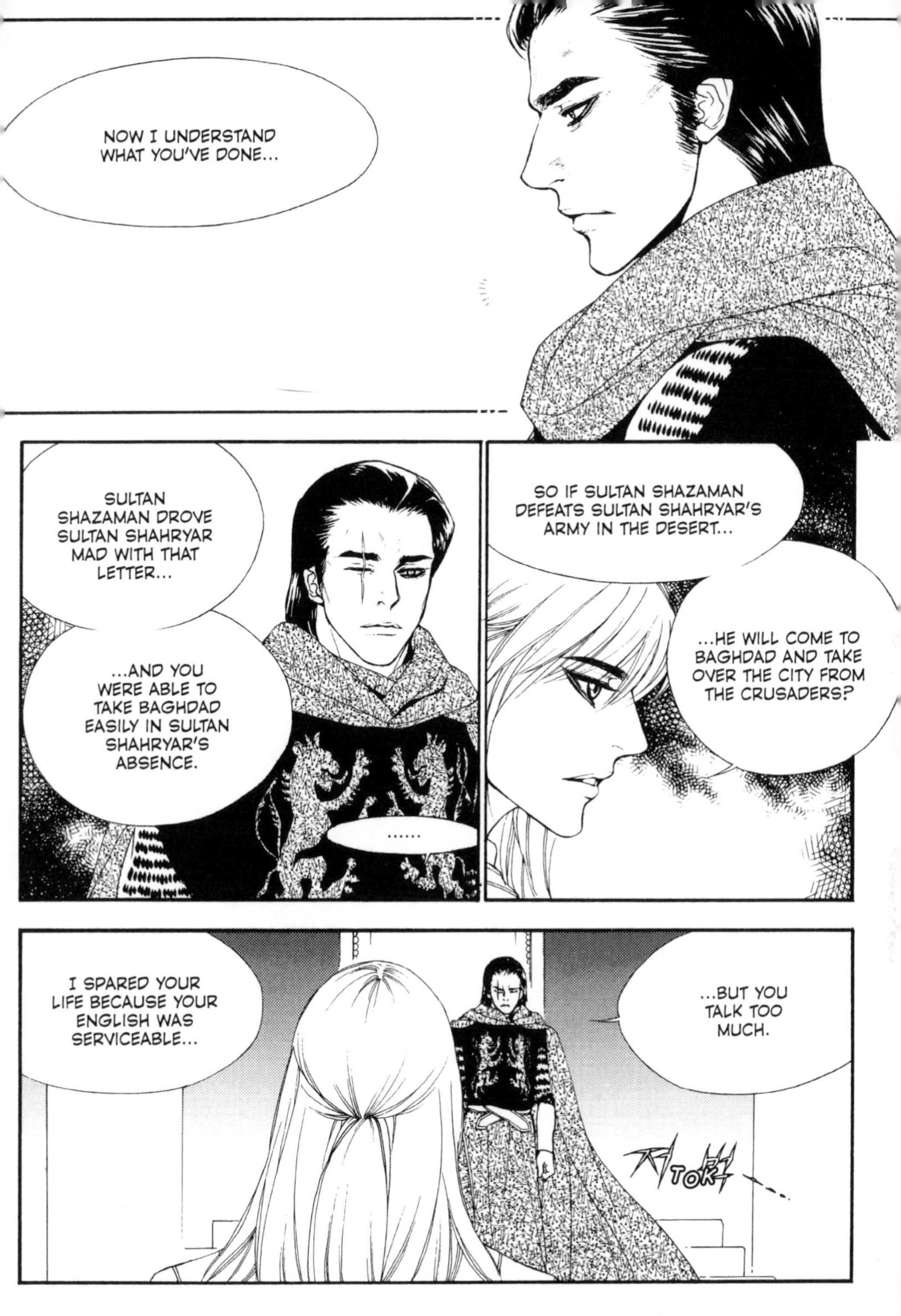
NOW I UNDERSTAND WHAT YOU'VE DONE...
SULTAN SHAZAMAN DROVE SULTAN SHAHRYAR MAD WITH THAT LETTER...
...AND YOU WERE ABLE TO TAKE BAGHDAD EASILY IN SULTAN SHAHRYAR'S ABSENCE.
......
SO IF SULTAN SHAZAMAN DEFEATS SULTAN SHAHRYAR'S ARMY IN THE DESERT...
...HE WILL COME TO BAGHDAD AND TAKE OVER THE CITY FROM THE CRUSADERS?
I SPARED YOUR LIFE BECAUSE YOUR ENGLISH WAS SERVICEABLE...
...BUT YOU TALK TOO MUCH.
TOK

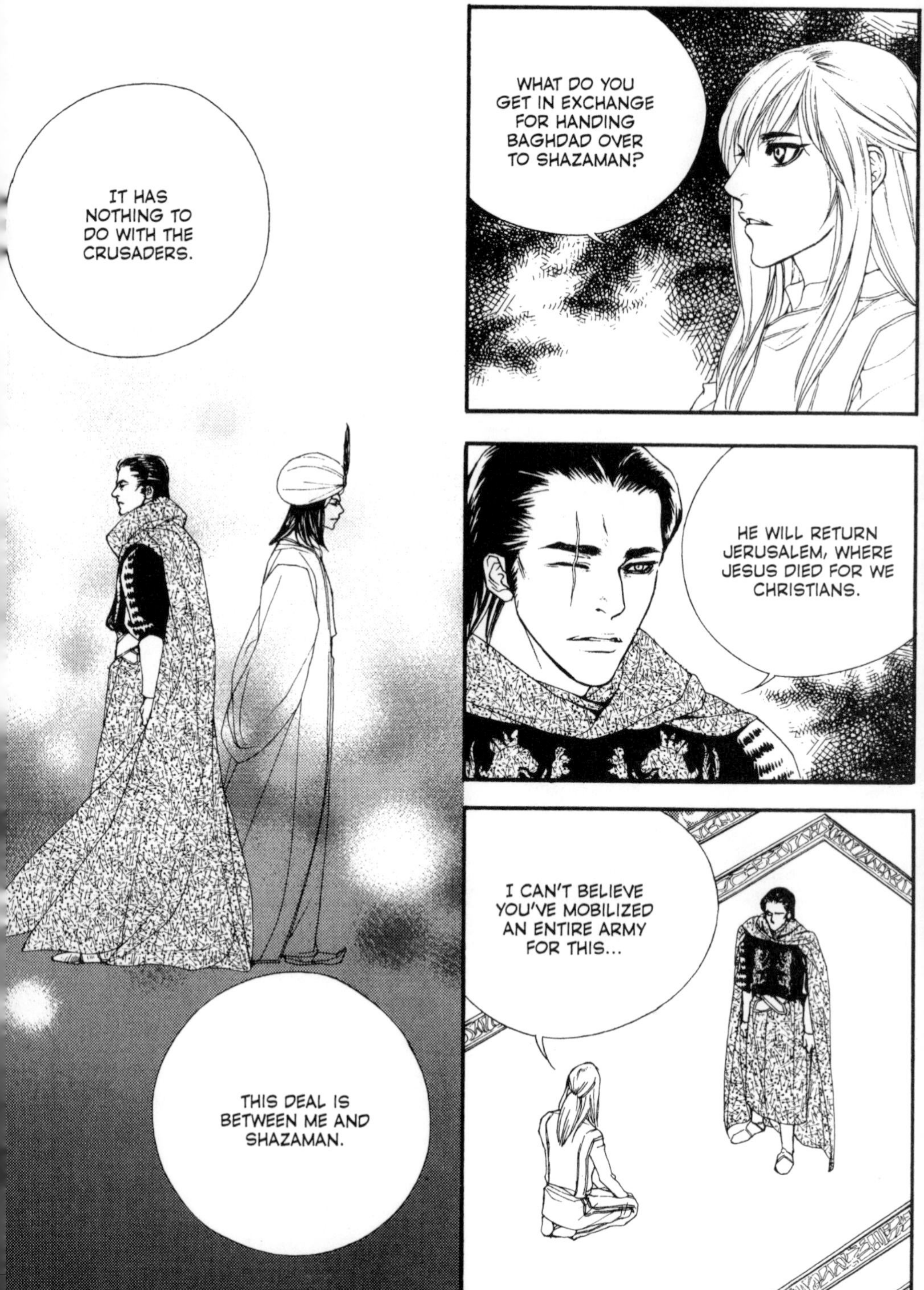
IT HAS NOTHING TO DO WITH THE CRUSADERS.
THIS DEAL IS BETWEEN ME AND SHAZAMAN.
WHAT DO YOU GET IN EXCHANGE FOR HANDING BAGHDAD OVER TO SHAZAMAN?
HE WILL RETURN JERUSALEM, WHERE JESUS DIED FOR WE CHRISTIANS.
I CAN'T BELIEVE YOU'VE MOBILIZED AN ENTIRE ARMY FOR THIS...

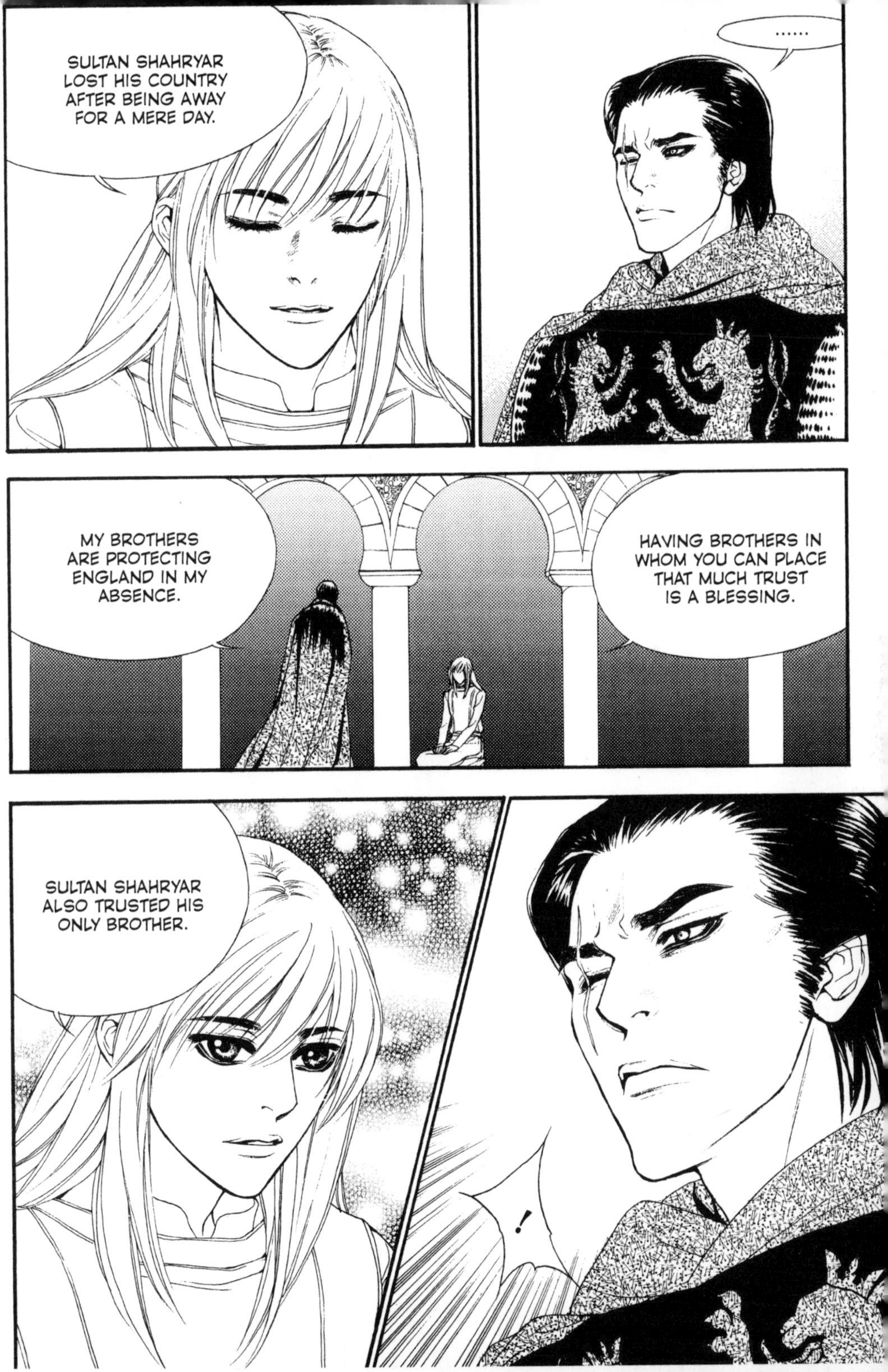
SULTAN SHAHRYAR LOST HIS COUNTRY AFTER BEING AWAY FOR A MERE DAY.
......
MY BROTHERS ARE PROTECTING ENGLAND IN MY ABSENCE.
HAVING BROTHERS IN WHOM YOU CAN PLACE THAT MUCH TRUST IS A BLESSING.
SULTAN SHAHRYAR ALSO TRUSTED HIS ONLY BROTHER.
!

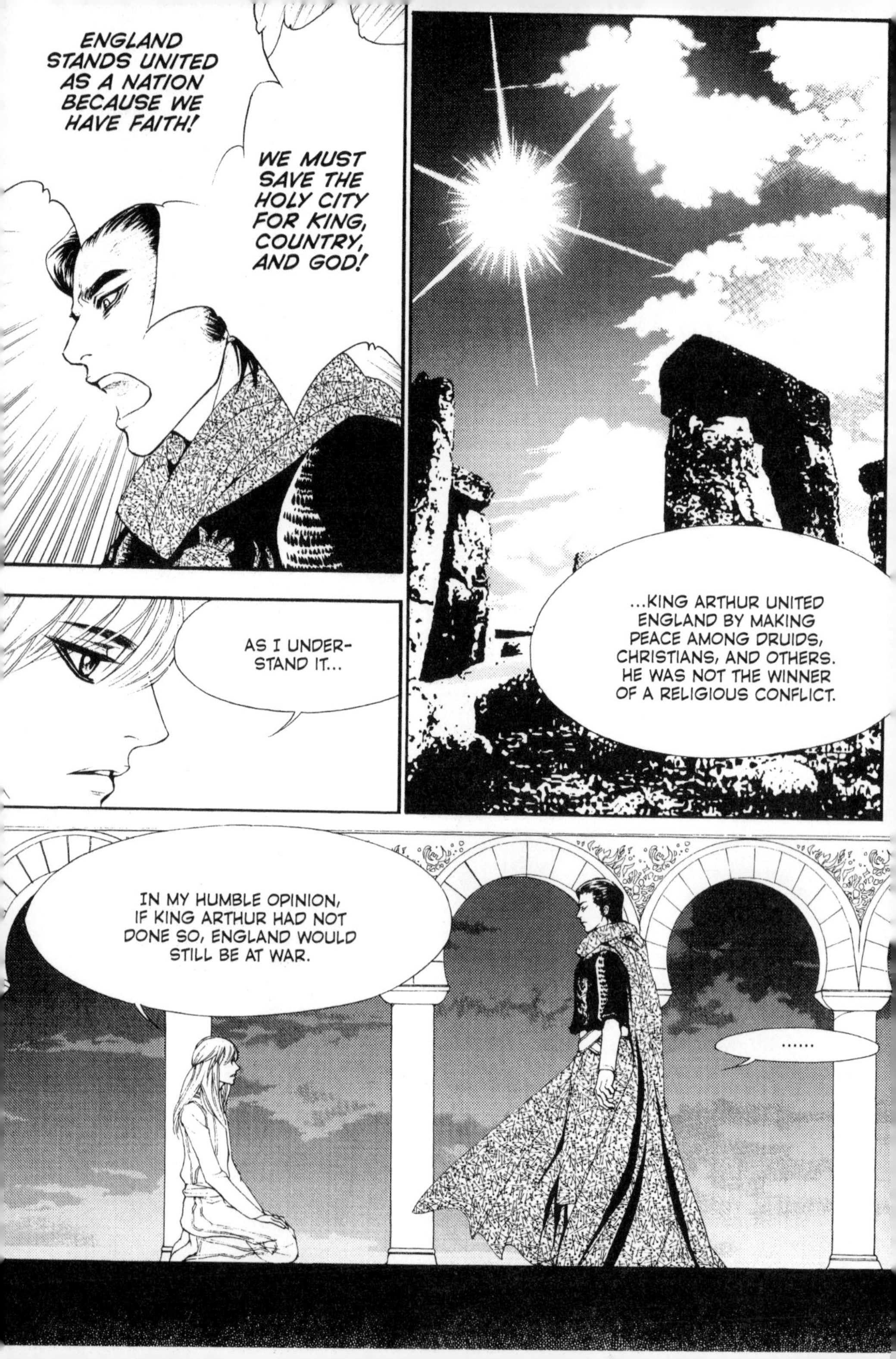
ENGLAND STANDS UNITED AS A NATION BECAUSE WE HAVE FAITH!
WE MUST SAVE THE HOLY CITY FOR KING, COUNTRY, AND GOD!
AS I UNDER-STAND IT...
...KING ARTHUR UNITED ENGLAND BY MAKING PEACE AMONG DRUIDS, CHRISTIANS, AND OTHERS. HE WAS NOT THE WINNER OF A RELIGIOUS CONFLICT.
IN MY HUMBLE OPINION, IF KING ARTHUR HAD NOT DONE SO, ENGLAND WOULD STILL BE AT WAR.
......

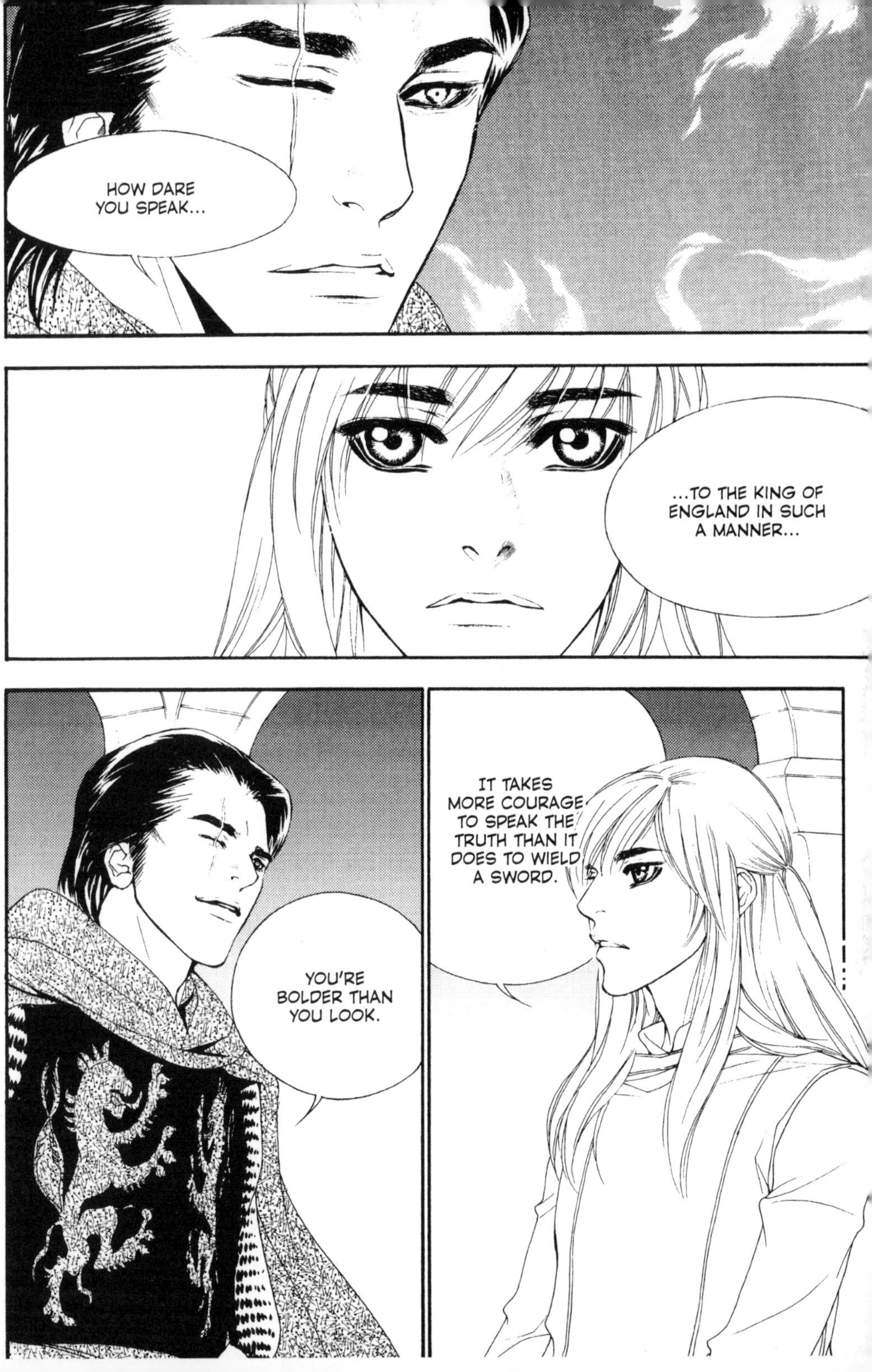
HOW DARE YOU SPEAK...
...TO THE KING OF ENGLAND IN SUCH A MANNER...
YOU'RE BOLDER THAN YOU LOOK.
IT TAKES MORE COURAGE TO SPEAK THE TRUTH THAN IT DOES TO WIELD A SWORD.

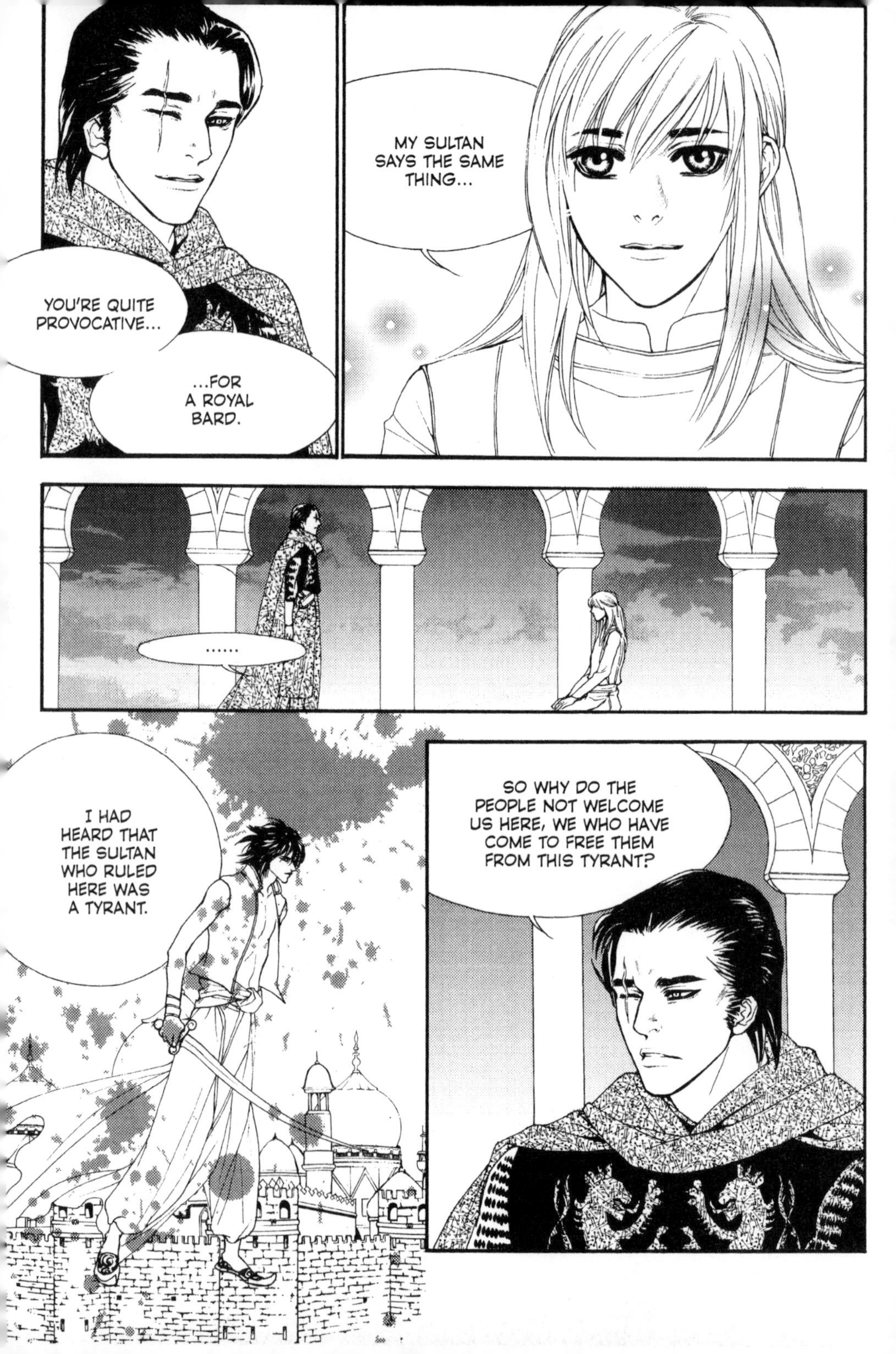
YOU'RE QUITE PROVOCATIVE...
...FOR A ROYAL BARD.
MY SULTAN SAYS THE SAME THING...
......
I HAD HEARD THAT THE SULTAN WHO RULED HERE WAS A TYRANT.
SO WHY DO THE PEOPLE NOT WELCOME US HERE, WE WHO HAVE COME TO FREE THEM FROM THIS TYRANT?

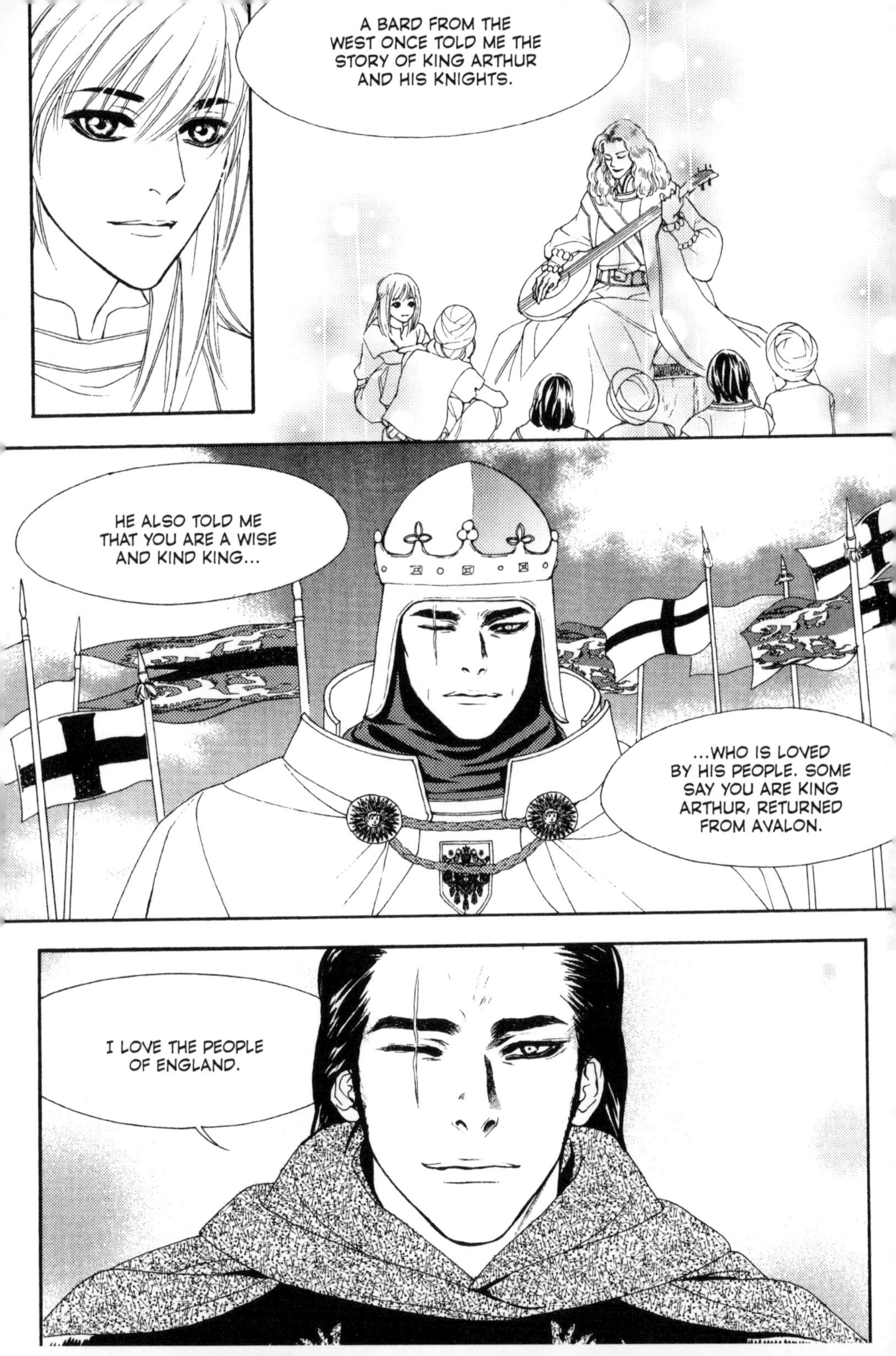
A BARD FROM THE WEST ONCE TOLD ME THE STORY OF KING ARTHUR AND HIS KNIGHTS.
HE ALSO TOLD ME THAT YOU ARE A WISE AND KIND KING...
...WHO IS LOVED BY HIS PEOPLE. SOME SAY YOU ARE KING ARTHUR, RETURNED FROM AVALON.
I LOVE THE PEOPLE OF ENGLAND.

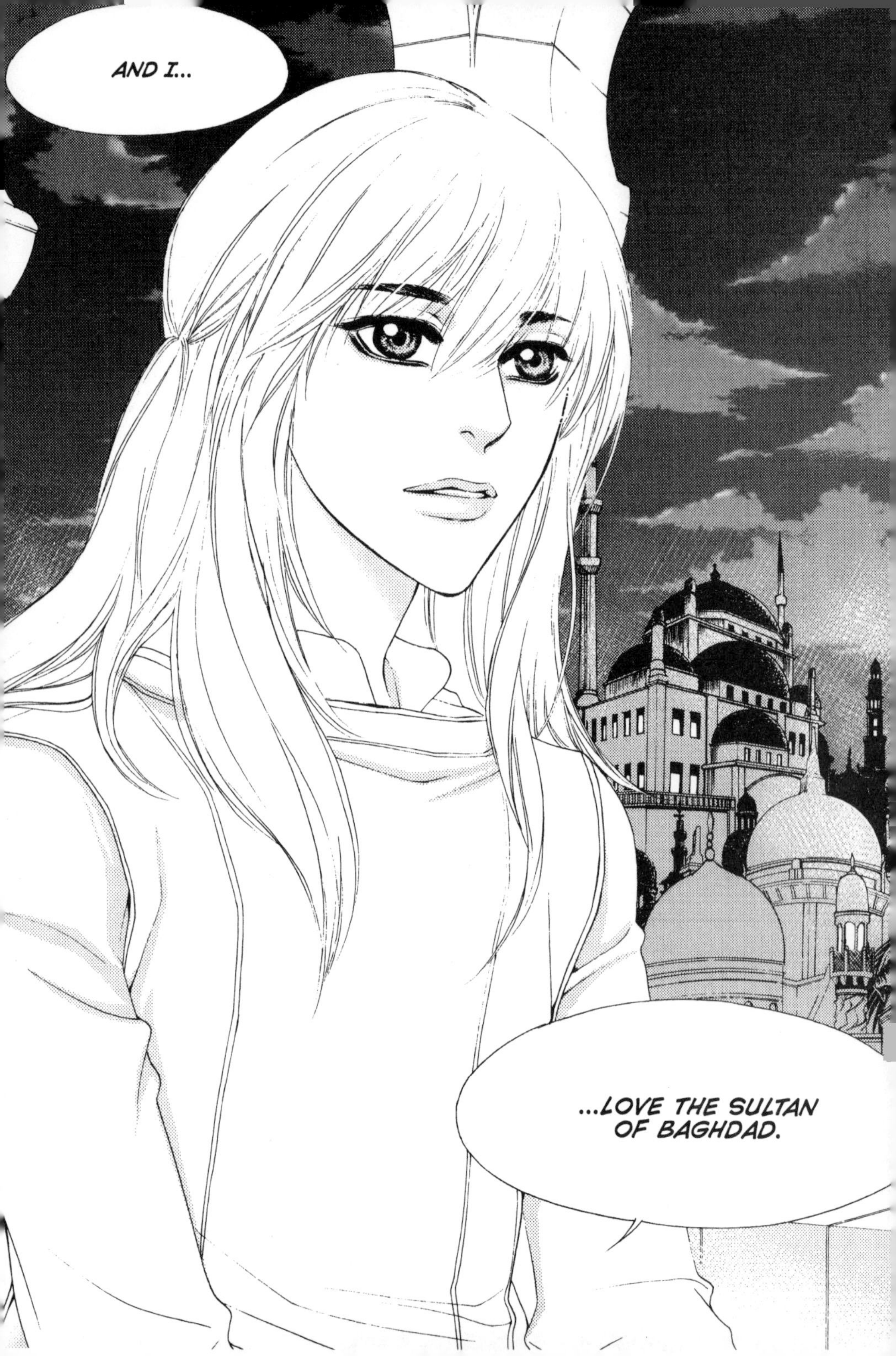
AND I...
...LOVE THE SULTAN OF BAGHDAD.

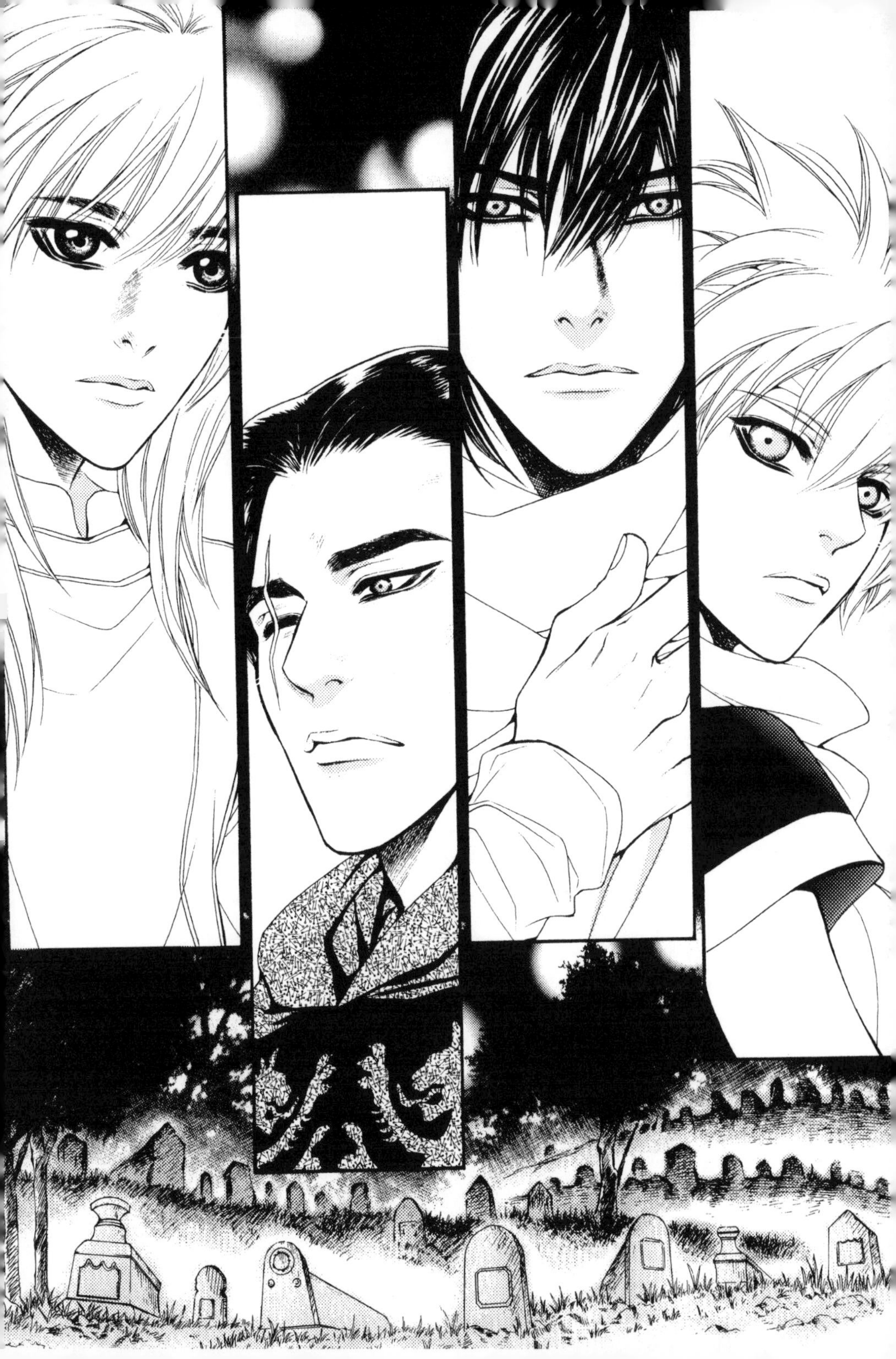

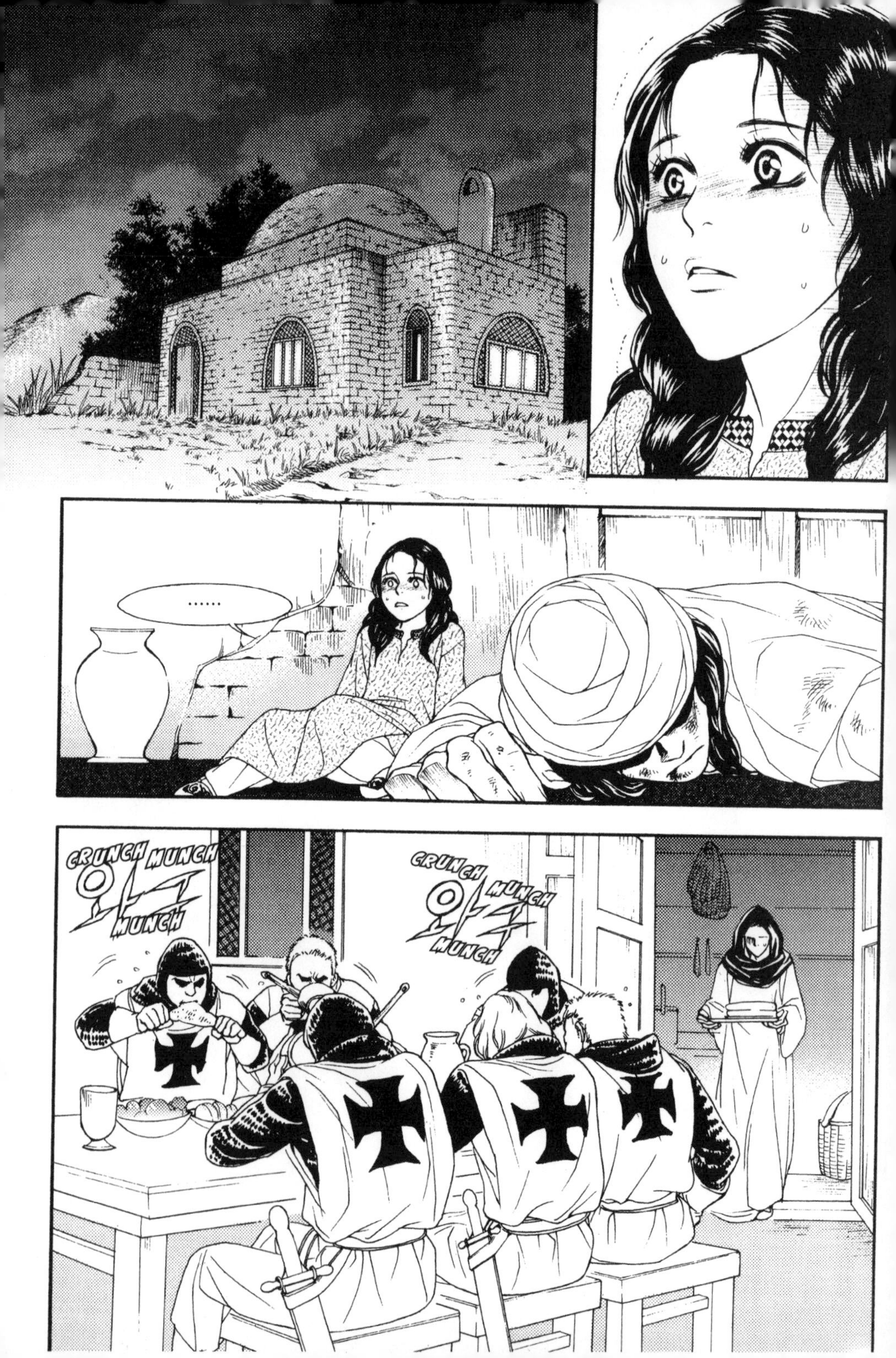

......
CRUNCH MUNCH
MUNCH
CRUNCH MUNCH
MUNCH

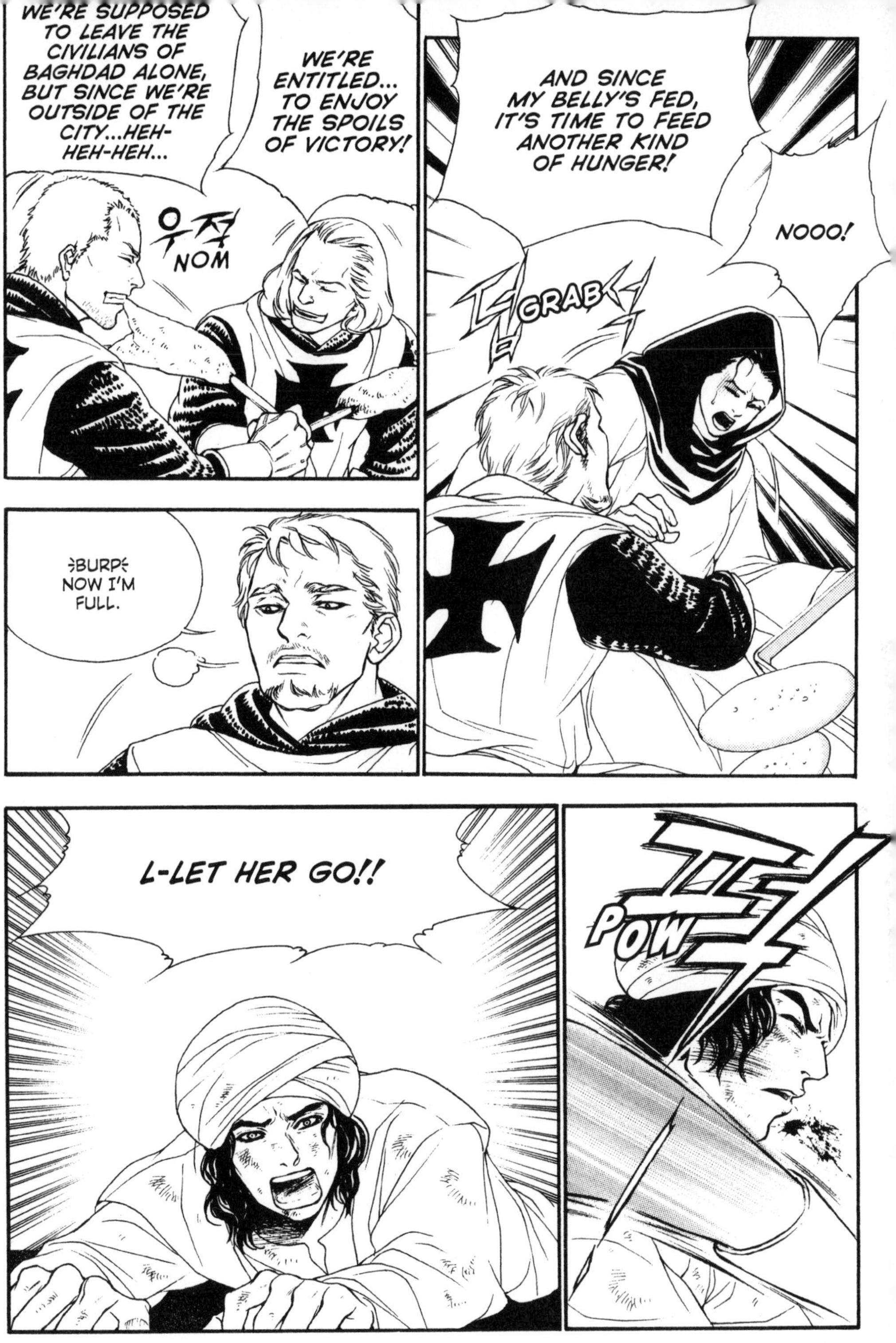
WE'RE SUPPOSED TO LEAVE THE CIVILIANS OF BAGHDAD ALONE, BUT SINCE WE'RE OUTSIDE OF THE CITY...HEH-HEH-HEH...
WE'RE ENTITLED... TO ENJOY THE SPOILS OF VICTORY!
우적
NOM
BURP
NOW I'M FULL.
AND SINCE MY BELLY'S FED, IT'S TIME TO FEED ANOTHER KIND OF HUNGER!
NOOO!
GRAB
L-LET HER GO!!
POW

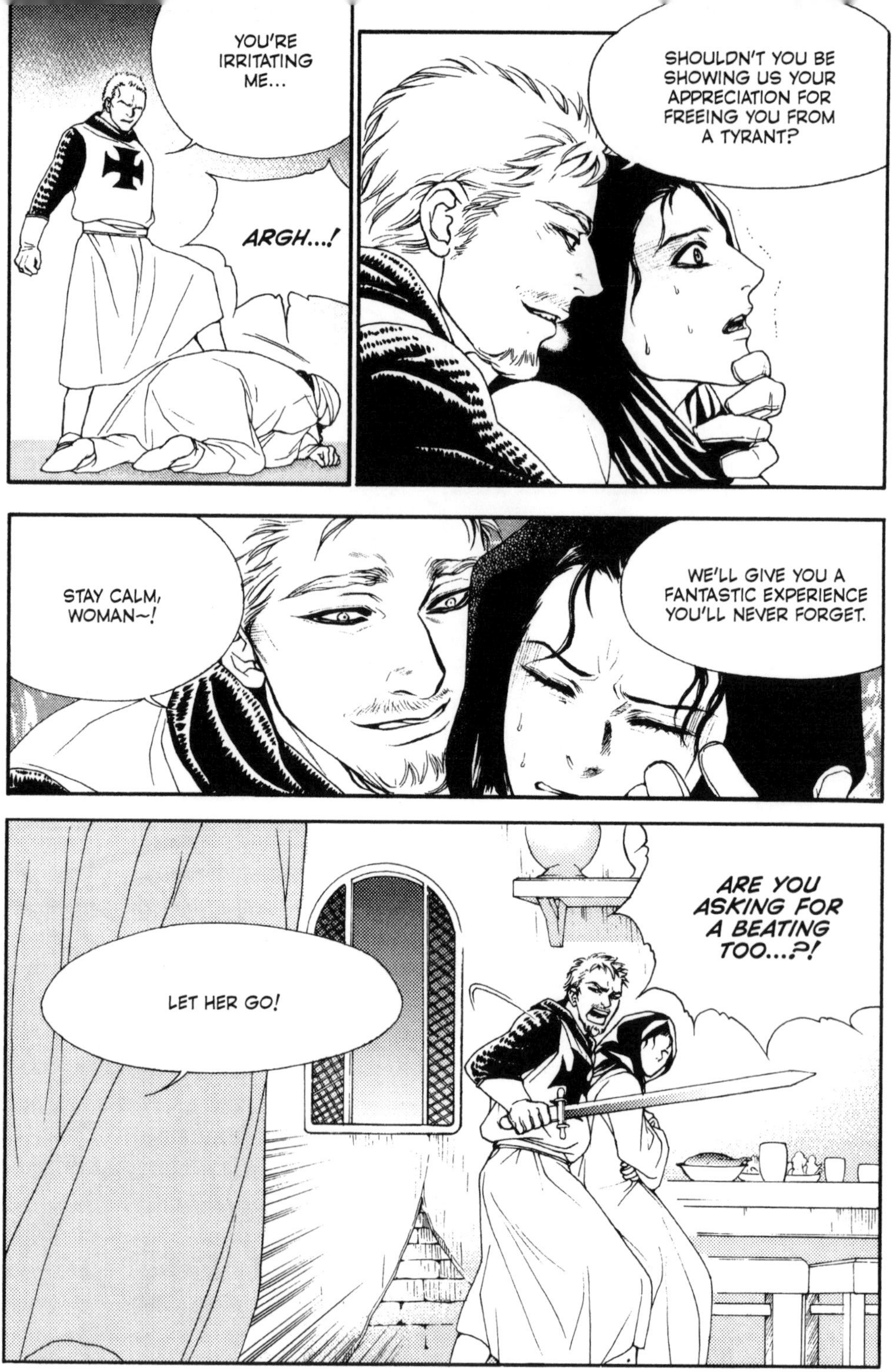

YOU'RE IRRITATING ME...
ARGH...!
SHOULDN'T YOU BE SHOWING US YOUR APPRECIATION FOR FREEING YOU FROM A TYRANT?
STAY CALM, WOMAN~!
WE'LL GIVE YOU A FANTASTIC EXPERIENCE YOU'LL NEVER FORGET.
LET HER GO!
ARE YOU ASKING FOR A BEATING TOO...?!

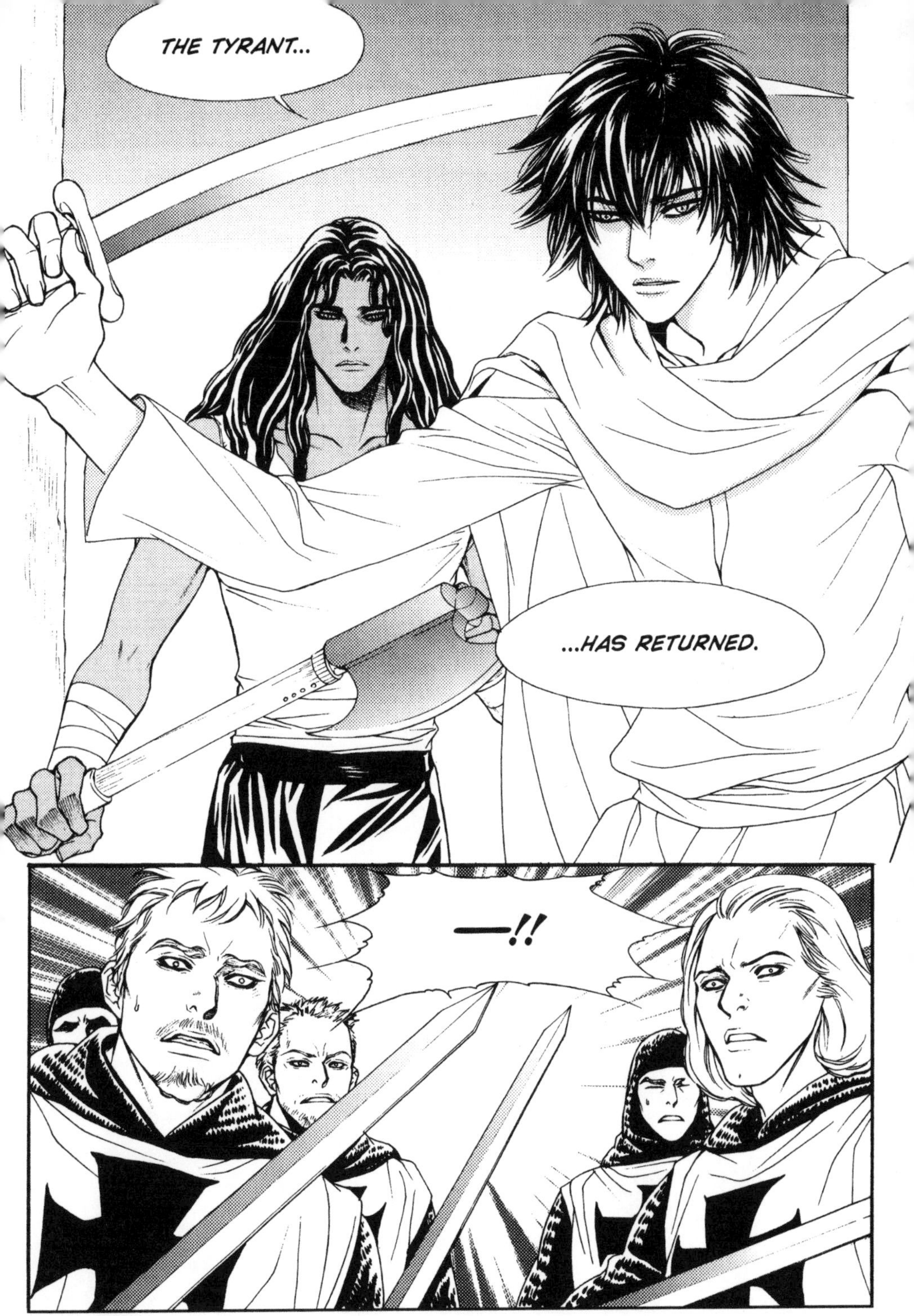
THE TYRANT...
...HAS RETURNED.
—!!

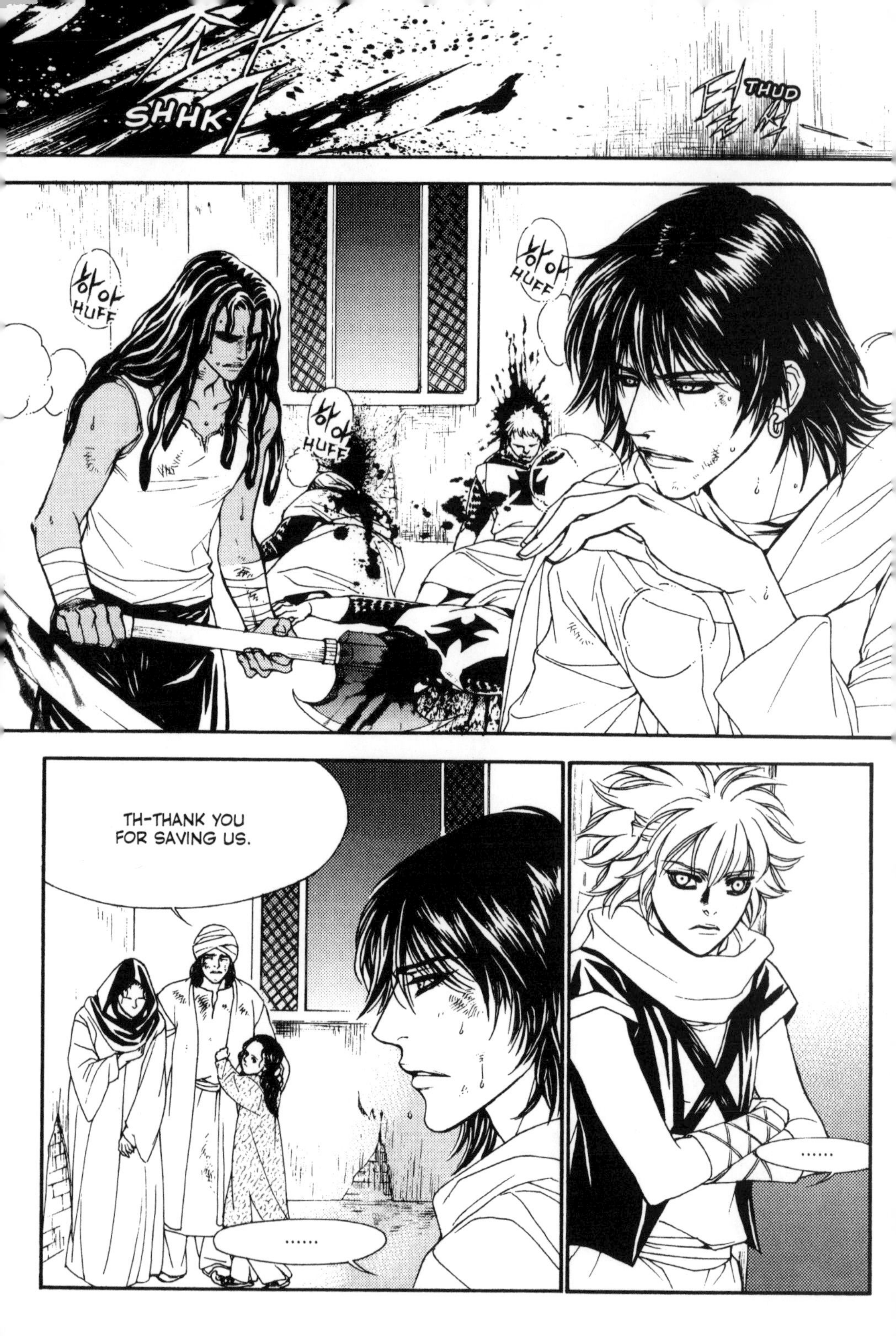

SHHK
THUD
하아 HUFF
하아 HUFF
하아 HUFF
TH-THANK YOU FOR SAVING US.
......
......

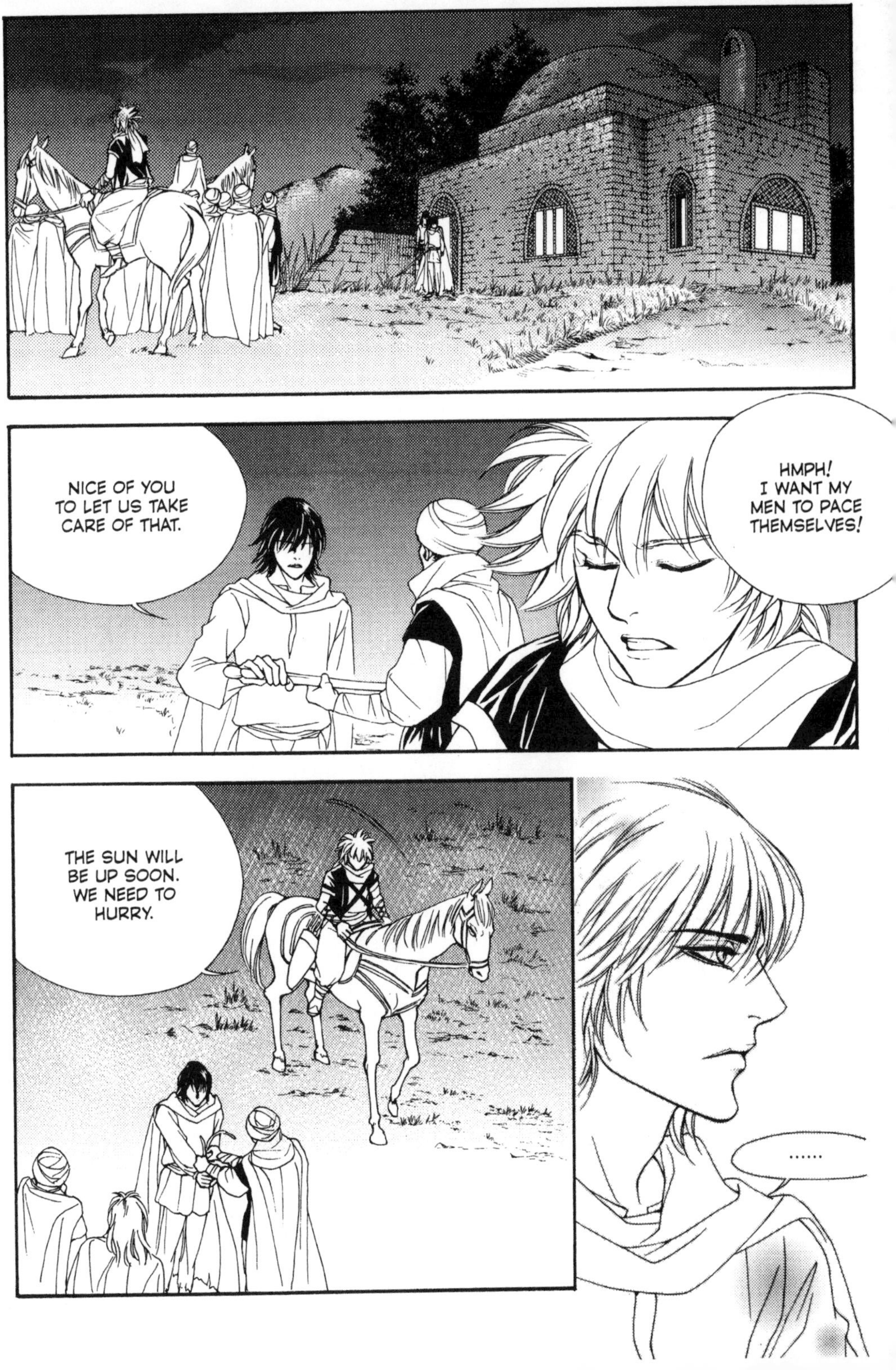
NICE OF YOU TO LET US TAKE CARE OF THAT.
HMPH! I WANT MY MEN TO PACE THEMSELVES!
THE SUN WILL BE UP SOON. WE NEED TO HURRY.
......

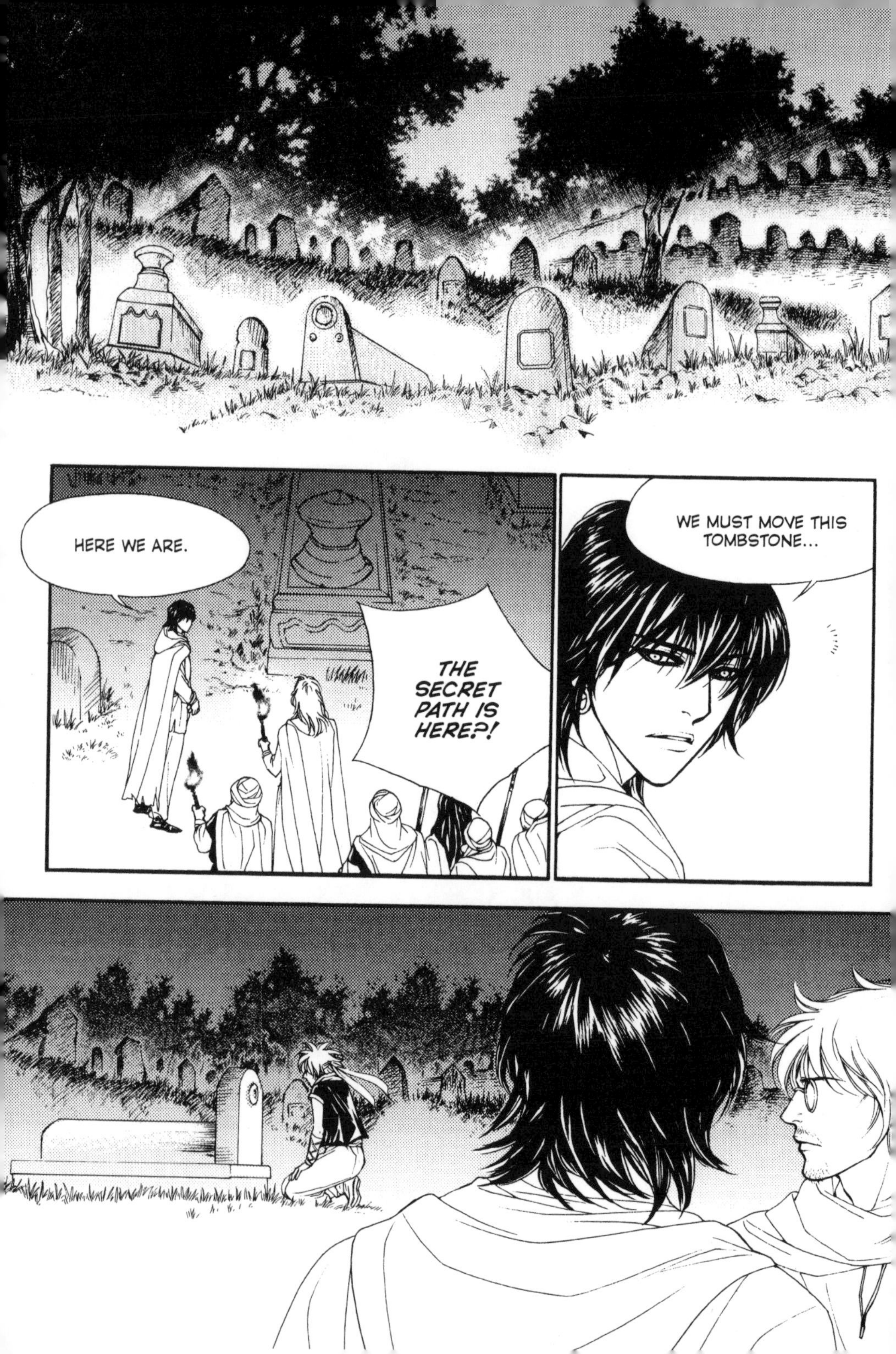
HERE WE ARE.
THE SECRET PATH IS HERE?!
WE MUST MOVE THIS TOMBSTONE...

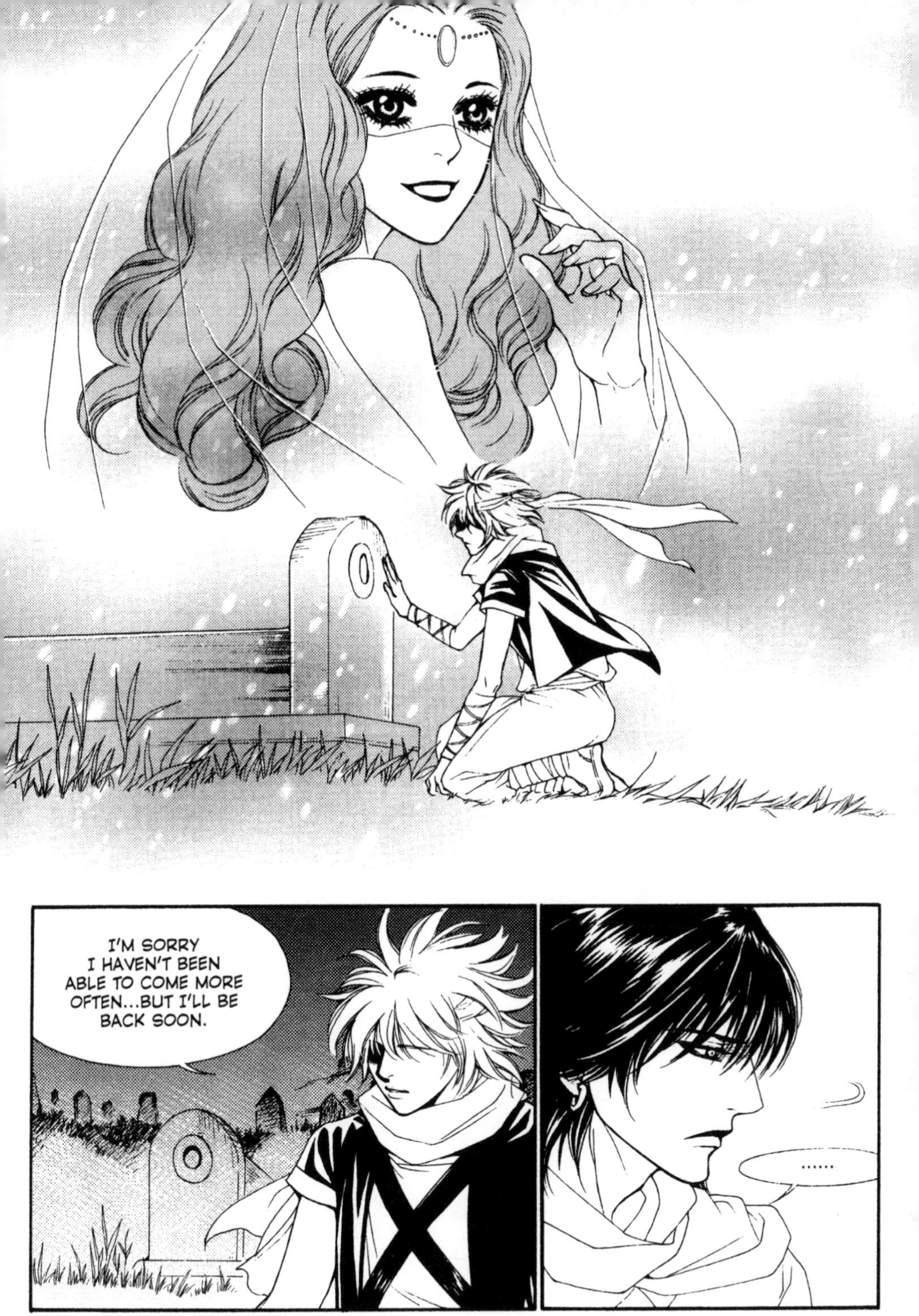
I'M SORRY I HAVEN'T BEEN ABLE TO COME MORE OFTEN...BUT I'LL BE BACK SOON.
......

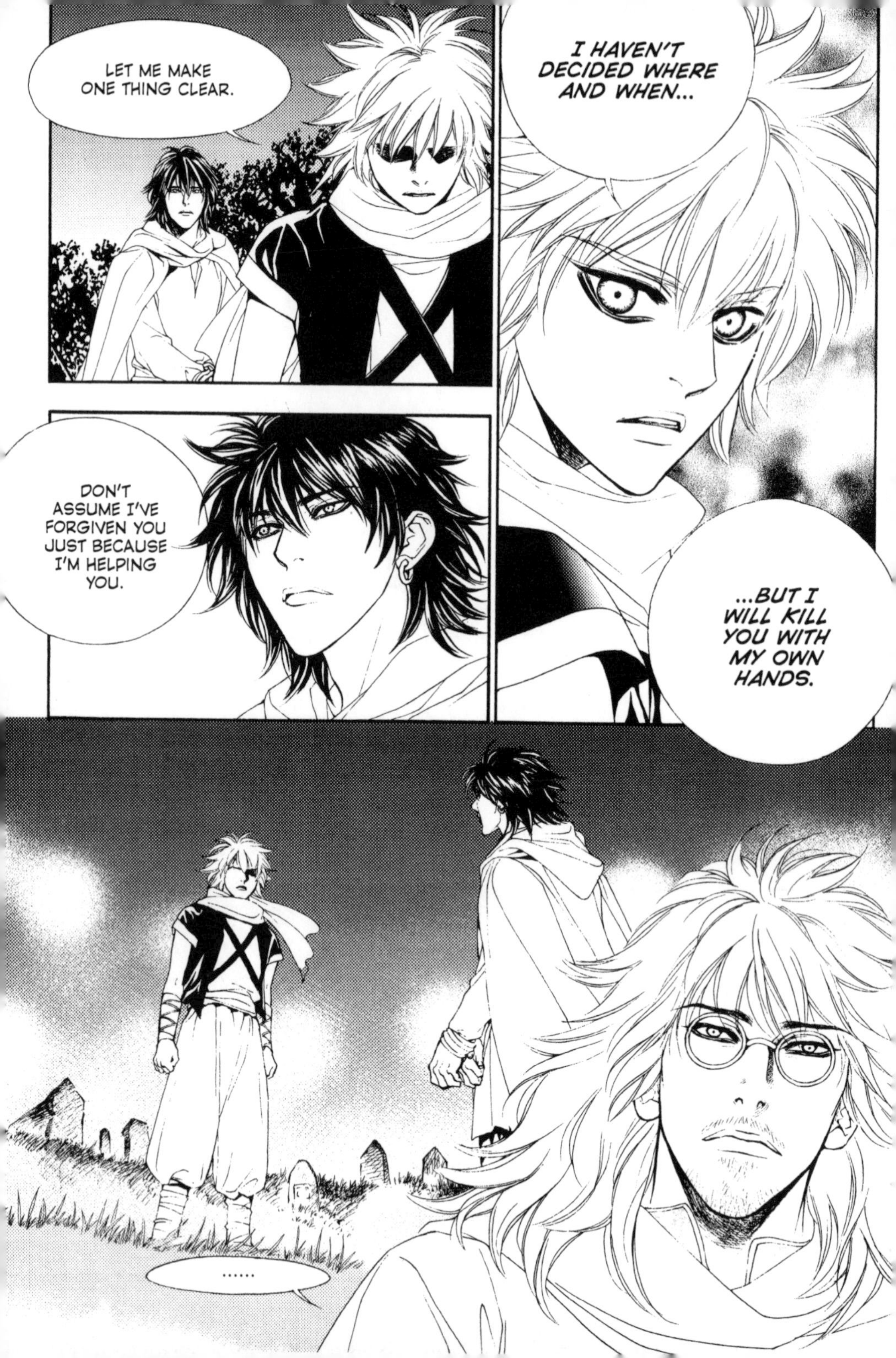
LET ME MAKE ONE THING CLEAR.
I HAVEN'T DECIDED WHERE AND WHEN...
DON'T ASSUME I'VE FORGIVEN YOU JUST BECAUSE I'M HELPING YOU.
...BUT I WILL KILL YOU WITH MY OWN HANDS.
......

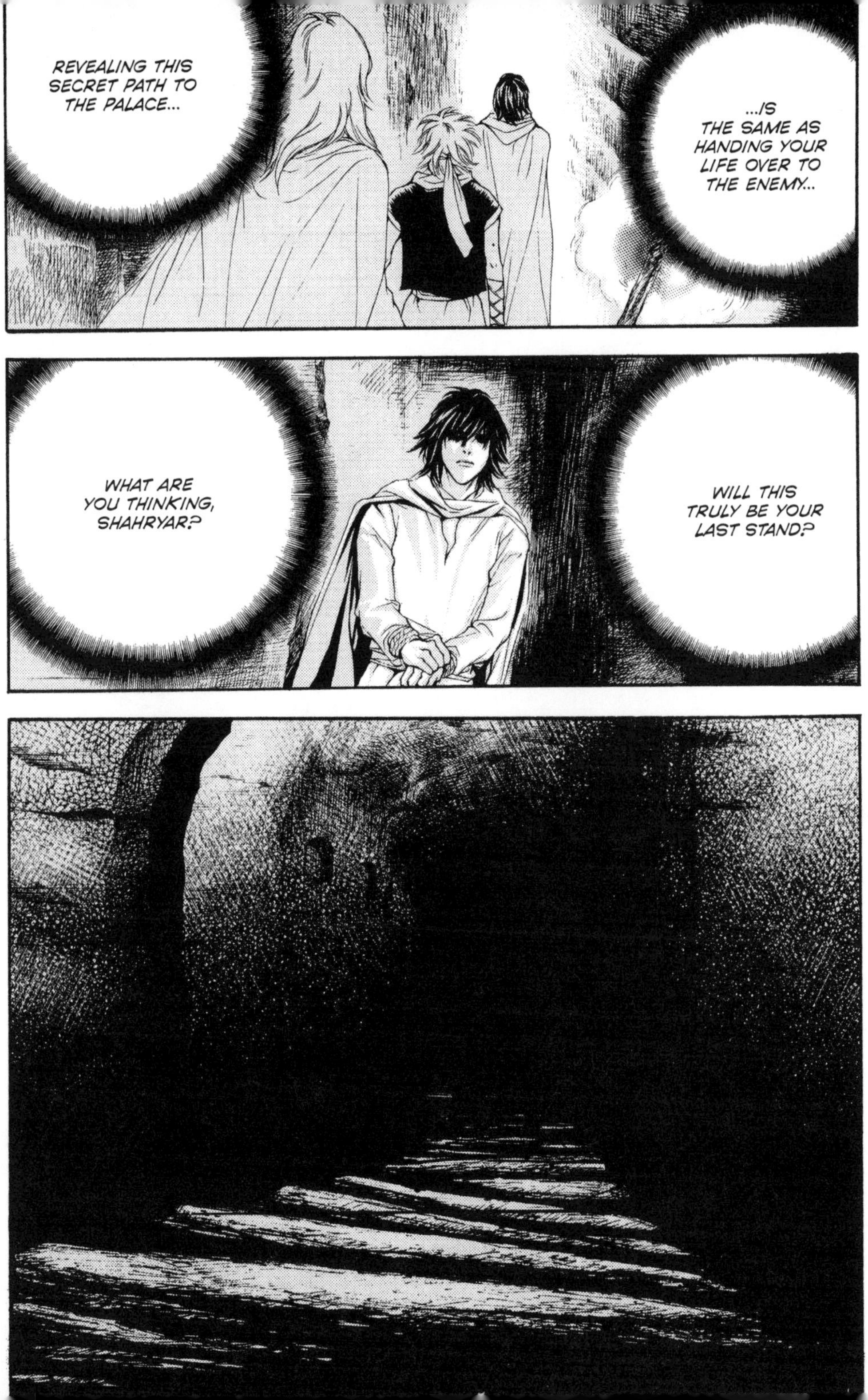
REVEALING THIS SECRET PATH TO THE PALACE...
...IS THE SAME AS HANDING YOUR LIFE OVER TO THE ENEMY...
WHAT ARE YOU THINKING, SHAHRYAR?
WILL THIS TRULY BE YOUR LAST STAND?

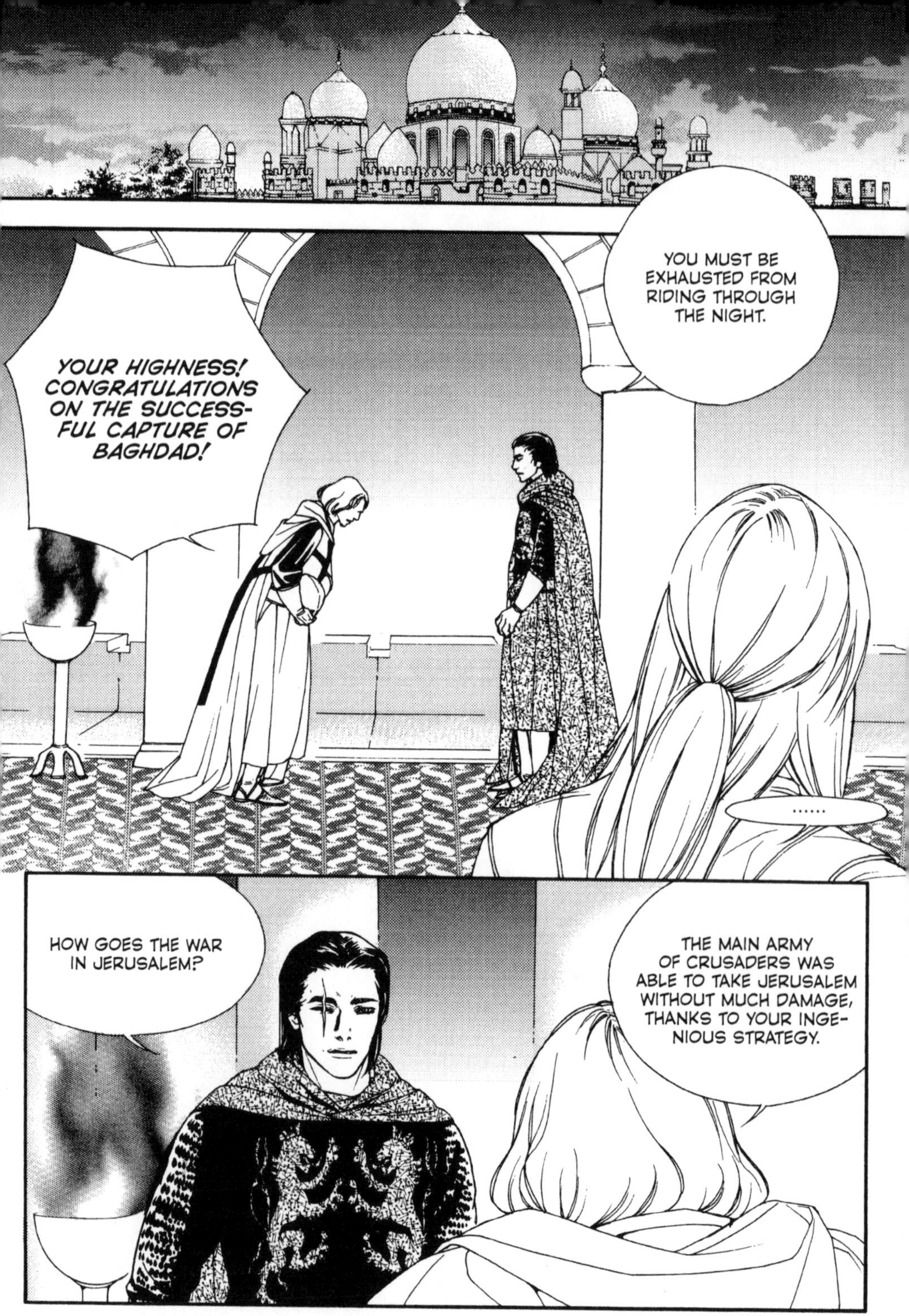
YOUR HIGHNESS! CONGRATULATIONS ON THE SUCCESS-FUL CAPTURE OF BAGHDAD!
YOU MUST BE EXHAUSTED FROM RIDING THROUGH THE NIGHT.
......
HOW GOES THE WAR IN JERUSALEM?
THE MAIN ARMY OF CRUSADERS WAS ABLE TO TAKE JERUSALEM WITHOUT MUCH DAMAGE, THANKS TO YOUR INGE-NIOUS STRATEGY.

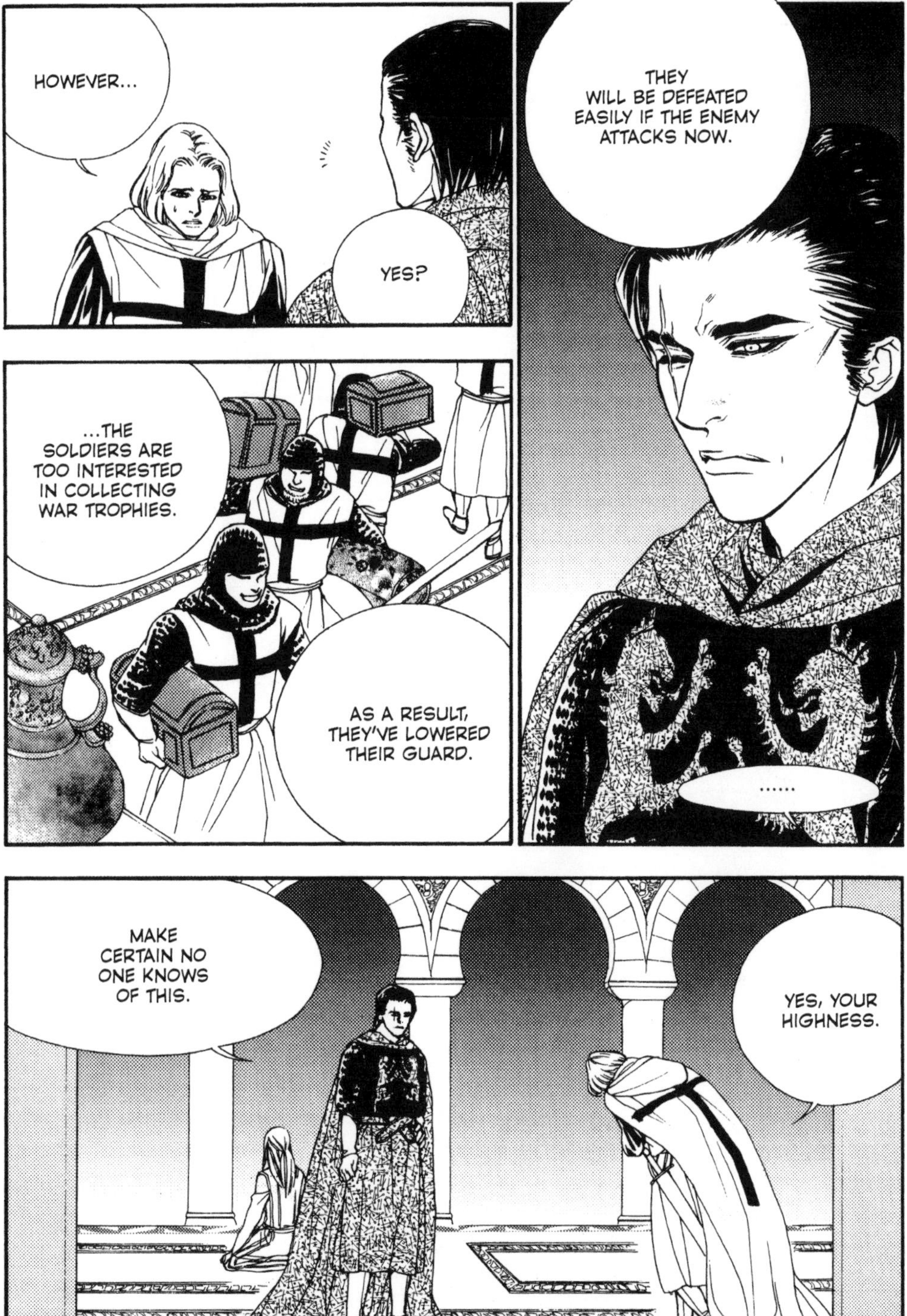
HOWEVER...
YES?
...THE SOLDIERS ARE TOO INTERESTED IN COLLECTING WAR TROPHIES.
AS A RESULT, THEY'VE LOWERED THEIR GUARD.
THEY WILL BE DEFEATED EASILY IF THE ENEMY ATTACKS NOW.
......
MAKE CERTAIN NO ONE KNOWS OF THIS.
YES, YOUR HIGHNESS.

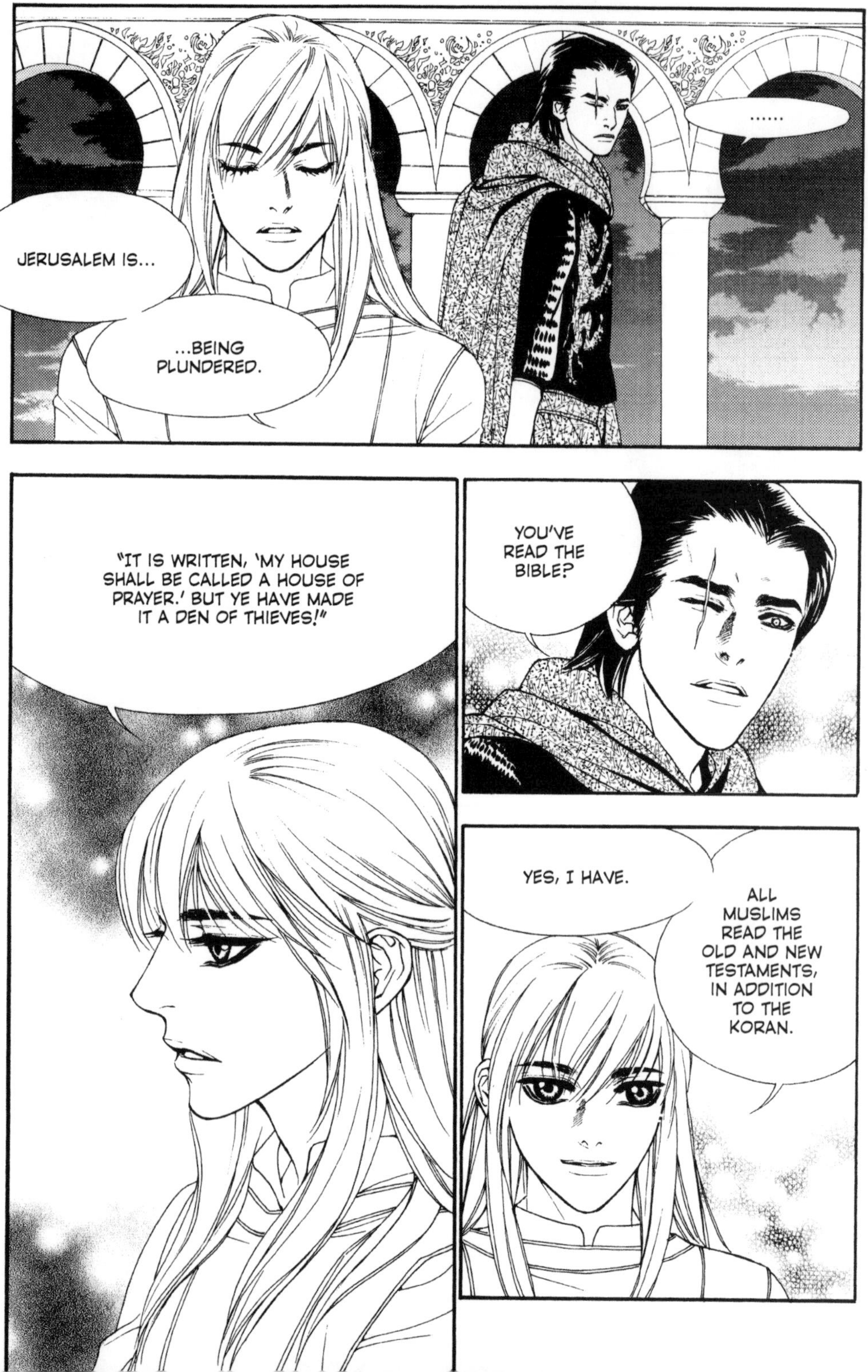
JERUSALEM IS...
...BEING PLUNDERED.
......
"IT IS WRITTEN, 'MY HOUSE SHALL BE CALLED A HOUSE OF PRAYER.' BUT YE HAVE MADE IT A DEN OF THIEVES!"
YOU'VE READ THE BIBLE?
YES, I HAVE.
ALL MUSLIMS READ THE OLD AND NEW TESTAMENTS, IN ADDITION TO THE KORAN.

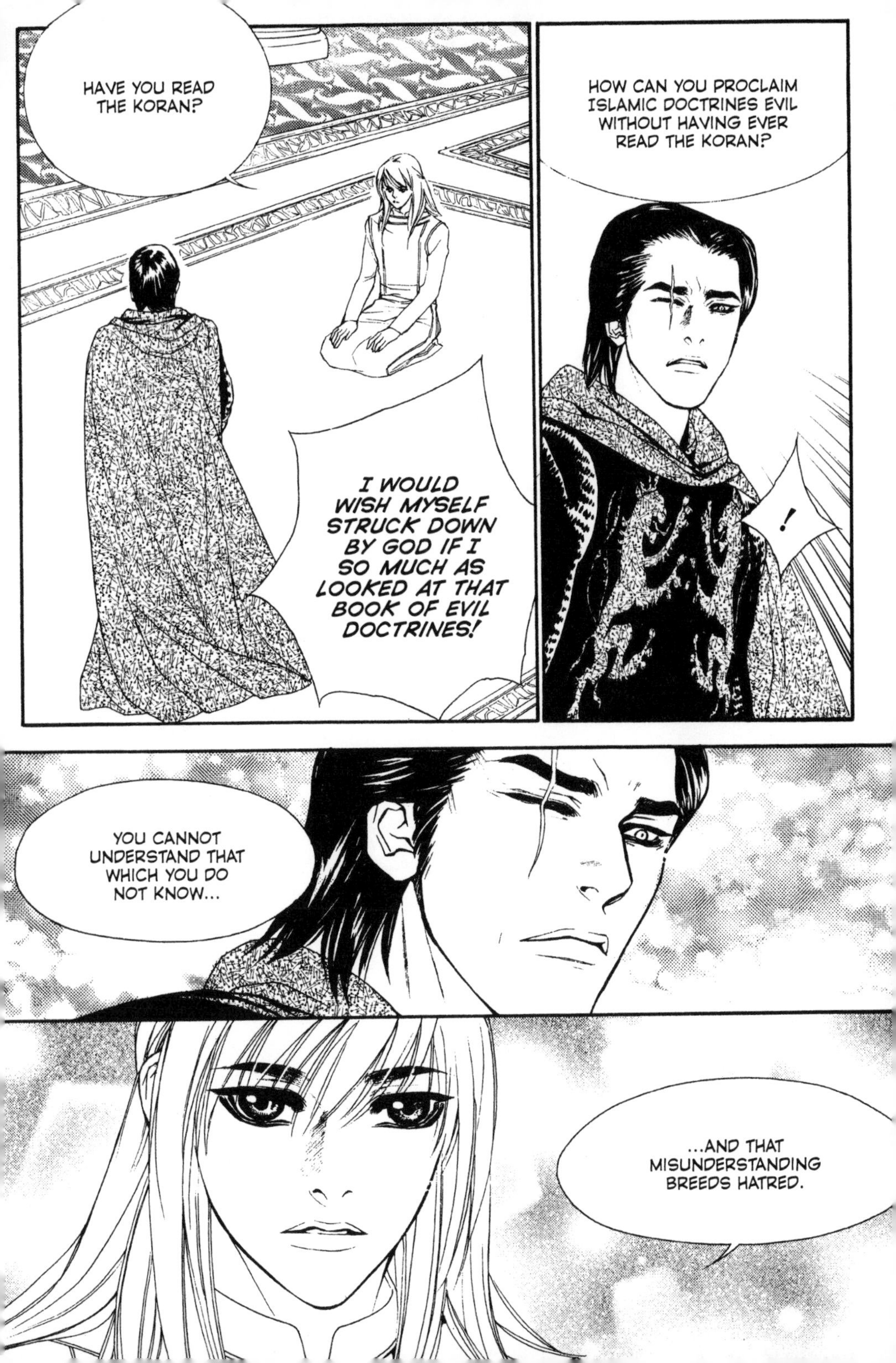
HAVE YOU READ THE KORAN?
I WOULD WISH MYSELF STRUCK DOWN BY GOD IF I SO MUCH AS LOOKED AT THAT BOOK OF EVIL DOCTRINES!
HOW CAN YOU PROCLAIM ISLAMIC DOCTRINES EVIL WITHOUT HAVING EVER READ THE KORAN?
!
YOU CANNOT UNDERSTAND THAT WHICH YOU DO NOT KNOW...
...AND THAT MISUNDERSTANDING BREEDS HATRED.

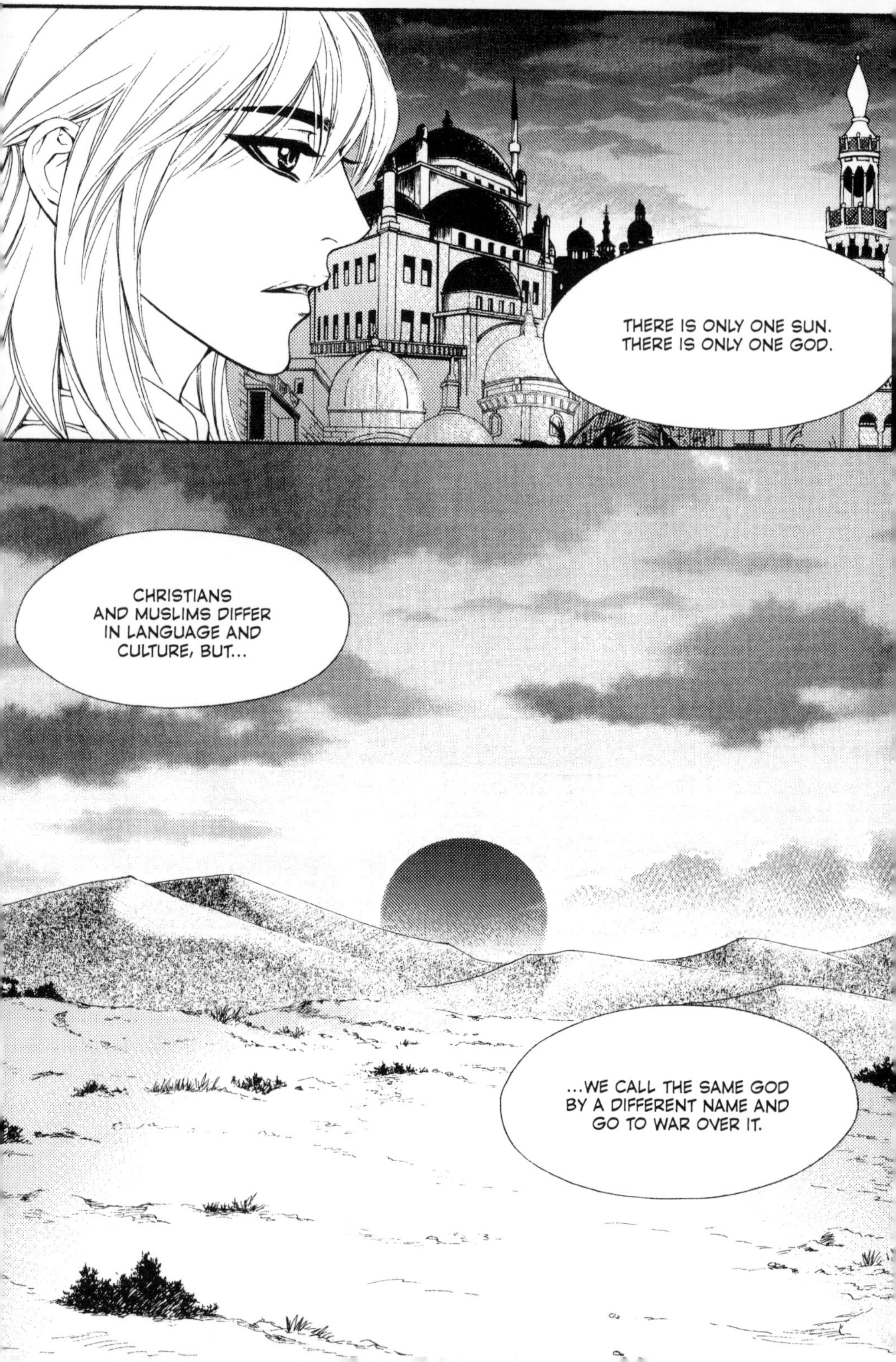
THERE IS ONLY ONE SUN. THERE IS ONLY ONE GOD.
CHRISTIANS AND MUSLIMS DIFFER IN LANGUAGE AND CULTURE, BUT...
...WE CALL THE SAME GOD BY A DIFFERENT NAME AND GO TO WAR OVER IT.

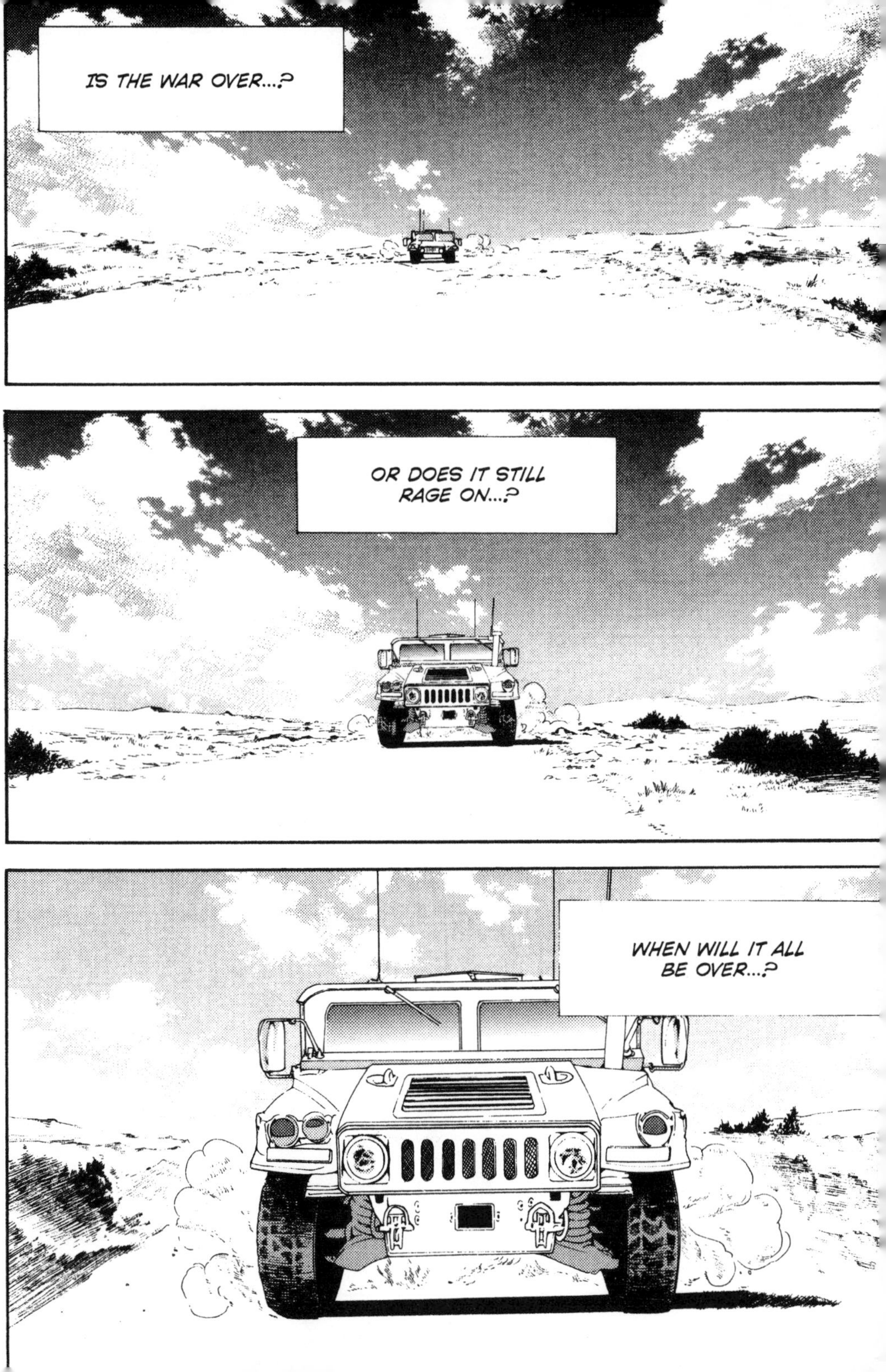
IS THE WAR OVER...?
OR DOES IT STILL RAGE ON...?
WHEN WILL IT ALL BE OVER...?

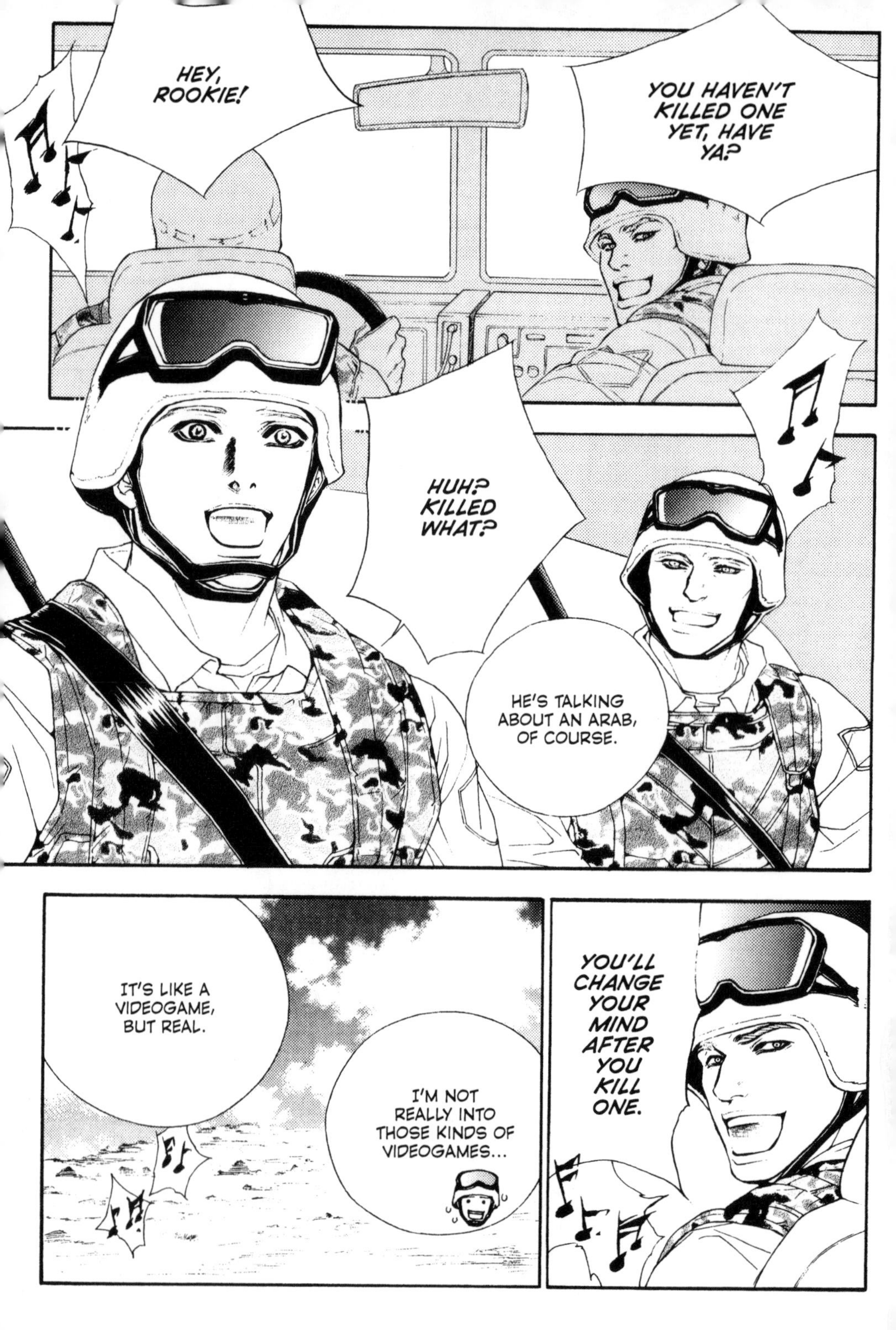
HEY, ROOKIE!
YOU HAVEN'T KILLED ONE YET, HAVE YA?
HUH? KILLED WHAT?
HE'S TALKING ABOUT AN ARAB, OF COURSE.
IT'S LIKE A VIDEOGAME, BUT REAL.
I'M NOT REALLY INTO THOSE KINDS OF VIDEOGAMES...
YOU'LL CHANGE YOUR MIND AFTER YOU KILL ONE.

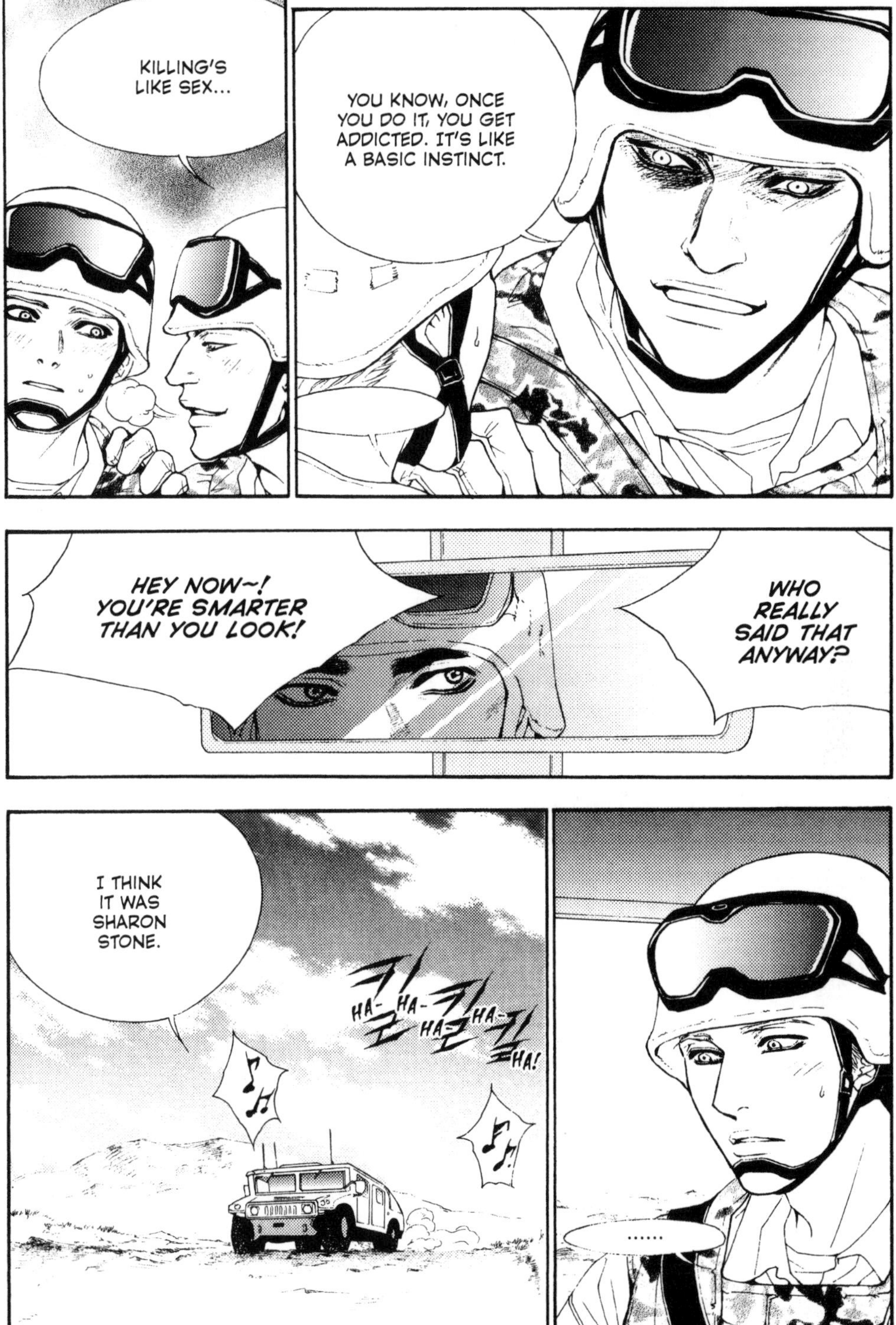
KILLING'S LIKE SEX...
YOU KNOW, ONCE YOU DO IT, YOU GET ADDICTED. IT'S LIKE A BASIC INSTINCT.
HEY NOW~! YOU'RE SMARTER THAN YOU LOOK!
WHO REALLY SAID THAT ANYWAY?
I THINK IT WAS SHARON STONE.
HA-HA-HA-HA-HA!
......

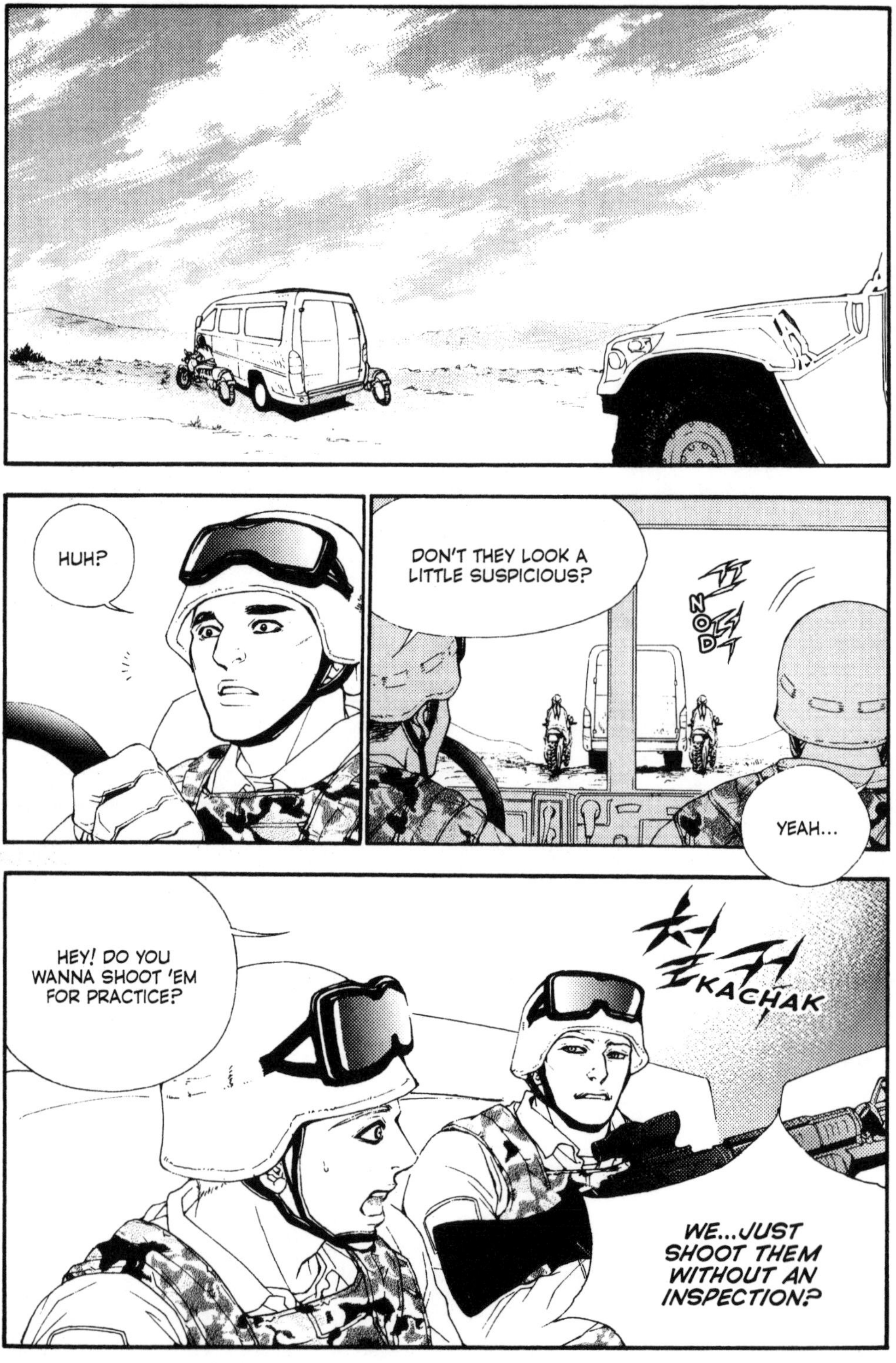
HUH?
DON'T THEY LOOK A LITTLE SUSPICIOUS?
NOD
YEAH...
HEY! DO YOU WANNA SHOOT 'EM FOR PRACTICE?
KACHAK
WE...JUST SHOOT THEM WITHOUT AN INSPECTION?

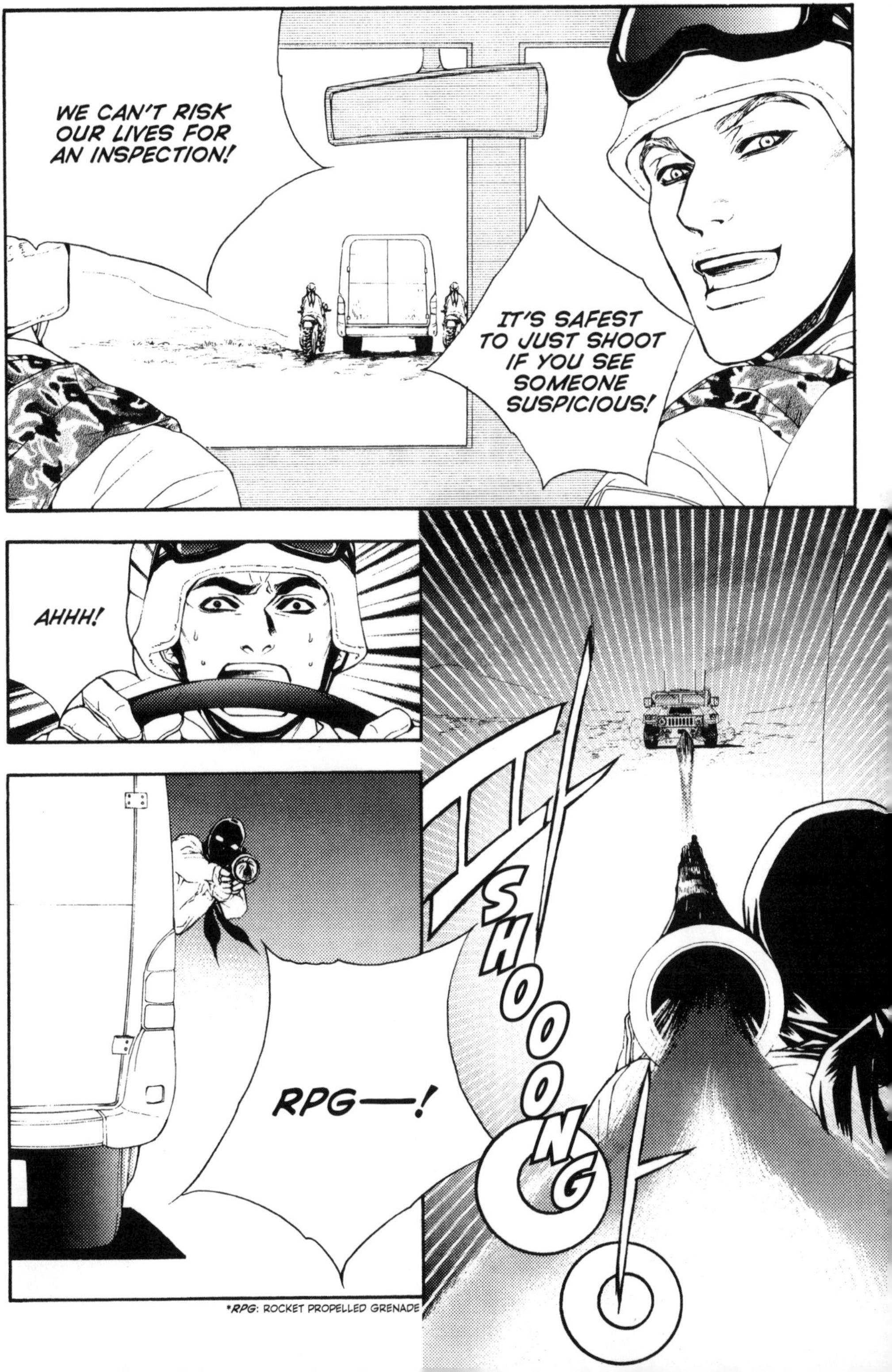
WE CAN'T RISK OUR LIVES FOR AN INSPECTION!
IT'S SAFEST TO JUST SHOOT IF YOU SEE SOMEONE SUSPICIOUS!
AHHH!
RPG—!
SHOOOONG

*RPG: ROCKET PROPELLED GRENADE

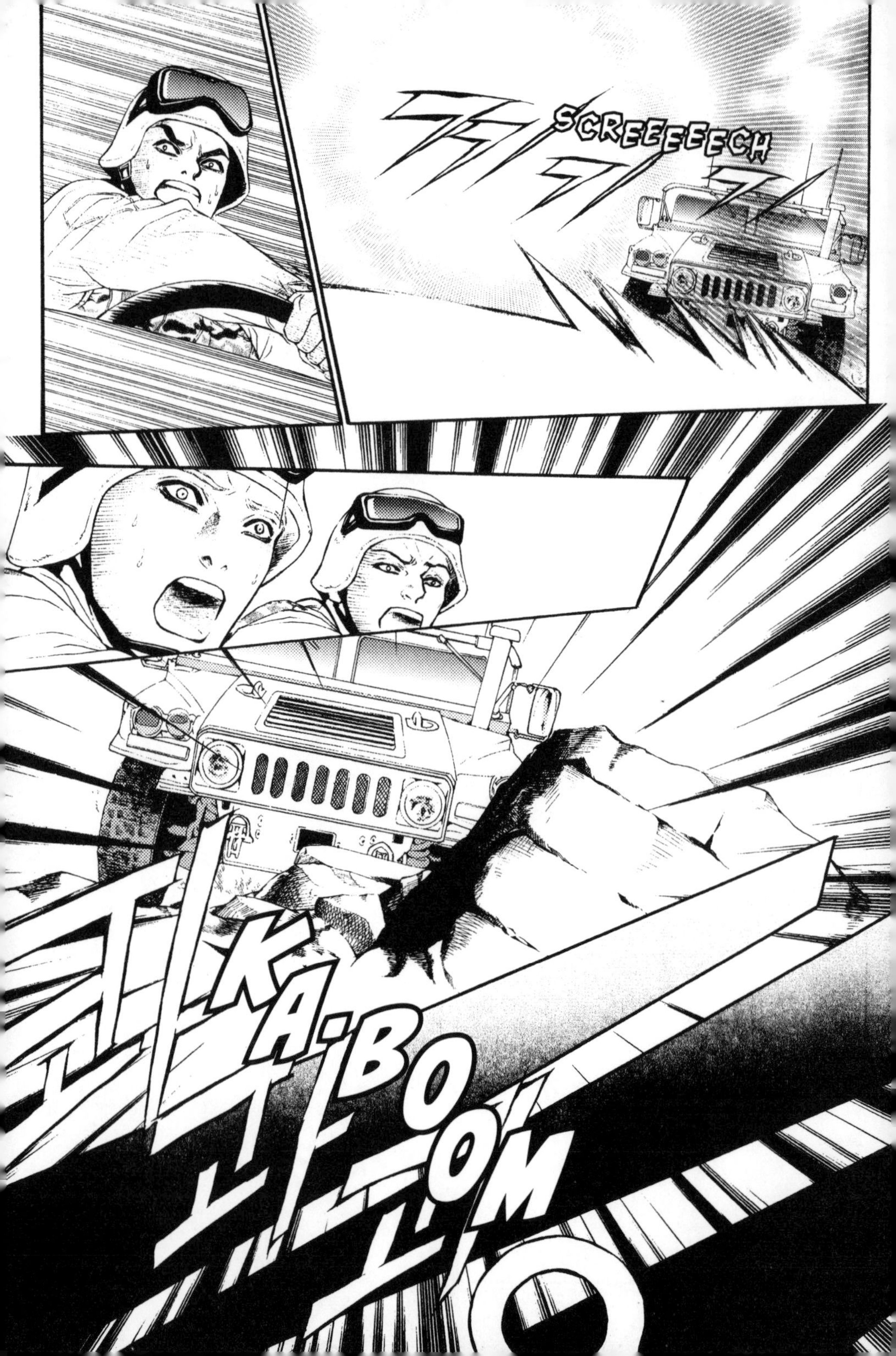
SCREEEEEECH
KA-BOOM

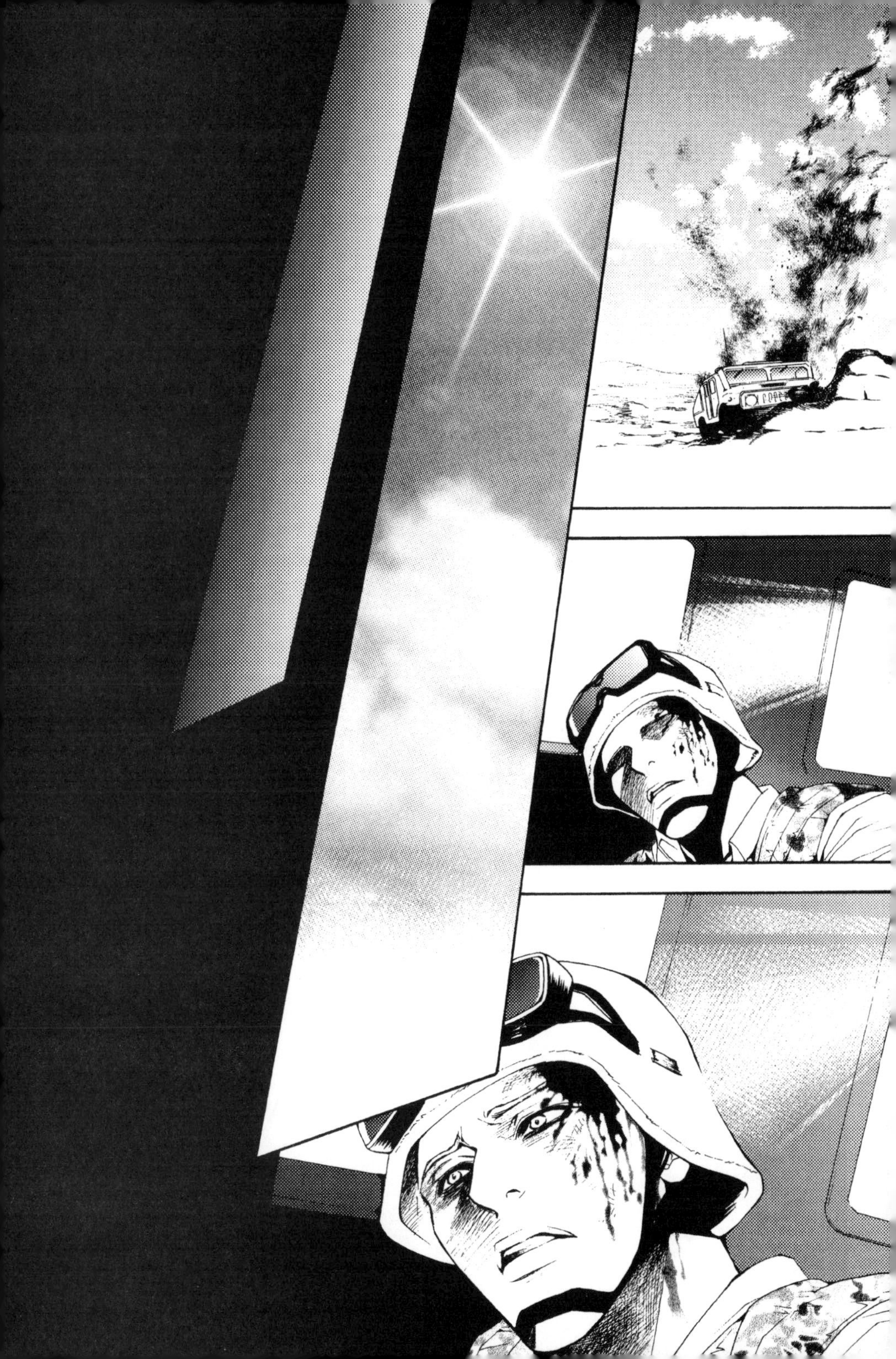

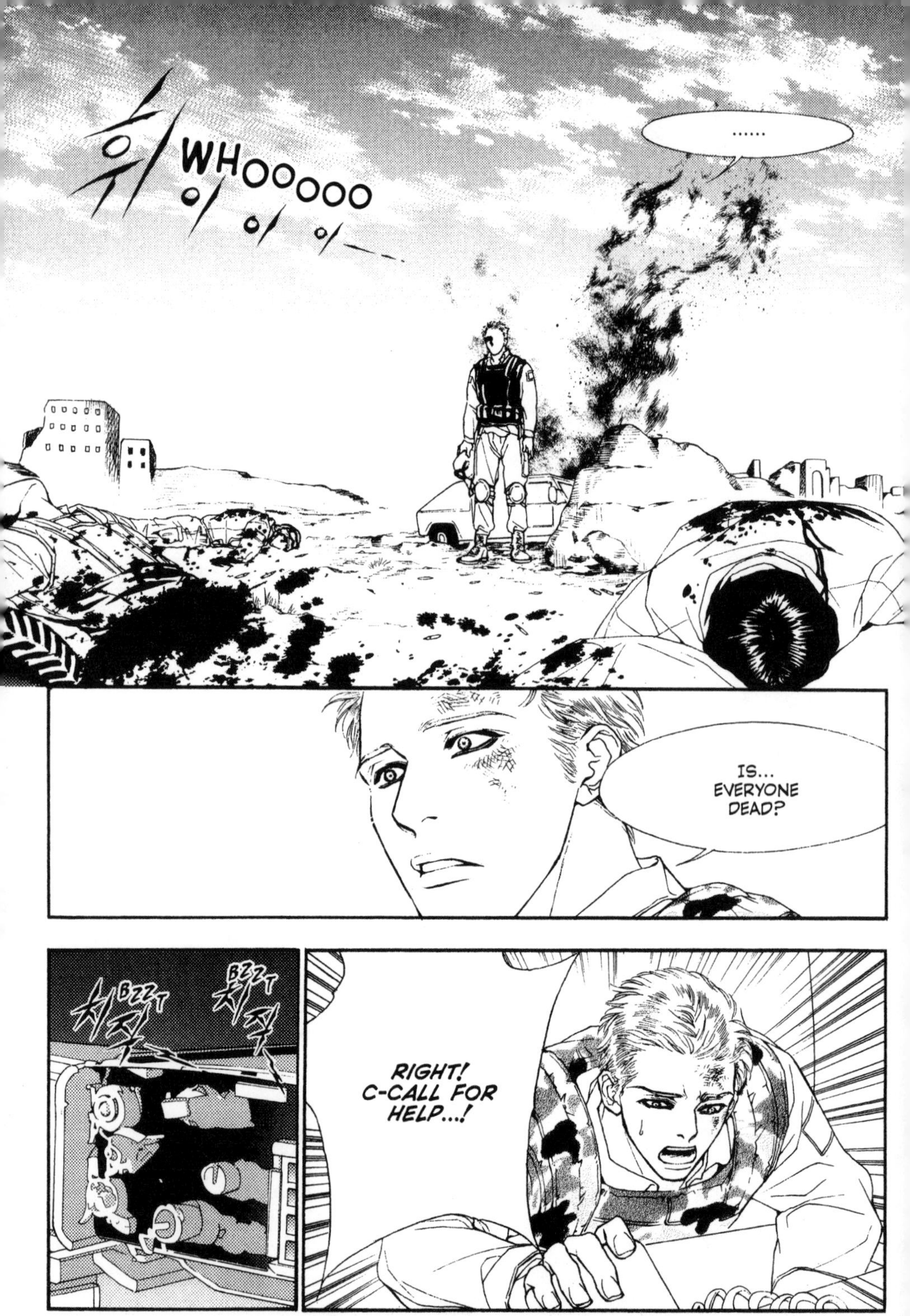
휘이이이
WHOOOOO
......
IS... EVERYONE DEAD?
치직
BZZT
치직
BZZT
RIGHT! C-CALL FOR HELP...!

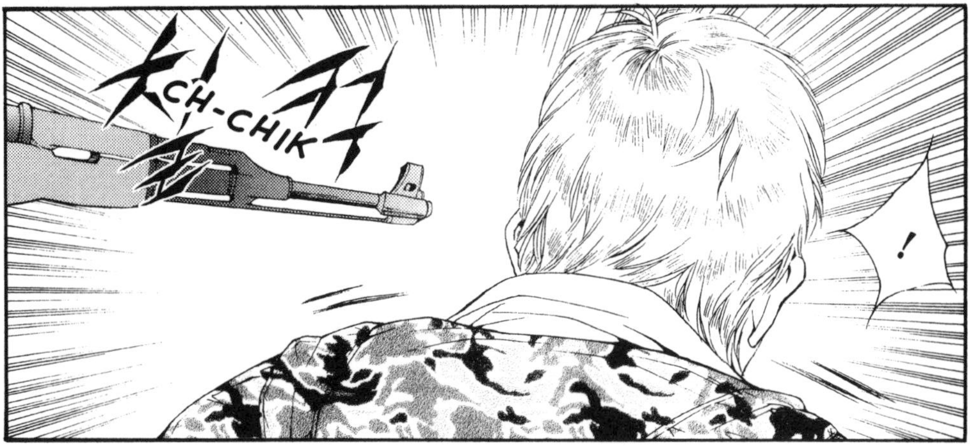
CH-CHIK
!

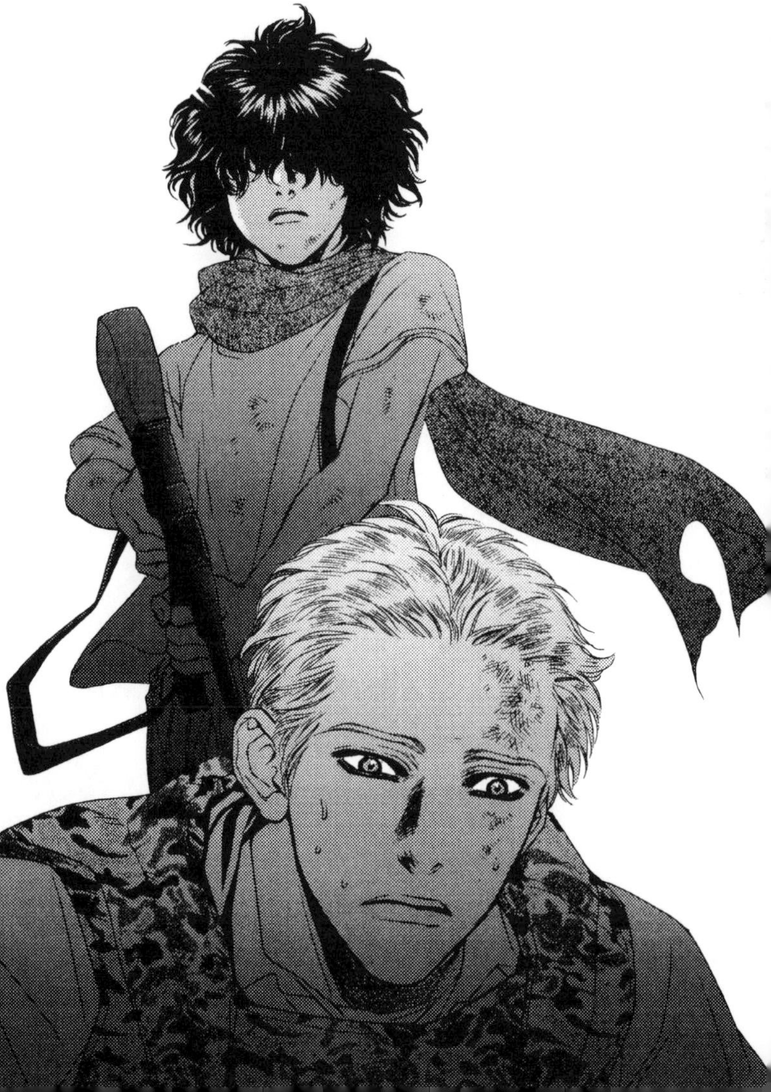

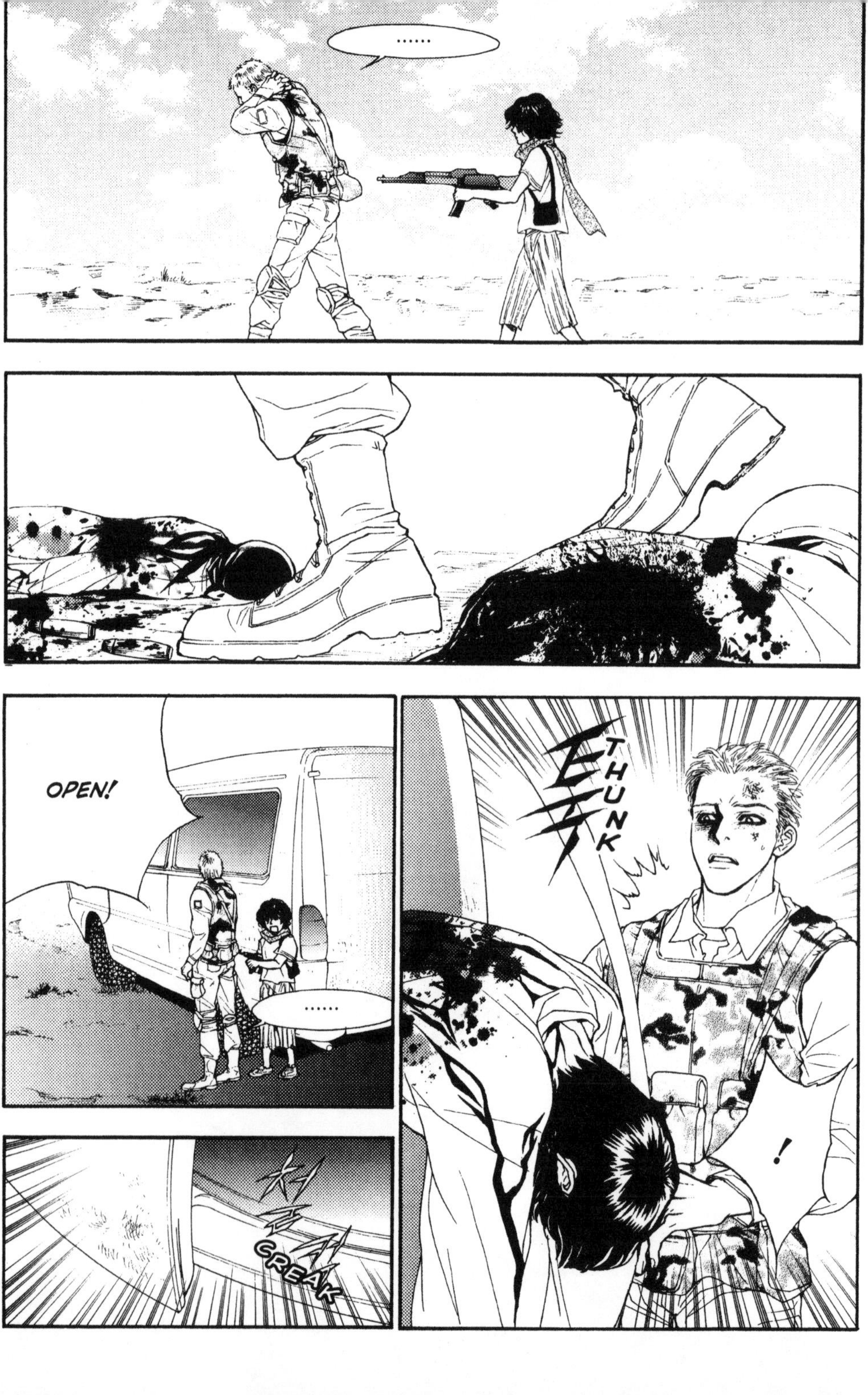
......
OPEN!
......
CREAK
THUNK
!

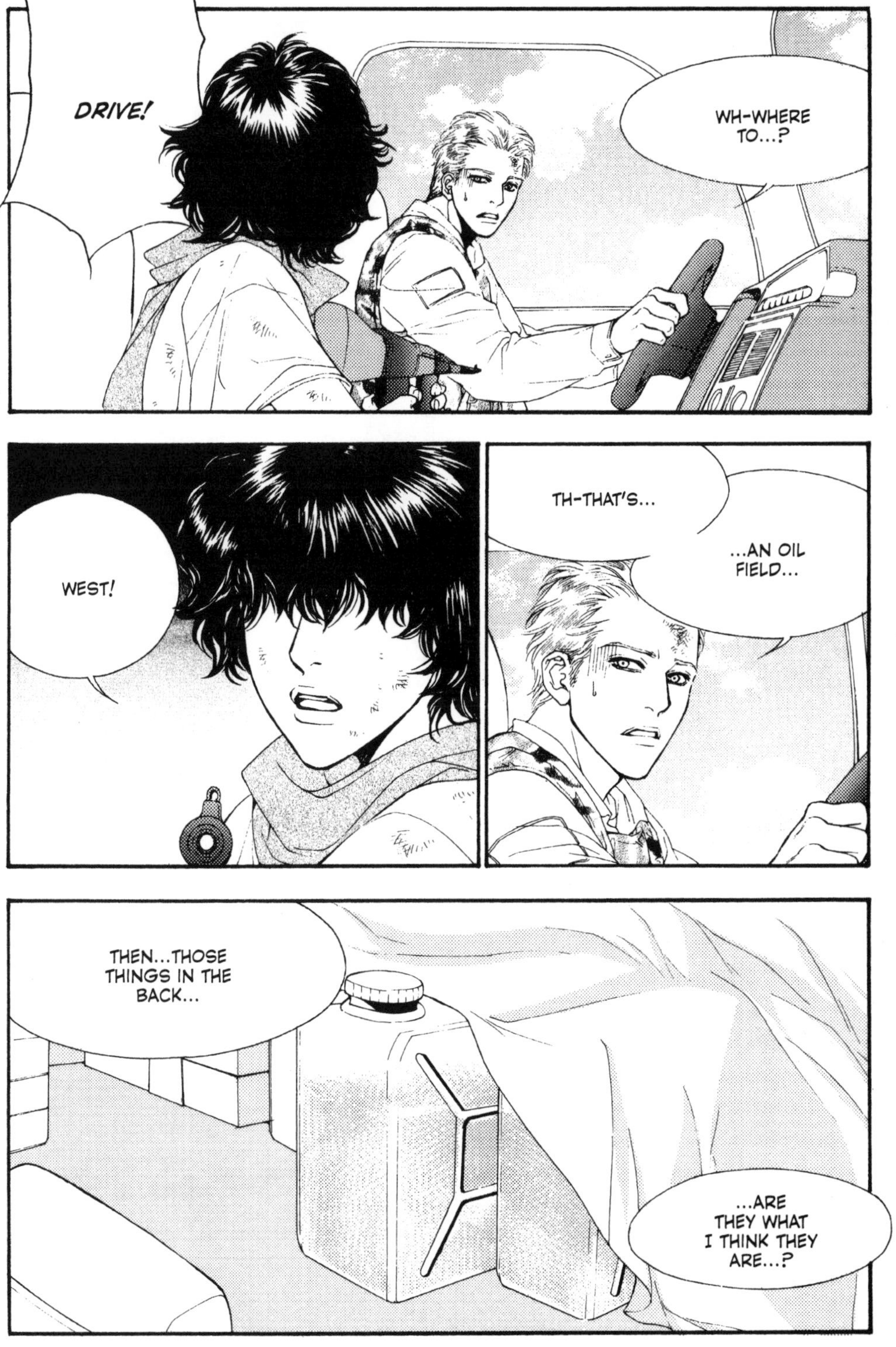
DRIVE!
WH-WHERE TO...?
WEST!
TH-THAT'S...
...AN OIL FIELD...
THEN...THOSE THINGS IN THE BACK...
...ARE THEY WHAT I THINK THEY ARE...?

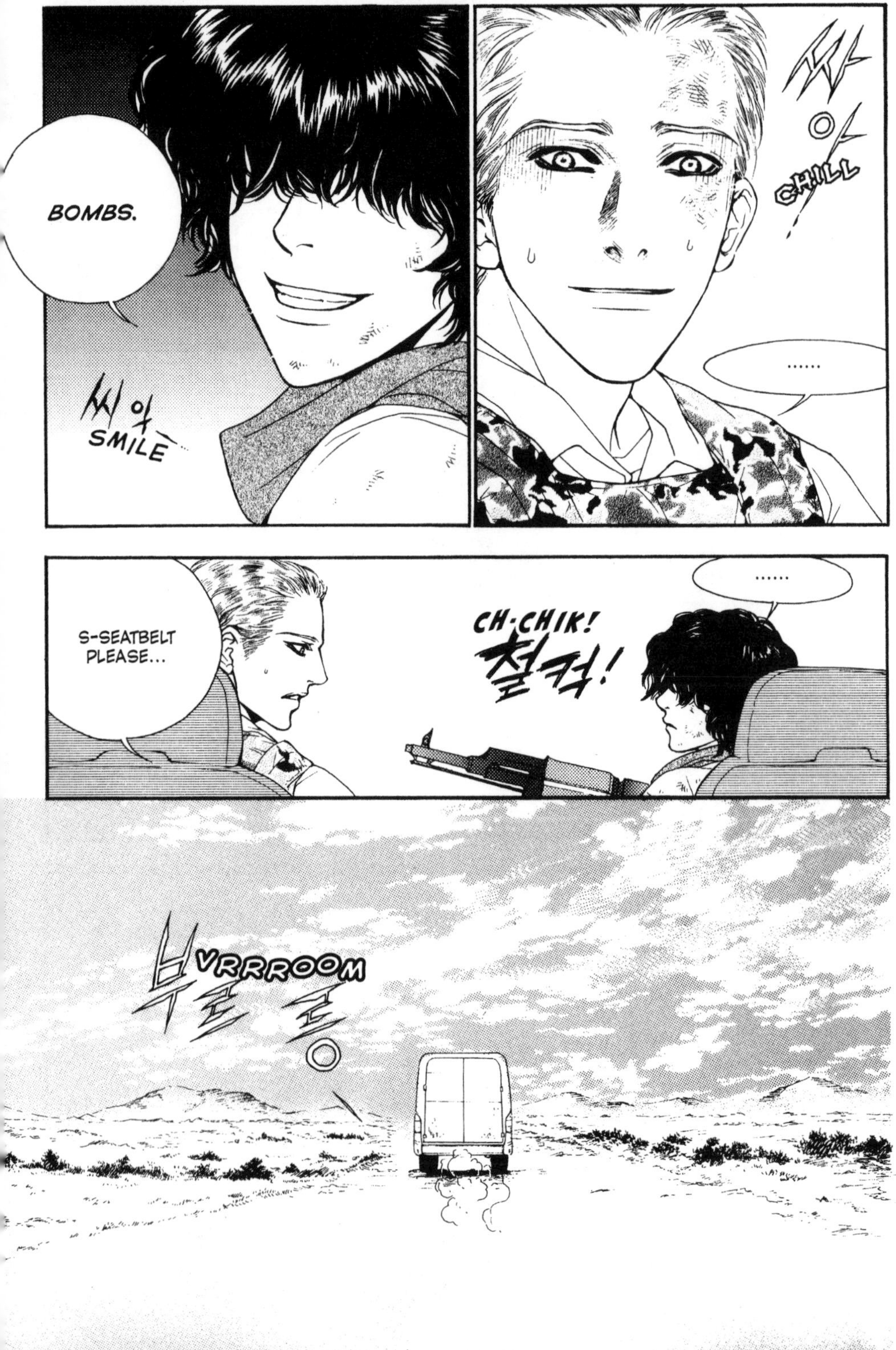
BOMBS.
씨익
SMILE
CHILL
......
S-SEATBELT PLEASE...
......
CH-CHIK!
철컥!
VRRROOM
부르릉

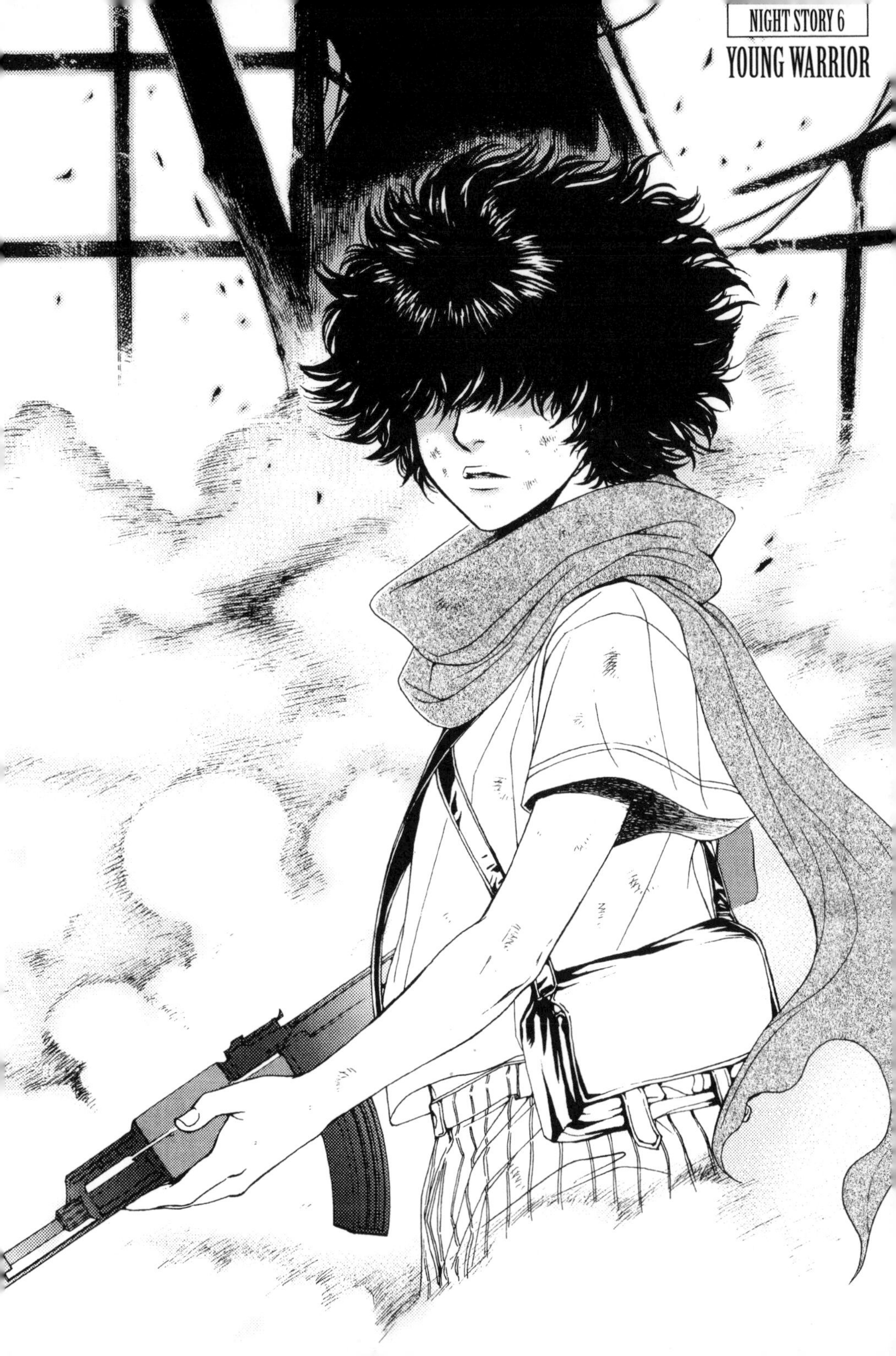
NIGHT STORY 6
YOUNG WARRIOR

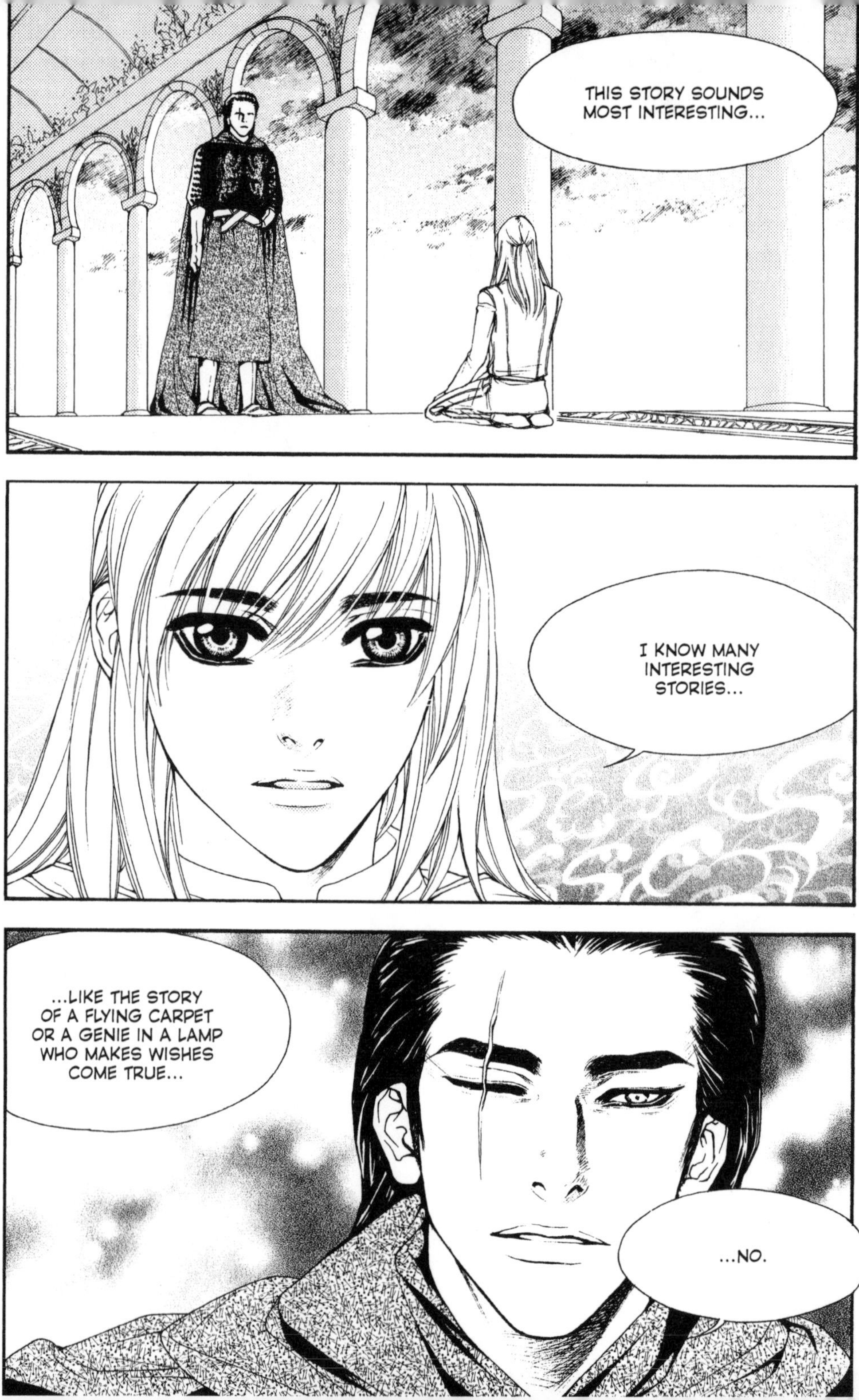
THIS STORY SOUNDS MOST INTERESTING...
I KNOW MANY INTERESTING STORIES...
...LIKE THE STORY OF A FLYING CARPET OR A GENIE IN A LAMP WHO MAKES WISHES COME TRUE...
...NO.

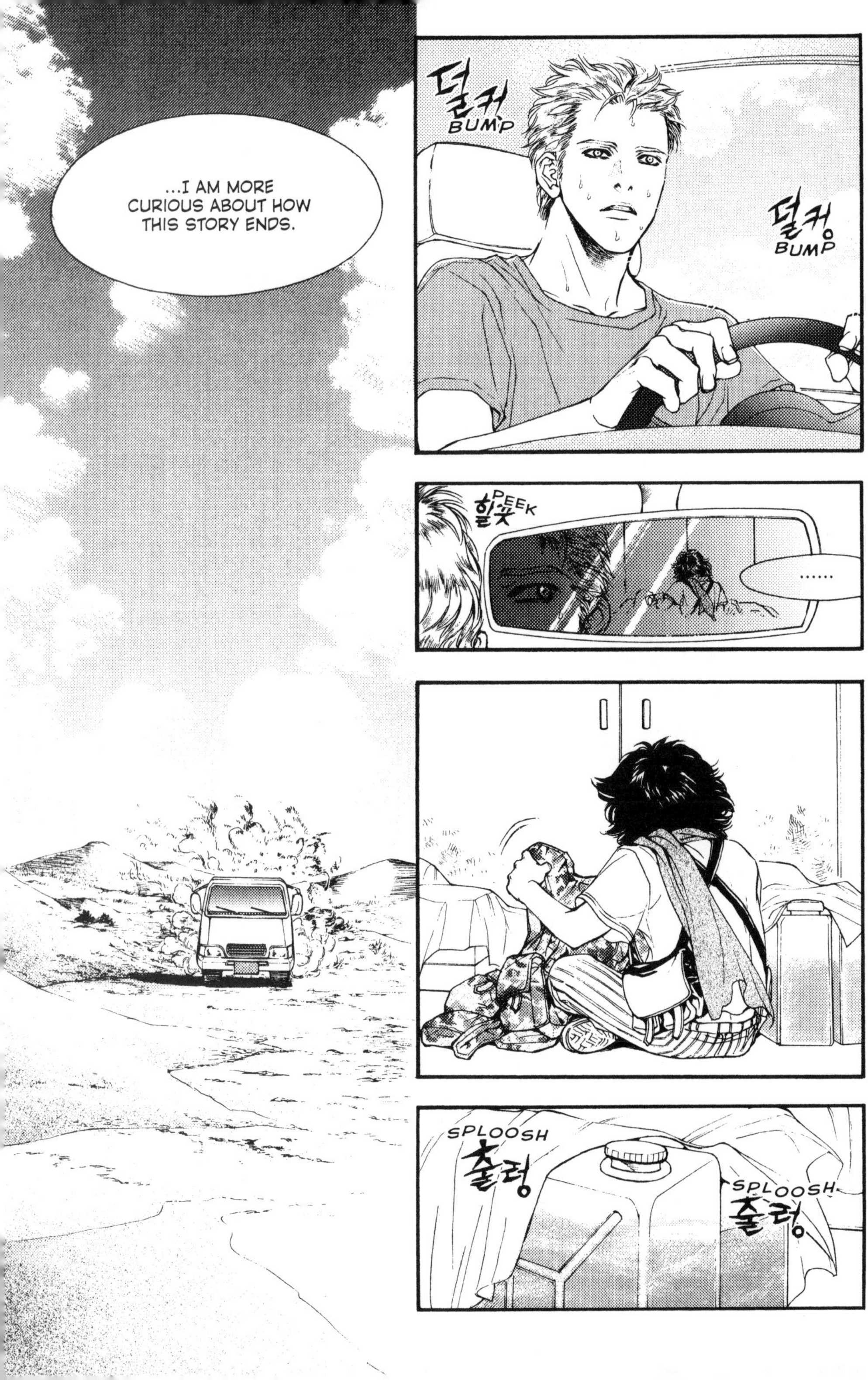
...I AM MORE CURIOUS ABOUT HOW THIS STORY ENDS.
덜컥
BUMP
덜컹
BUMP
힐끗
PEEK
......
SPLOOSH
출렁
SPLOOSH
출렁

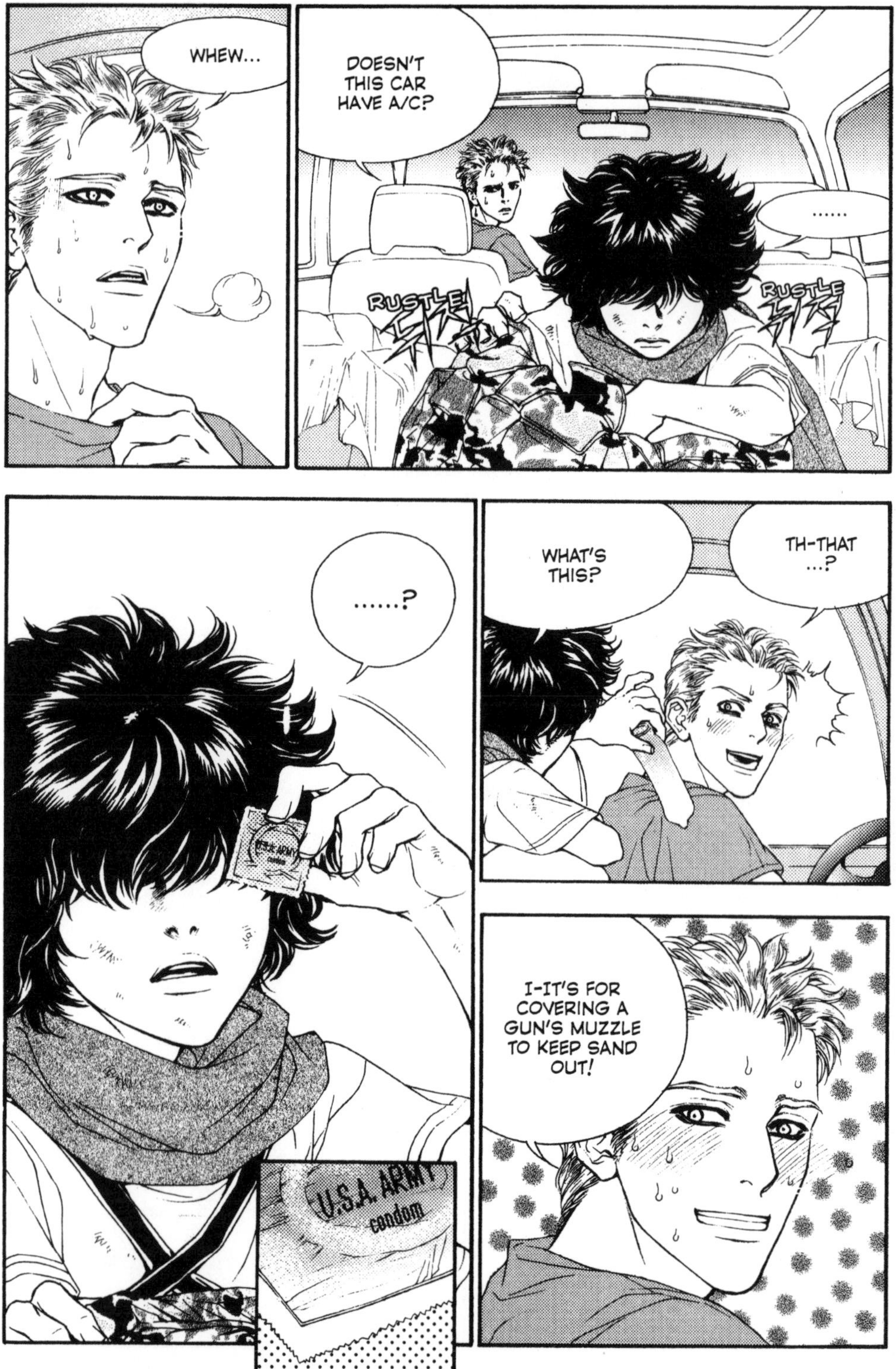
WHEW...
DOESN'T THIS CAR HAVE A/C?
RUSTLE
RUSTLE
......
......?
U.S.A. ARMY condom
U.S.A. ARMY condom
WHAT'S THIS?
TH-THAT ...?
I-IT'S FOR COVERING A GUN'S MUZZLE TO KEEP SAND OUT!

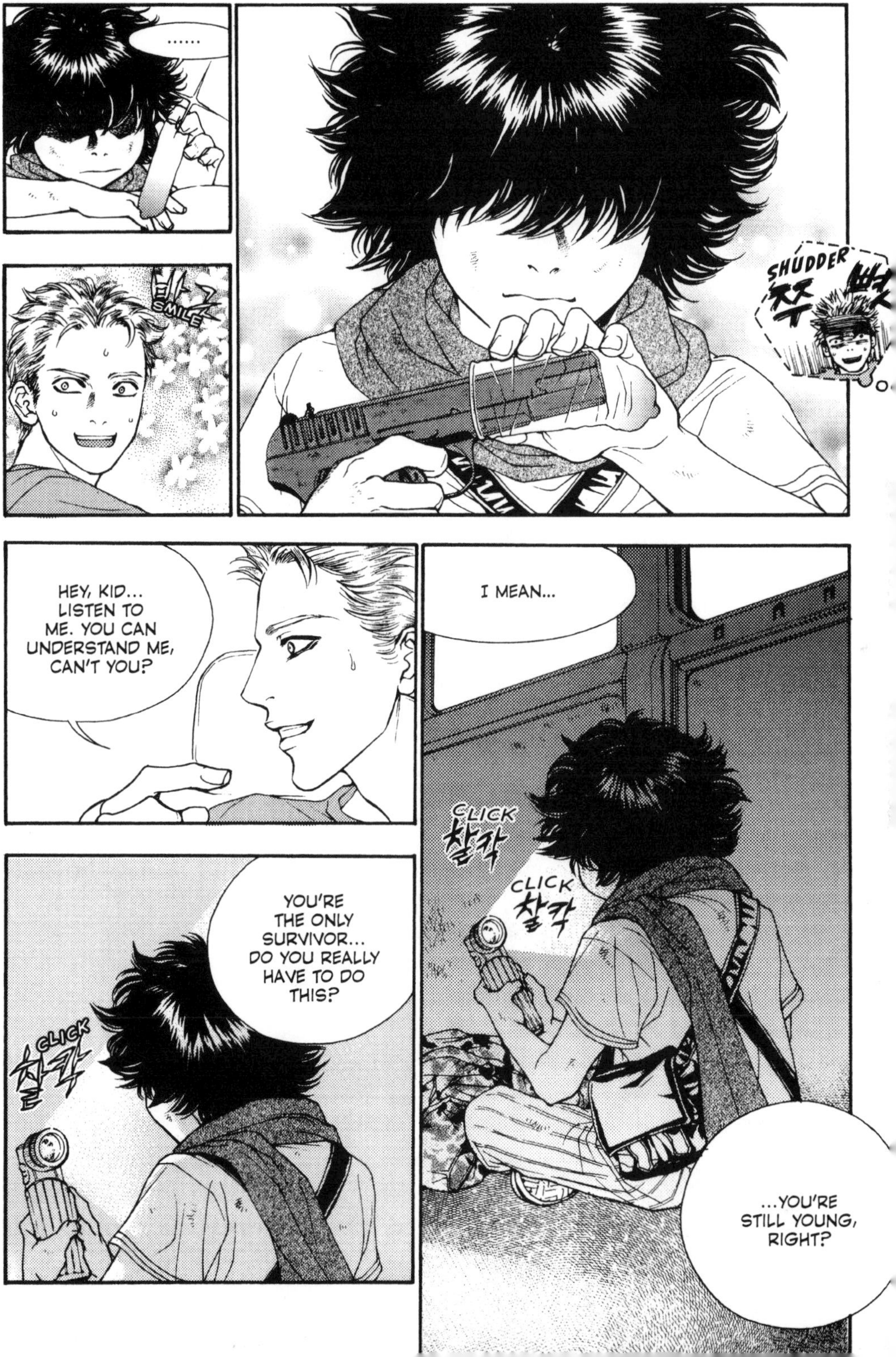
......
SMILE
SHUDDER
쭈뼛
HEY, KID... LISTEN TO ME. YOU CAN UNDERSTAND ME, CAN'T YOU?
YOU'RE THE ONLY SURVIVOR... DO YOU REALLY HAVE TO DO THIS?
CLICK
찰칵
I MEAN...
CLICK
찰칵
CLICK
찰칵
...YOU'RE STILL YOUNG, RIGHT?

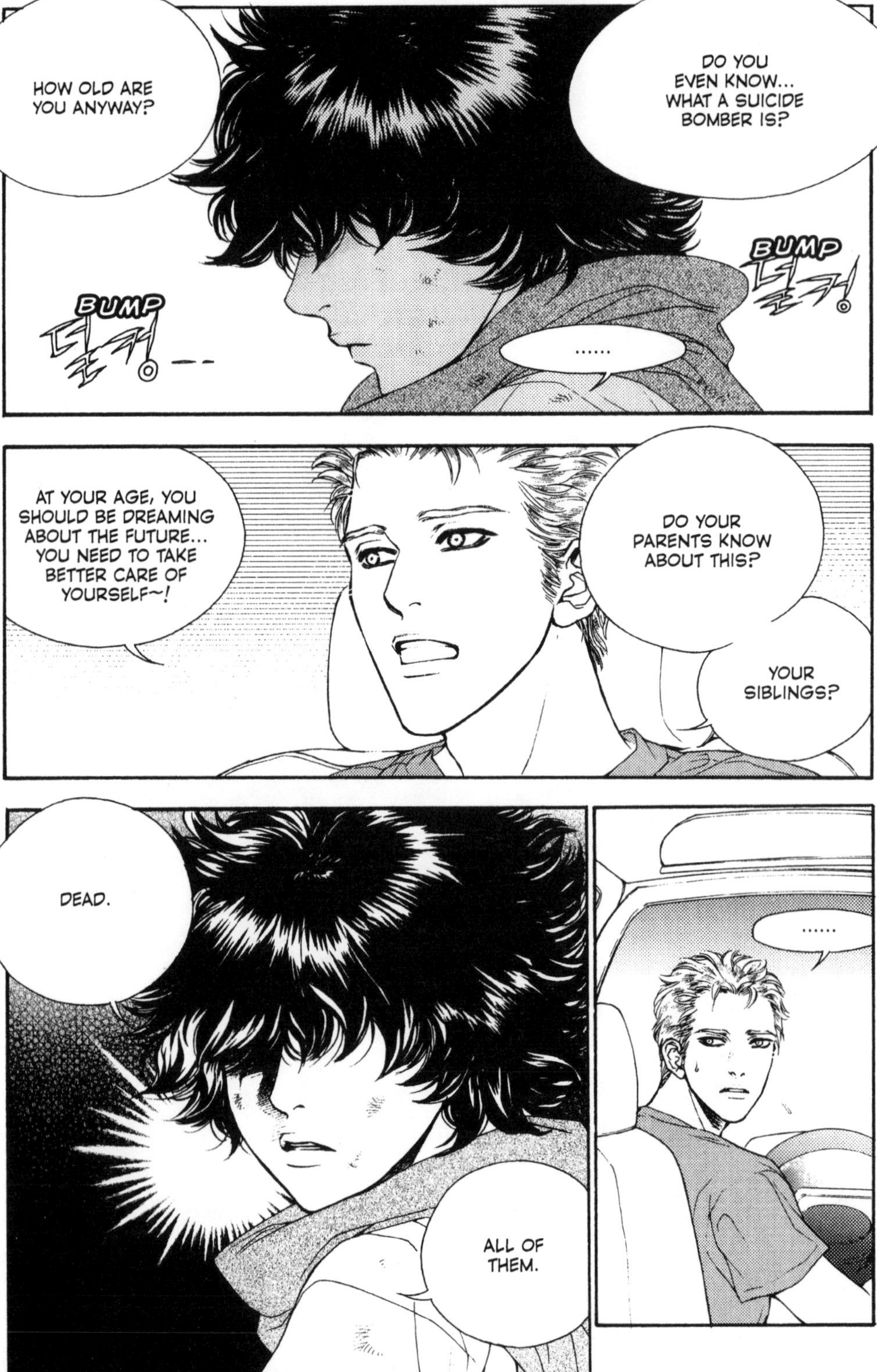
HOW OLD ARE YOU ANYWAY?
DO YOU EVEN KNOW... WHAT A SUICIDE BOMBER IS?
BUMP
BUMP
......
AT YOUR AGE, YOU SHOULD BE DREAMING ABOUT THE FUTURE... YOU NEED TO TAKE BETTER CARE OF YOURSELF~!
DO YOUR PARENTS KNOW ABOUT THIS?
YOUR SIBLINGS?
DEAD.
ALL OF THEM.
......

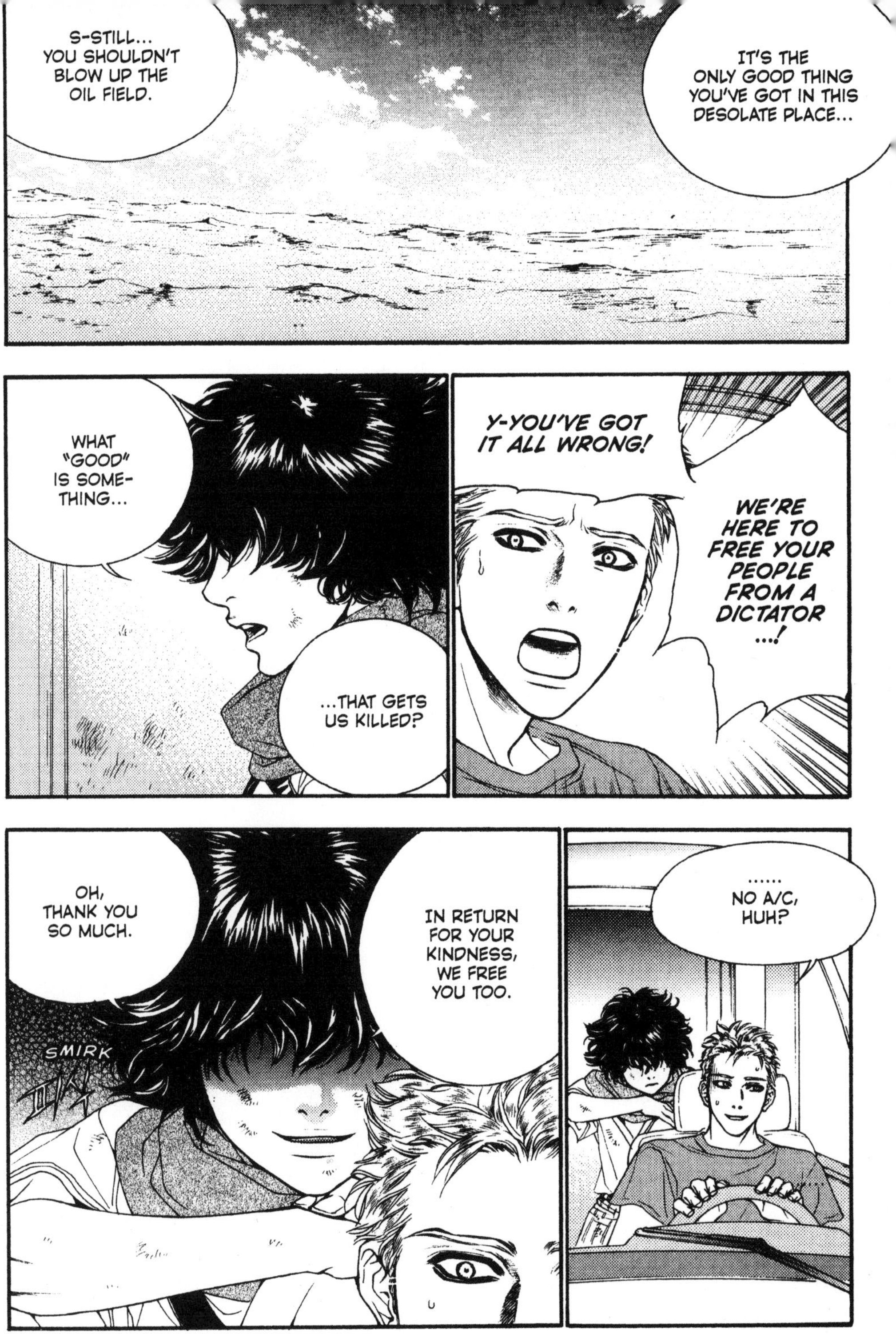
S-STILL... YOU SHOULDN'T BLOW UP THE OIL FIELD.
IT'S THE ONLY GOOD THING YOU'VE GOT IN THIS DESOLATE PLACE...
WHAT "GOOD" IS SOME-THING...
...THAT GETS US KILLED?
Y-YOU'VE GOT IT ALL WRONG!
WE'RE HERE TO FREE YOUR PEOPLE FROM A DICTATOR ...!
OH, THANK YOU SO MUCH.
IN RETURN FOR YOUR KINDNESS, WE FREE YOU TOO.
SMIRK
...... NO A/C, HUH?

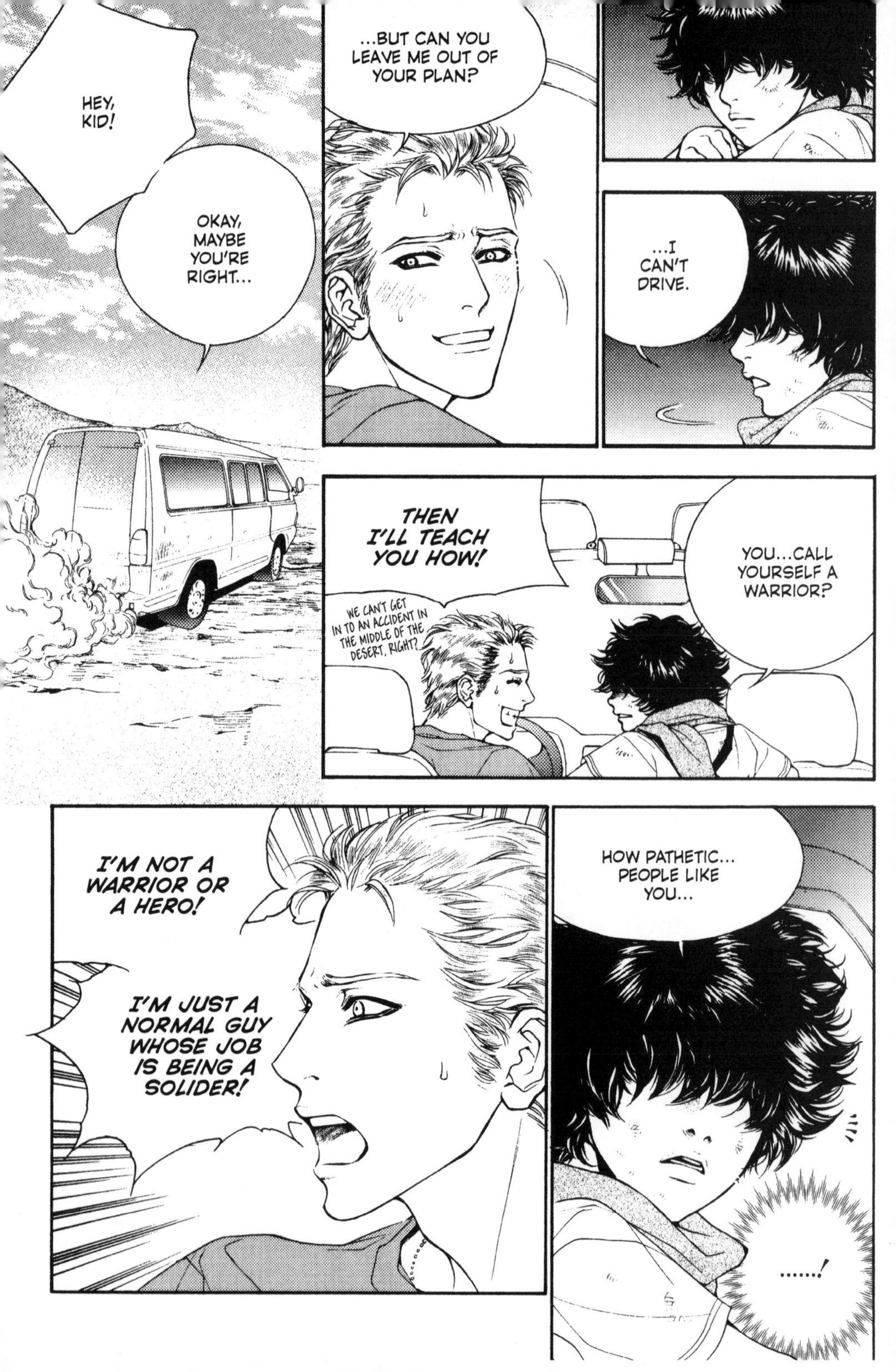
HEY, KID!
OKAY, MAYBE YOU'RE RIGHT...
...BUT CAN YOU LEAVE ME OUT OF YOUR PLAN?
...I CAN'T DRIVE.
THEN I'LL TEACH YOU HOW!
WE CAN'T GET IN TO AN ACCIDENT IN THE MIDDLE OF THE DESERT, RIGHT?
YOU...CALL YOURSELF A WARRIOR?
I'M NOT A WARRIOR OR A HERO!
I'M JUST A NORMAL GUY WHOSE JOB IS BEING A SOLIDER!
HOW PATHETIC... PEOPLE LIKE YOU...
......!

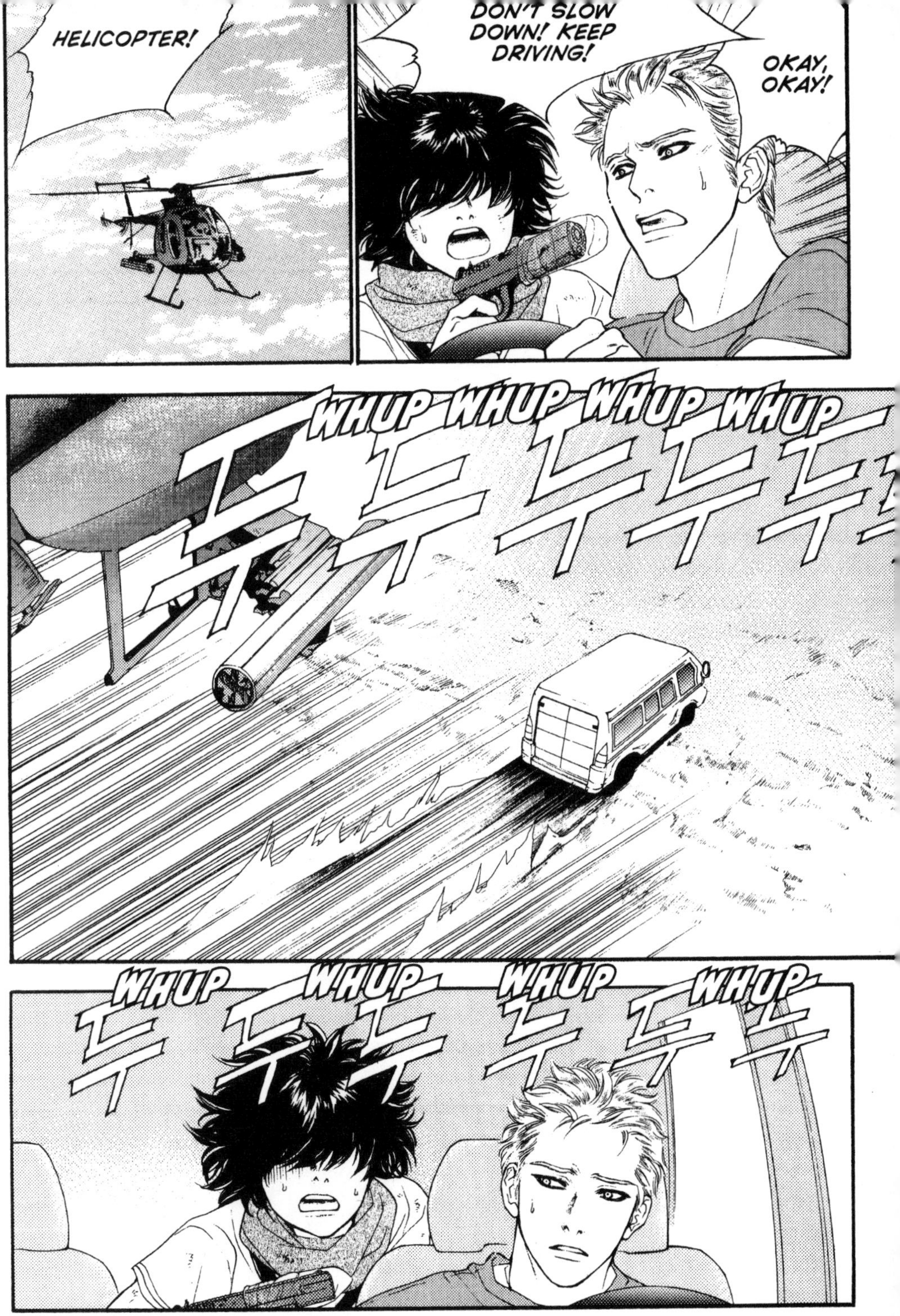
HELICOPTER!
DON'T SLOW DOWN! KEEP DRIVING!
OKAY, OKAY!
WHUP WHUP WHUP WHUP
WHUP
WHUP
WHUP
WHUP

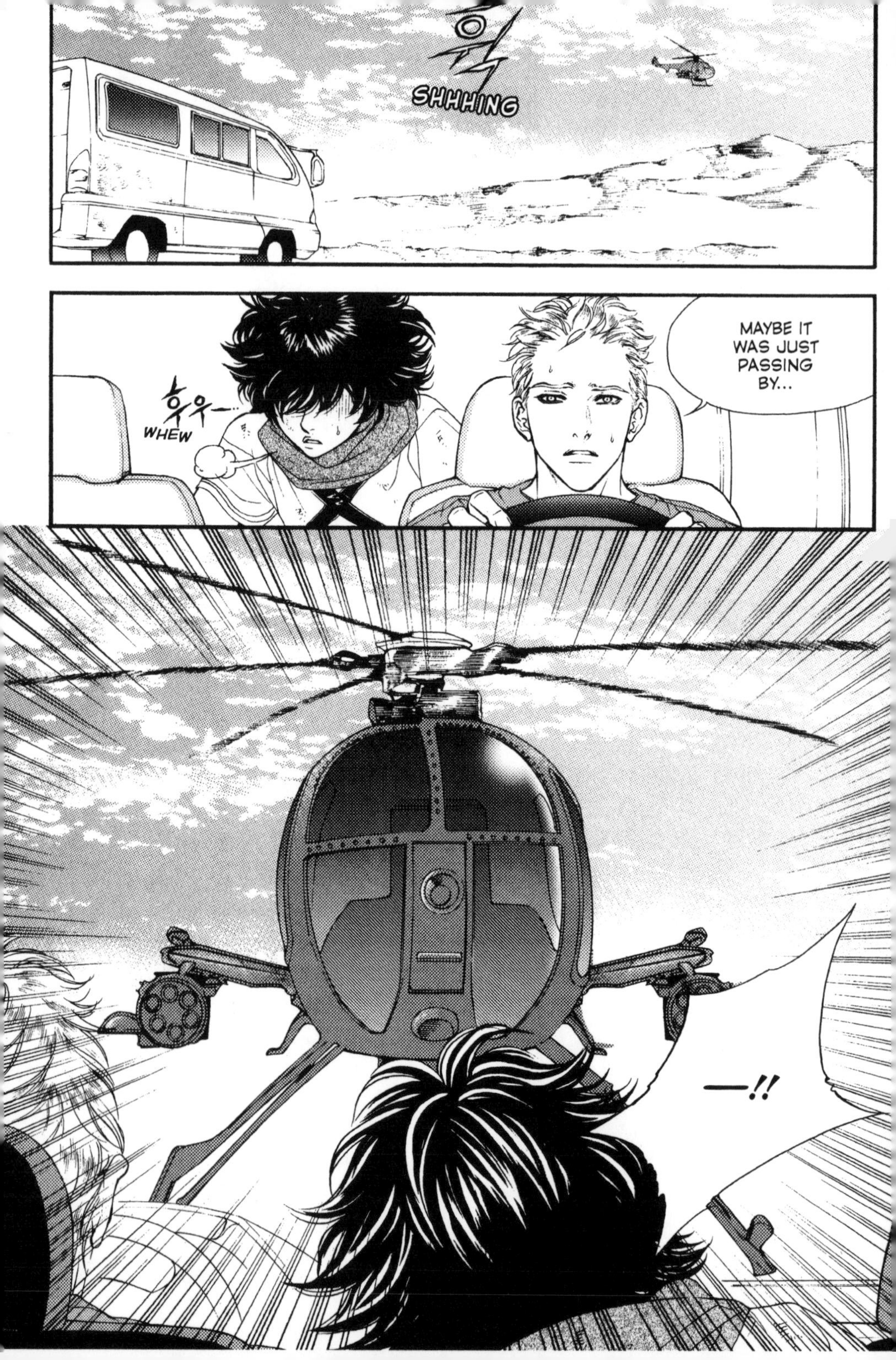
SHHHING
후우—…
WHEW
MAYBE IT WAS JUST PASSING BY…
—!!

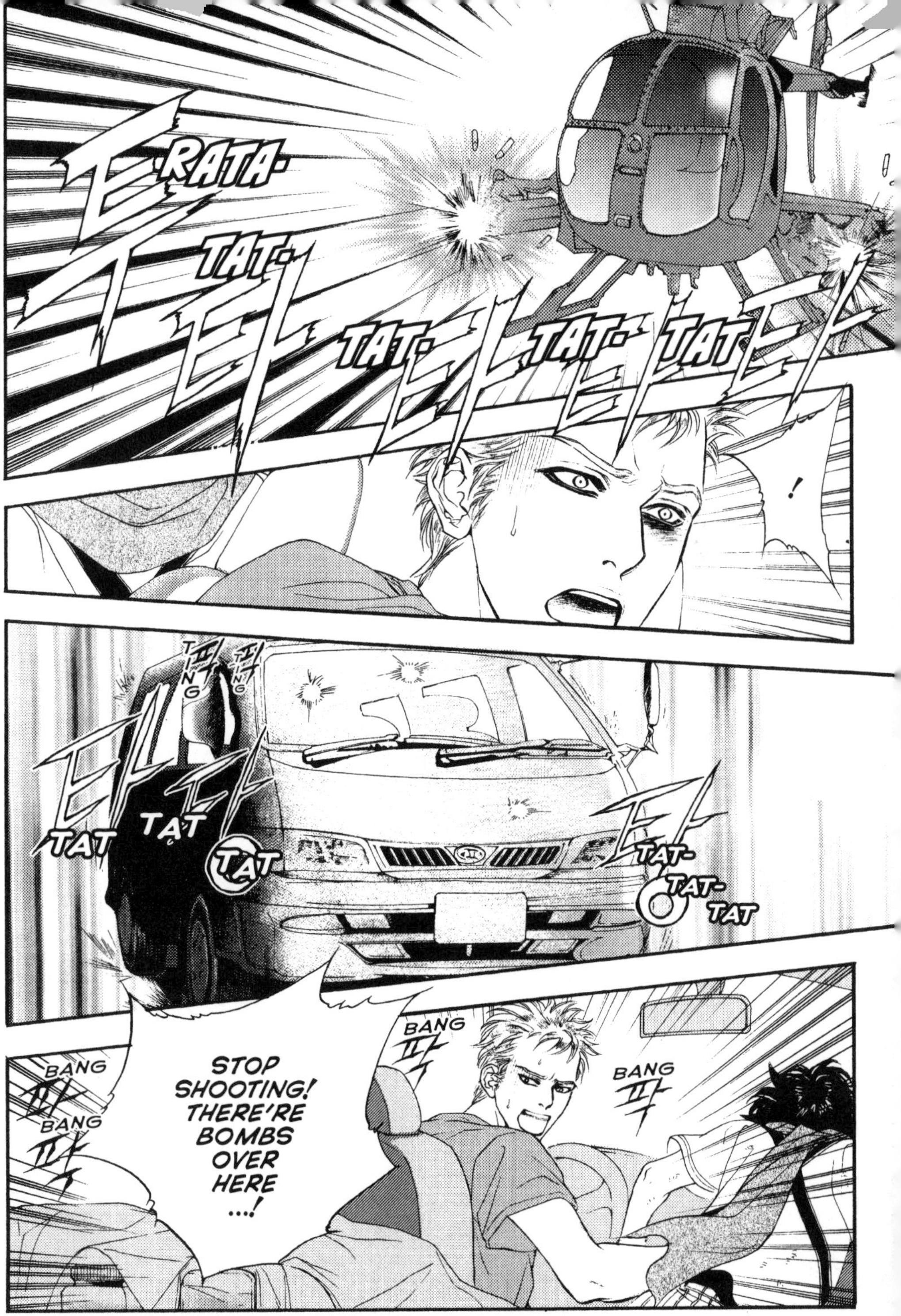

RATA-
TAT-
TAT-
TAT-
TAT
!
TING
TING
TAT
TAT
TAT
TAT-
TAT-
TAT
BANG
BANG
STOP SHOOTING! THERE'RE BOMBS OVER HERE ...!
BANG
BANG

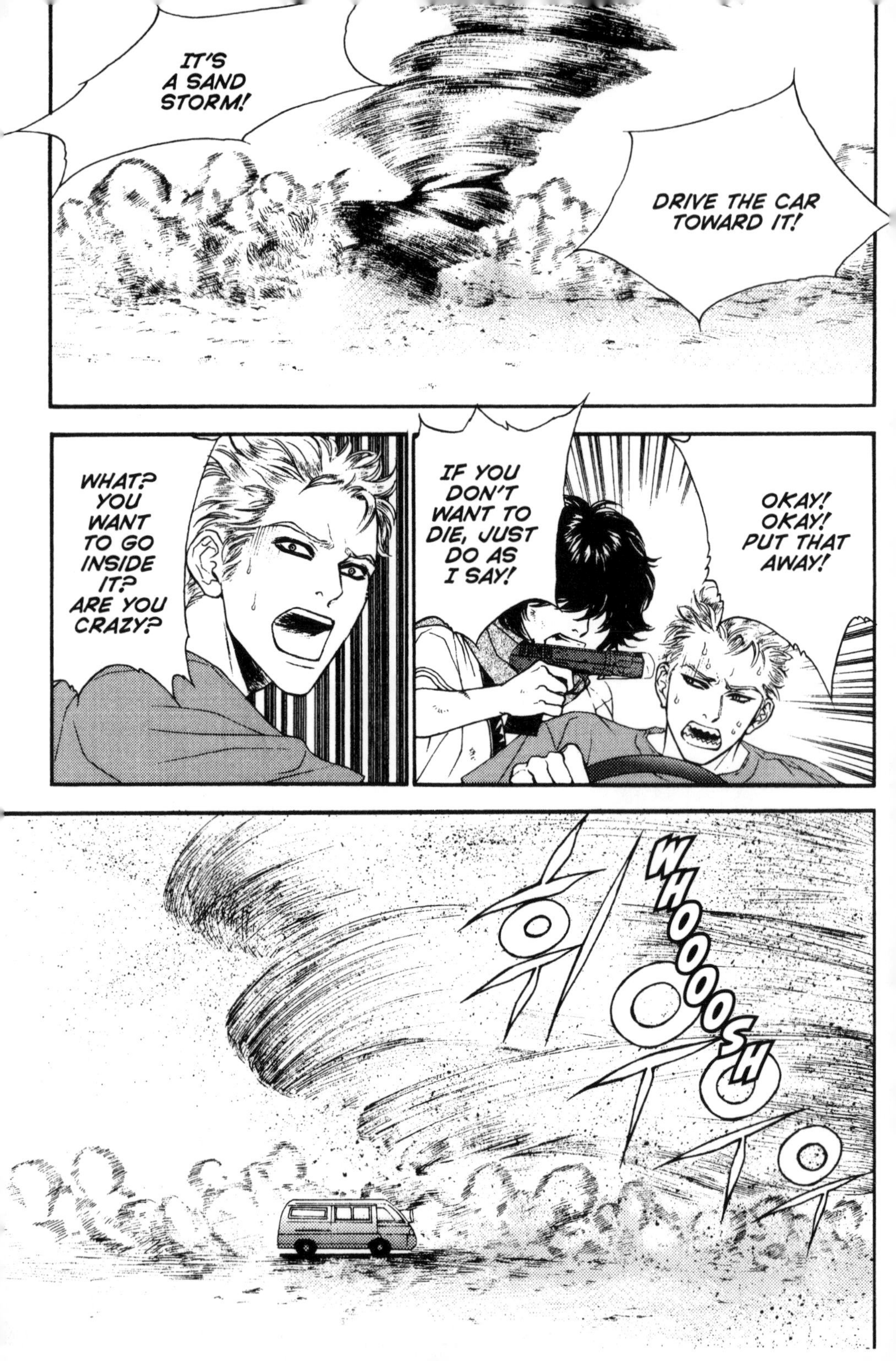
IT'S A SAND STORM!
DRIVE THE CAR TOWARD IT!
WHAT? YOU WANT TO GO INSIDE IT? ARE YOU CRAZY?
IF YOU DON'T WANT TO DIE, JUST DO AS I SAY!
OKAY! OKAY! PUT THAT AWAY!
WHOOOOSH

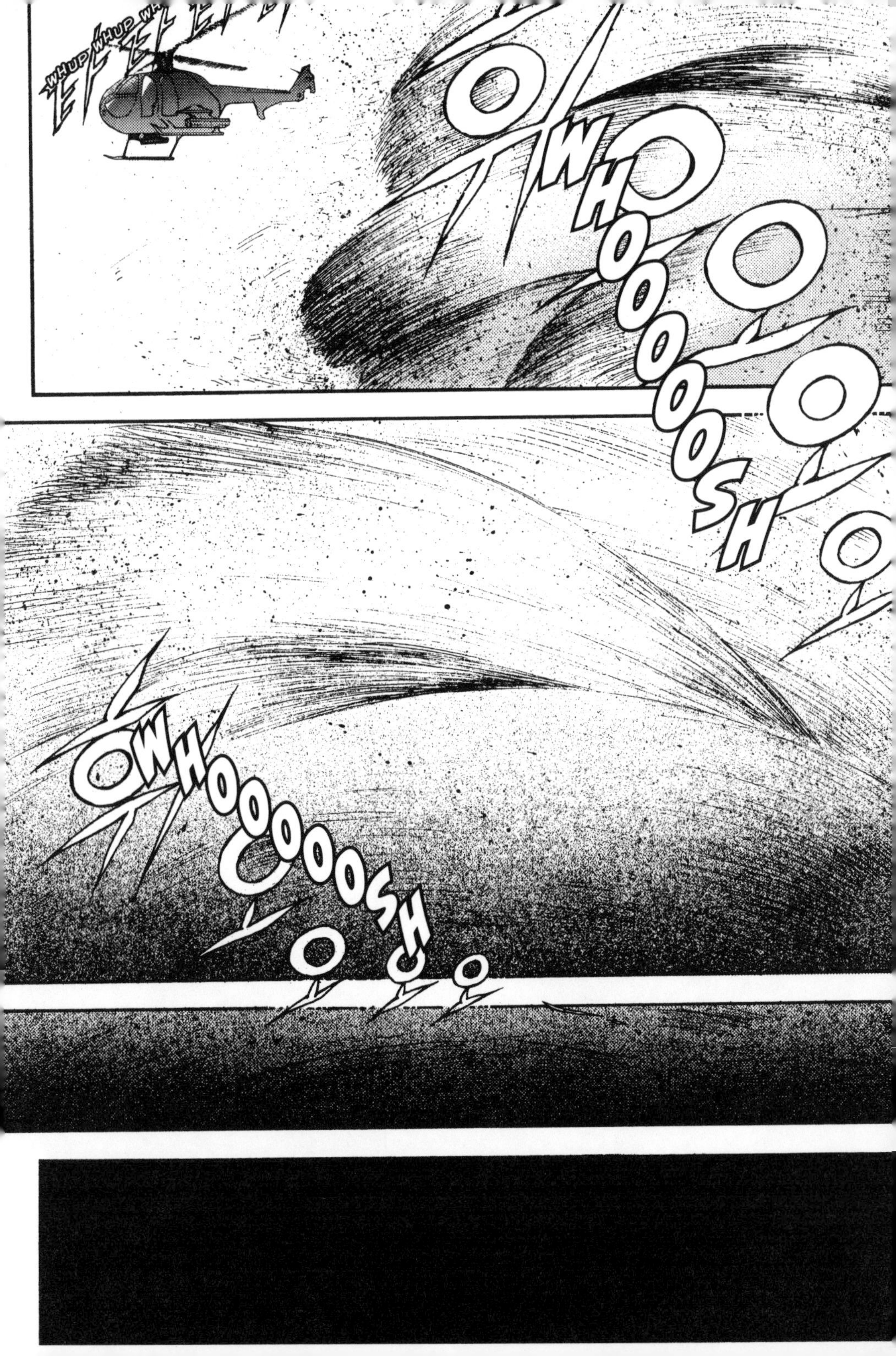
WHUP WHUP
WHOOOOOSH
WHOOOOOSH

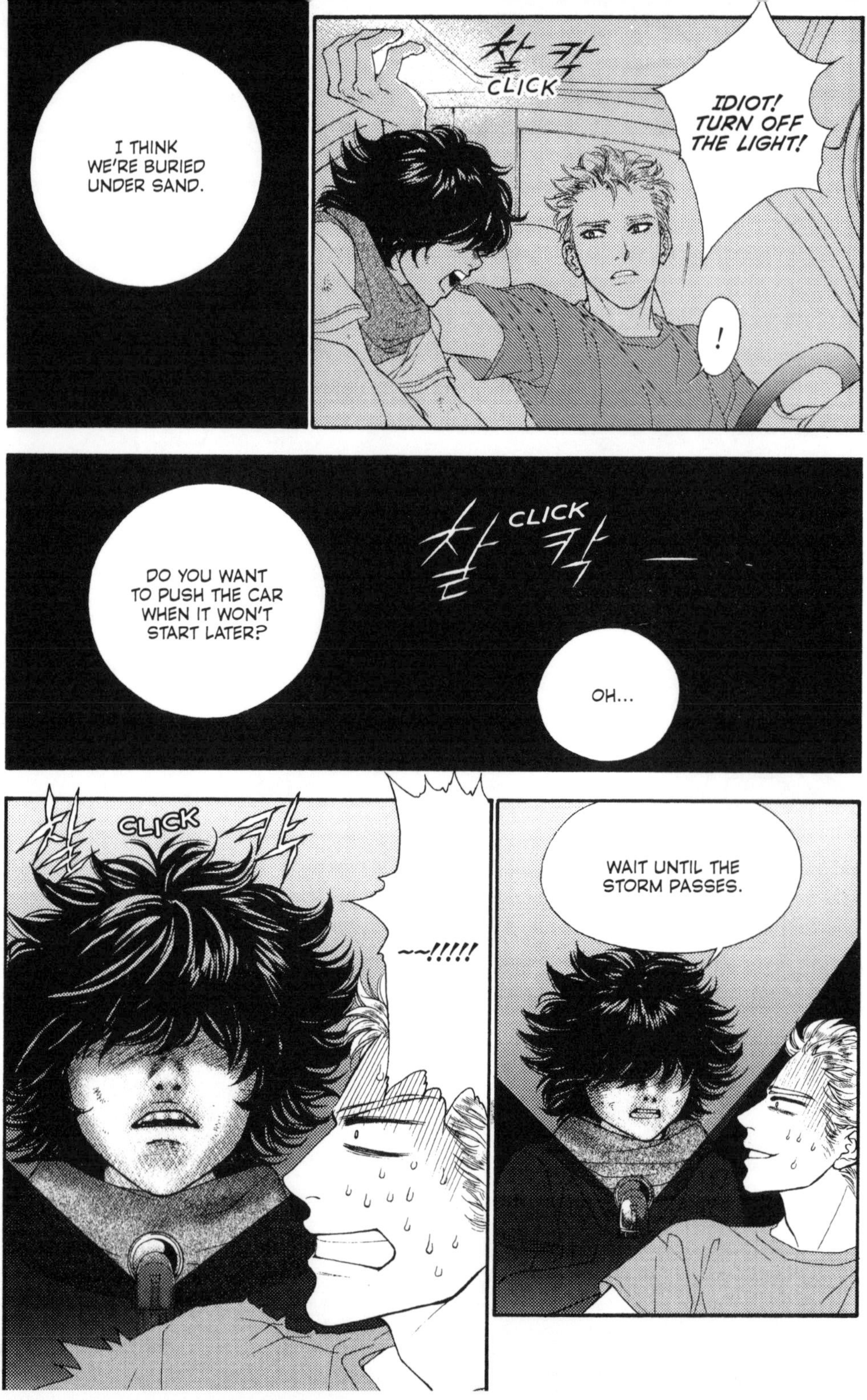
I THINK WE'RE BURIED UNDER SAND.
찰칵
CLICK
IDIOT! TURN OFF THE LIGHT!
!
찰칵
CLICK
DO YOU WANT TO PUSH THE CAR WHEN IT WON'T START LATER?
OH...
찰칵
CLICK
~~!!!!!
WAIT UNTIL THE STORM PASSES.

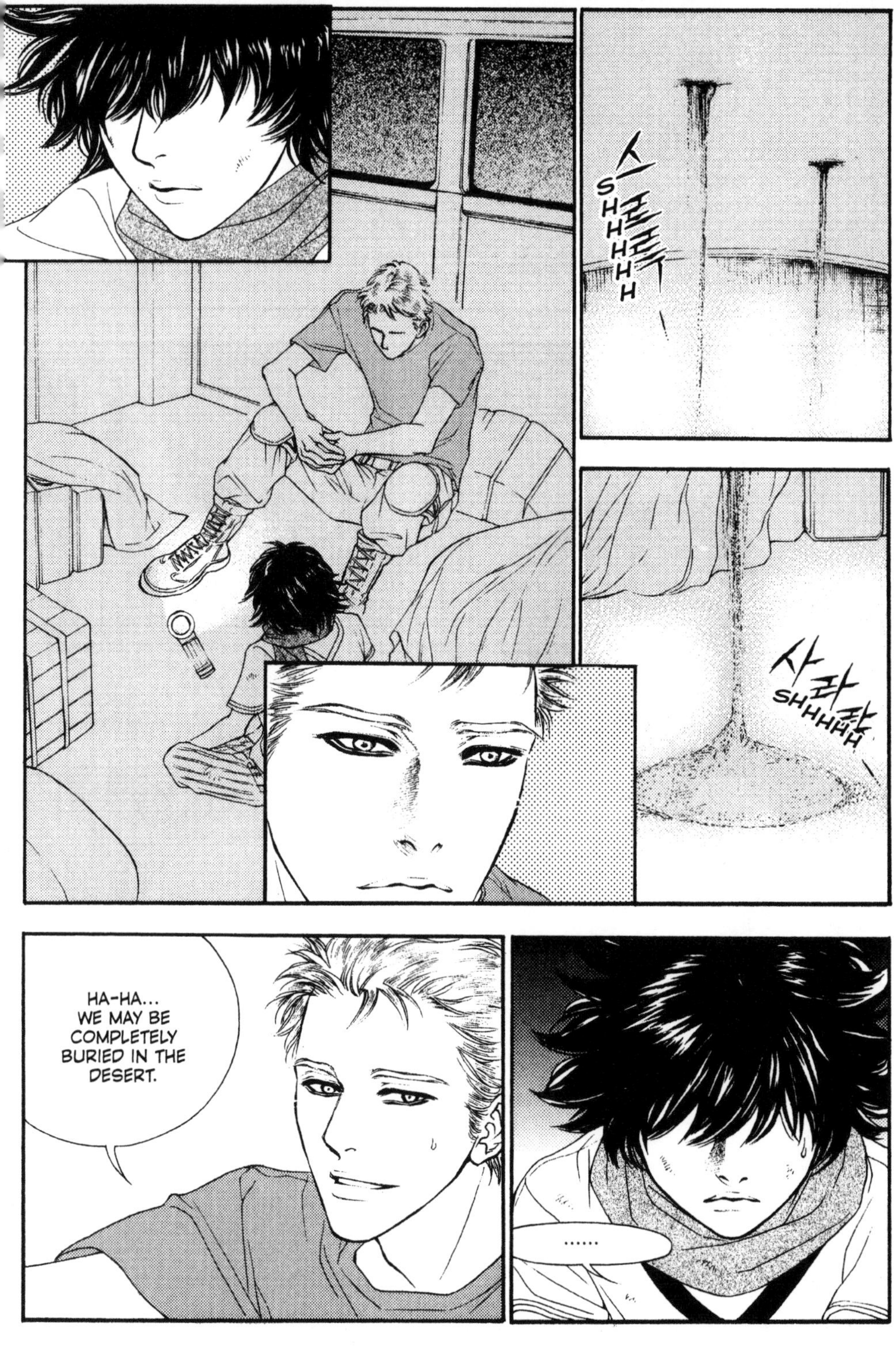
스르륵
SHHHHHH
사라락
SHHHHH
HA-HA... WE MAY BE COMPLETELY BURIED IN THE DESERT.
......

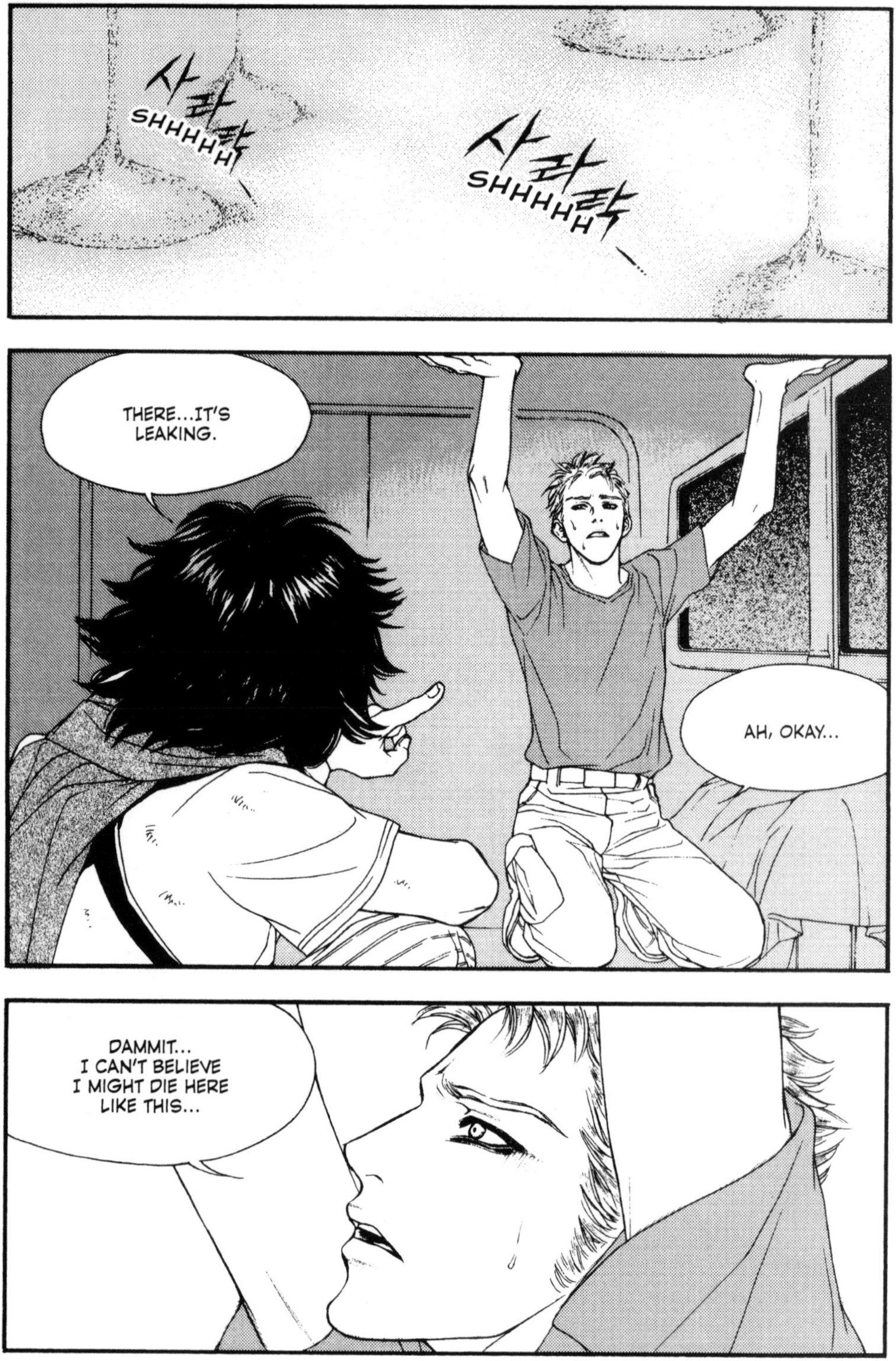
사라락
SHHHHH
사라락
SHHHHH
THERE...IT'S LEAKING.
AH, OKAY...
DAMMIT... I CAN'T BELIEVE I MIGHT DIE HERE LIKE THIS...

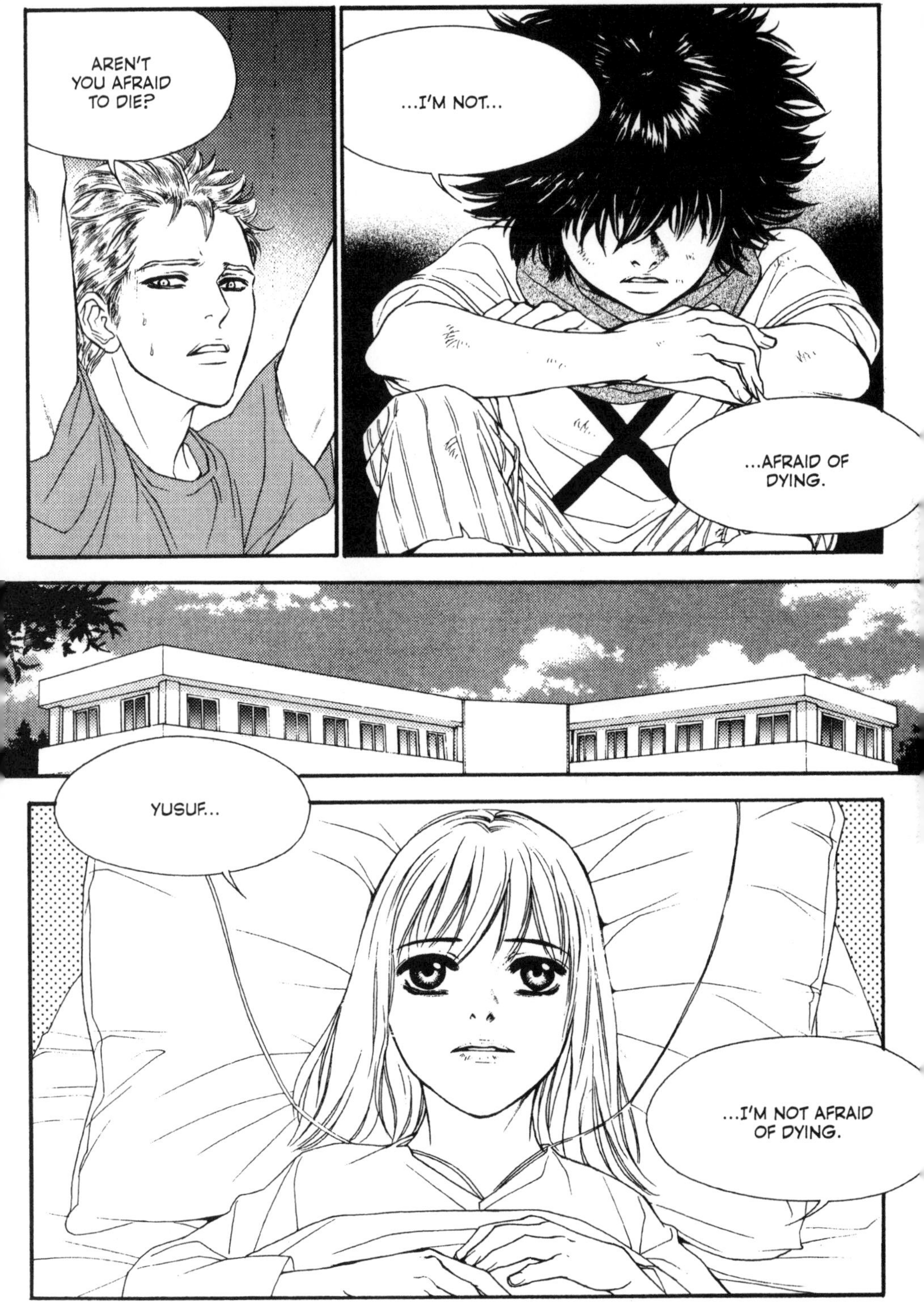
AREN'T YOU AFRAID TO DIE?
...I'M NOT...
...AFRAID OF DYING.
YUSUF...
...I'M NOT AFRAID OF DYING.

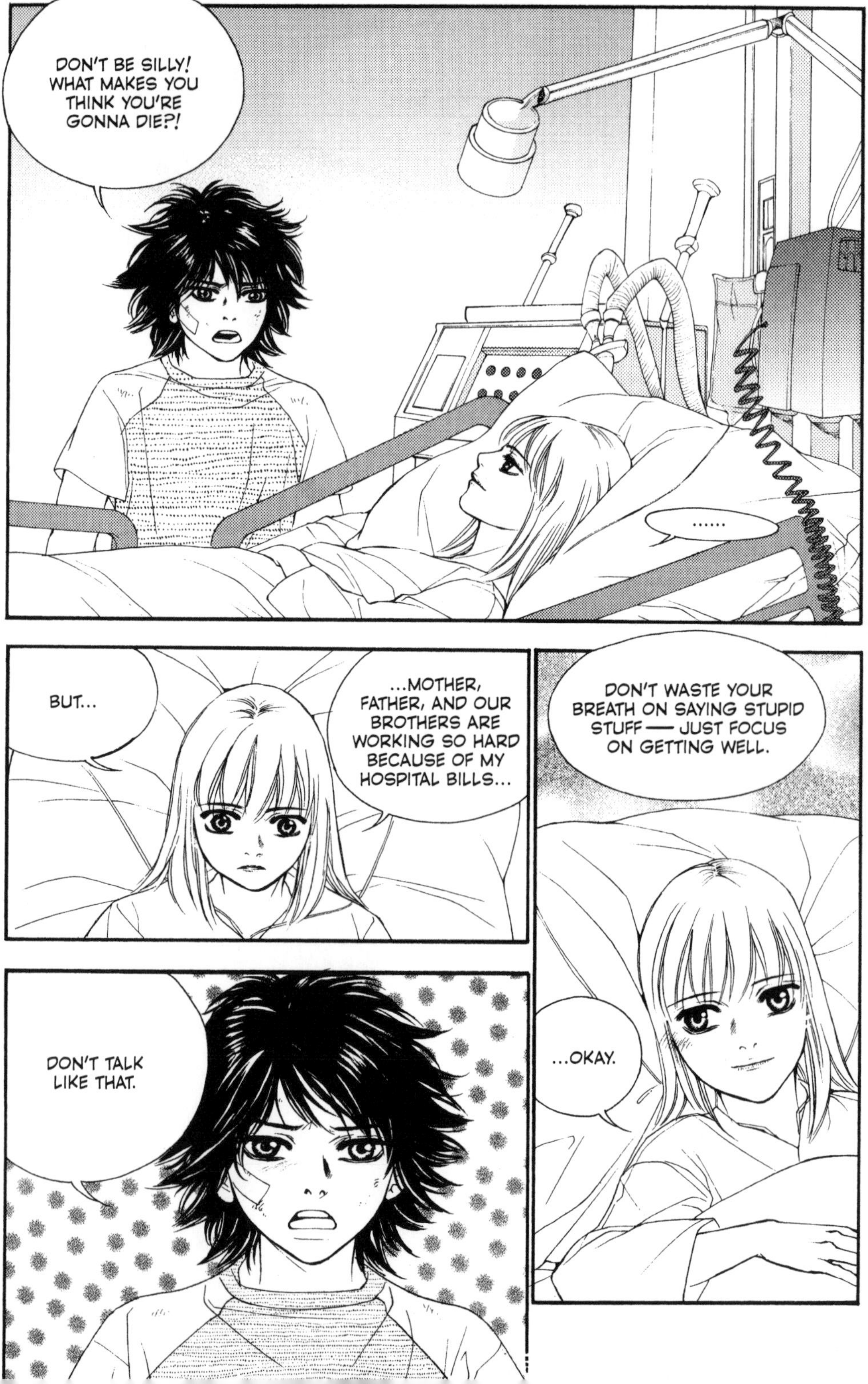
DON'T BE SILLY! WHAT MAKES YOU THINK YOU'RE GONNA DIE?!
......
BUT...
...MOTHER, FATHER, AND OUR BROTHERS ARE WORKING SO HARD BECAUSE OF MY HOSPITAL BILLS...
DON'T TALK LIKE THAT.
DON'T WASTE YOUR BREATH ON SAYING STUPID STUFF — JUST FOCUS ON GETTING WELL.
...OKAY.

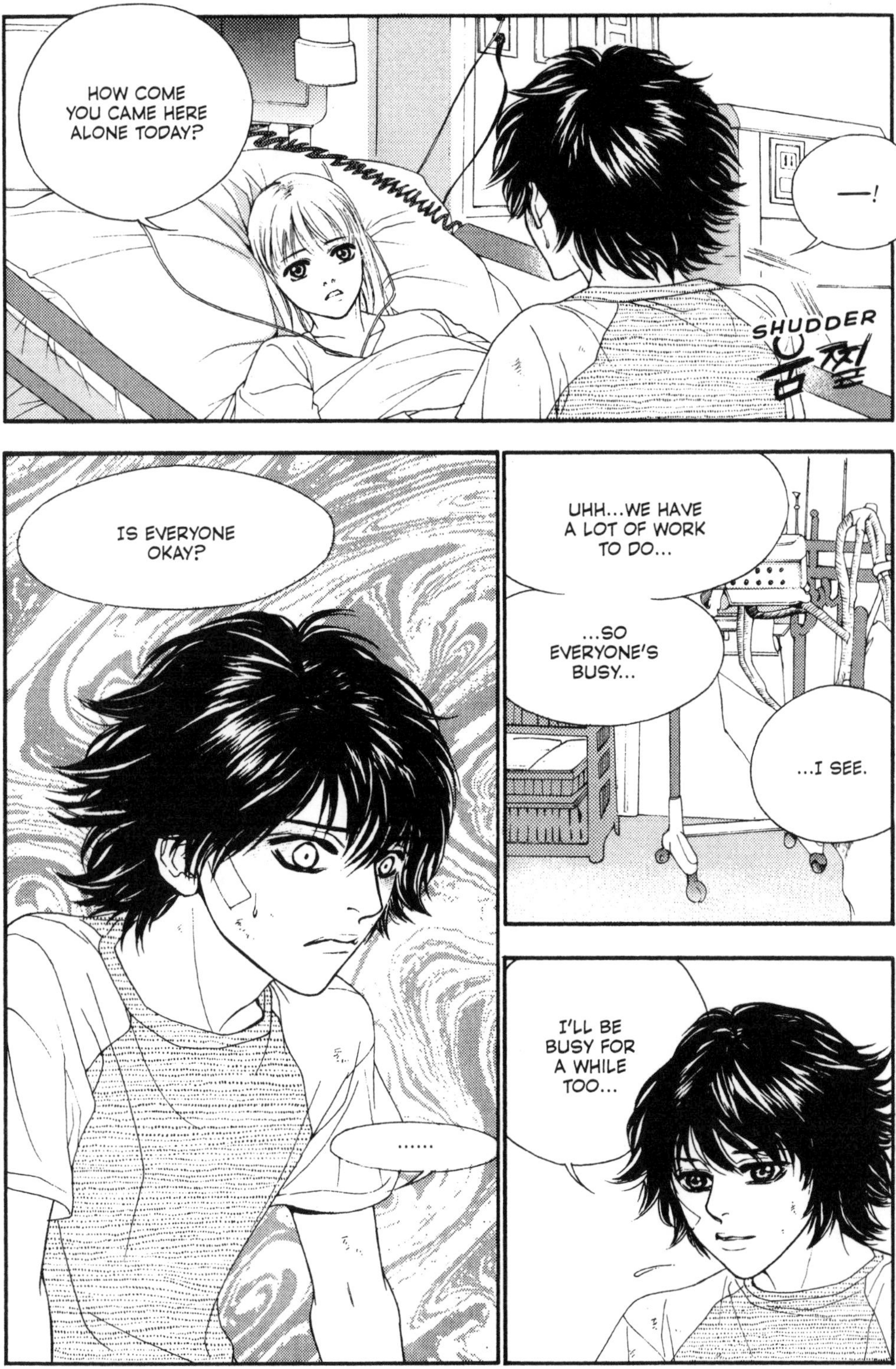
HOW COME YOU CAME HERE ALONE TODAY?
—!
SHUDDER
움찔
IS EVERYONE OKAY?
......
UHH...WE HAVE A LOT OF WORK TO DO...
...SO EVERYONE'S BUSY...
...I SEE.
I'LL BE BUSY FOR A WHILE TOO...

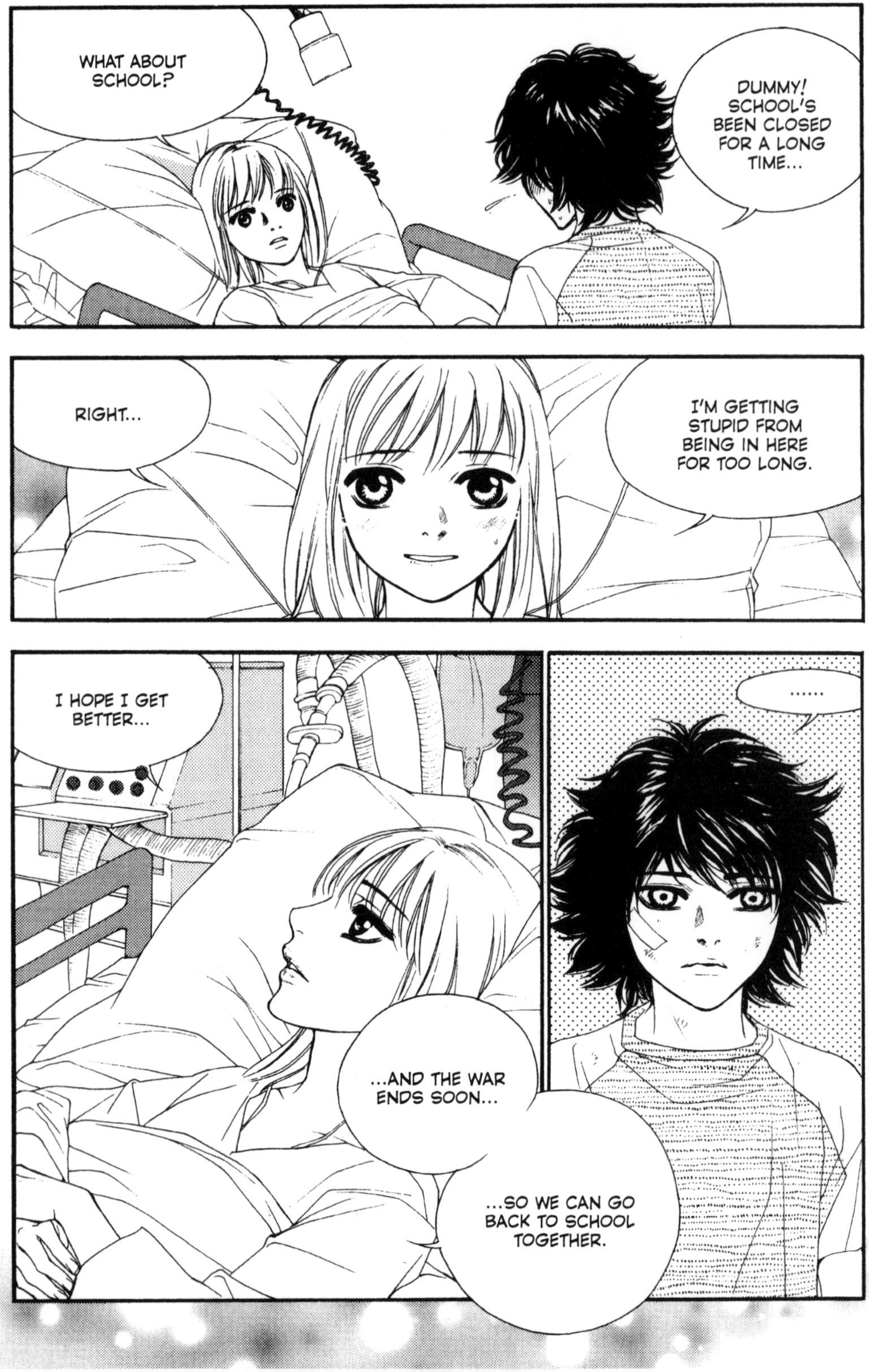
WHAT ABOUT SCHOOL?
DUMMY! SCHOOL'S BEEN CLOSED FOR A LONG TIME...
RIGHT...
I'M GETTING STUPID FROM BEING IN HERE FOR TOO LONG.
I HOPE I GET BETTER...
...AND THE WAR ENDS SOON...
...SO WE CAN GO BACK TO SCHOOL TOGETHER.
......

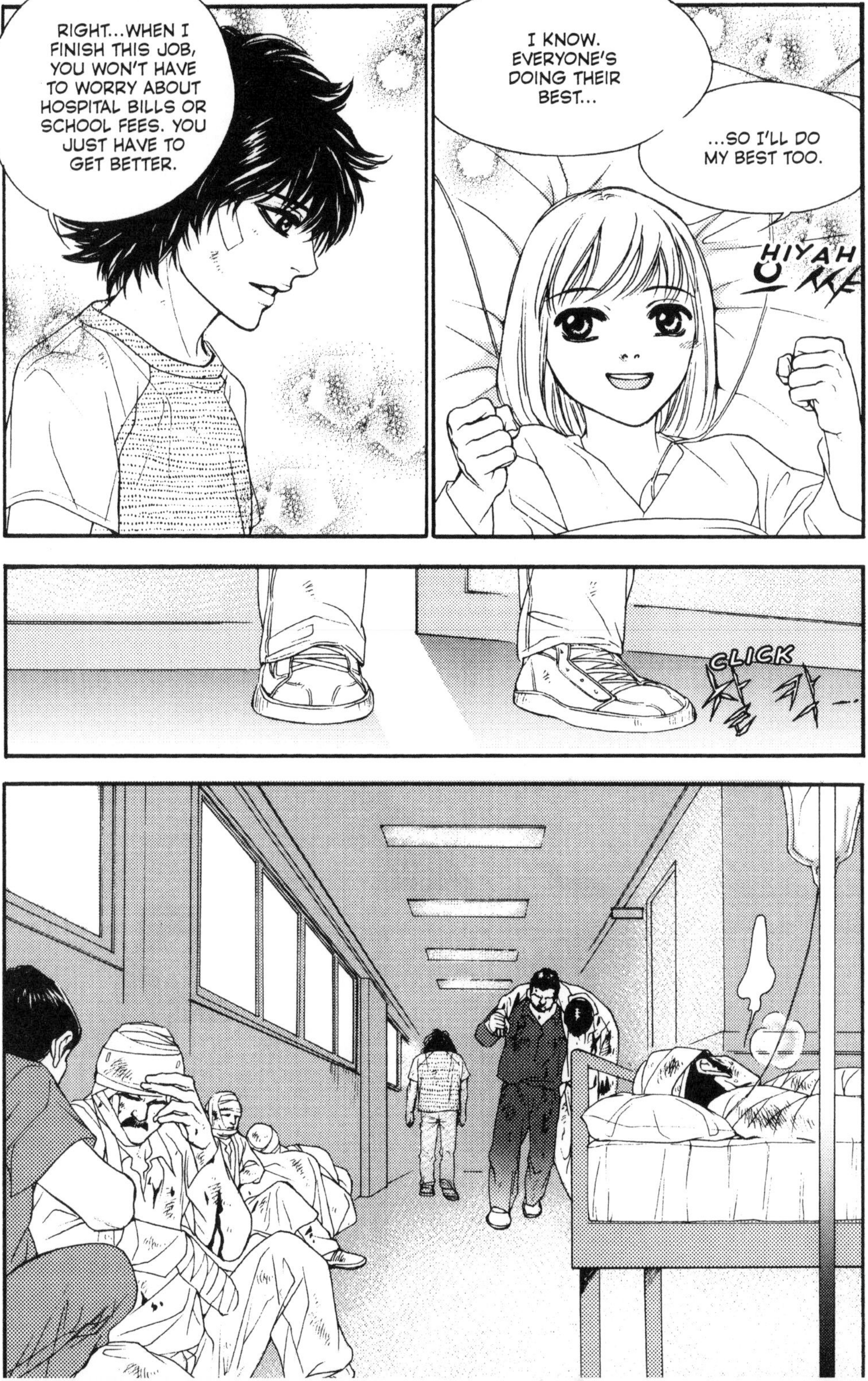
RIGHT...WHEN I FINISH THIS JOB, YOU WON'T HAVE TO WORRY ABOUT HOSPITAL BILLS OR SCHOOL FEES. YOU JUST HAVE TO GET BETTER.
I KNOW. EVERYONE'S DOING THEIR BEST...
...SO I'LL DO MY BEST TOO.
HIYAH
CLICK

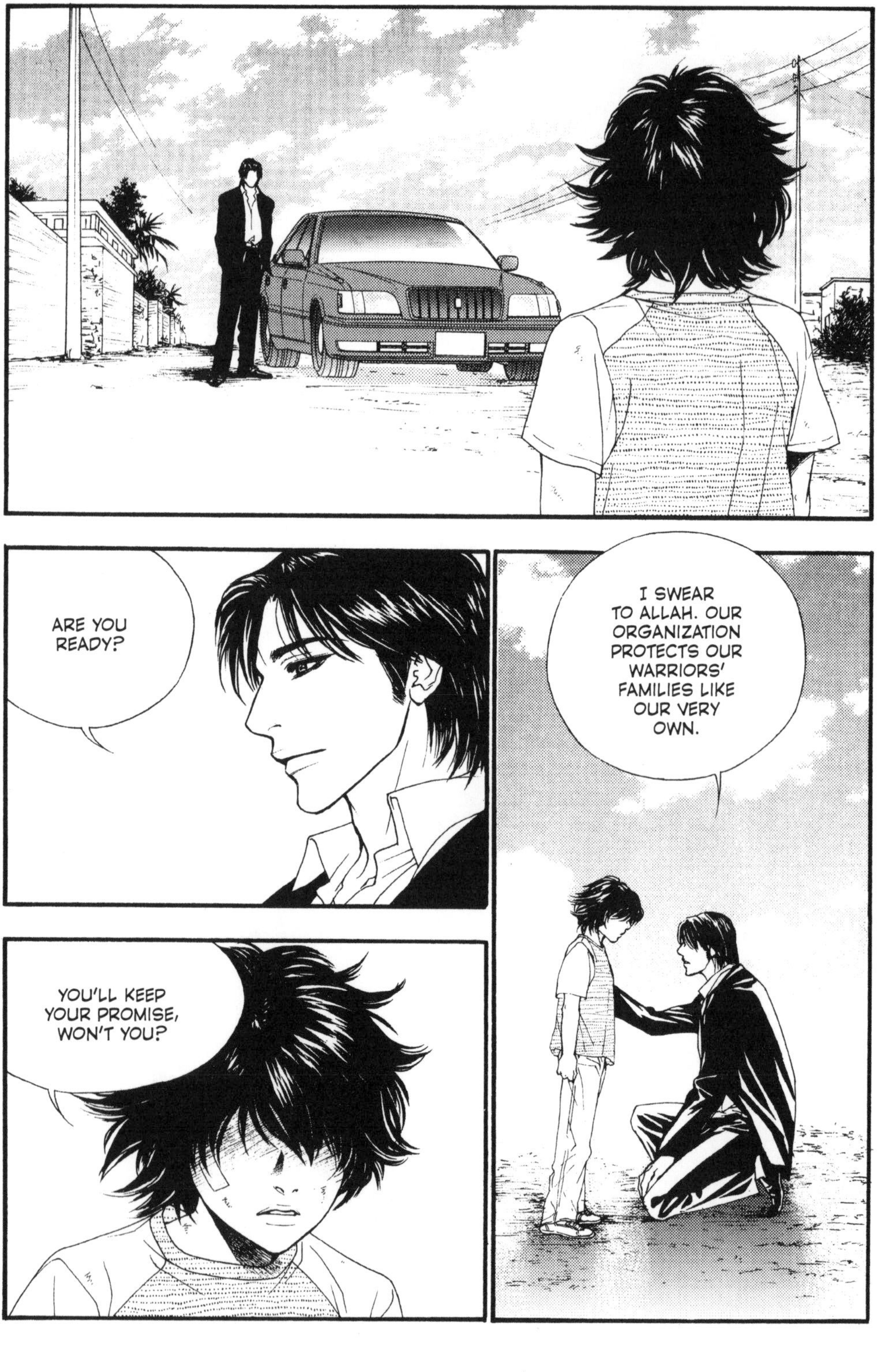
ARE YOU READY?
YOU'LL KEEP YOUR PROMISE, WON'T YOU?
I SWEAR TO ALLAH. OUR ORGANIZATION PROTECTS OUR WARRIORS' FAMILIES LIKE OUR VERY OWN.

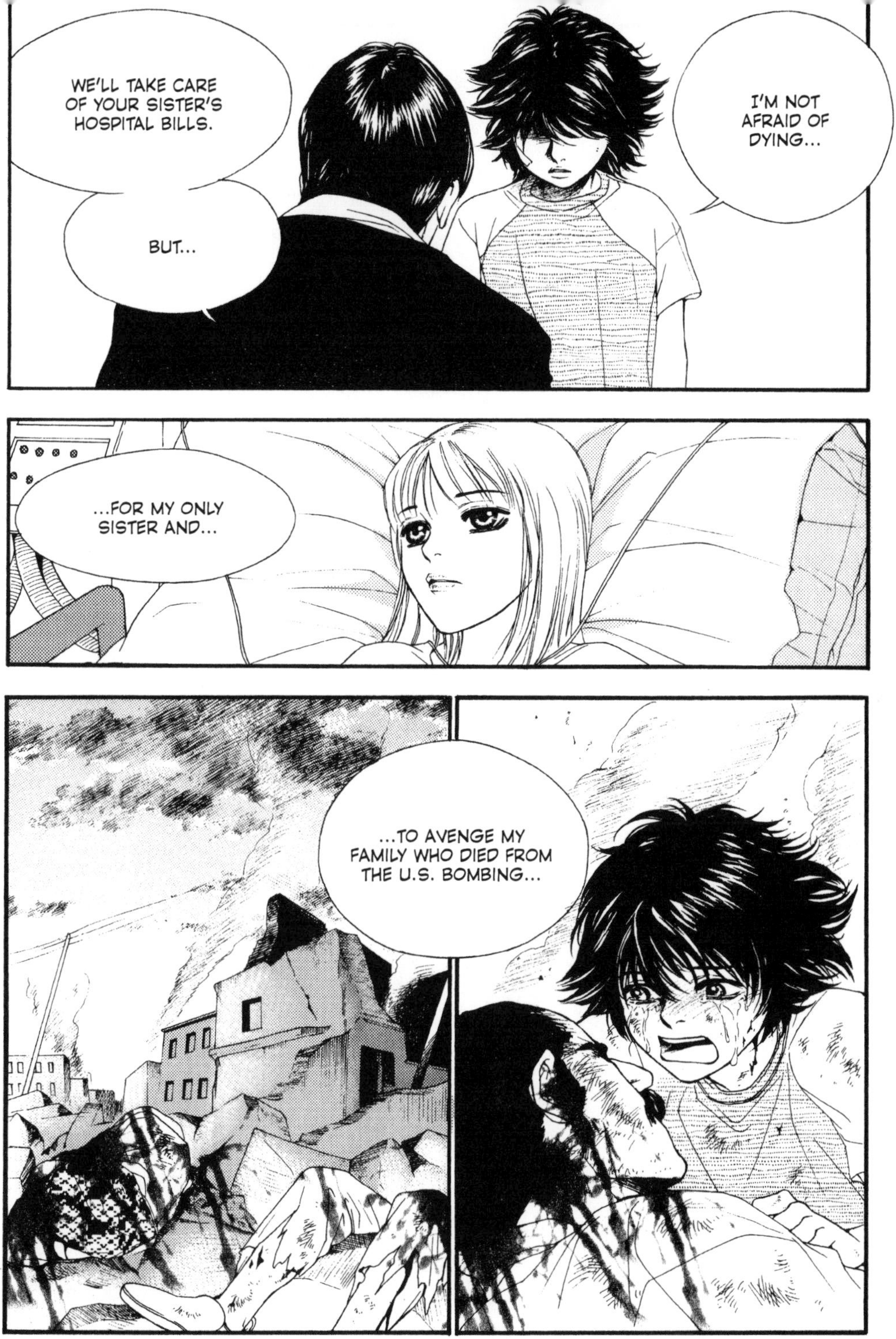
WE'LL TAKE CARE OF YOUR SISTER'S HOSPITAL BILLS.
BUT...
I'M NOT AFRAID OF DYING...
...FOR MY ONLY SISTER AND...
...TO AVENGE MY FAMILY WHO DIED FROM THE U.S. BOMBING...

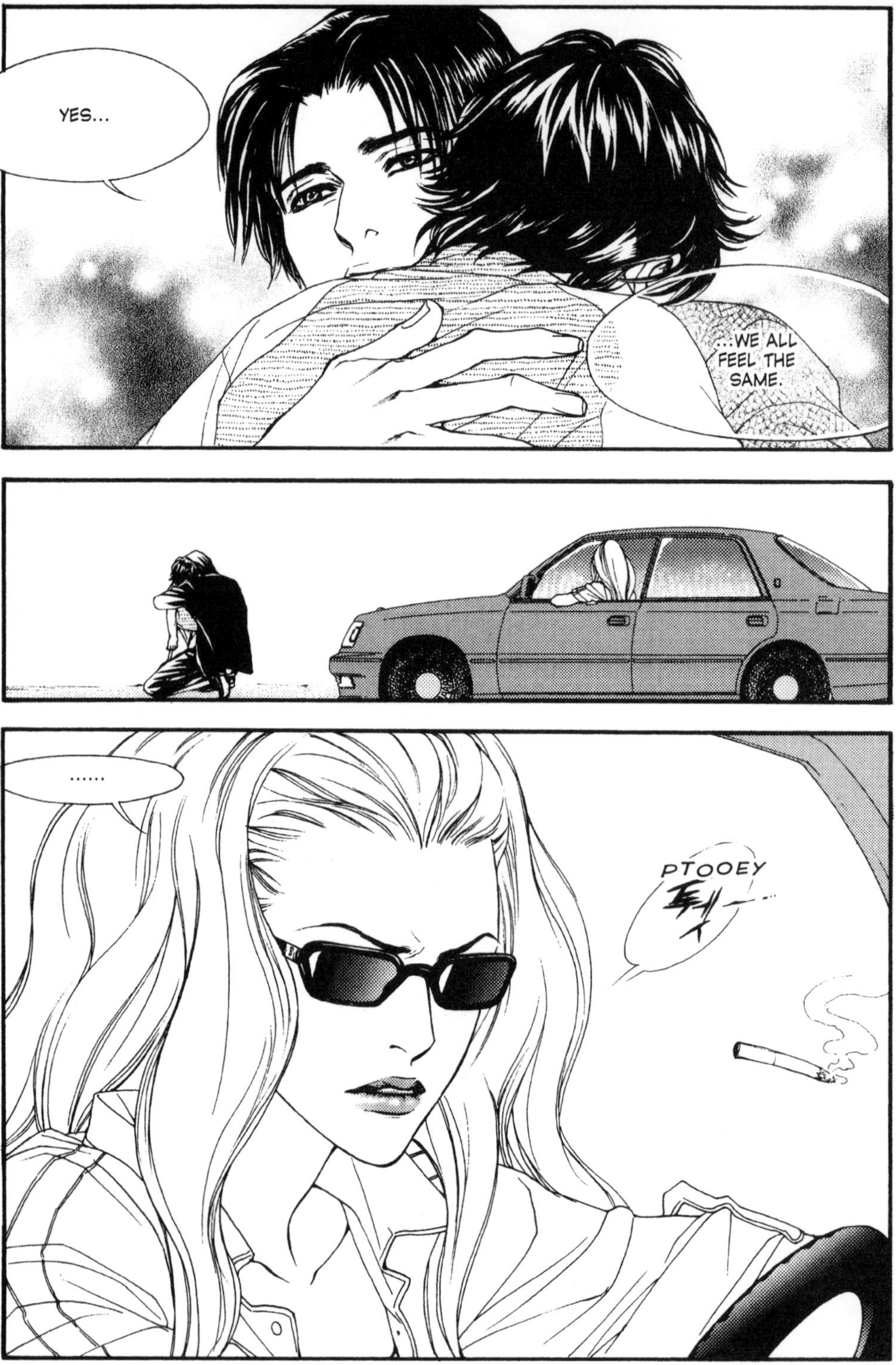
YES...
...WE ALL FEEL THE SAME.
......
PTOOEY

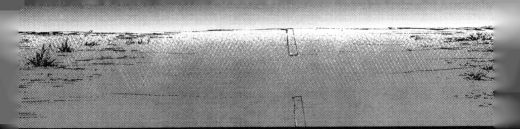

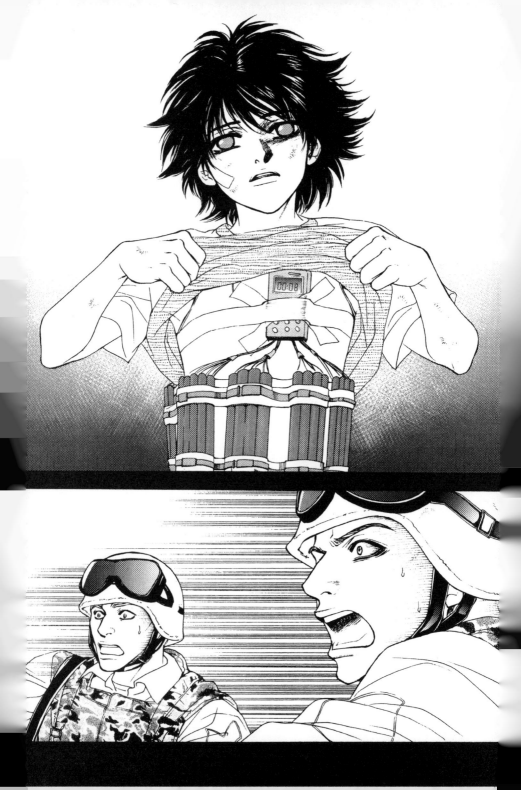

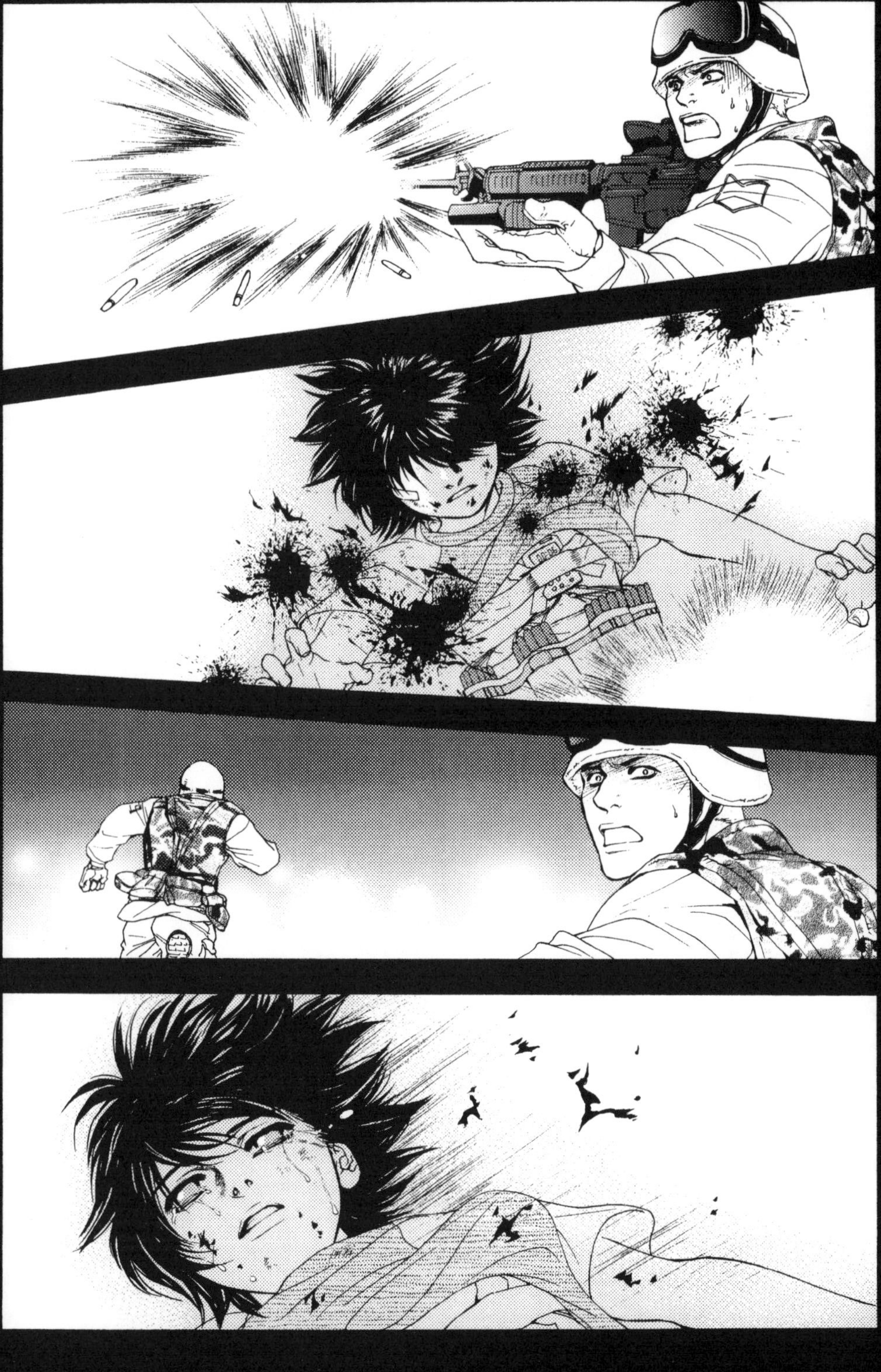

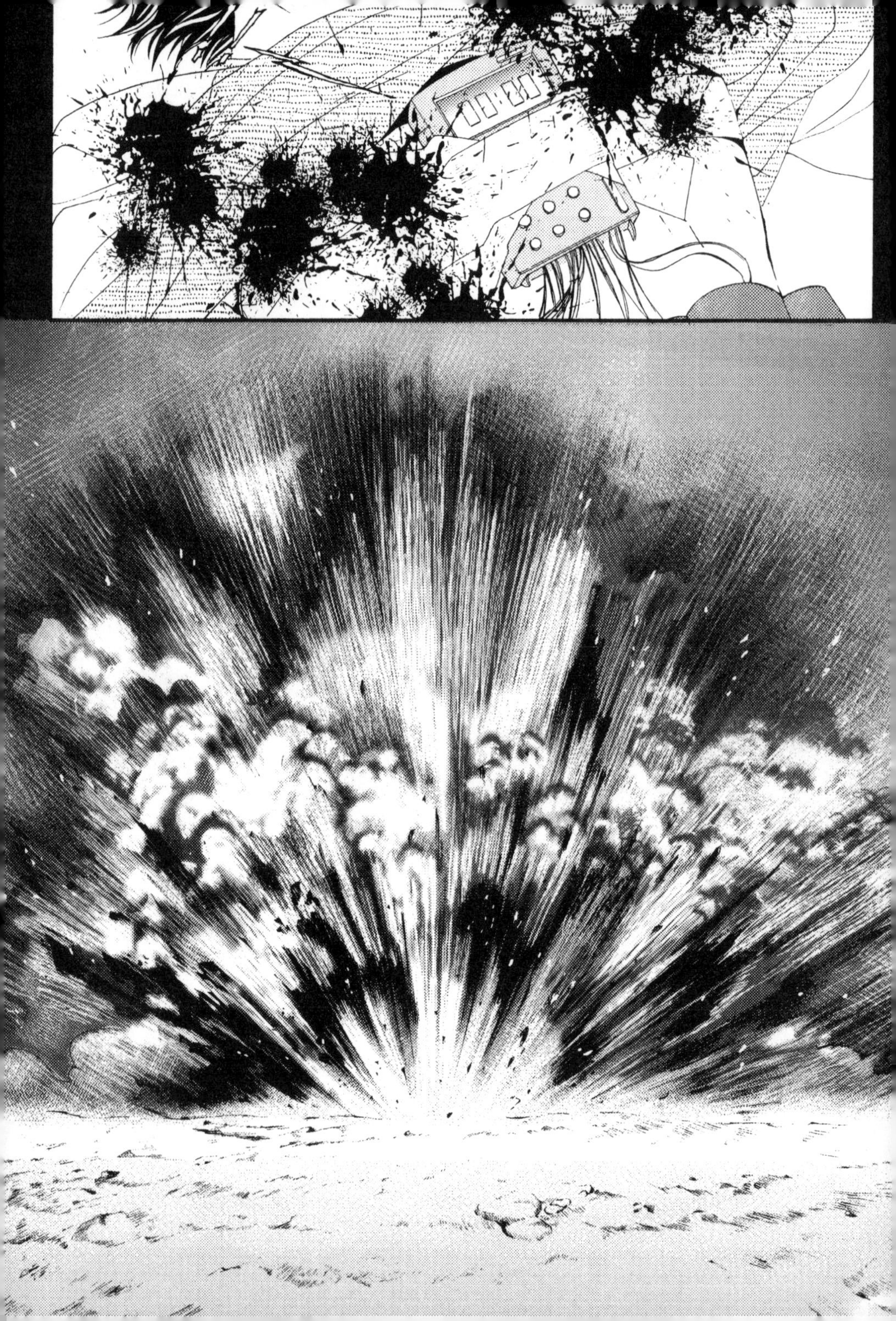

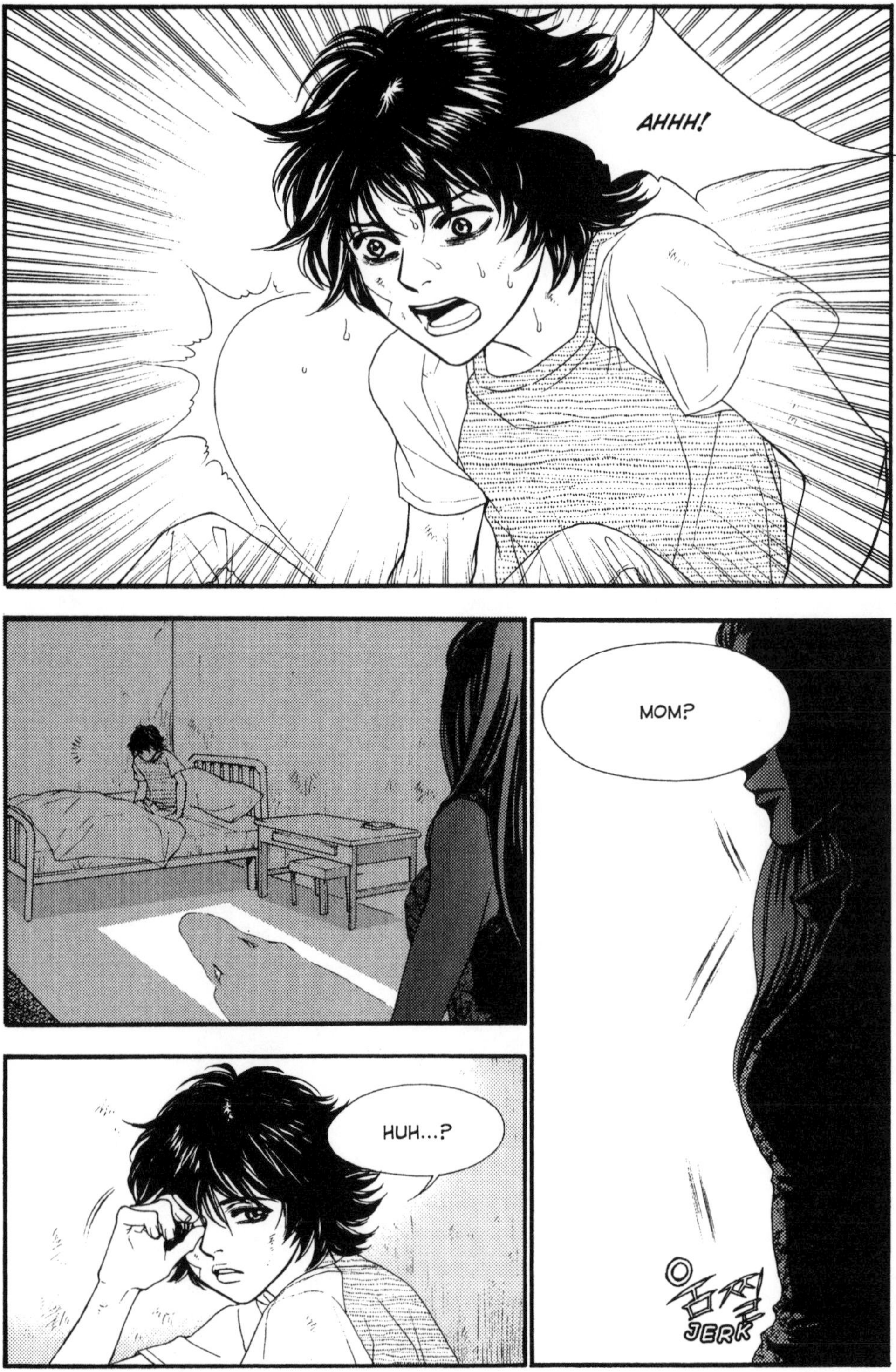
AHHH!
HUH...?
MOM?
움찔
JERK

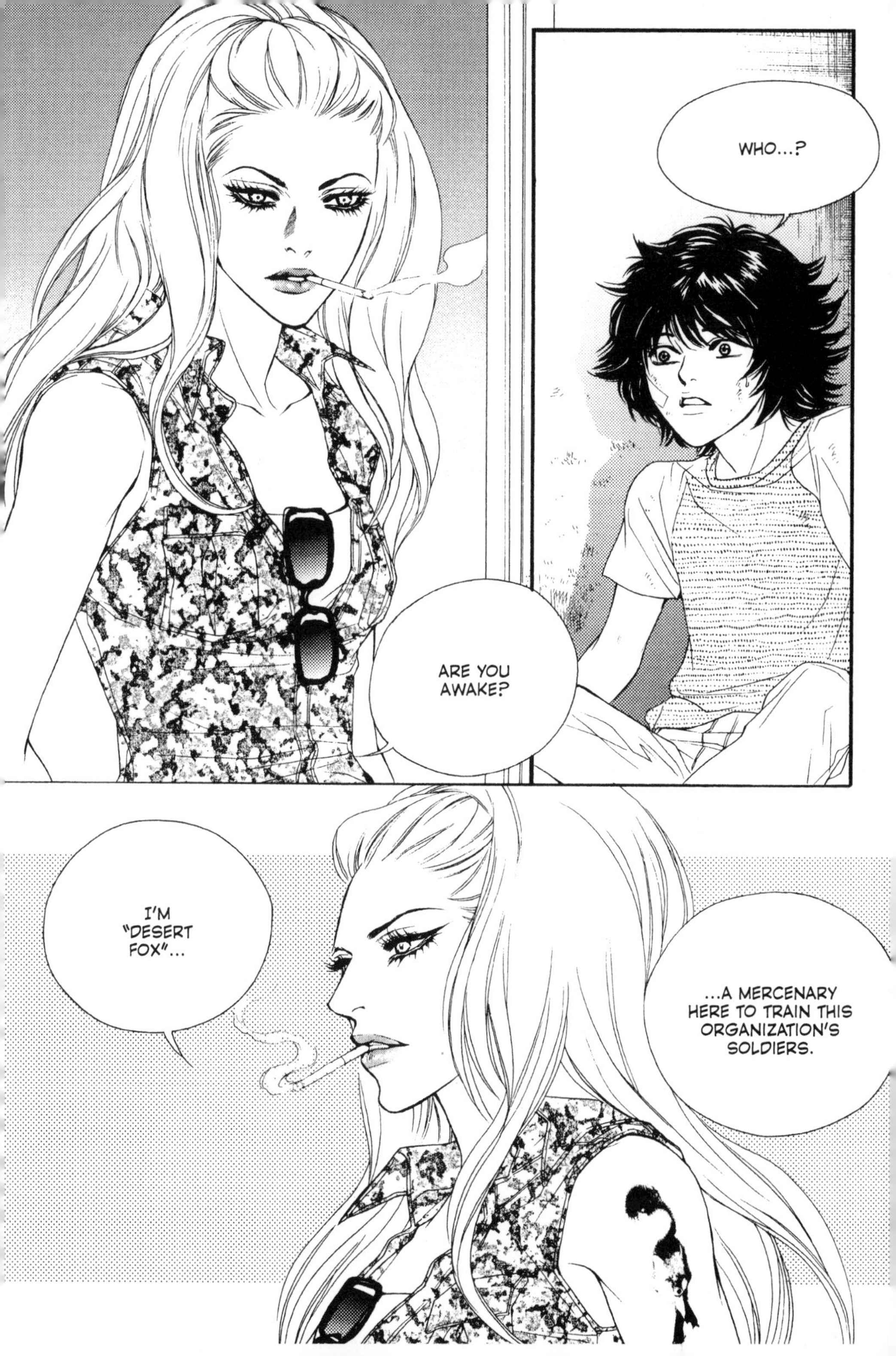
ARE YOU AWAKE?
WHO...?
I'M "DESERT FOX"...
...A MERCENARY HERE TO TRAIN THIS ORGANIZATION'S SOLDIERS.

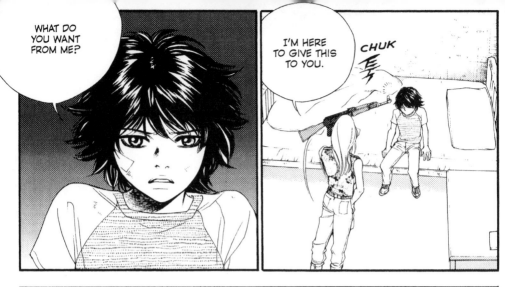

WHAT DO YOU WANT FROM ME?

I'M HERE TO GIVE THIS TO YOU.

CHUK

THAT'S A...

IT'S AN AK-47.

IT'S A BIG GUN WITH A BIG KICK.

BUT IT'S DURABLE AND EASY TO USE, PERFECT FOR AN AMATEUR LIKE YOU.

I DON'T NEED IT.

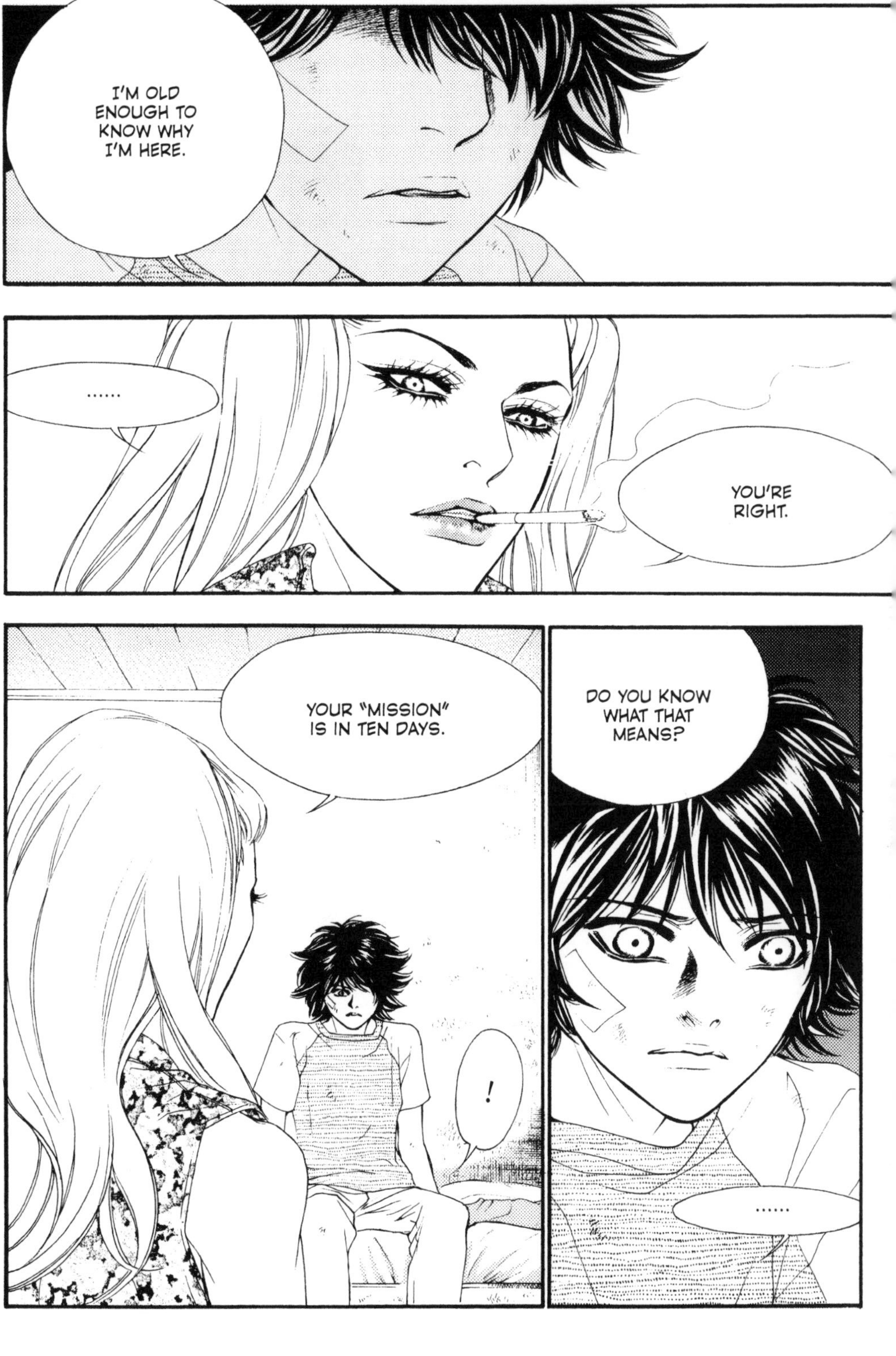
I'M OLD ENOUGH TO KNOW WHY I'M HERE.
......
YOU'RE RIGHT.
YOUR "MISSION" IS IN TEN DAYS.
!
DO YOU KNOW WHAT THAT MEANS?
......

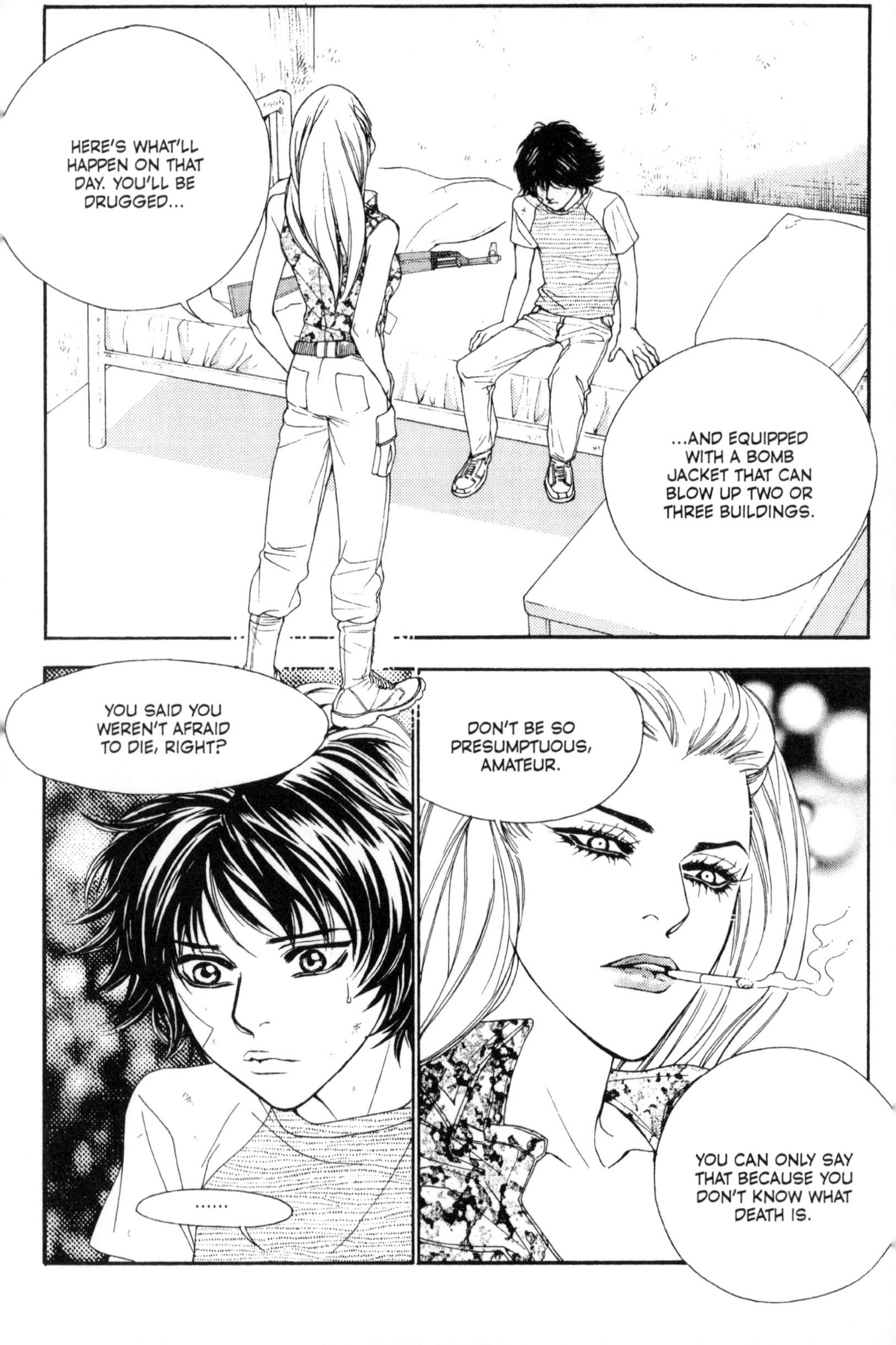
HERE'S WHAT'LL HAPPEN ON THAT DAY. YOU'LL BE DRUGGED...
...AND EQUIPPED WITH A BOMB JACKET THAT CAN BLOW UP TWO OR THREE BUILDINGS.
YOU SAID YOU WEREN'T AFRAID TO DIE, RIGHT?
......
DON'T BE SO PRESUMPTUOUS, AMATEUR.
YOU CAN ONLY SAY THAT BECAUSE YOU DON'T KNOW WHAT DEATH IS.

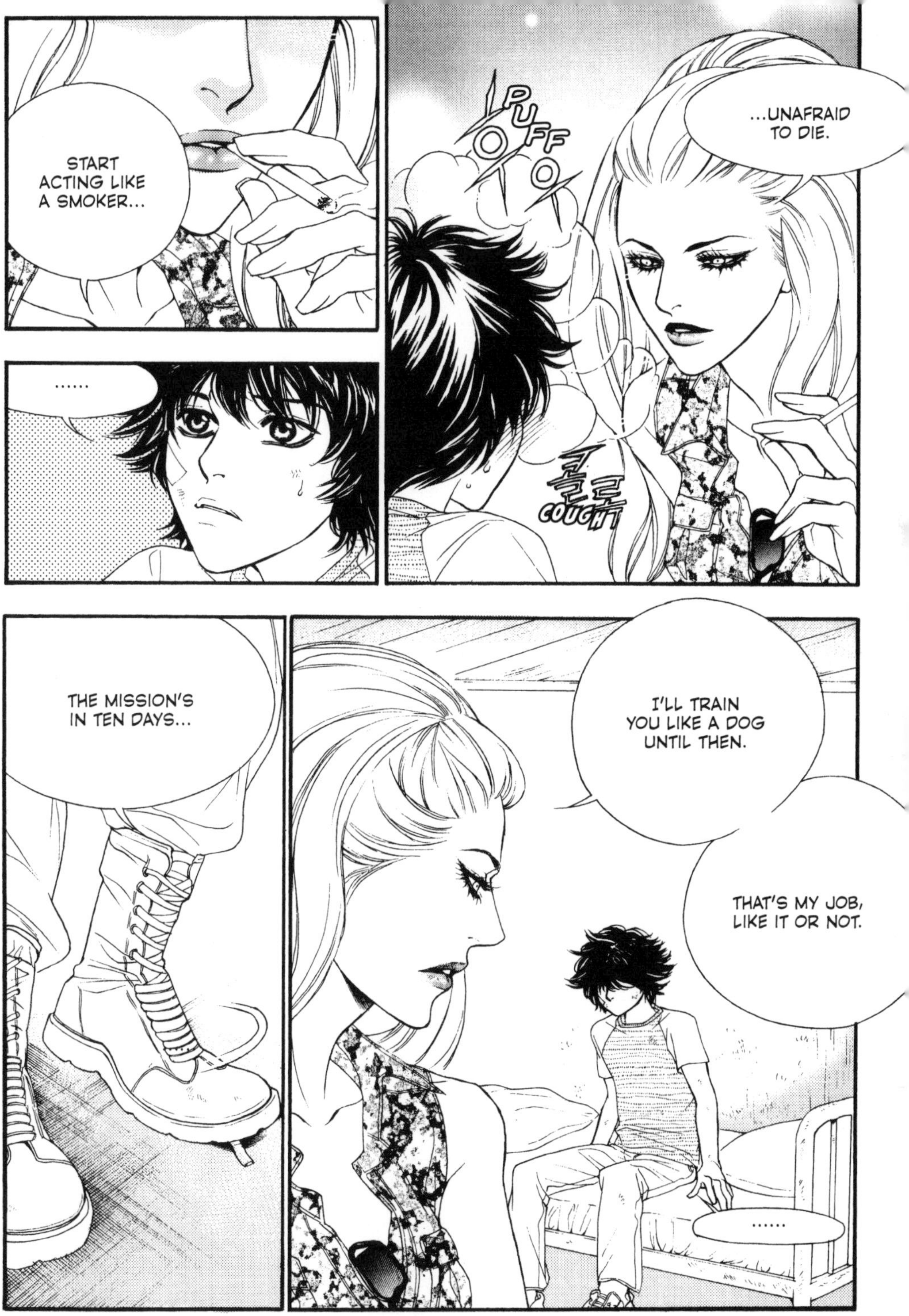
START ACTING LIKE A SMOKER...
......
PUFF
...UNAFRAID TO DIE.
콜록
COUGH
THE MISSION'S IN TEN DAYS...
I'LL TRAIN YOU LIKE A DOG UNTIL THEN.
THAT'S MY JOB, LIKE IT OR NOT.
......

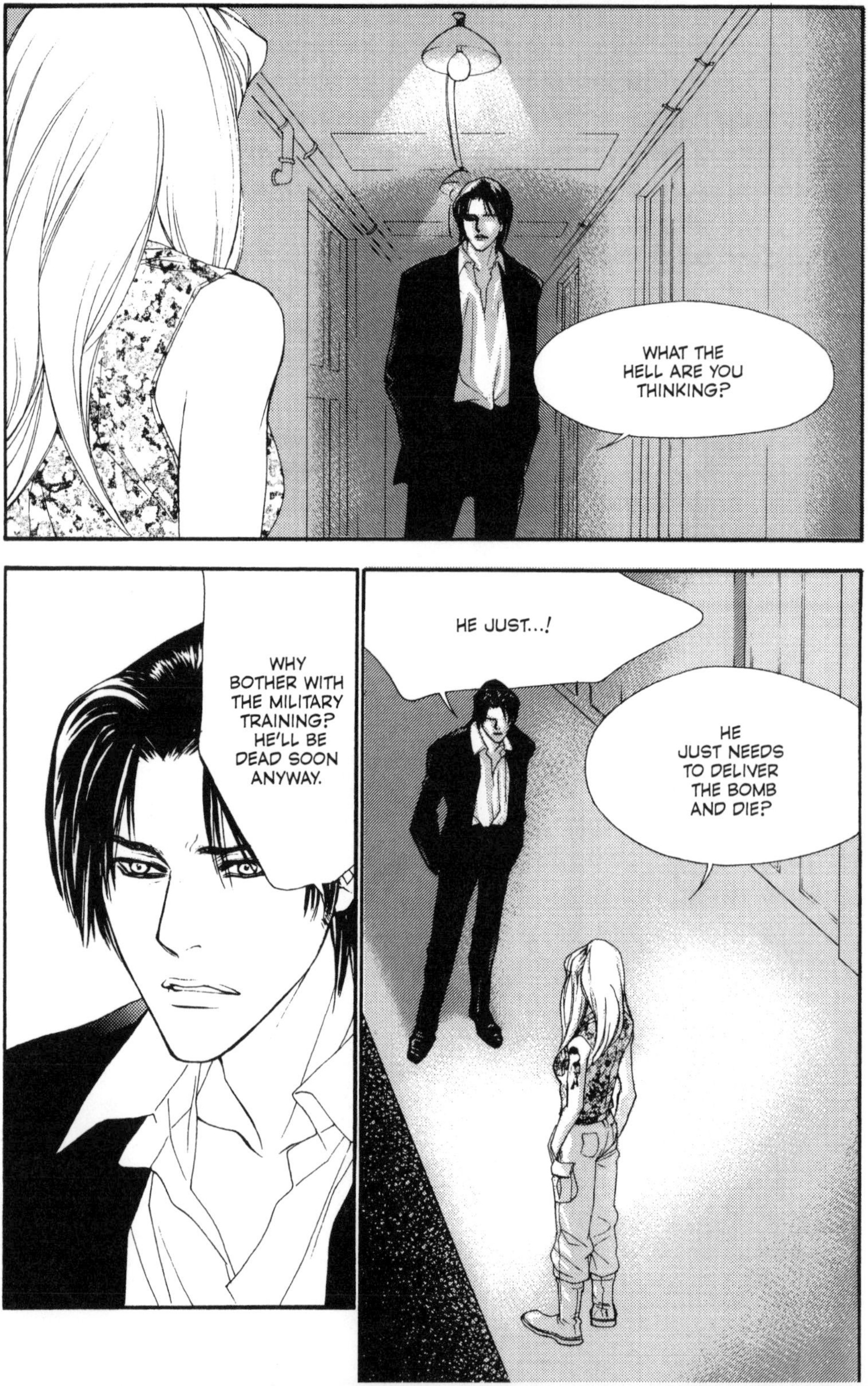
WHAT THE HELL ARE YOU THINKING?
WHY BOTHER WITH THE MILITARY TRAINING? HE'LL BE DEAD SOON ANYWAY.
HE JUST...!
HE JUST NEEDS TO DELIVER THE BOMB AND DIE?

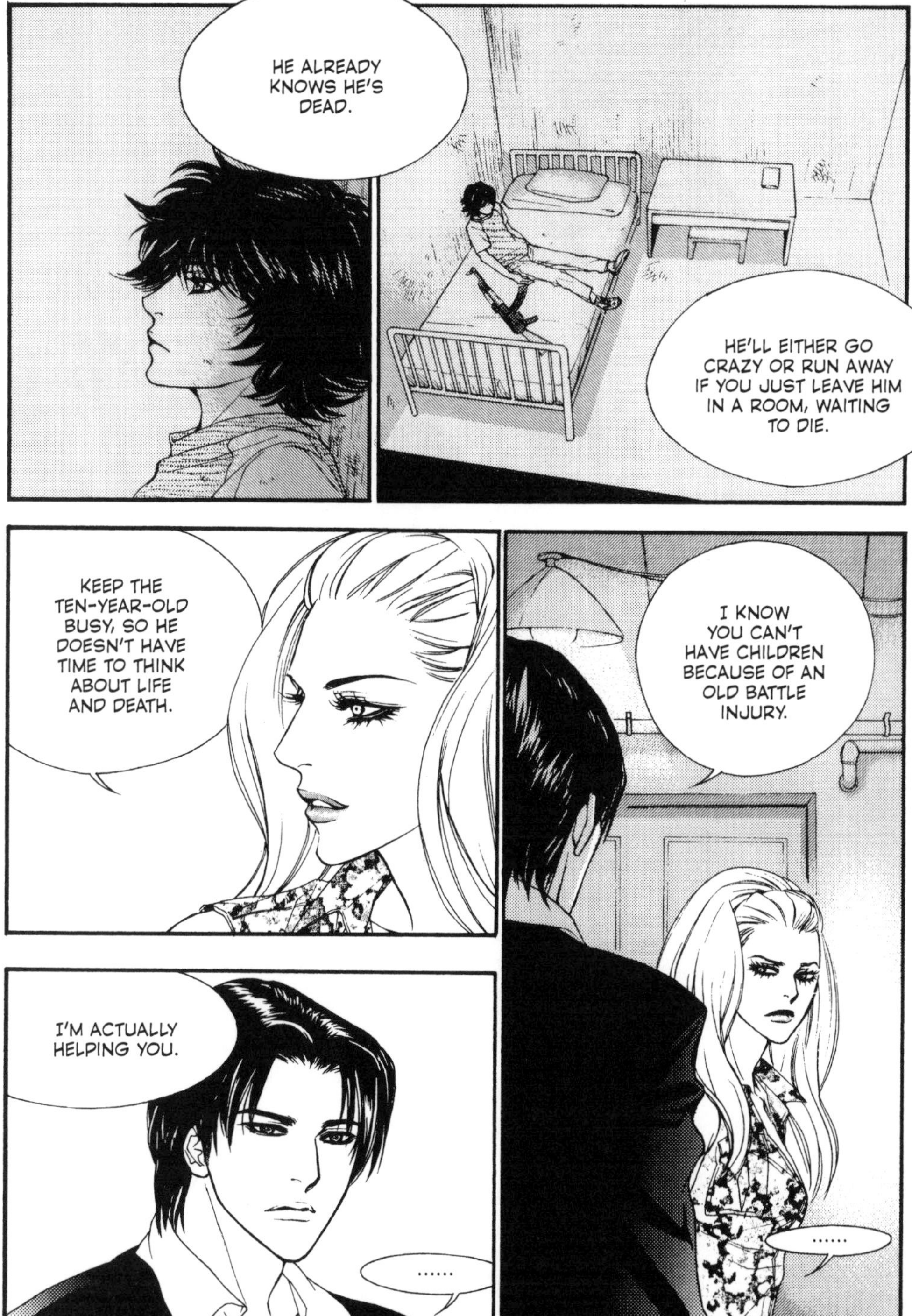
HE ALREADY KNOWS HE'S DEAD.
HE'LL EITHER GO CRAZY OR RUN AWAY IF YOU JUST LEAVE HIM IN A ROOM, WAITING TO DIE.
KEEP THE TEN-YEAR-OLD BUSY, SO HE DOESN'T HAVE TIME TO THINK ABOUT LIFE AND DEATH.
I'M ACTUALLY HELPING YOU.
......
I KNOW YOU CAN'T HAVE CHILDREN BECAUSE OF AN OLD BATTLE INJURY.
......

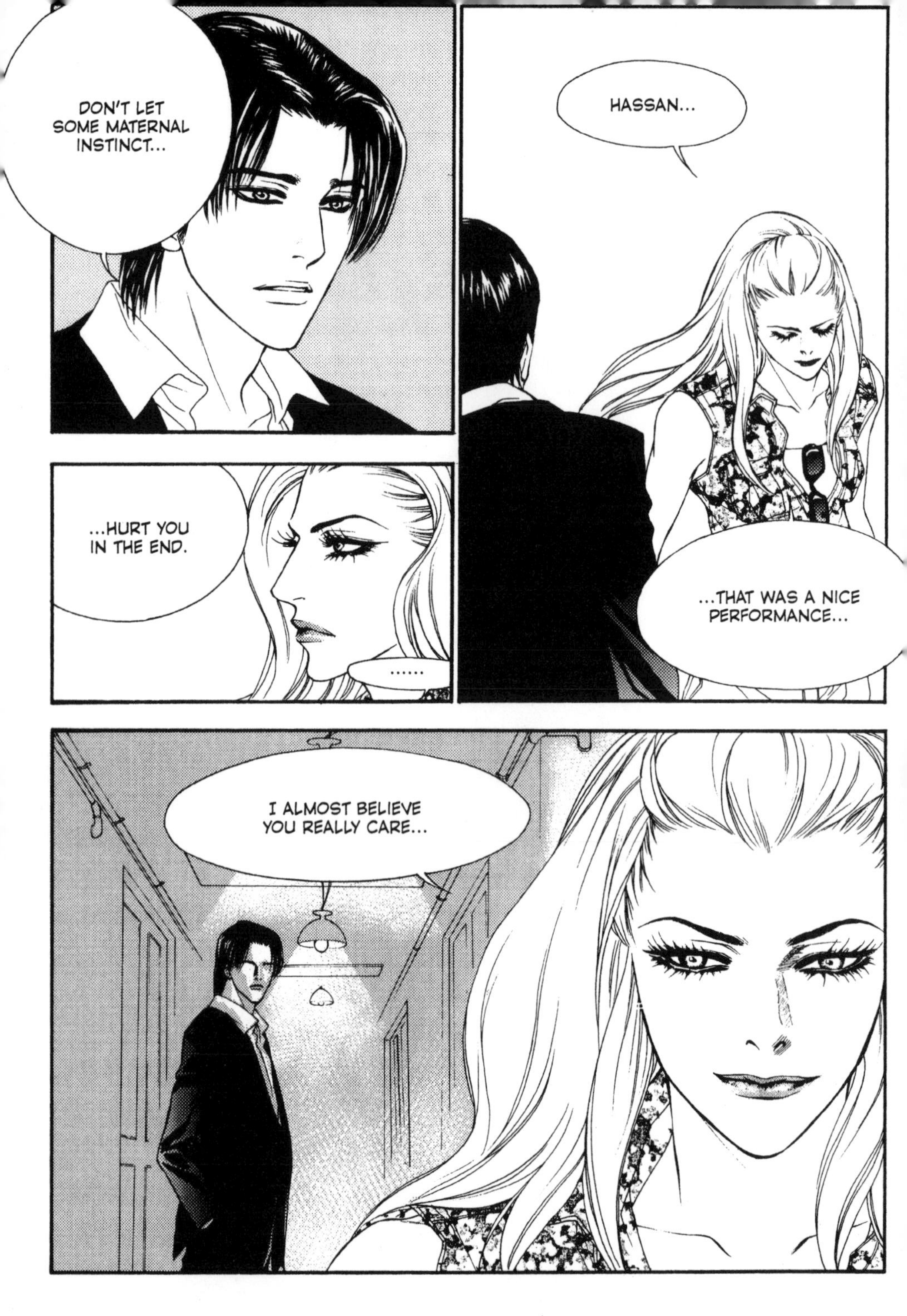
DON'T LET SOME MATERNAL INSTINCT...
HASSAN...
...HURT YOU IN THE END.
......
...THAT WAS A NICE PERFORMANCE...
I ALMOST BELIEVE YOU REALLY CARE...

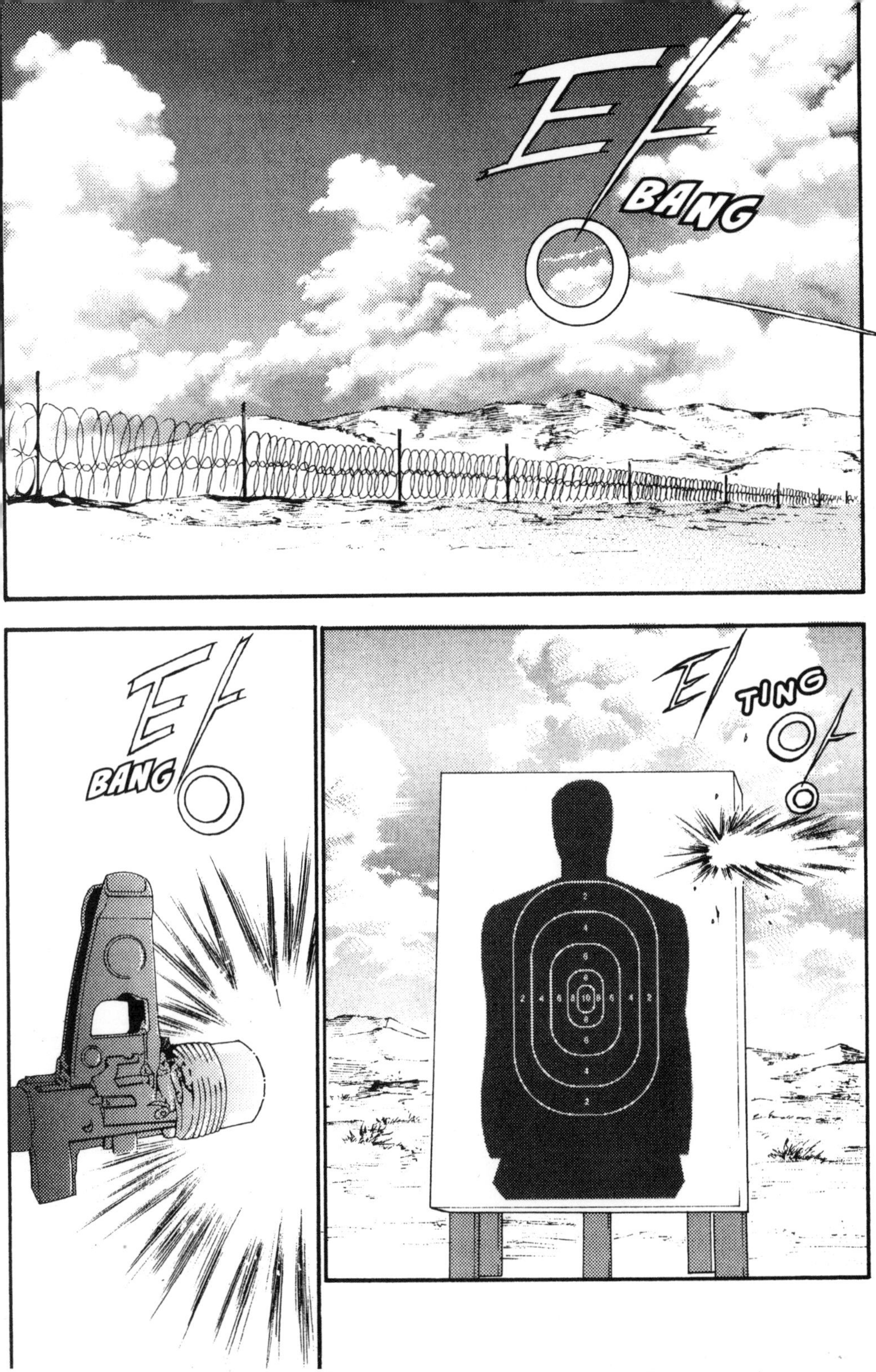
BANG
BANG
TING

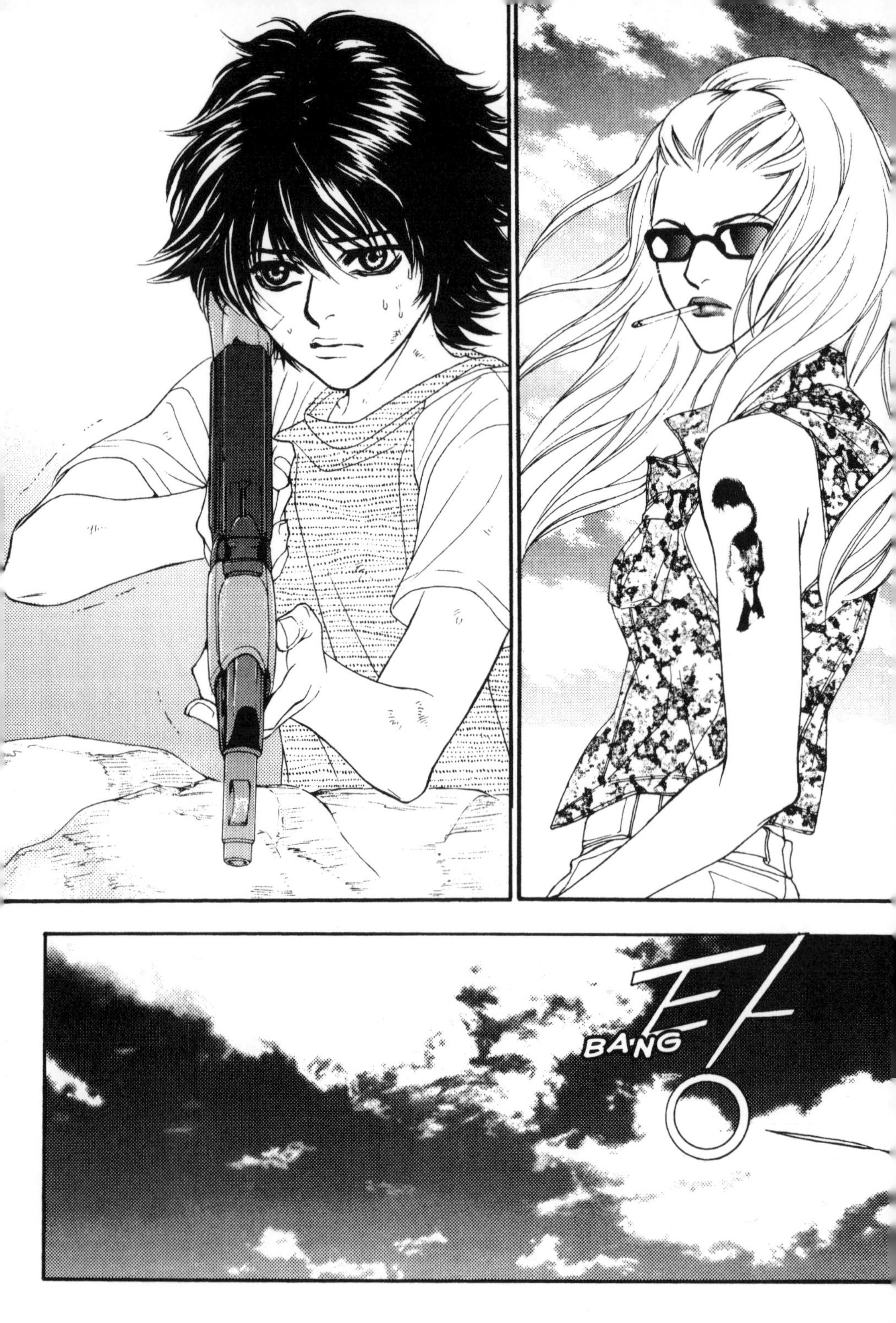
BANG

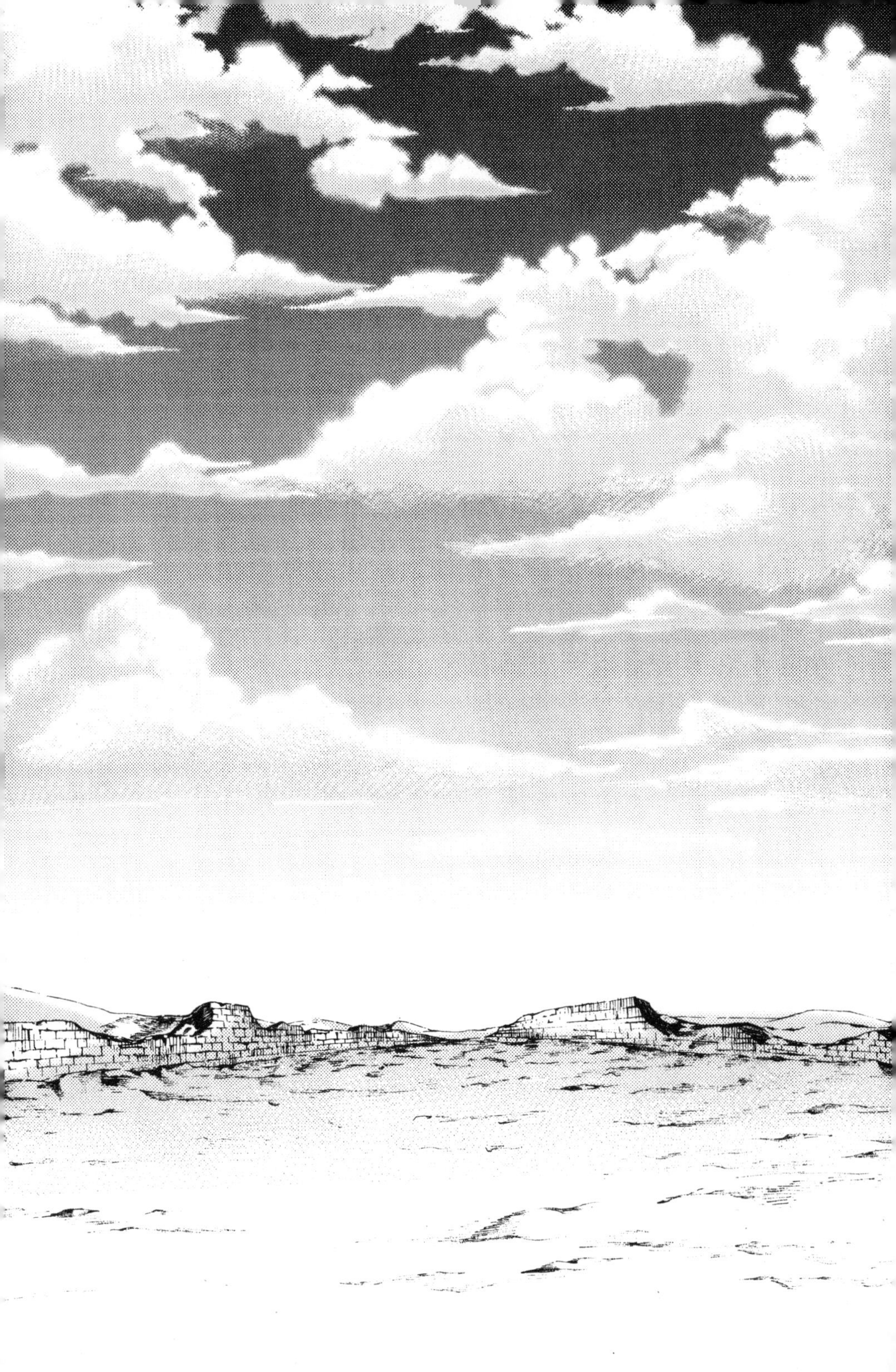

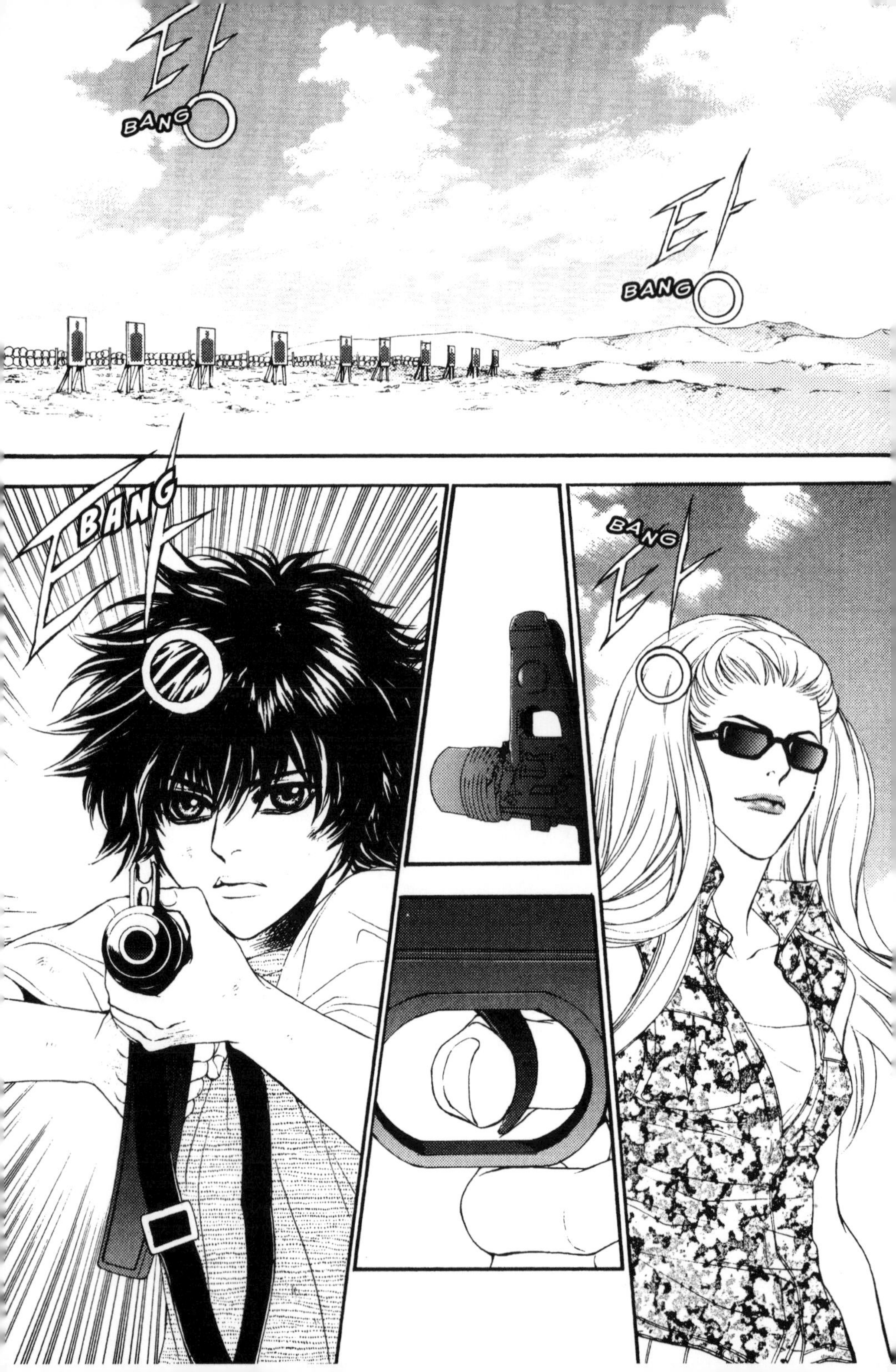
탕 BANG
탕 BANG
탕 BANG
탕 BANG

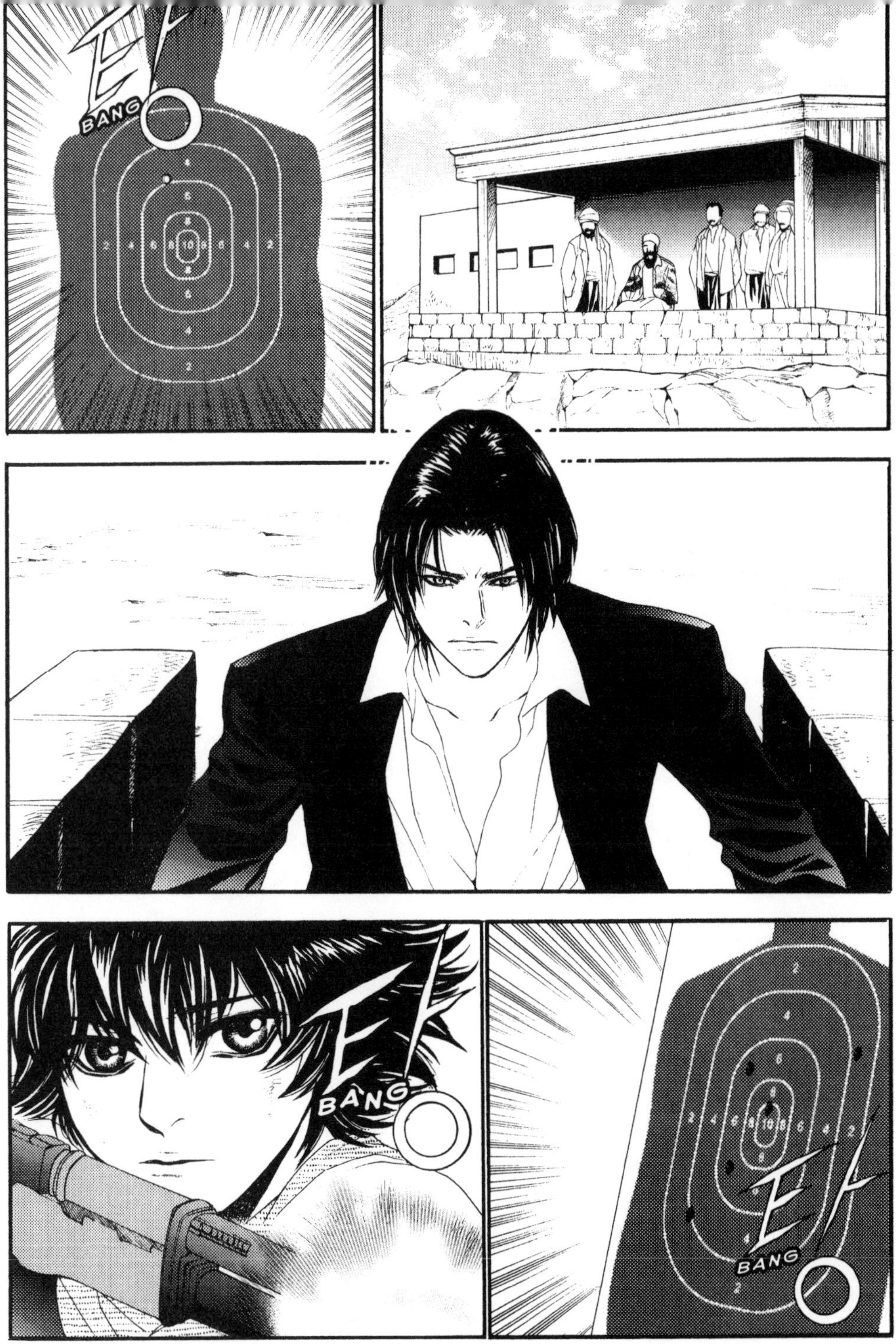
BANG
BANG
BANG

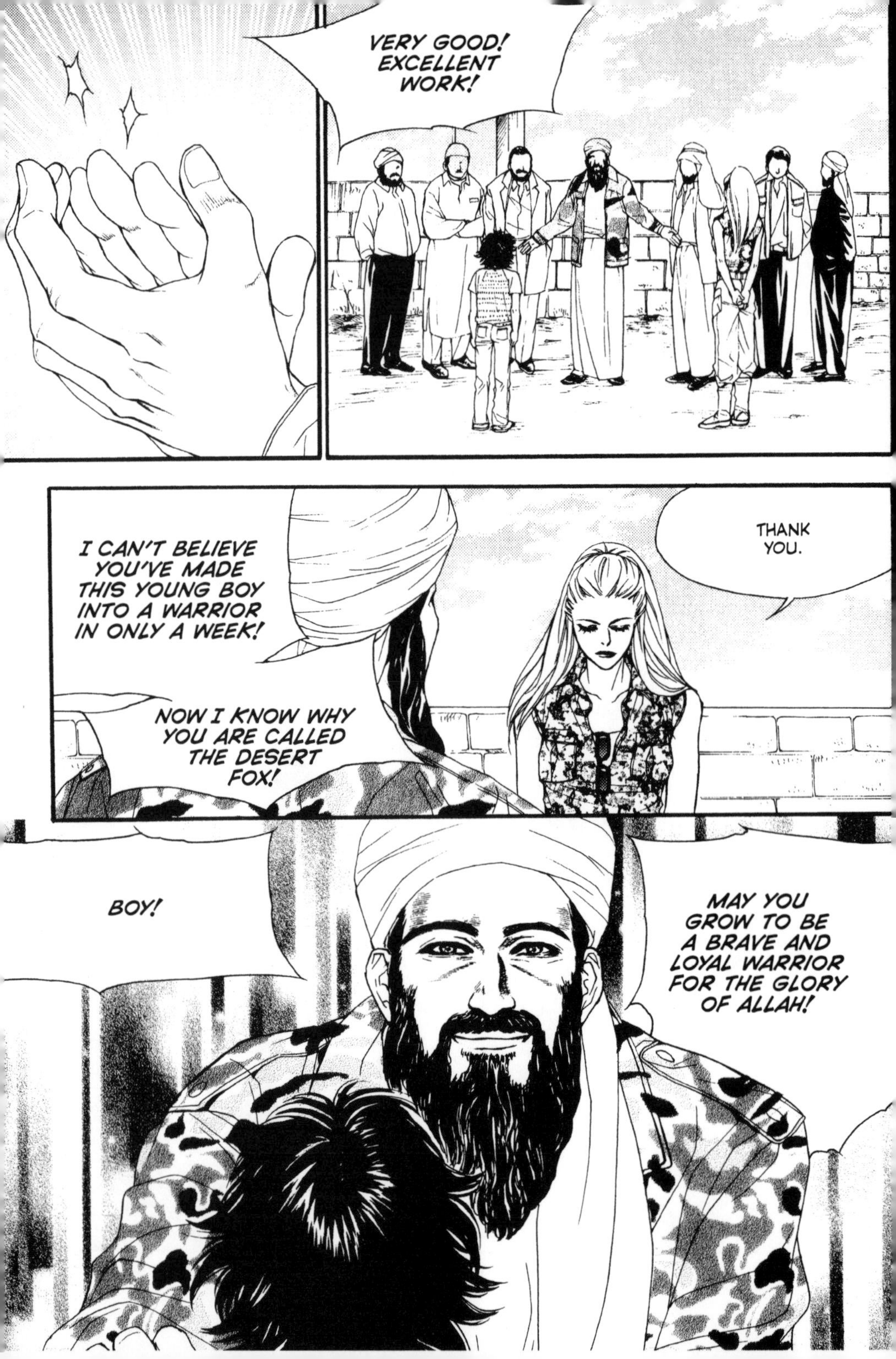
VERY GOOD! EXCELLENT WORK!
I CAN'T BELIEVE YOU'VE MADE THIS YOUNG BOY INTO A WARRIOR IN ONLY A WEEK!
NOW I KNOW WHY YOU ARE CALLED THE DESERT FOX!
THANK YOU.
BOY!
MAY YOU GROW TO BE A BRAVE AND LOYAL WARRIOR FOR THE GLORY OF ALLAH!

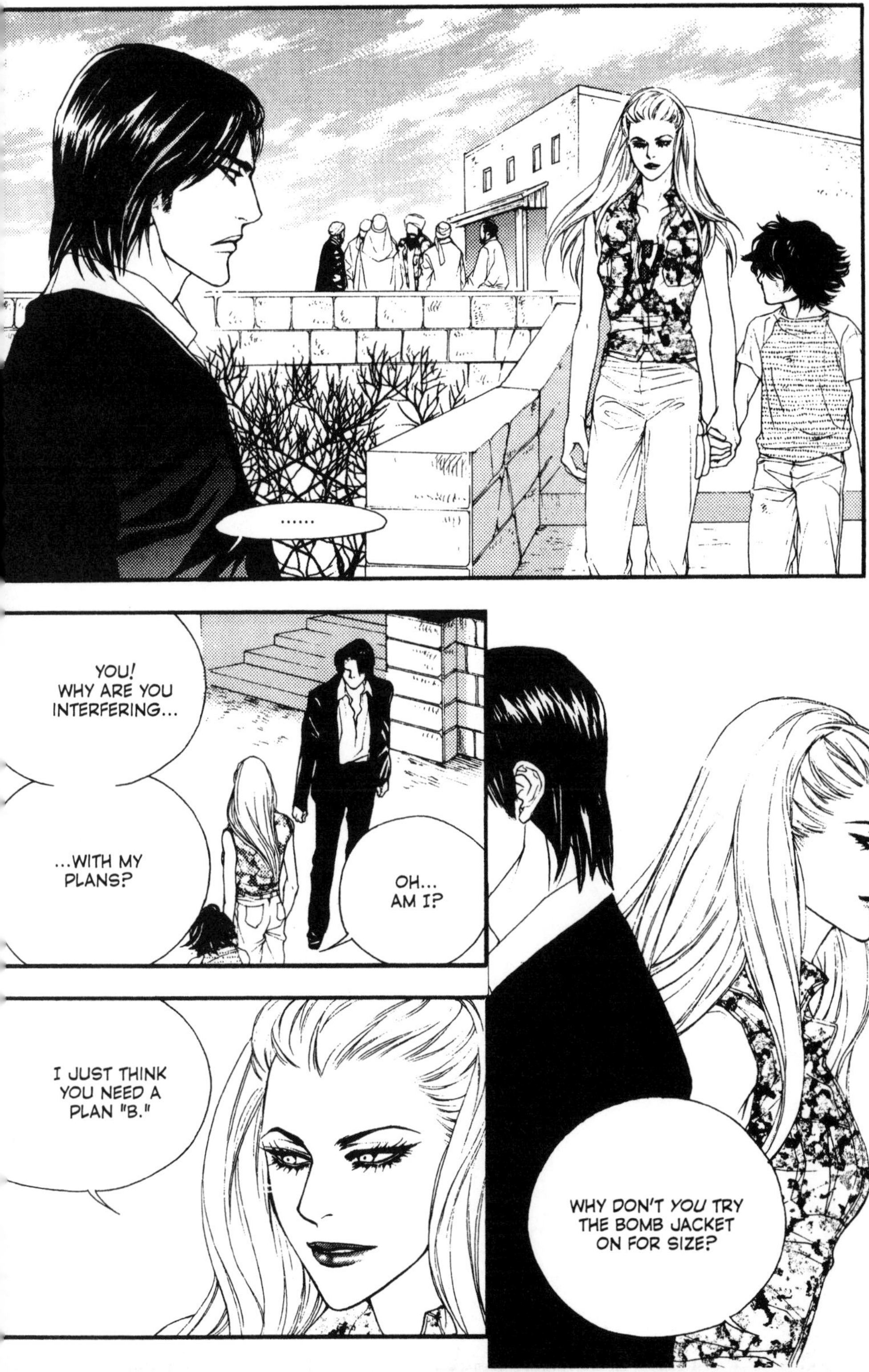
......
YOU! WHY ARE YOU INTERFERING...
...WITH MY PLANS?
OH... AM I?
I JUST THINK YOU NEED A PLAN "B."
WHY DON'T *YOU* TRY THE BOMB JACKET ON FOR SIZE?

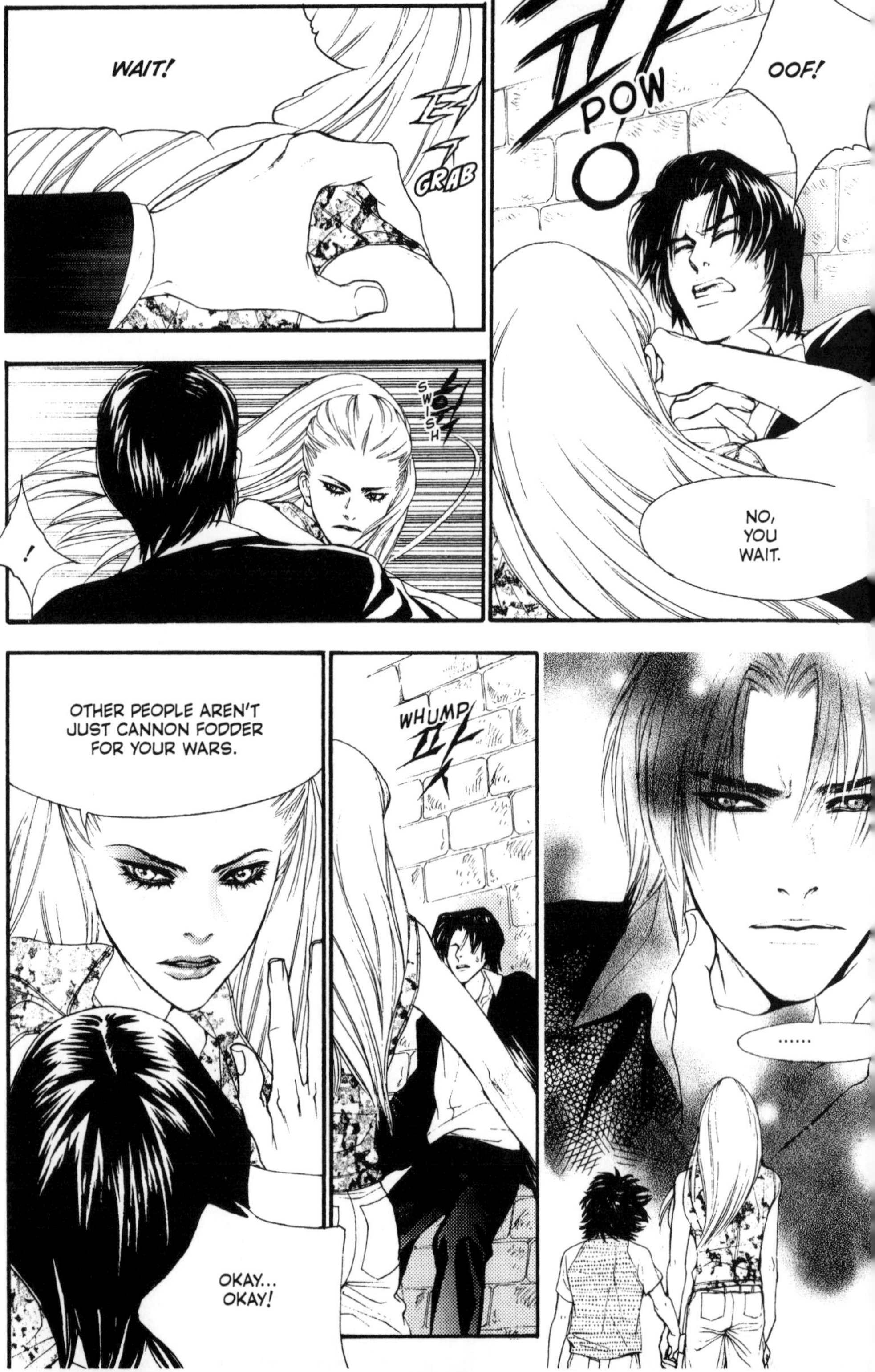
WAIT!
GRAB
SWISH
!
POW
OOF!
NO, YOU WAIT.
OTHER PEOPLE AREN'T JUST CANNON FODDER FOR YOUR WARS.
OKAY... OKAY!
WHUMP
......

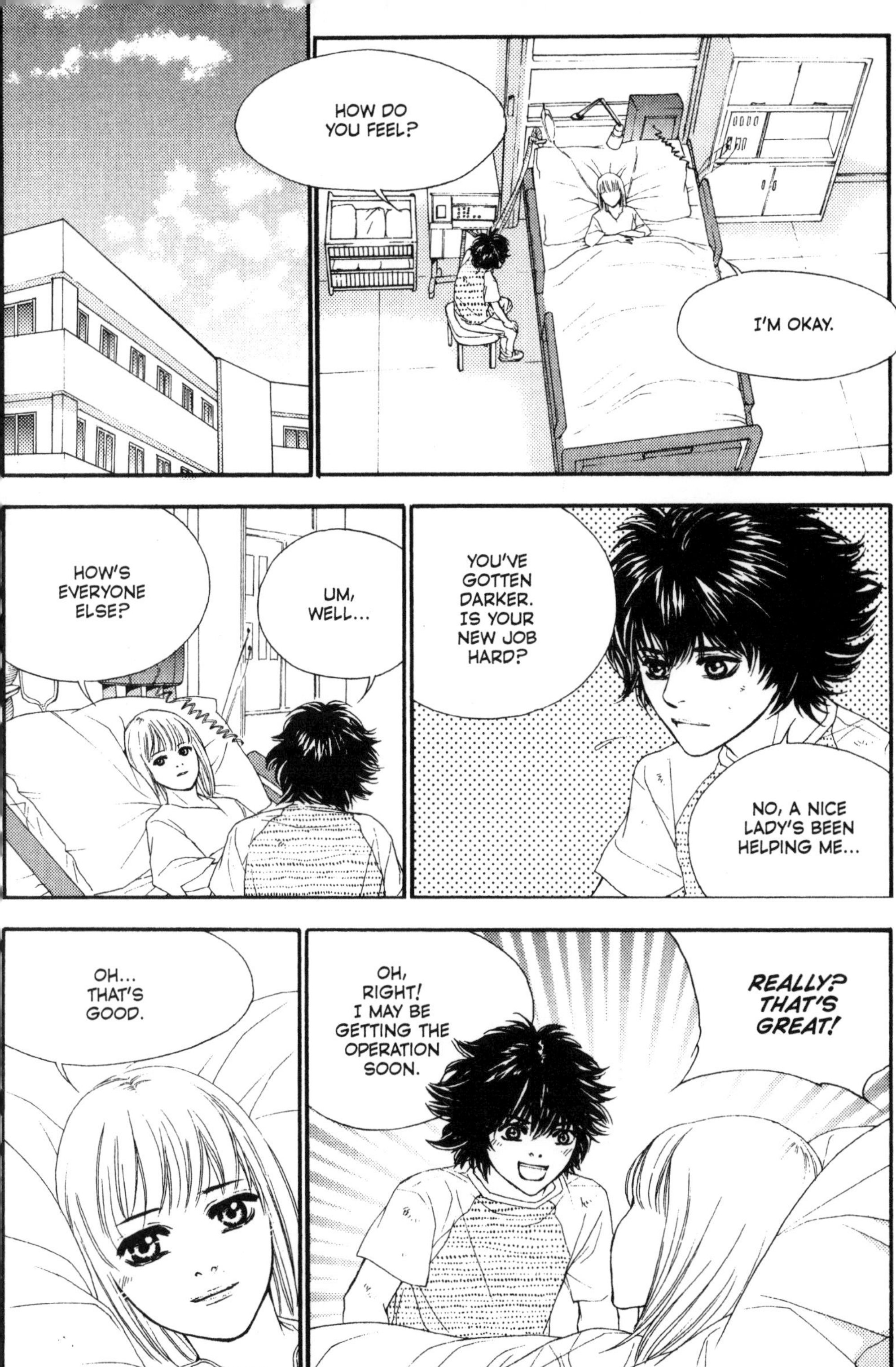
HOW DO YOU FEEL?
I'M OKAY.
HOW'S EVERYONE ELSE?
UM, WELL...
YOU'VE GOTTEN DARKER. IS YOUR NEW JOB HARD?
NO, A NICE LADY'S BEEN HELPING ME...
OH... THAT'S GOOD.
OH, RIGHT! I MAY BE GETTING THE OPERATION SOON.
REALLY? THAT'S GREAT!

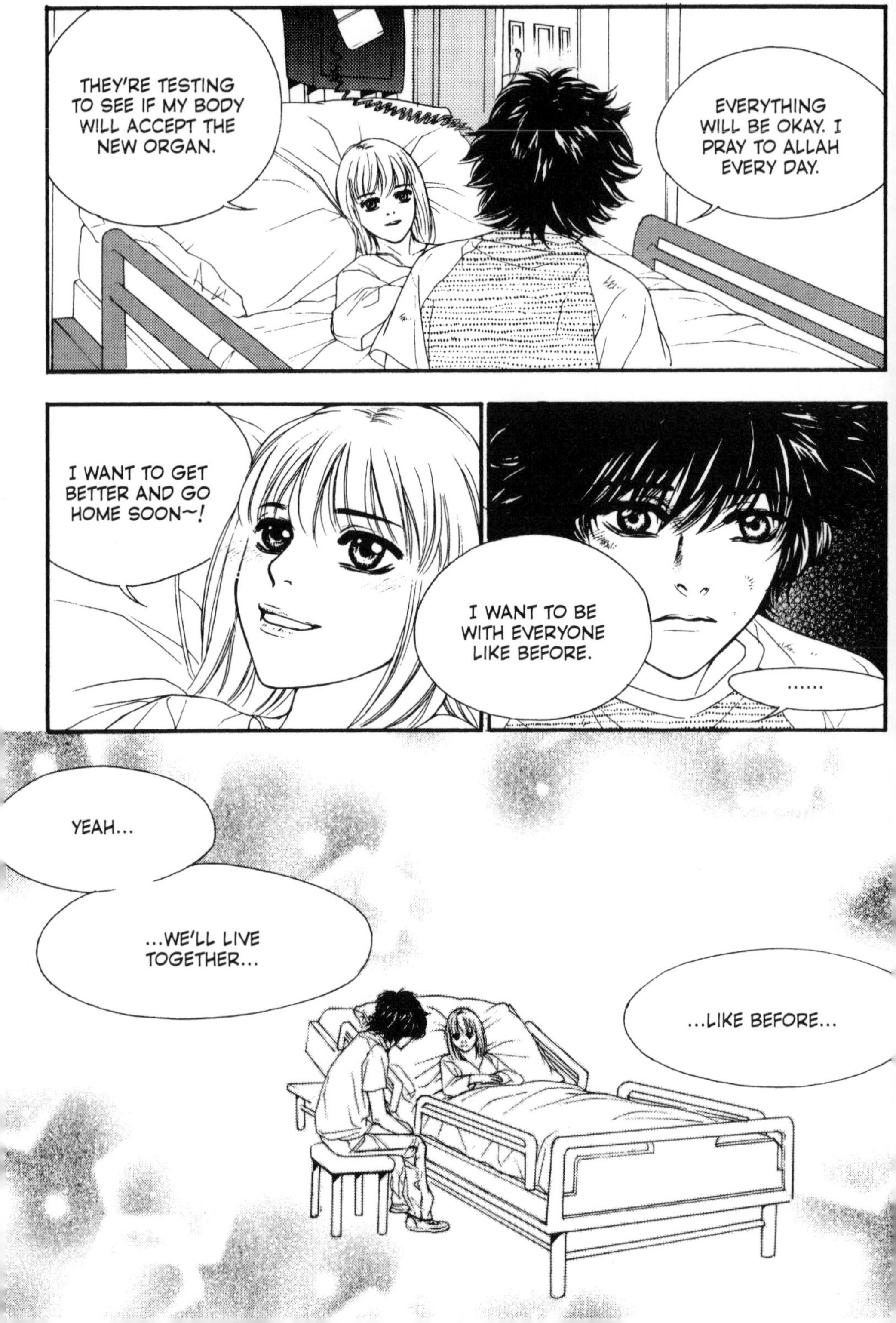
THEY'RE TESTING TO SEE IF MY BODY WILL ACCEPT THE NEW ORGAN.
EVERYTHING WILL BE OKAY. I PRAY TO ALLAH EVERY DAY.
I WANT TO GET BETTER AND GO HOME SOON~!
I WANT TO BE WITH EVERYONE LIKE BEFORE.
......
YEAH...
...WE'LL LIVE TOGETHER...
...LIKE BEFORE...

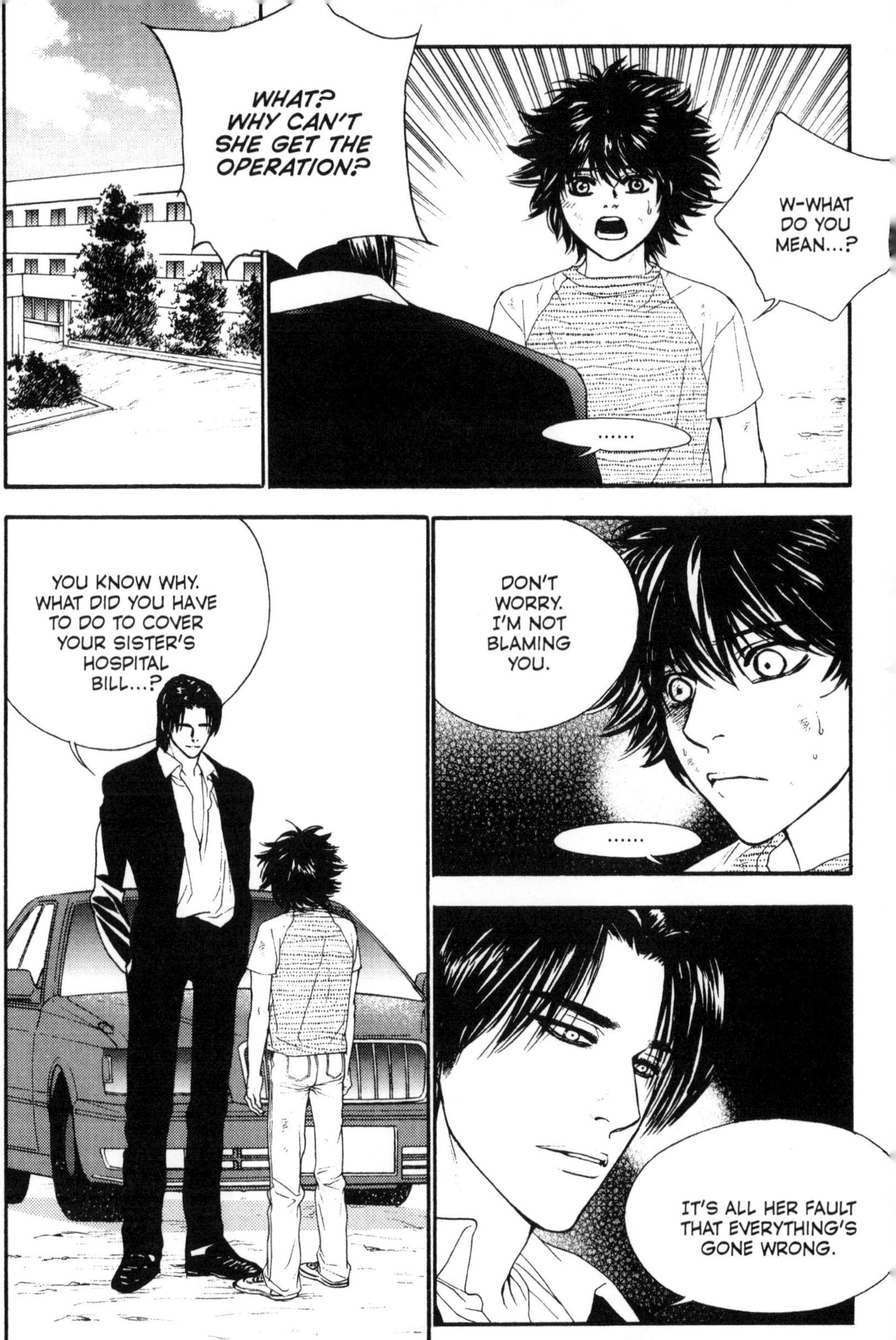
WHAT? WHY CAN'T SHE GET THE OPERATION?
W-WHAT DO YOU MEAN...?
......
YOU KNOW WHY. WHAT DID YOU HAVE TO DO TO COVER YOUR SISTER'S HOSPITAL BILL...?
DON'T WORRY. I'M NOT BLAMING YOU.
......
IT'S ALL HER FAULT THAT EVERYTHING'S GONE WRONG.

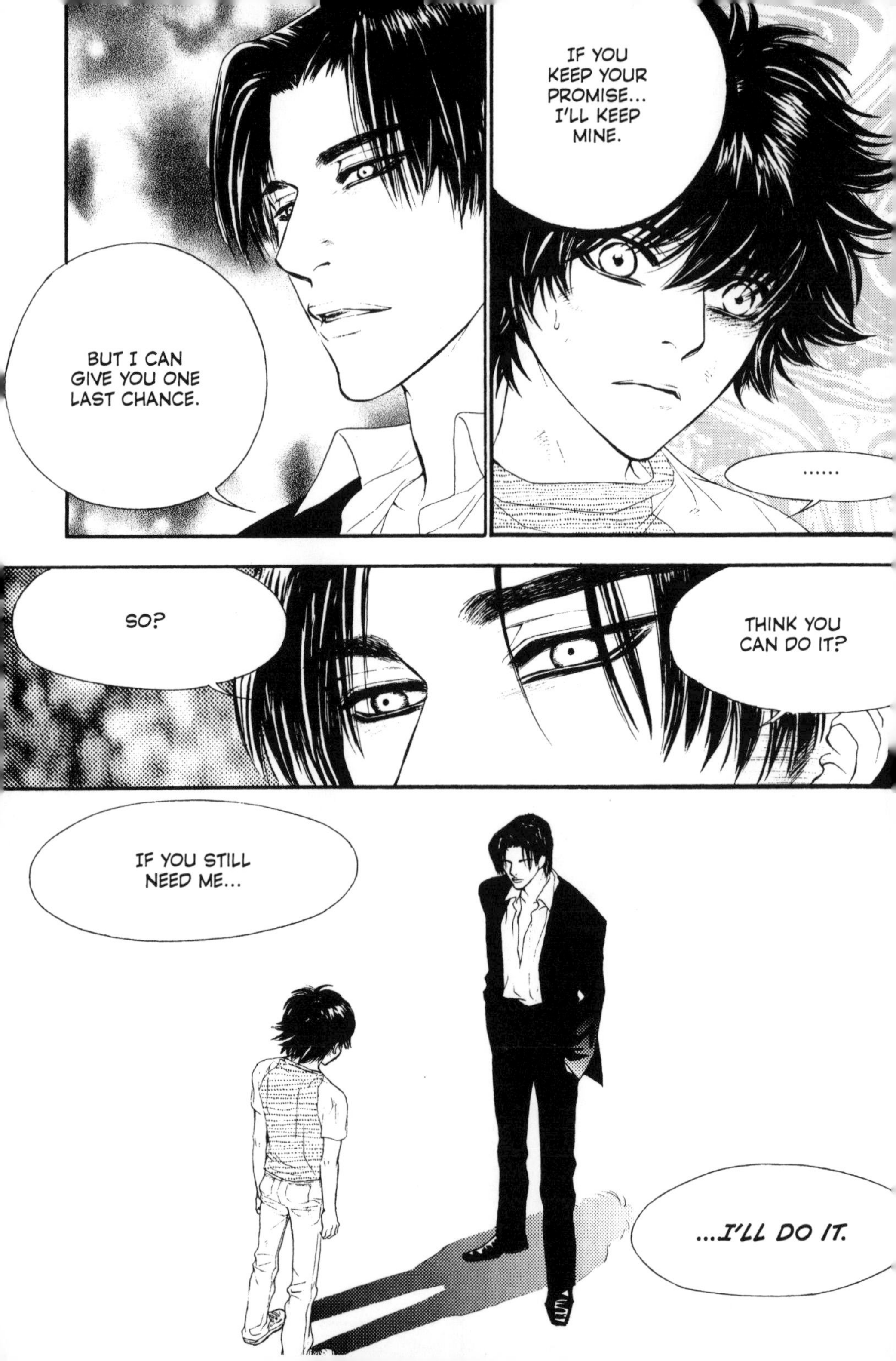
BUT I CAN GIVE YOU ONE LAST CHANCE.
IF YOU KEEP YOUR PROMISE... I'LL KEEP MINE.
......
SO?
THINK YOU CAN DO IT?
IF YOU STILL NEED ME...
...I'LL DO IT.

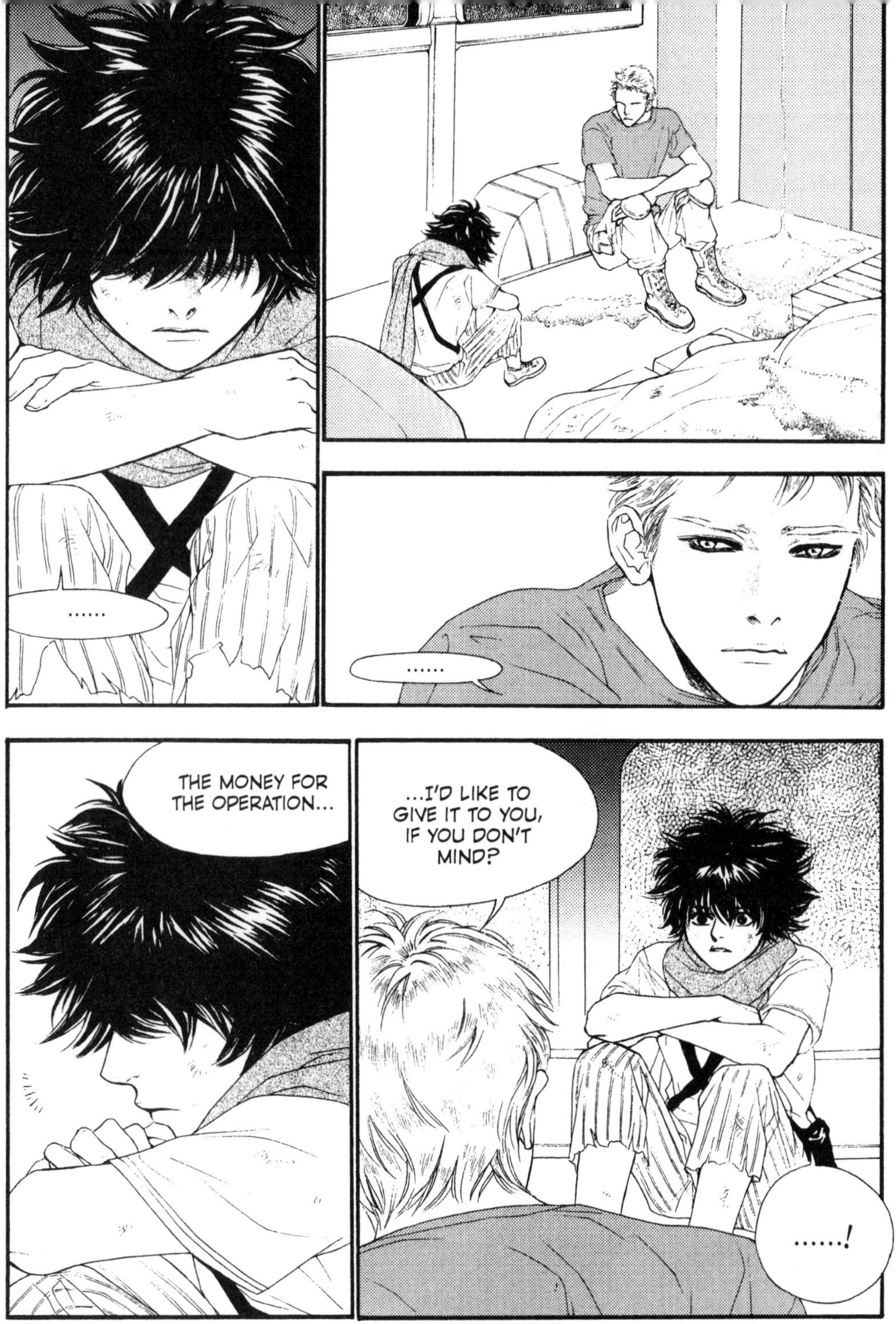
......
......
THE MONEY FOR THE OPERATION...
...I'D LIKE TO GIVE IT TO YOU, IF YOU DON'T MIND?
......!

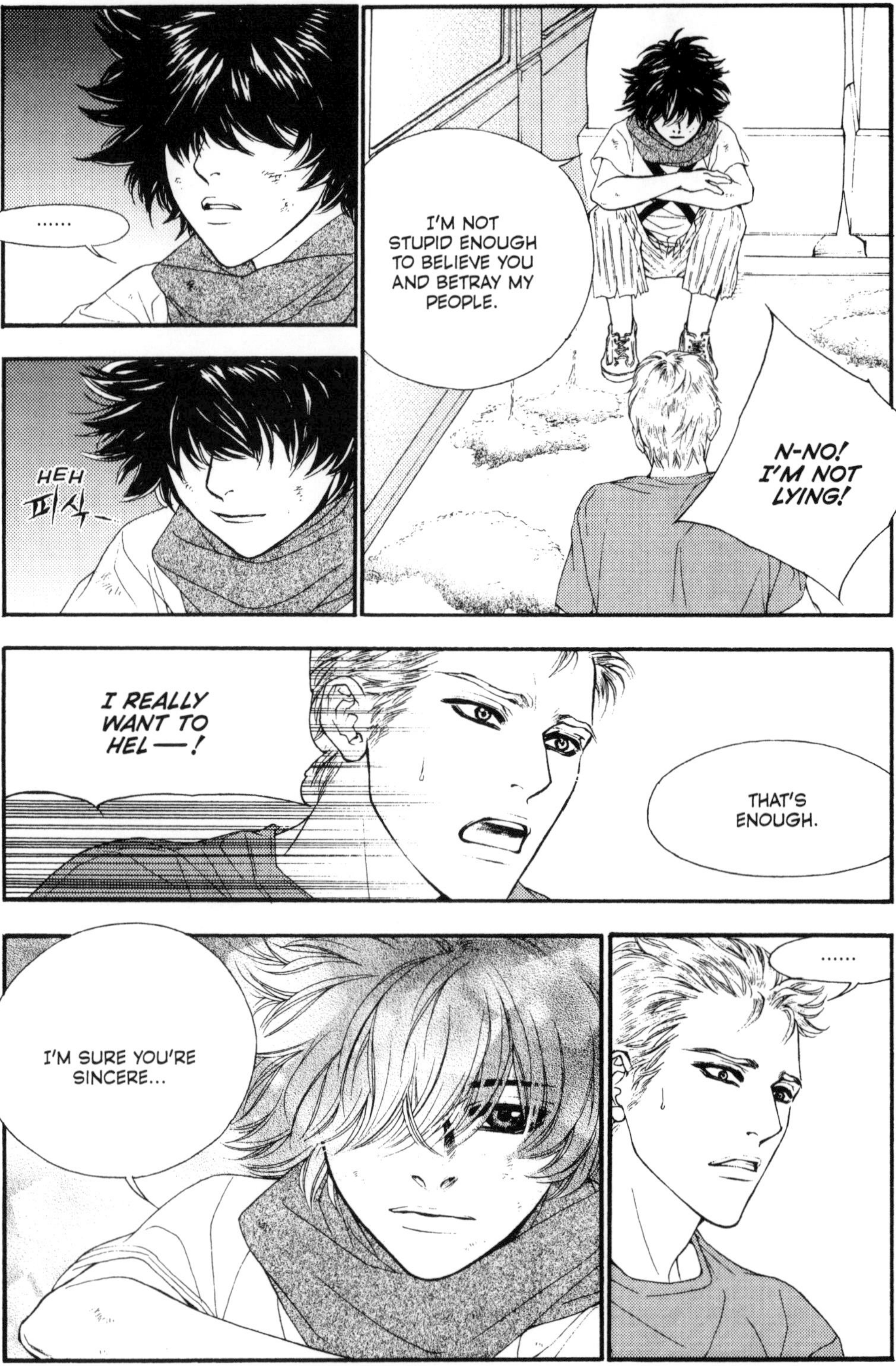
......
HEH
피식_
I'M NOT STUPID ENOUGH TO BELIEVE YOU AND BETRAY MY PEOPLE.
N-NO! I'M NOT LYING!
I REALLY WANT TO HEL—!
THAT'S ENOUGH.
I'M SURE YOU'RE SINCERE...
......

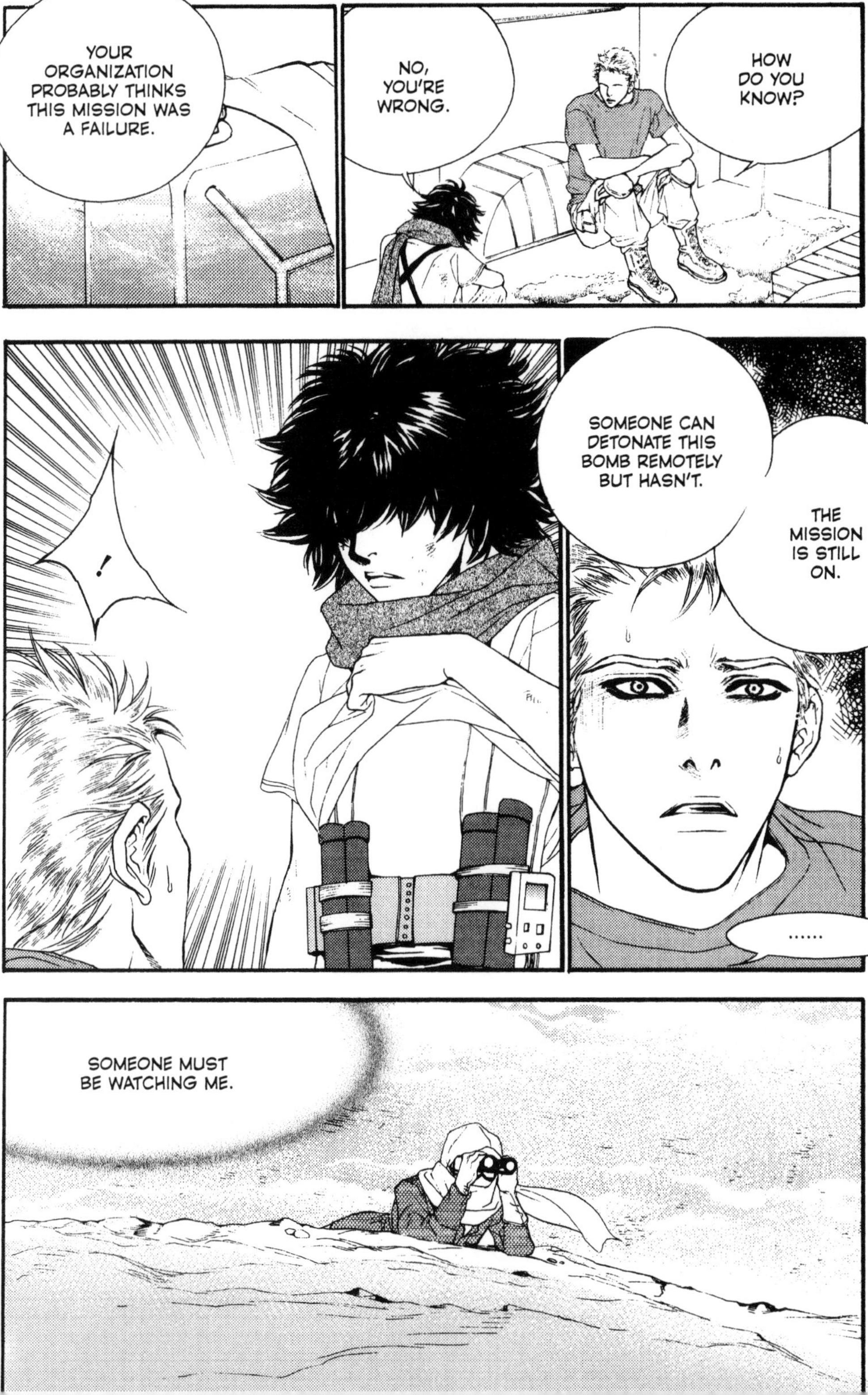
YOUR ORGANIZATION PROBABLY THINKS THIS MISSION WAS A FAILURE.
NO, YOU'RE WRONG.
HOW DO YOU KNOW?
!
SOMEONE CAN DETONATE THIS BOMB REMOTELY BUT HASN'T.
THE MISSION IS STILL ON.
......
SOMEONE MUST BE WATCHING ME.

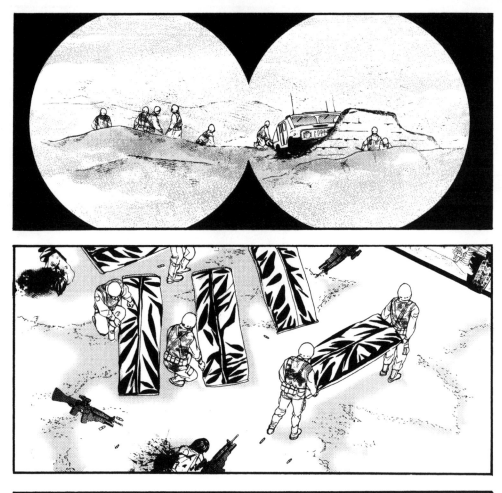

VROOOM

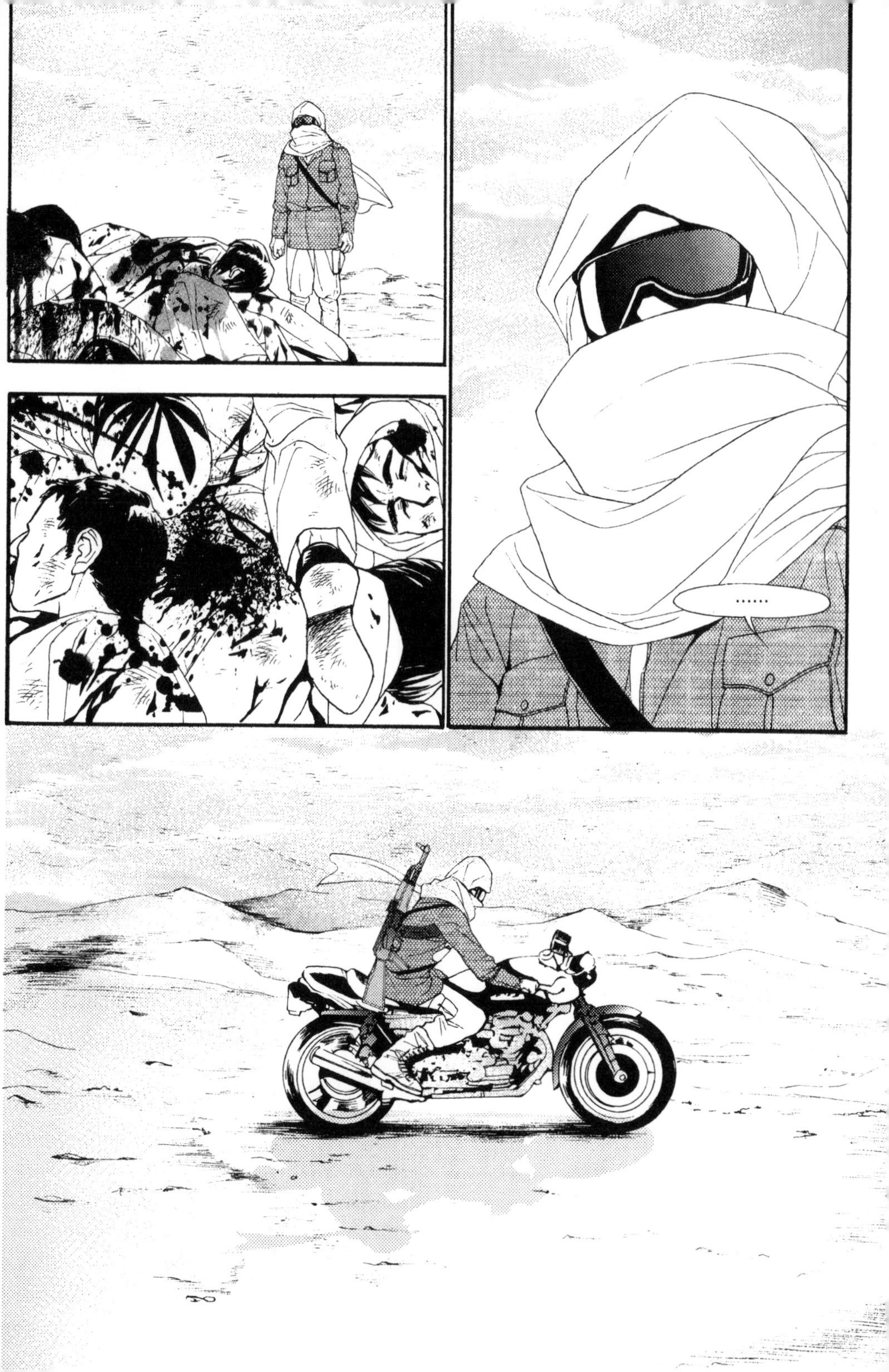

......

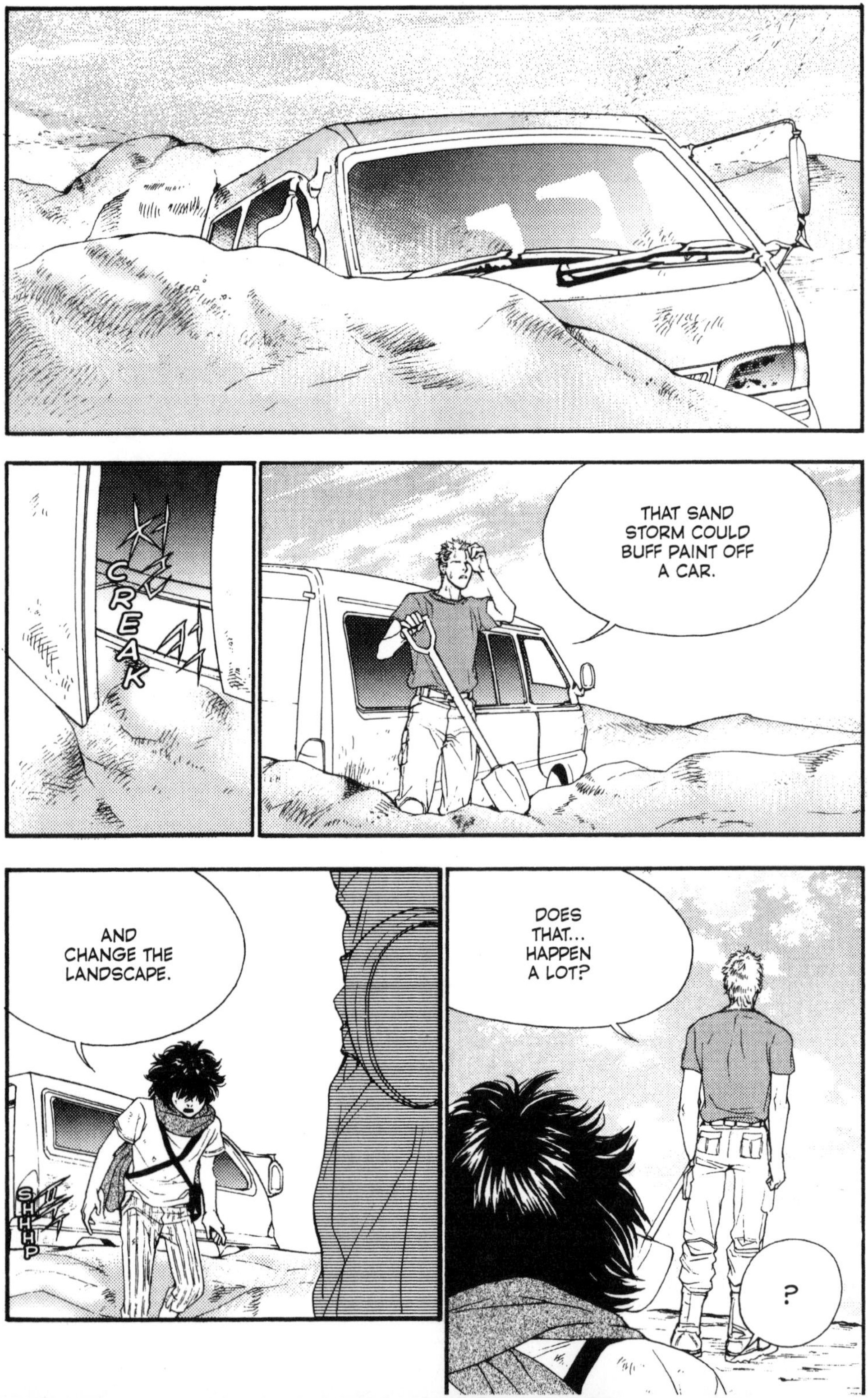
CREAK
THAT SAND STORM COULD BUFF PAINT OFF A CAR.
AND CHANGE THE LANDSCAPE.
SHHHP
DOES THAT... HAPPEN A LOT?
?

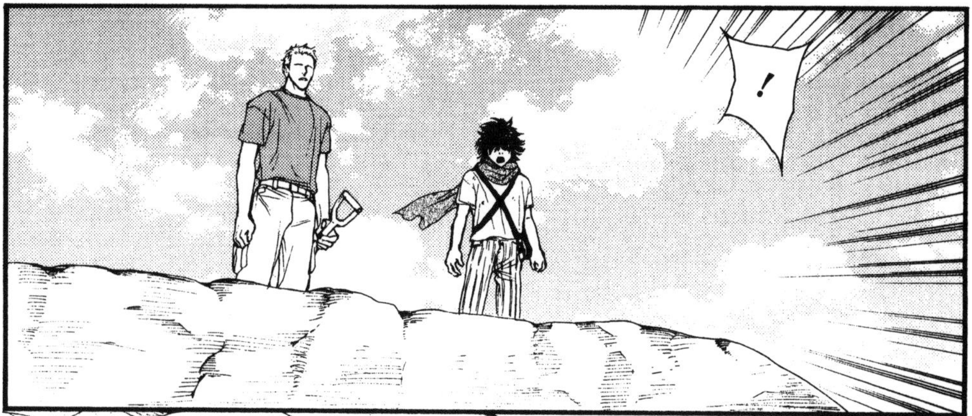
!
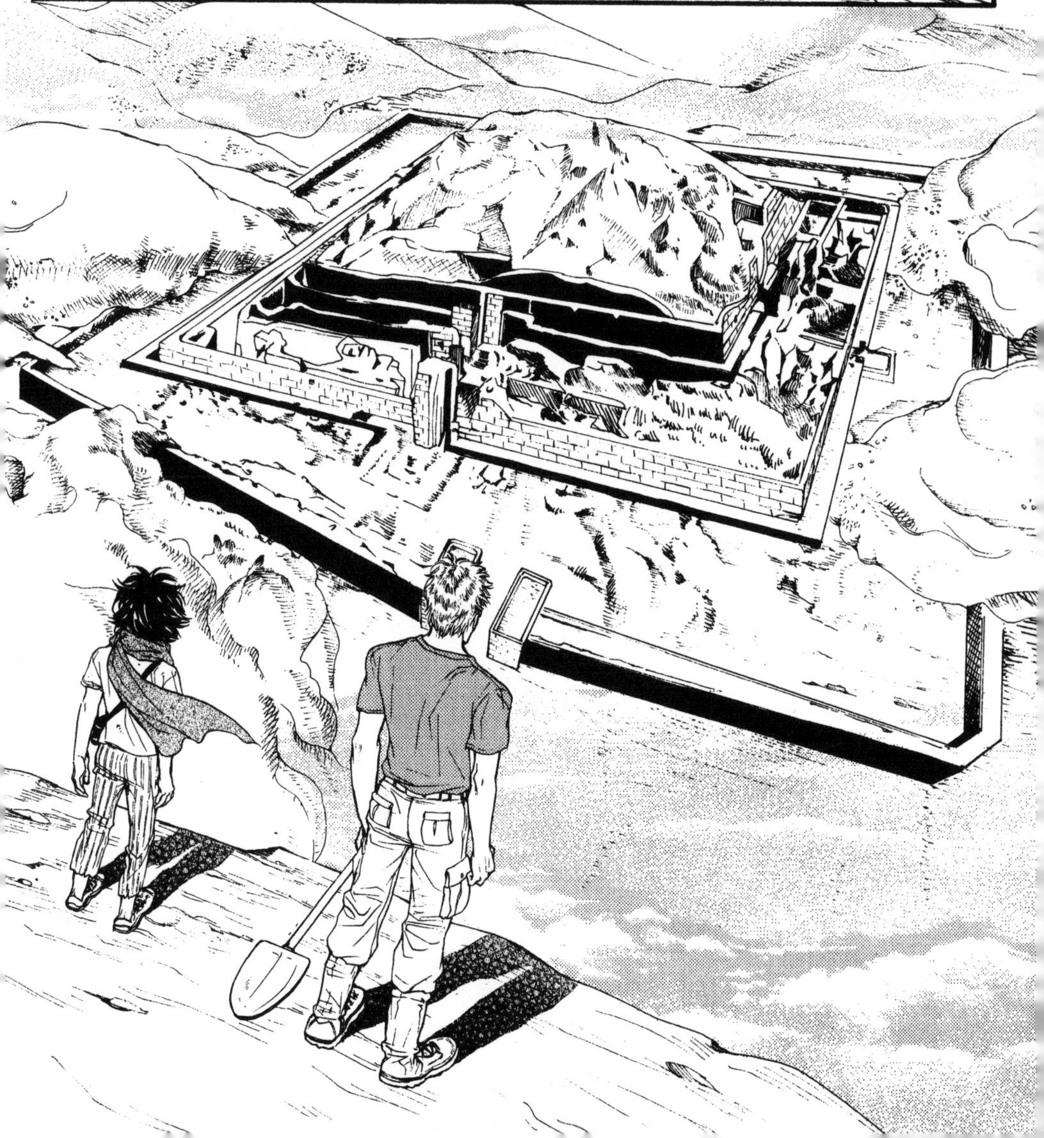

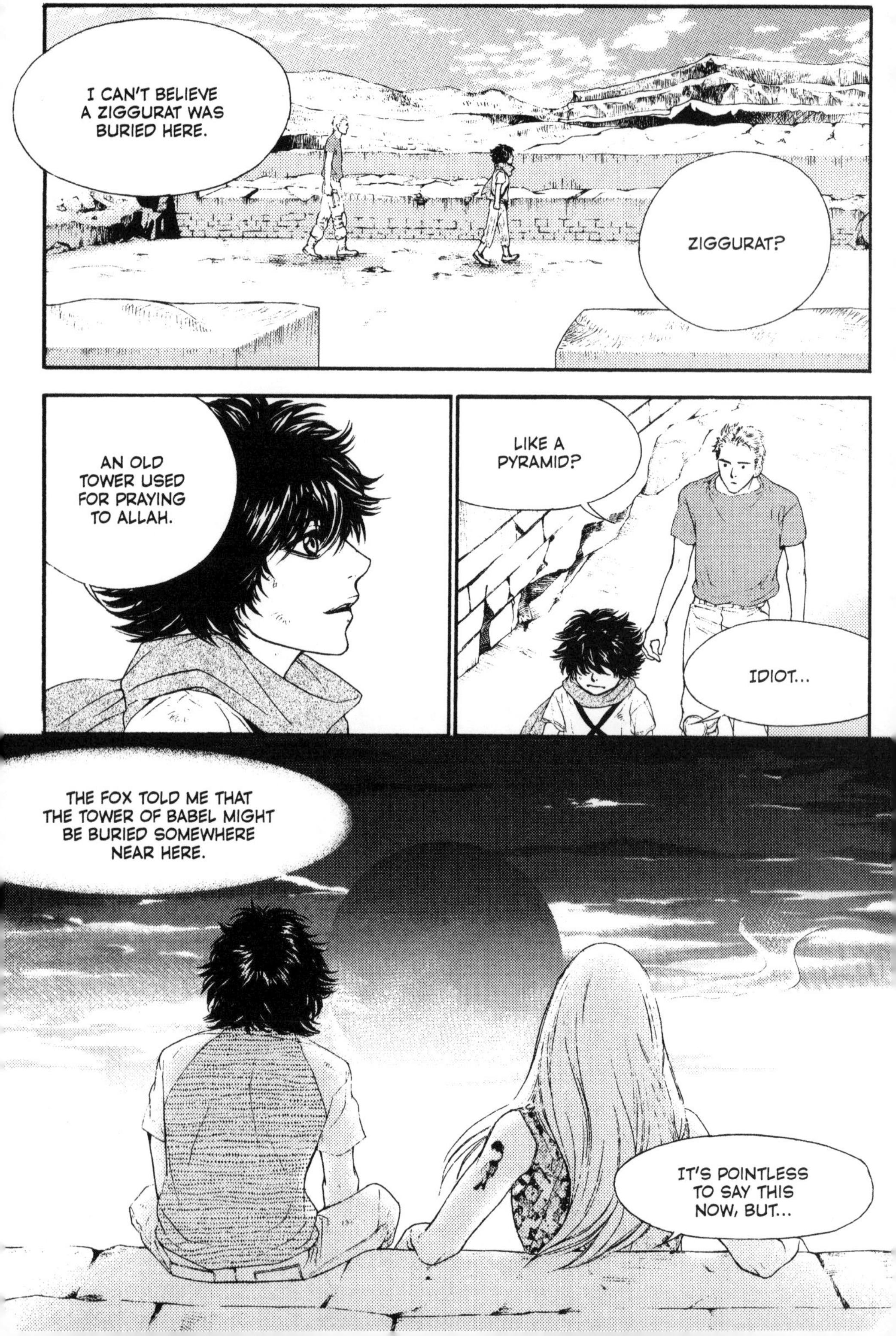
I CAN'T BELIEVE A ZIGGURAT WAS BURIED HERE.
ZIGGURAT?
AN OLD TOWER USED FOR PRAYING TO ALLAH.
LIKE A PYRAMID?
IDIOT...
THE FOX TOLD ME THAT THE TOWER OF BABEL MIGHT BE BURIED SOMEWHERE NEAR HERE.
IT'S POINTLESS TO SAY THIS NOW, BUT...

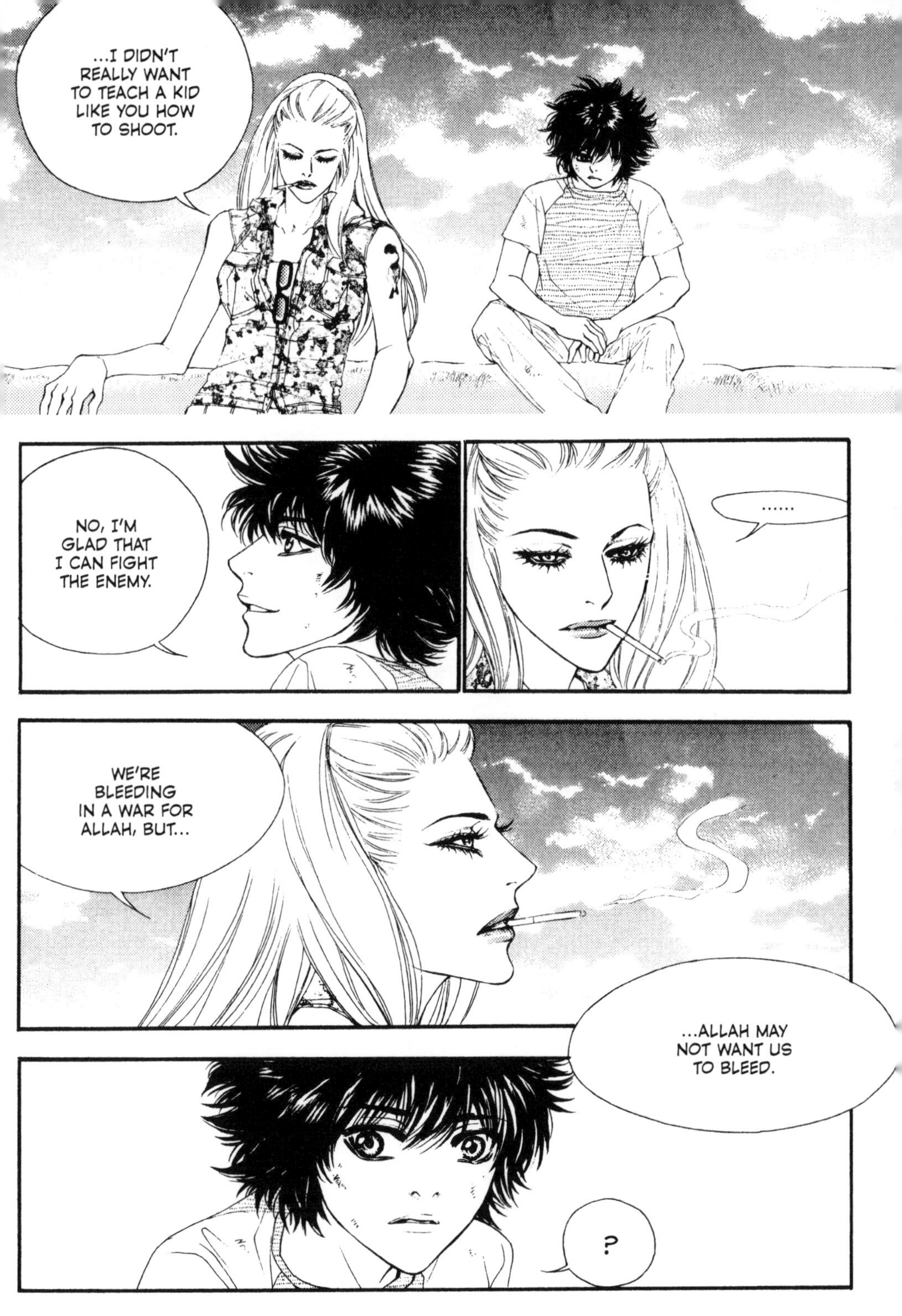
...I DIDN'T REALLY WANT TO TEACH A KID LIKE YOU HOW TO SHOOT.
NO, I'M GLAD THAT I CAN FIGHT THE ENEMY.
......
WE'RE BLEEDING IN A WAR FOR ALLAH, BUT...
...ALLAH MAY NOT WANT US TO BLEED.
?

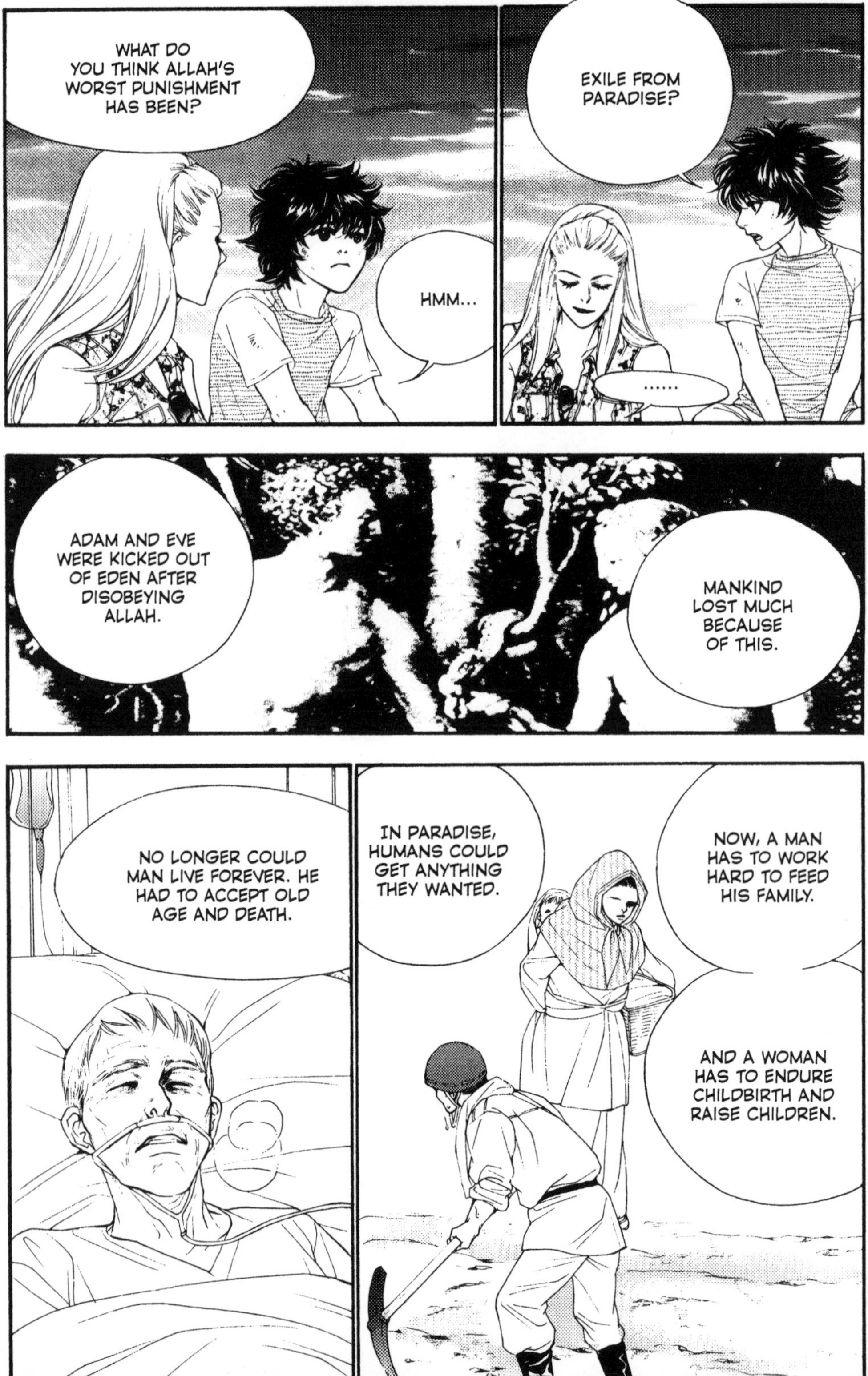
WHAT DO YOU THINK ALLAH'S WORST PUNISHMENT HAS BEEN?
HMM...
EXILE FROM PARADISE?
......
ADAM AND EVE WERE KICKED OUT OF EDEN AFTER DISOBEYING ALLAH.
MANKIND LOST MUCH BECAUSE OF THIS.
NO LONGER COULD MAN LIVE FOREVER. HE HAD TO ACCEPT OLD AGE AND DEATH.
IN PARADISE, HUMANS COULD GET ANYTHING THEY WANTED.
NOW, A MAN HAS TO WORK HARD TO FEED HIS FAMILY.
AND A WOMAN HAS TO ENDURE CHILDBIRTH AND RAISE CHILDREN.

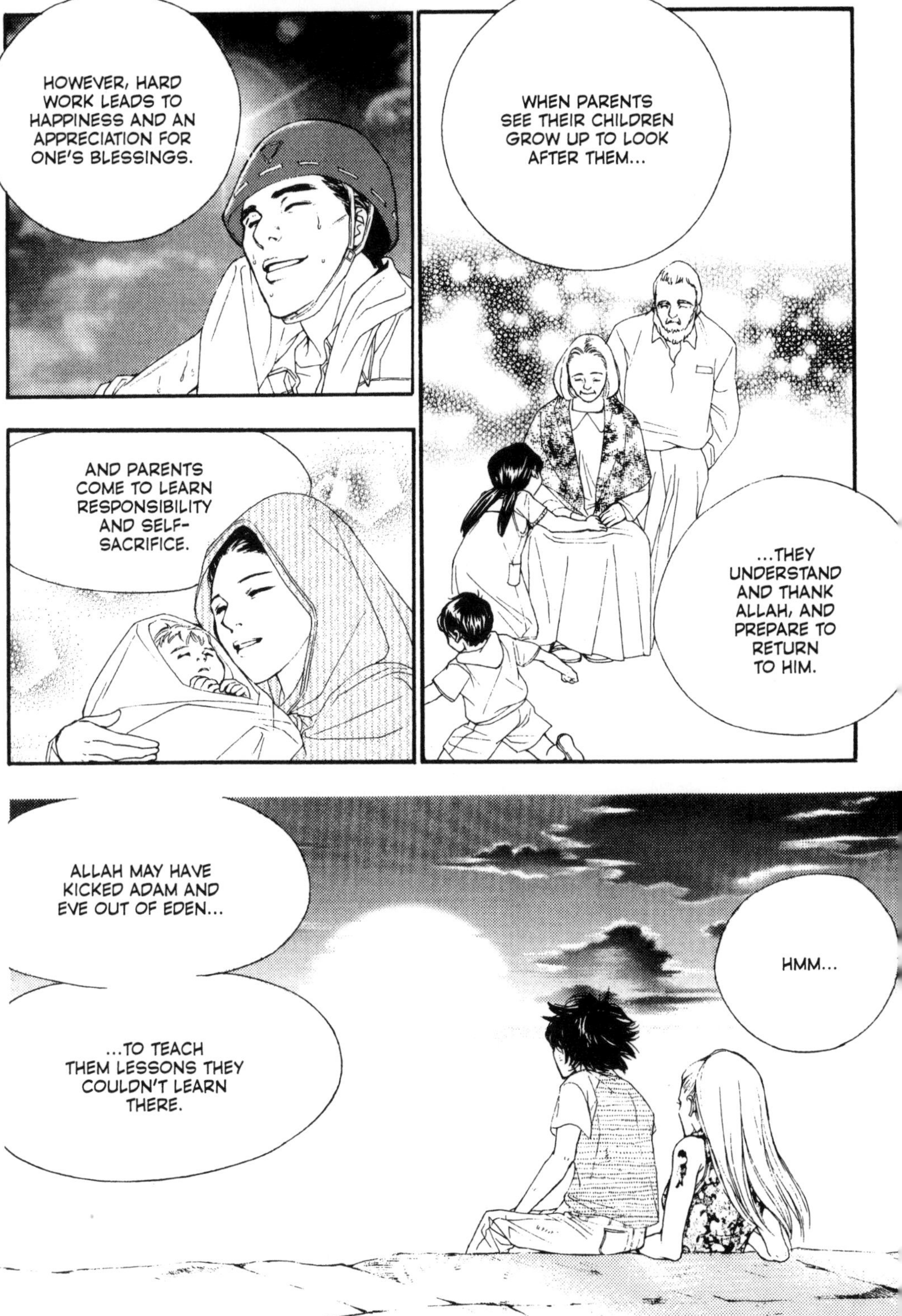
HOWEVER, HARD WORK LEADS TO HAPPINESS AND AN APPRECIATION FOR ONE'S BLESSINGS.
AND PARENTS COME TO LEARN RESPONSIBILITY AND SELF-SACRIFICE.
WHEN PARENTS SEE THEIR CHILDREN GROW UP TO LOOK AFTER THEM...
...THEY UNDERSTAND AND THANK ALLAH, AND PREPARE TO RETURN TO HIM.
ALLAH MAY HAVE KICKED ADAM AND EVE OUT OF EDEN...
...TO TEACH THEM LESSONS THEY COULDN'T LEARN THERE.
HMM...

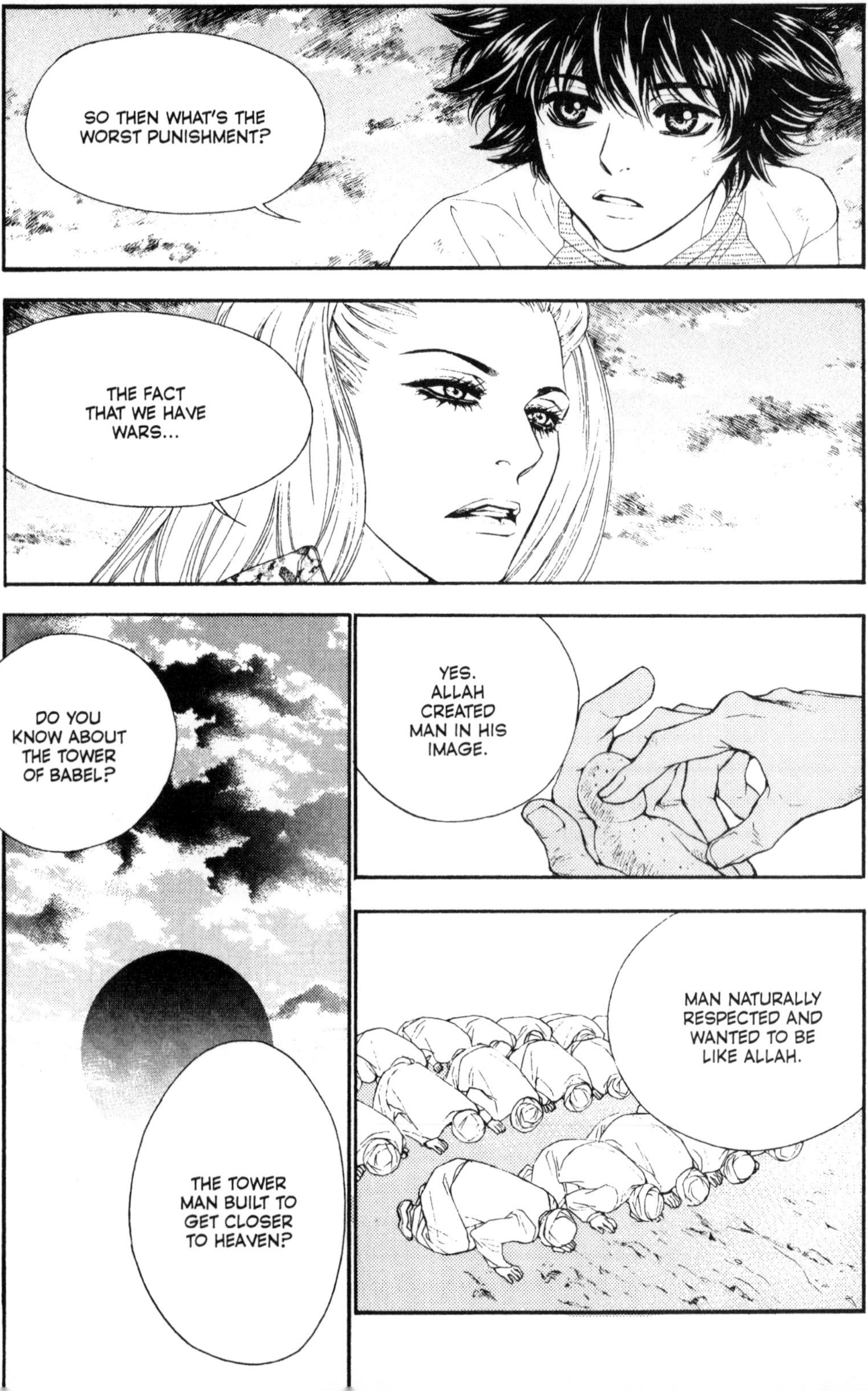
SO THEN WHAT'S THE WORST PUNISHMENT?
THE FACT THAT WE HAVE WARS...
DO YOU KNOW ABOUT THE TOWER OF BABEL?
THE TOWER MAN BUILT TO GET CLOSER TO HEAVEN?
YES. ALLAH CREATED MAN IN HIS IMAGE.
MAN NATURALLY RESPECTED AND WANTED TO BE LIKE ALLAH.

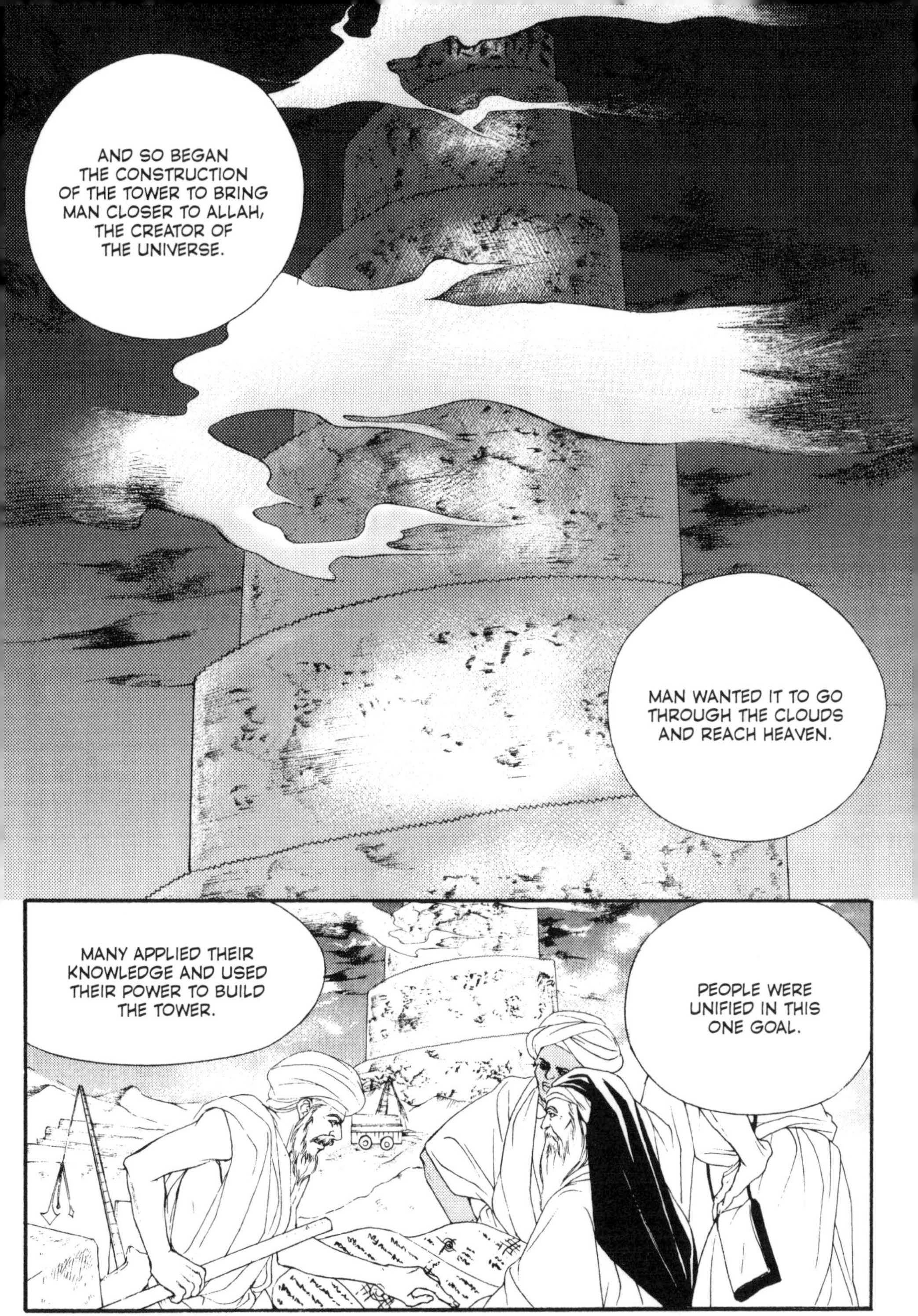
AND SO BEGAN THE CONSTRUCTION OF THE TOWER TO BRING MAN CLOSER TO ALLAH, THE CREATOR OF THE UNIVERSE.
MAN WANTED IT TO GO THROUGH THE CLOUDS AND REACH HEAVEN.
MANY APPLIED THEIR KNOWLEDGE AND USED THEIR POWER TO BUILD THE TOWER.
PEOPLE WERE UNIFIED IN THIS ONE GOAL.

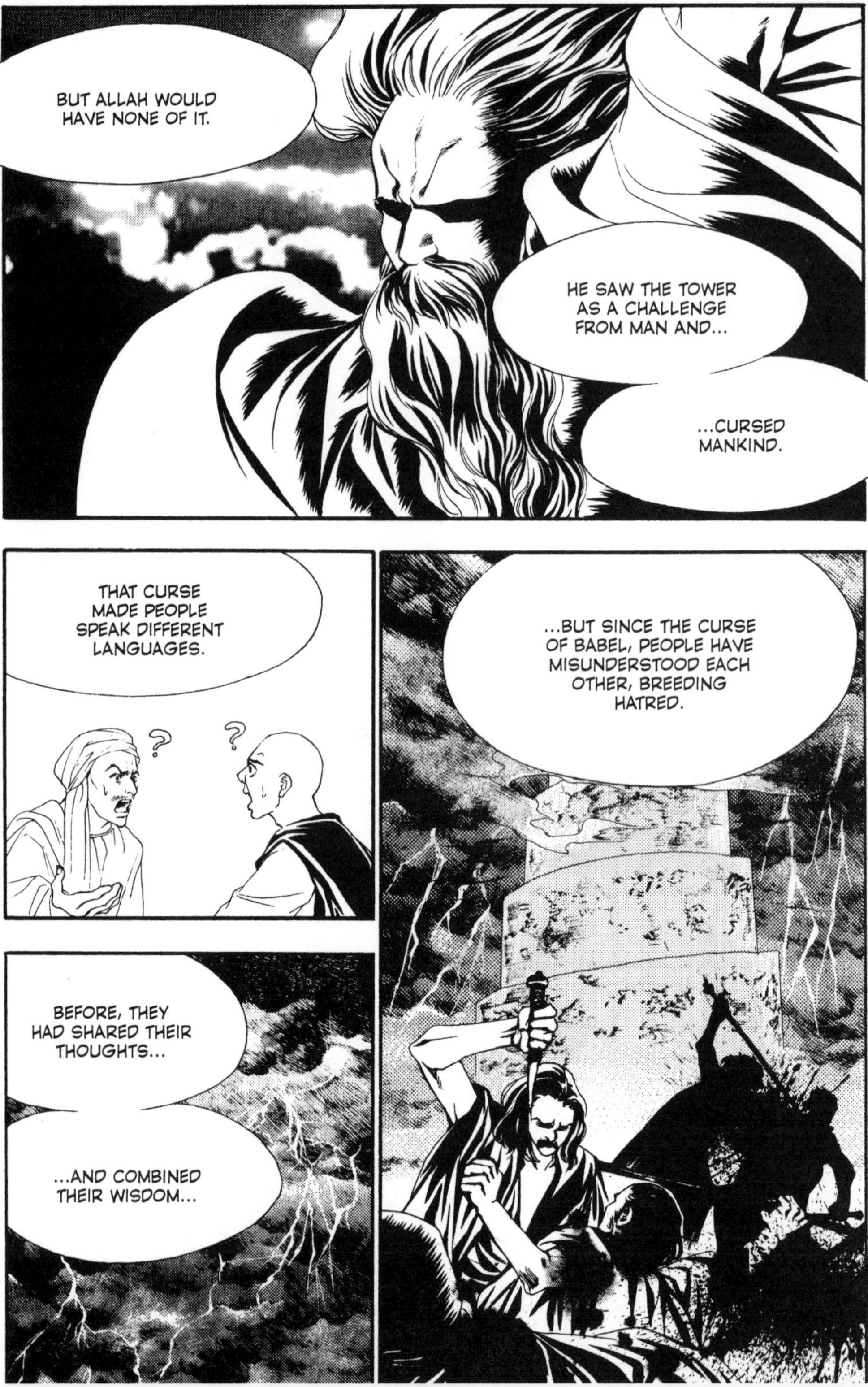
BUT ALLAH WOULD HAVE NONE OF IT.
HE SAW THE TOWER AS A CHALLENGE FROM MAN AND...
...CURSED MANKIND.
THAT CURSE MADE PEOPLE SPEAK DIFFERENT LANGUAGES.
?
?
BEFORE, THEY HAD SHARED THEIR THOUGHTS...
...AND COMBINED THEIR WISDOM...
...BUT SINCE THE CURSE OF BABEL, PEOPLE HAVE MISUNDERSTOOD EACH OTHER, BREEDING HATRED.

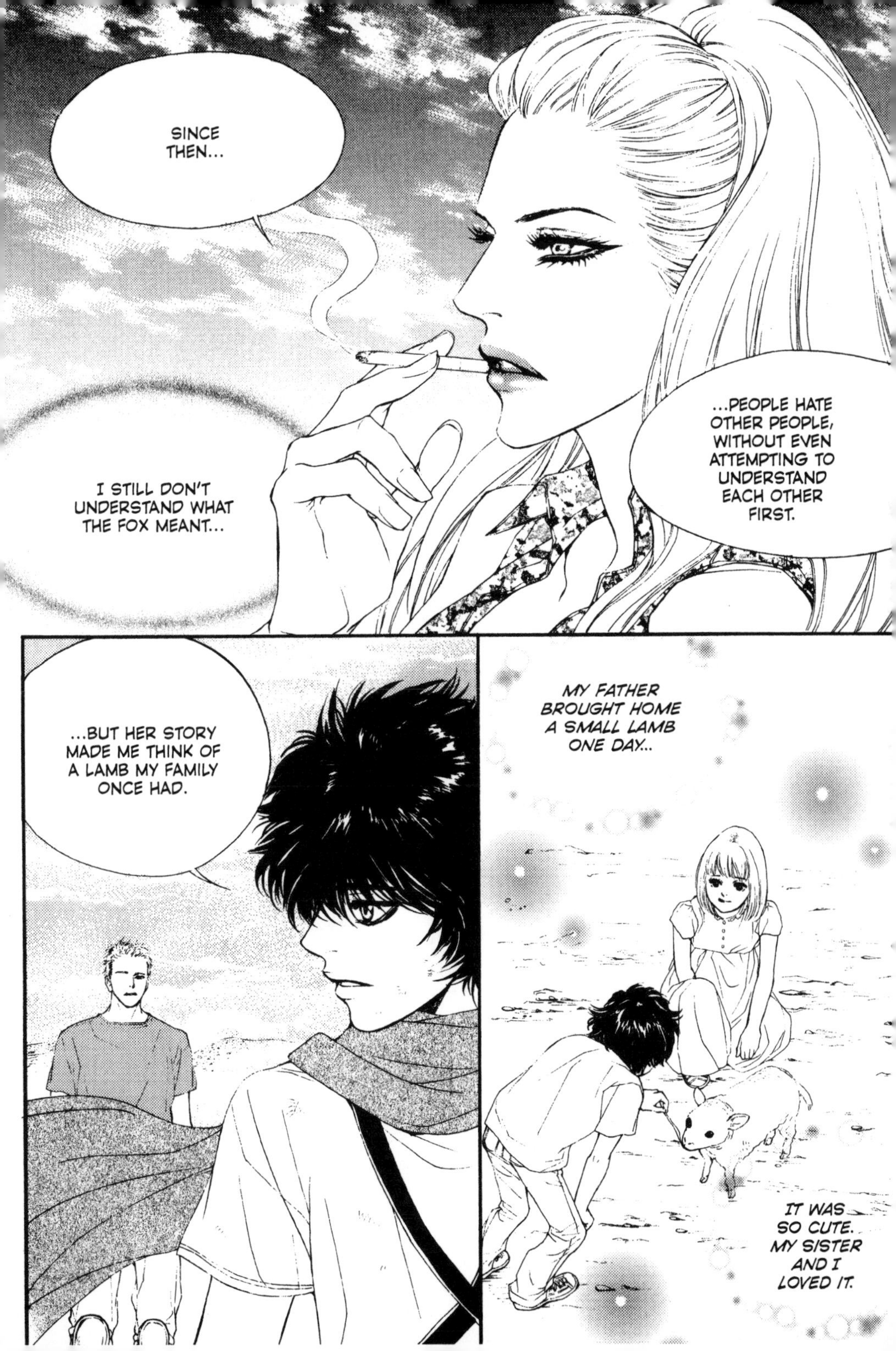
SINCE THEN...
...PEOPLE HATE OTHER PEOPLE, WITHOUT EVEN ATTEMPTING TO UNDERSTAND EACH OTHER FIRST.
I STILL DON'T UNDERSTAND WHAT THE FOX MEANT...
...BUT HER STORY MADE ME THINK OF A LAMB MY FAMILY ONCE HAD.
MY FATHER BROUGHT HOME A SMALL LAMB ONE DAY...
IT WAS SO CUTE. MY SISTER AND I LOVED IT.

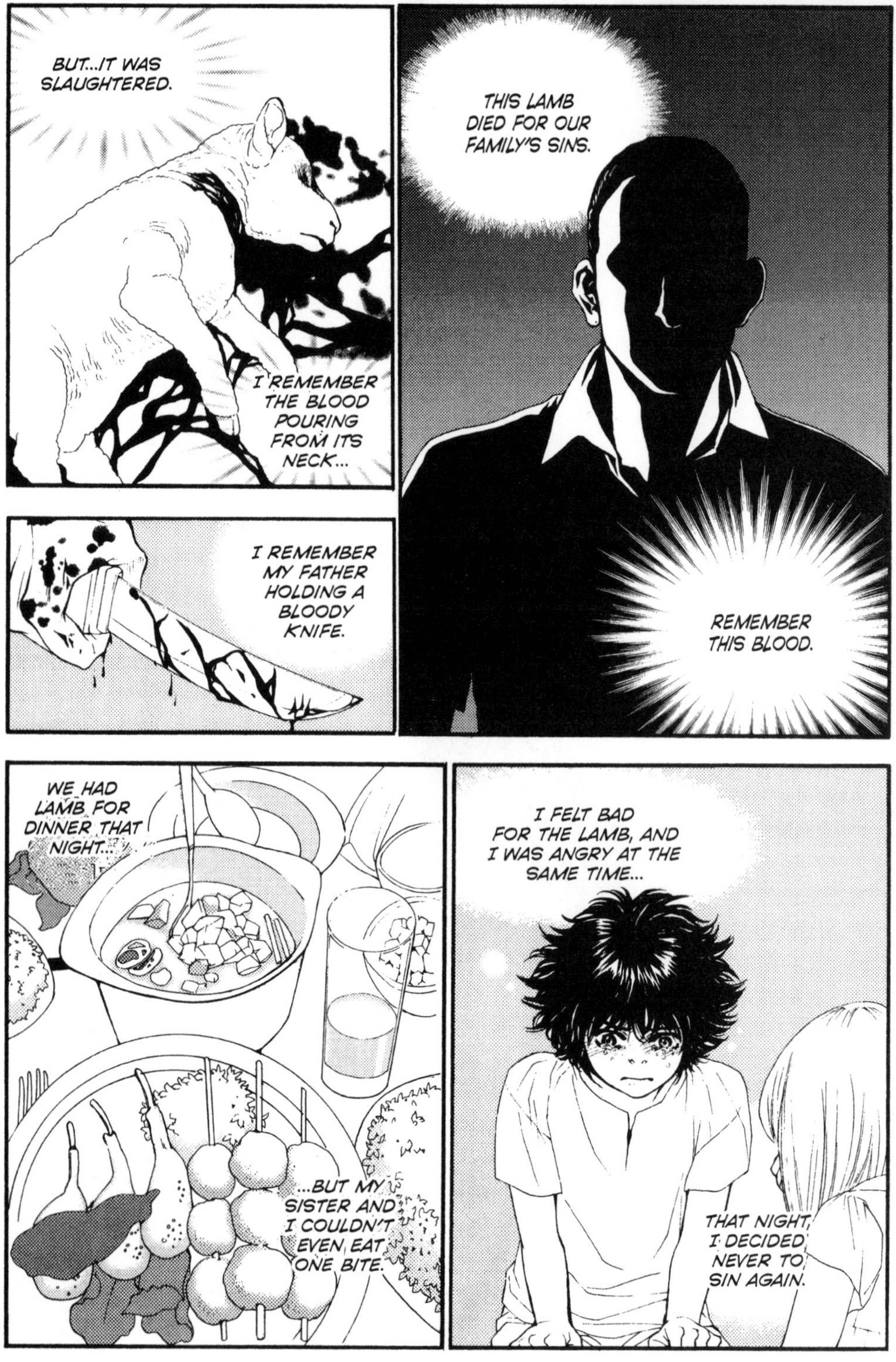
BUT...IT WAS SLAUGHTERED.
I REMEMBER THE BLOOD POURING FROM ITS NECK...
I REMEMBER MY FATHER HOLDING A BLOODY KNIFE.
THIS LAMB DIED FOR OUR FAMILY'S SINS.
REMEMBER THIS BLOOD.
WE HAD LAMB FOR DINNER THAT NIGHT...
...BUT MY SISTER AND I COULDN'T EVEN EAT ONE BITE.
I FELT BAD FOR THE LAMB, AND I WAS ANGRY AT THE SAME TIME...
THAT NIGHT, I DECIDED NEVER TO SIN AGAIN.

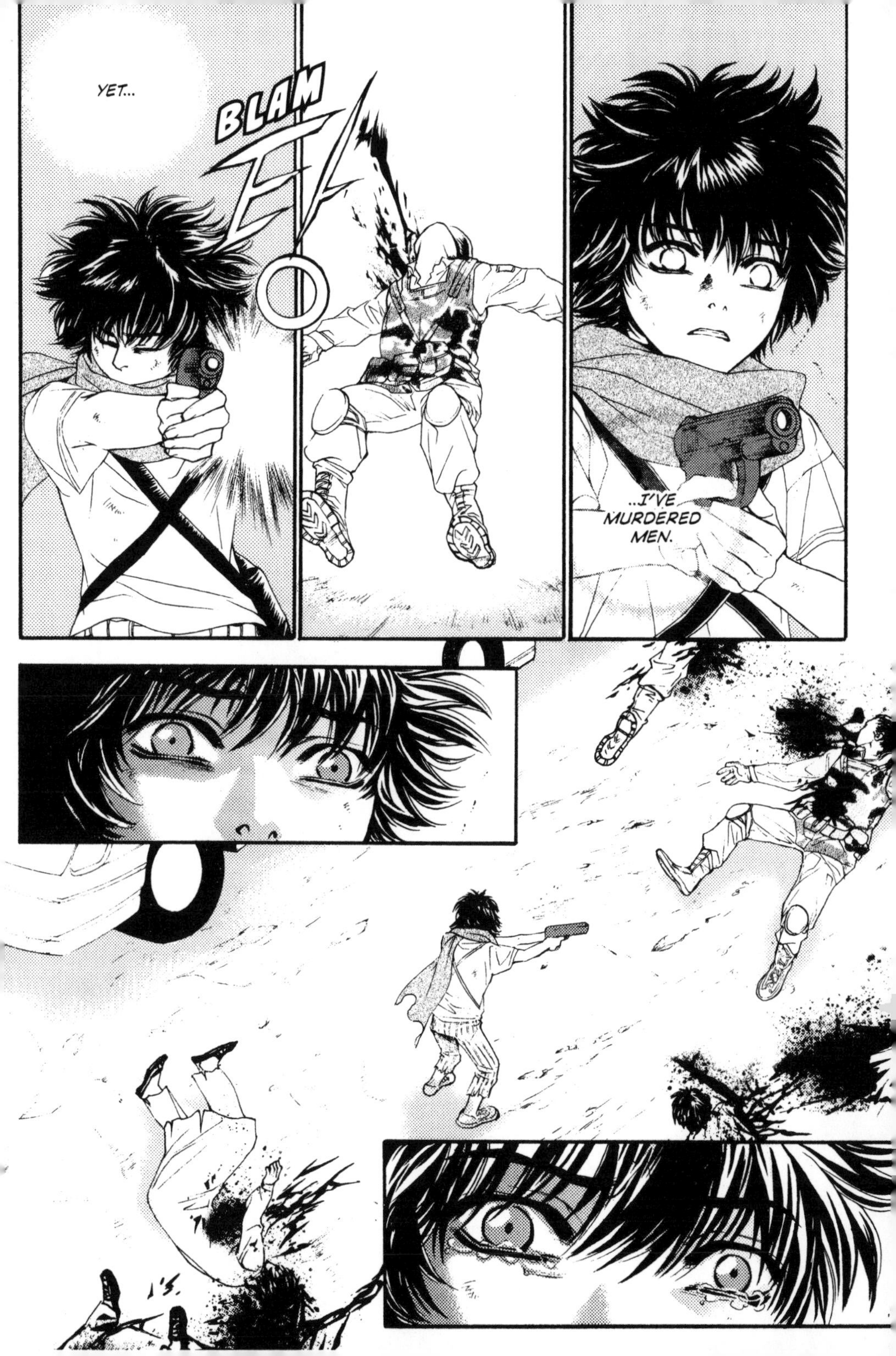
YET...
BLAM
...I'VE MURDERED MEN.

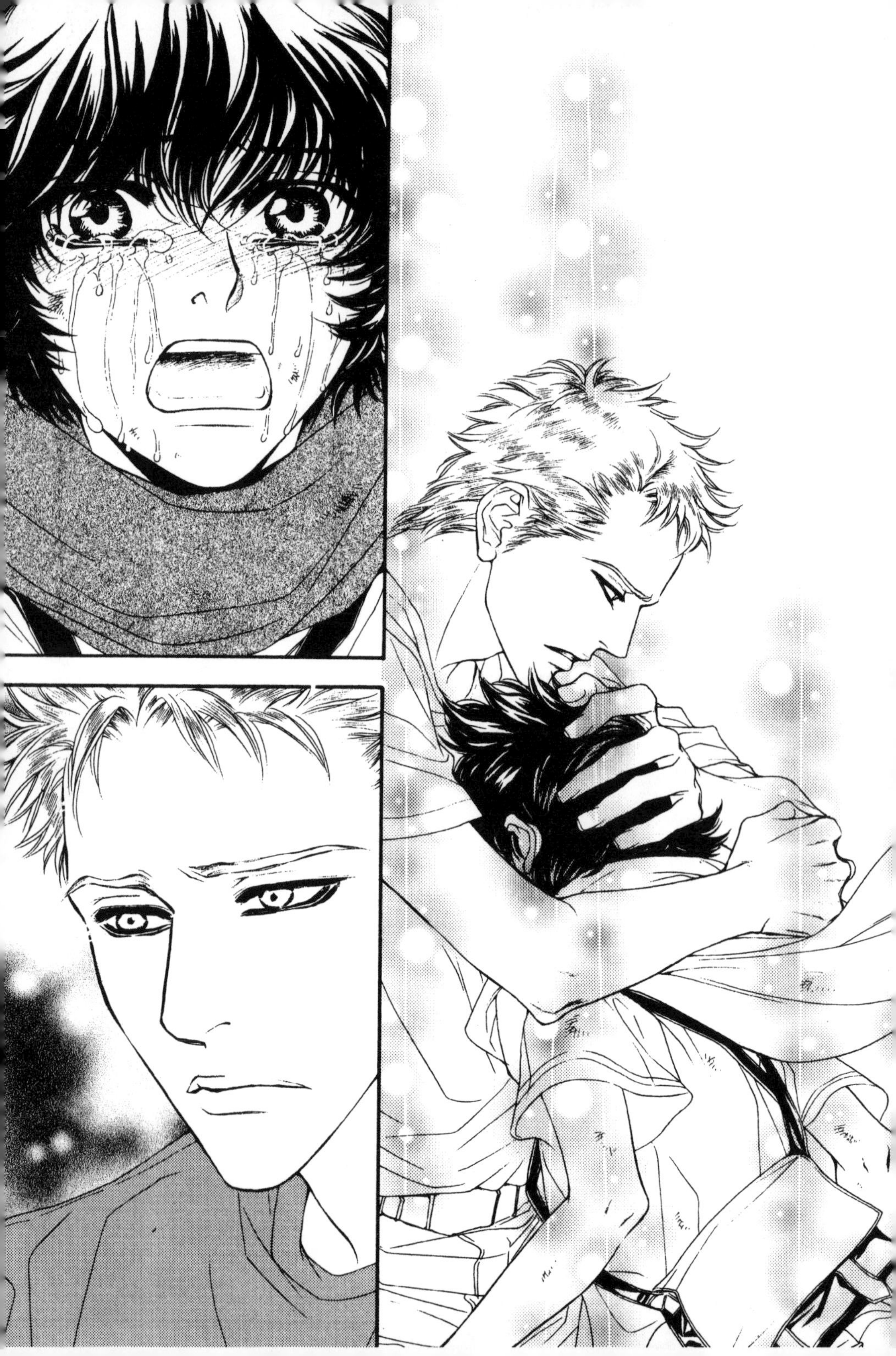

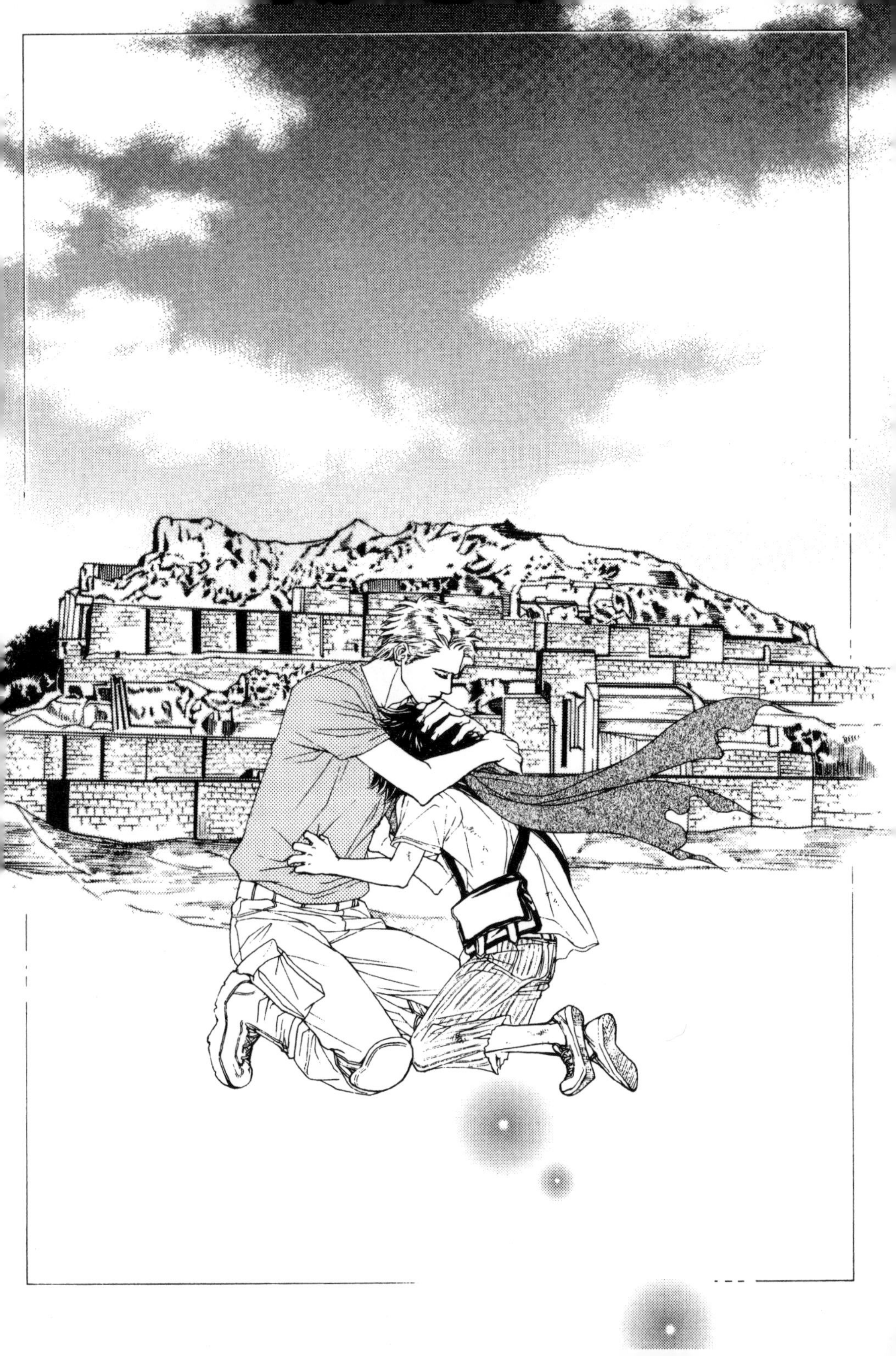

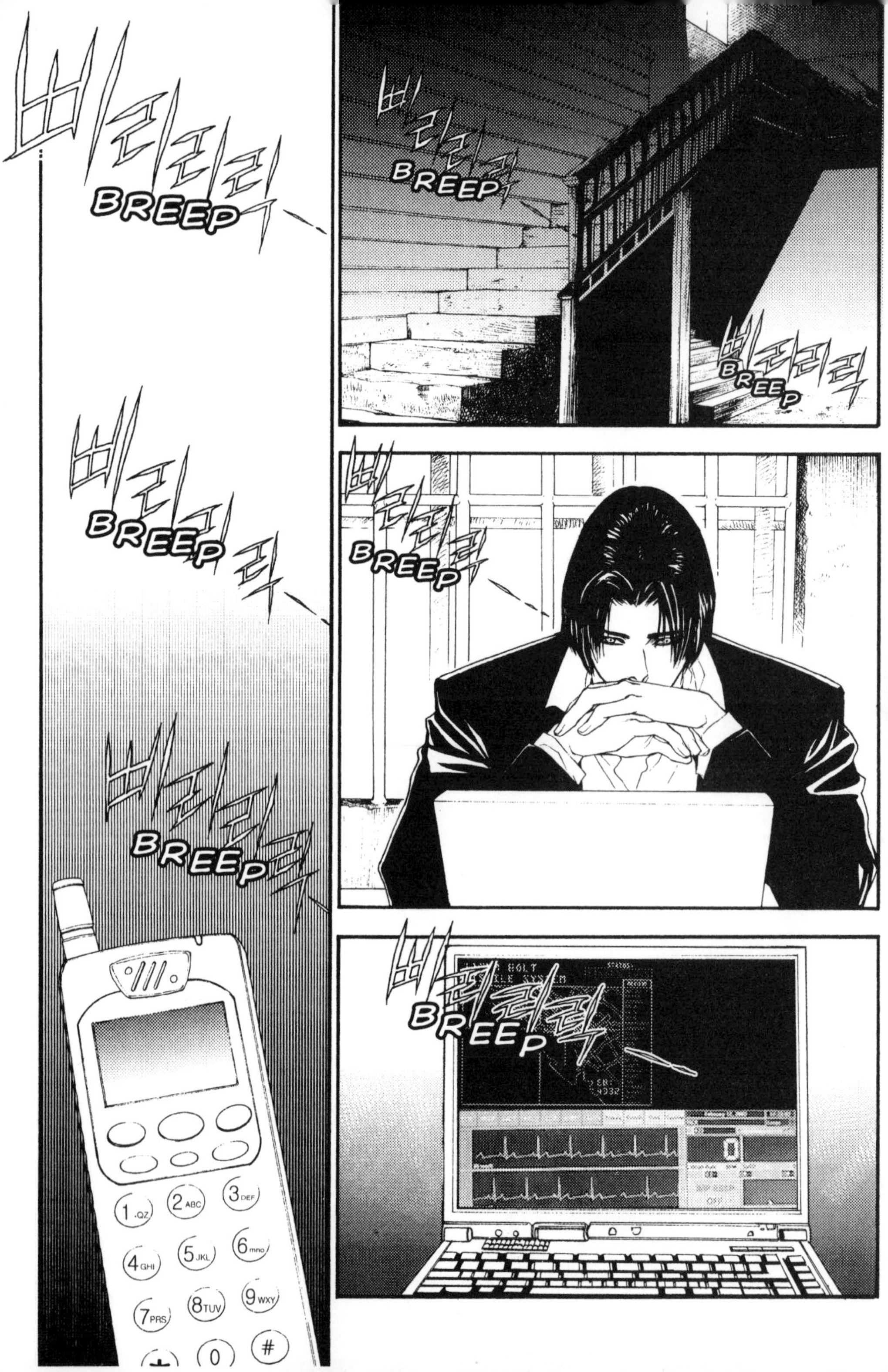
삐리리릭
BREEP
삐리리릭
BREEP
삐리리릭
BREEP
삐리리릭
BREEP
삐리리릭
BREEP
삐리리릭
BREEP
삐리리릭
BREEP

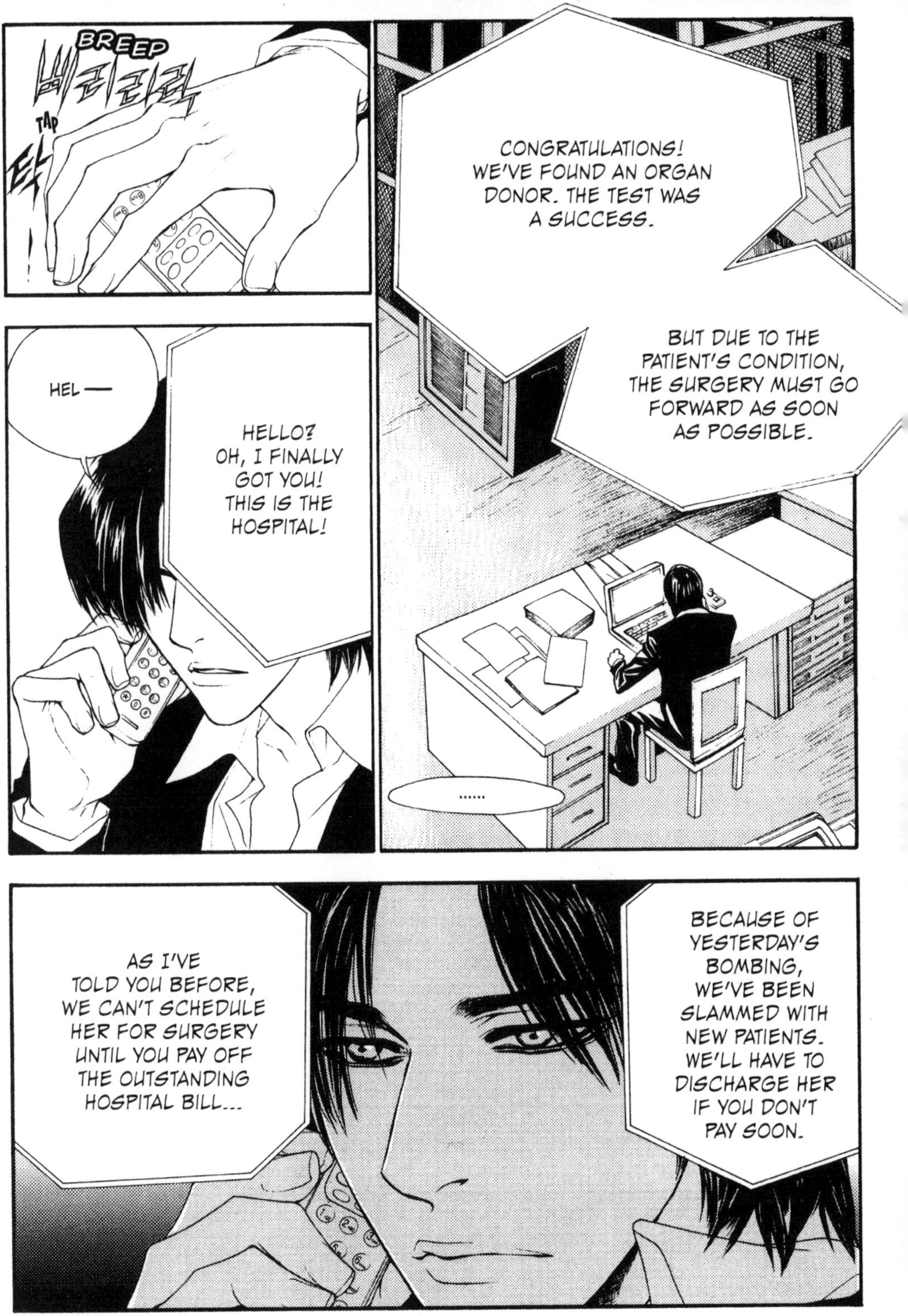
BREEP
삐리리릭
TAP
탁
CONGRATULATIONS! WE'VE FOUND AN ORGAN DONOR. THE TEST WAS A SUCCESS.
BUT DUE TO THE PATIENT'S CONDITION, THE SURGERY MUST GO FORWARD AS SOON AS POSSIBLE.
HEL—
HELLO? OH, I FINALLY GOT YOU! THIS IS THE HOSPITAL!
......
AS I'VE TOLD YOU BEFORE, WE CAN'T SCHEDULE HER FOR SURGERY UNTIL YOU PAY OFF THE OUTSTANDING HOSPITAL BILL...
BECAUSE OF YESTERDAY'S BOMBING, WE'VE BEEN SLAMMED WITH NEW PATIENTS. WE'LL HAVE TO DISCHARGE HER IF YOU DON'T PAY SOON.

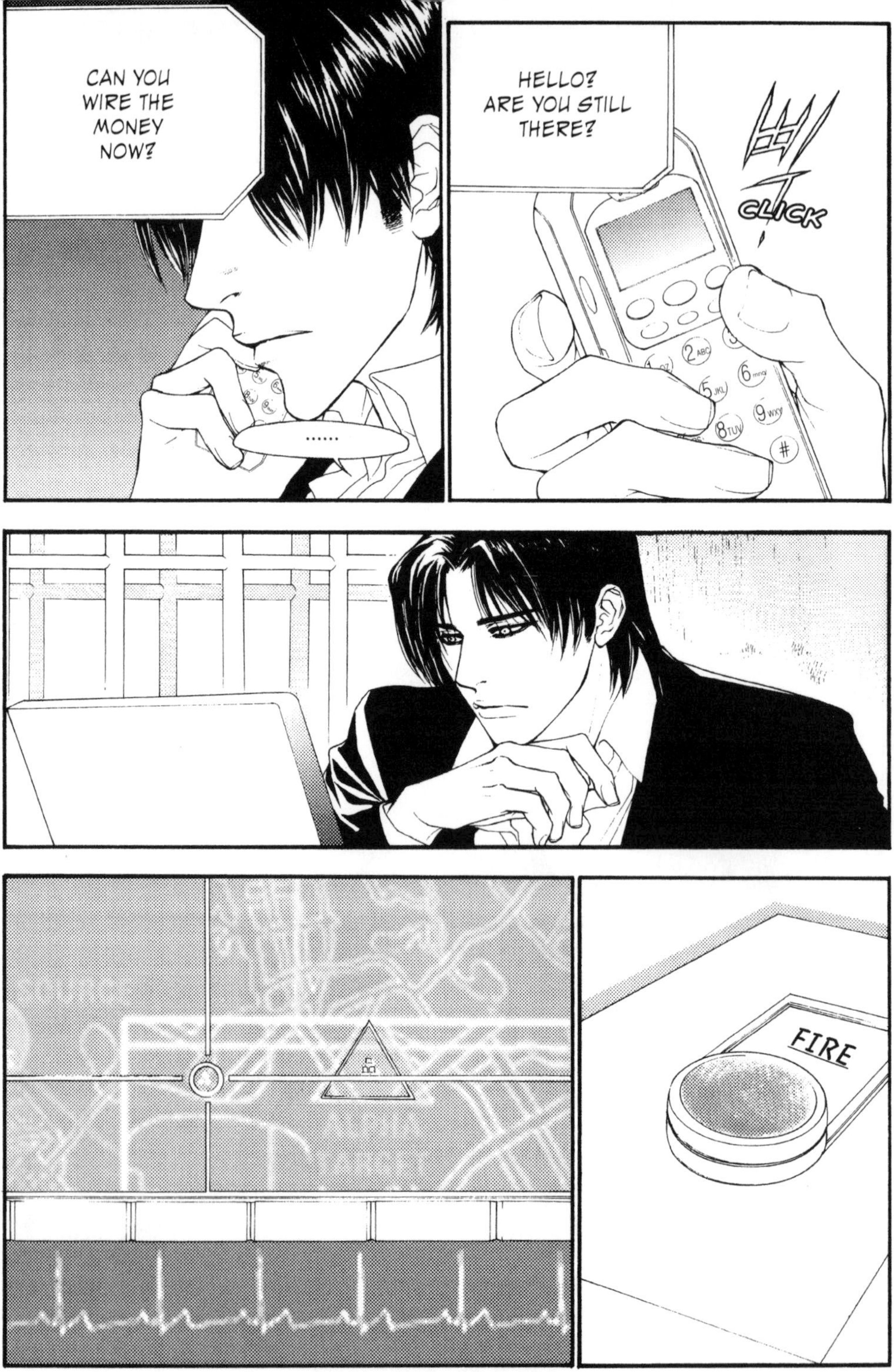

CAN YOU WIRE THE MONEY NOW?
......
HELLO? ARE YOU STILL THERE?
CLICK
FIRE

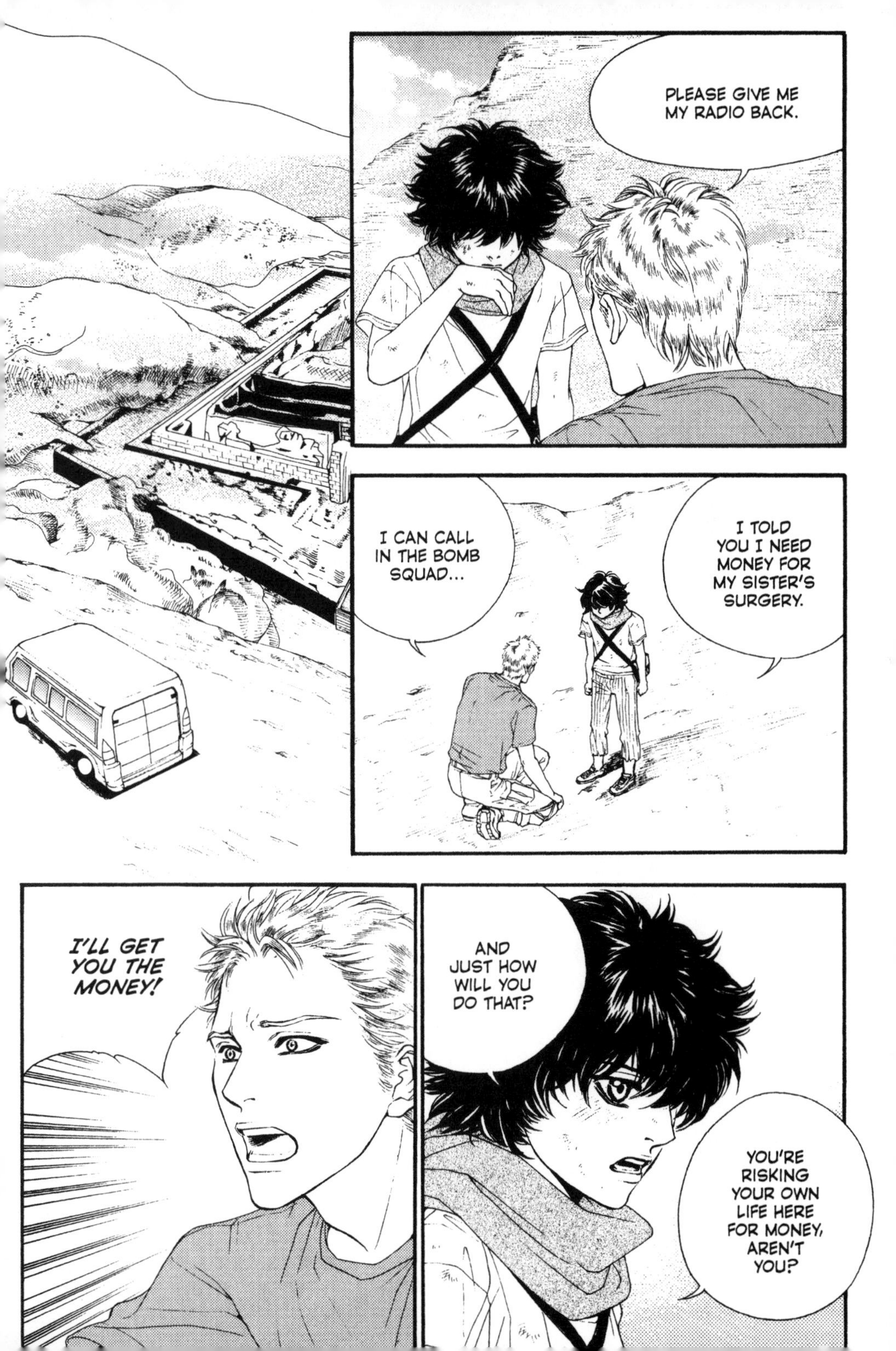
PLEASE GIVE ME MY RADIO BACK.
I TOLD YOU I NEED MONEY FOR MY SISTER'S SURGERY.
I CAN CALL IN THE BOMB SQUAD...
AND JUST HOW WILL YOU DO THAT?
YOU'RE RISKING YOUR OWN LIFE HERE FOR MONEY, AREN'T YOU?
I'LL GET YOU THE MONEY!

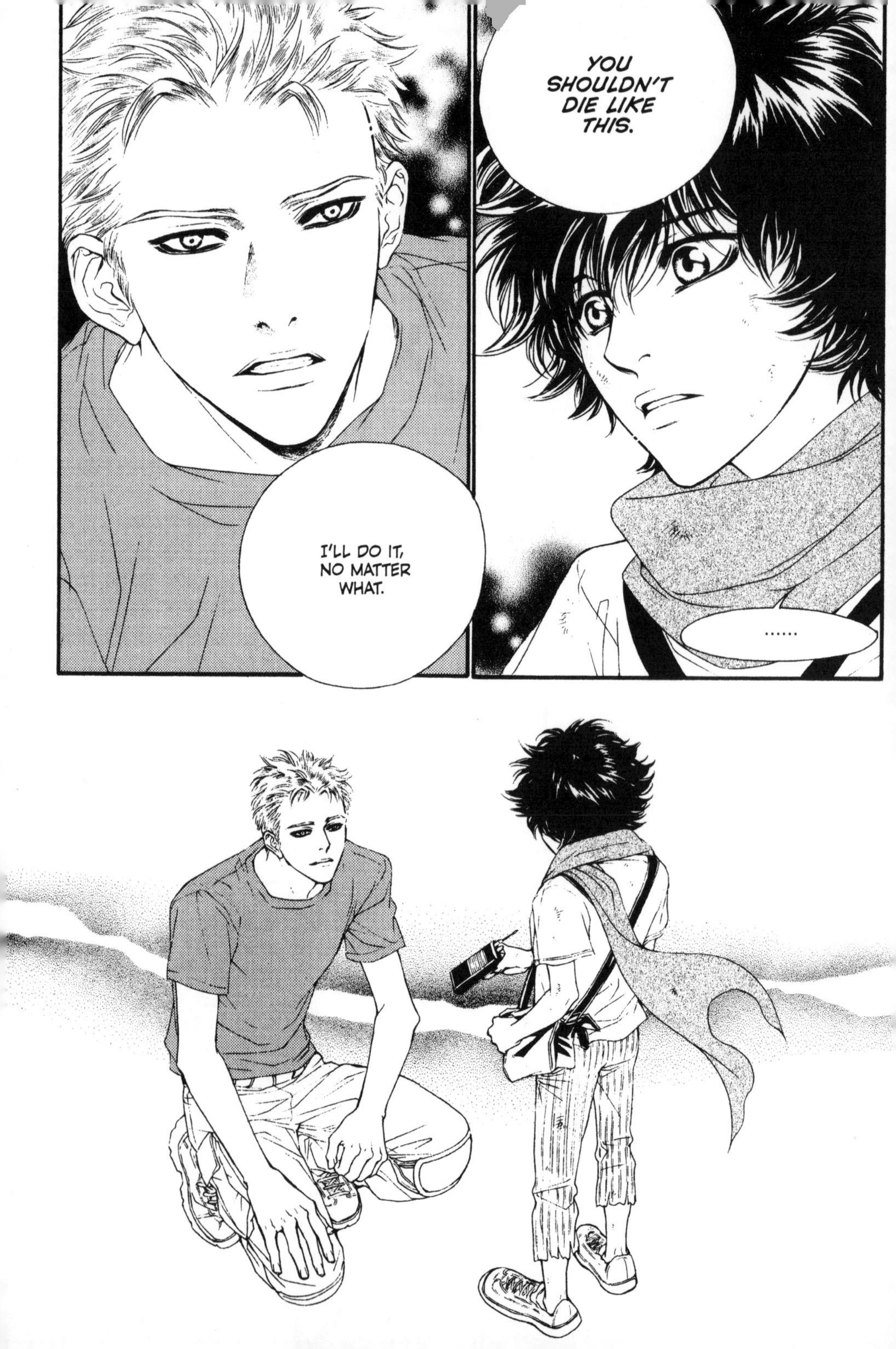
YOU SHOULDN'T DIE LIKE THIS.
I'LL DO IT, NO MATTER WHAT.
......

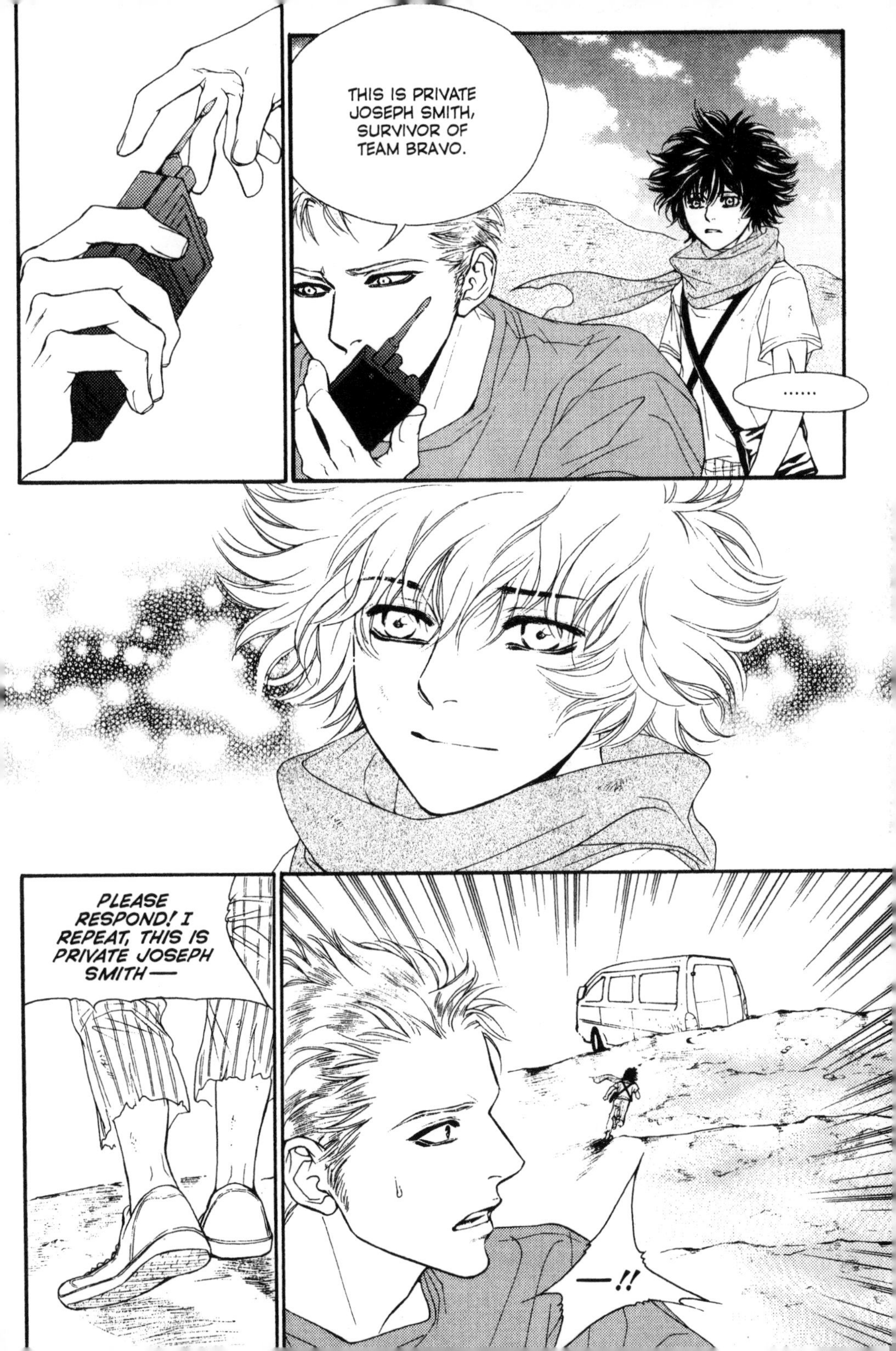
THIS IS PRIVATE JOSEPH SMITH, SURVIVOR OF TEAM BRAVO.
......
PLEASE RESPOND! I REPEAT, THIS IS PRIVATE JOSEPH SMITH—
—!!

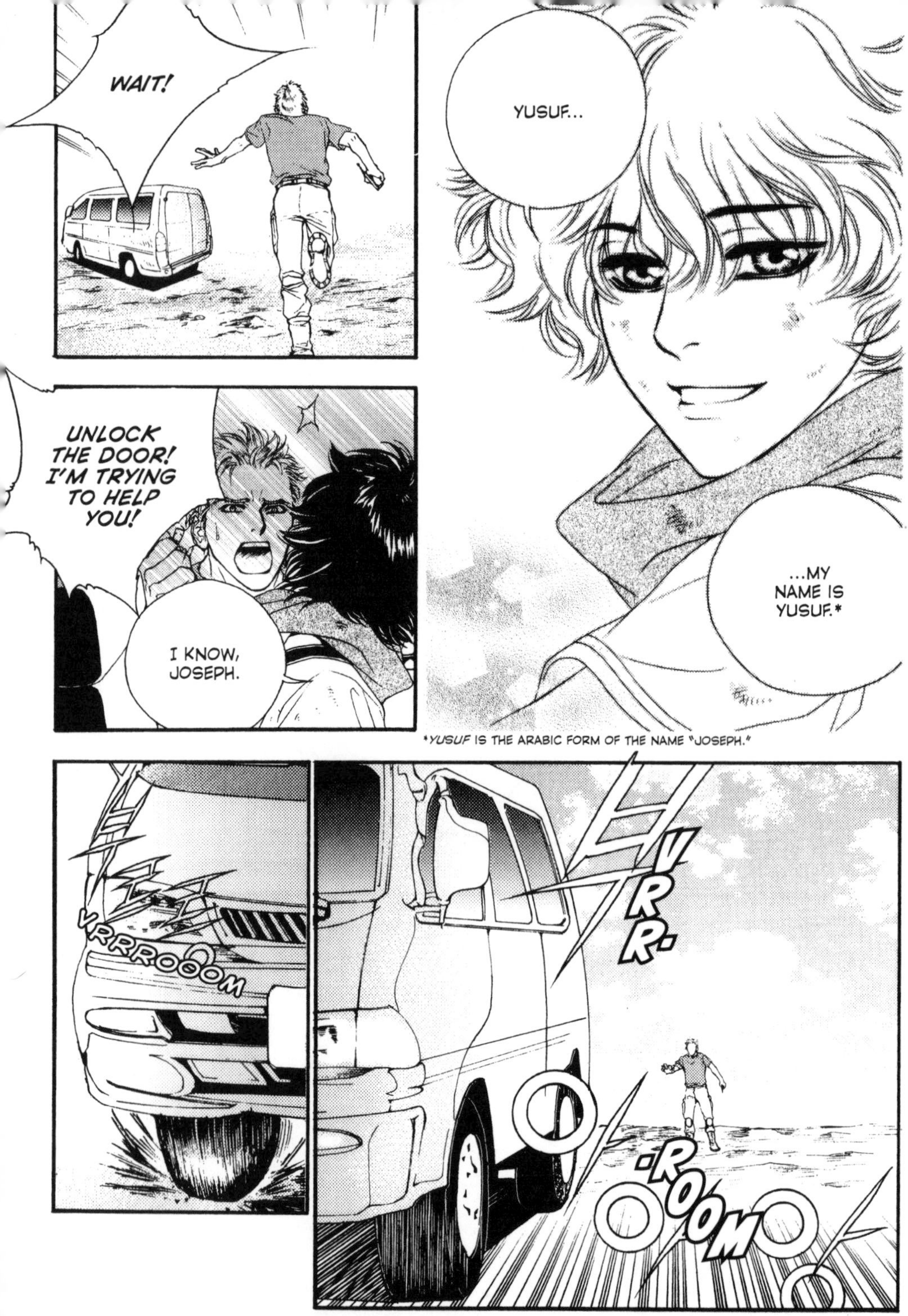
WAIT!
UNLOCK THE DOOR! I'M TRYING TO HELP YOU!
I KNOW, JOSEPH.
YUSUF...
...MY NAME IS YUSUF.*
VRRROOOM
VRR-
-ROOM

*YUSUF IS THE ARABIC FORM OF THE NAME "JOSEPH."

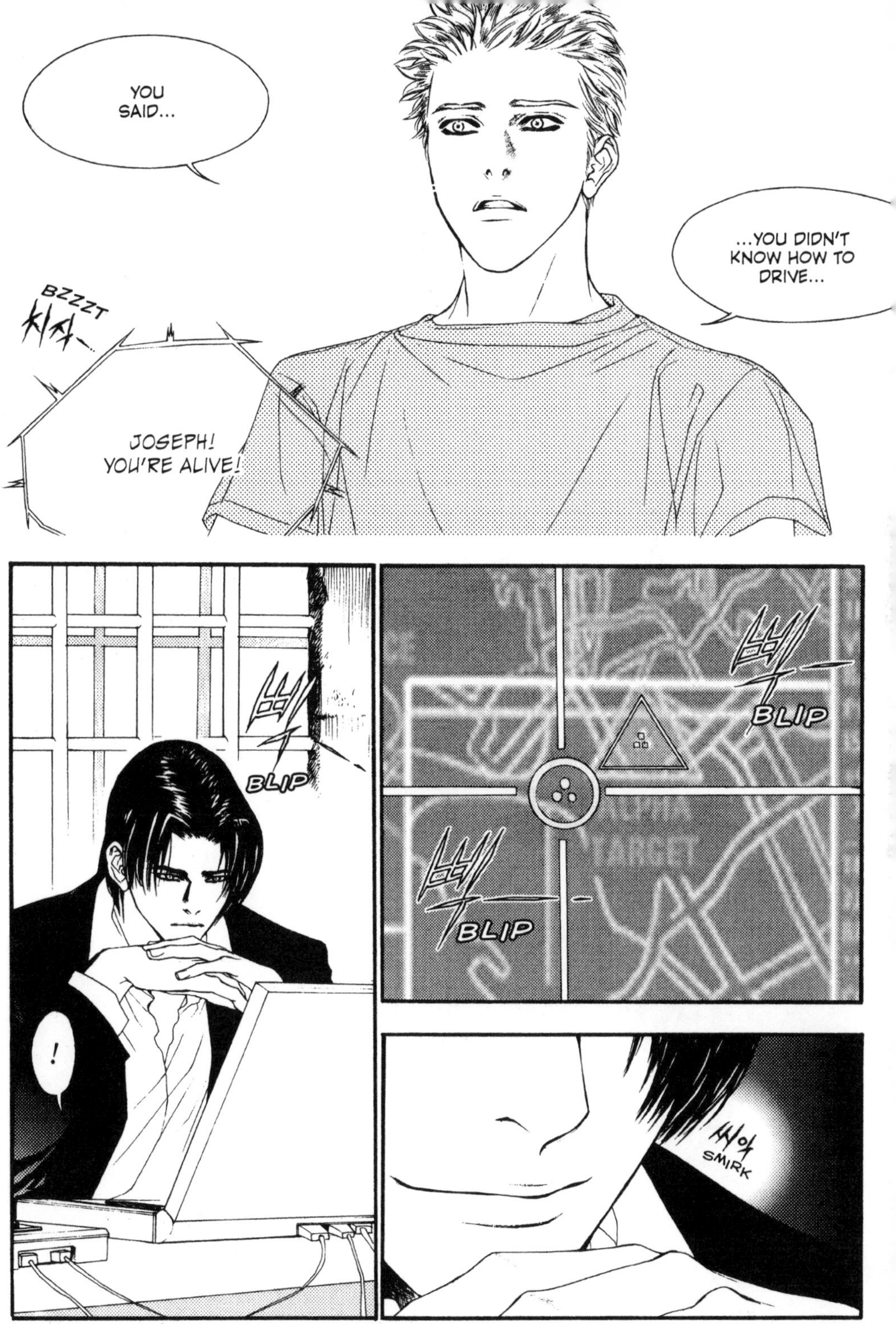
YOU SAID...
...YOU DIDN'T KNOW HOW TO DRIVE...
BZZZT
JOSEPH! YOU'RE ALIVE!
BLIP
BLIP
BLIP
!
SMIRK

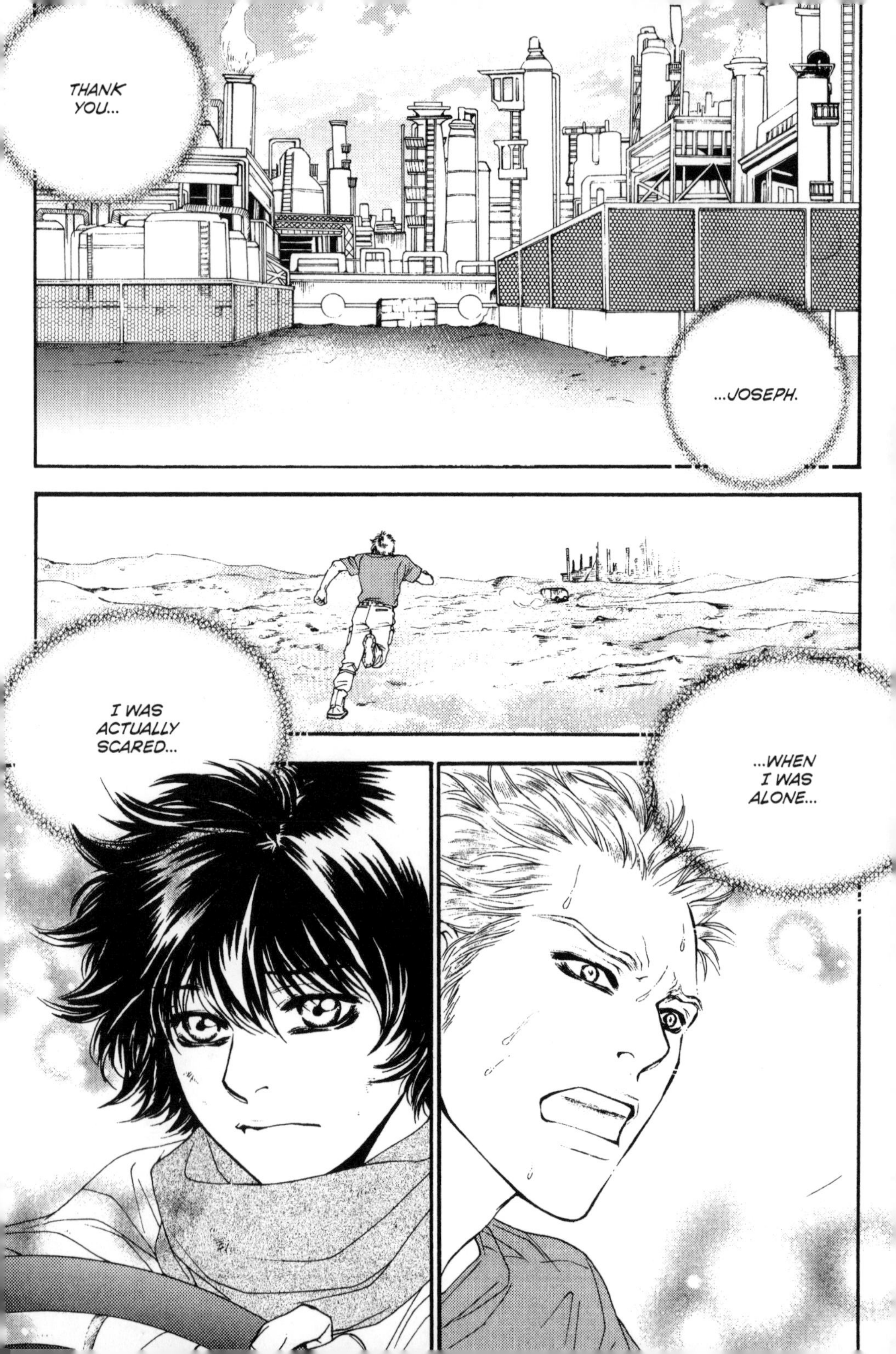
THANK YOU...
...JOSEPH.
I WAS ACTUALLY SCARED...
...WHEN I WAS ALONE...

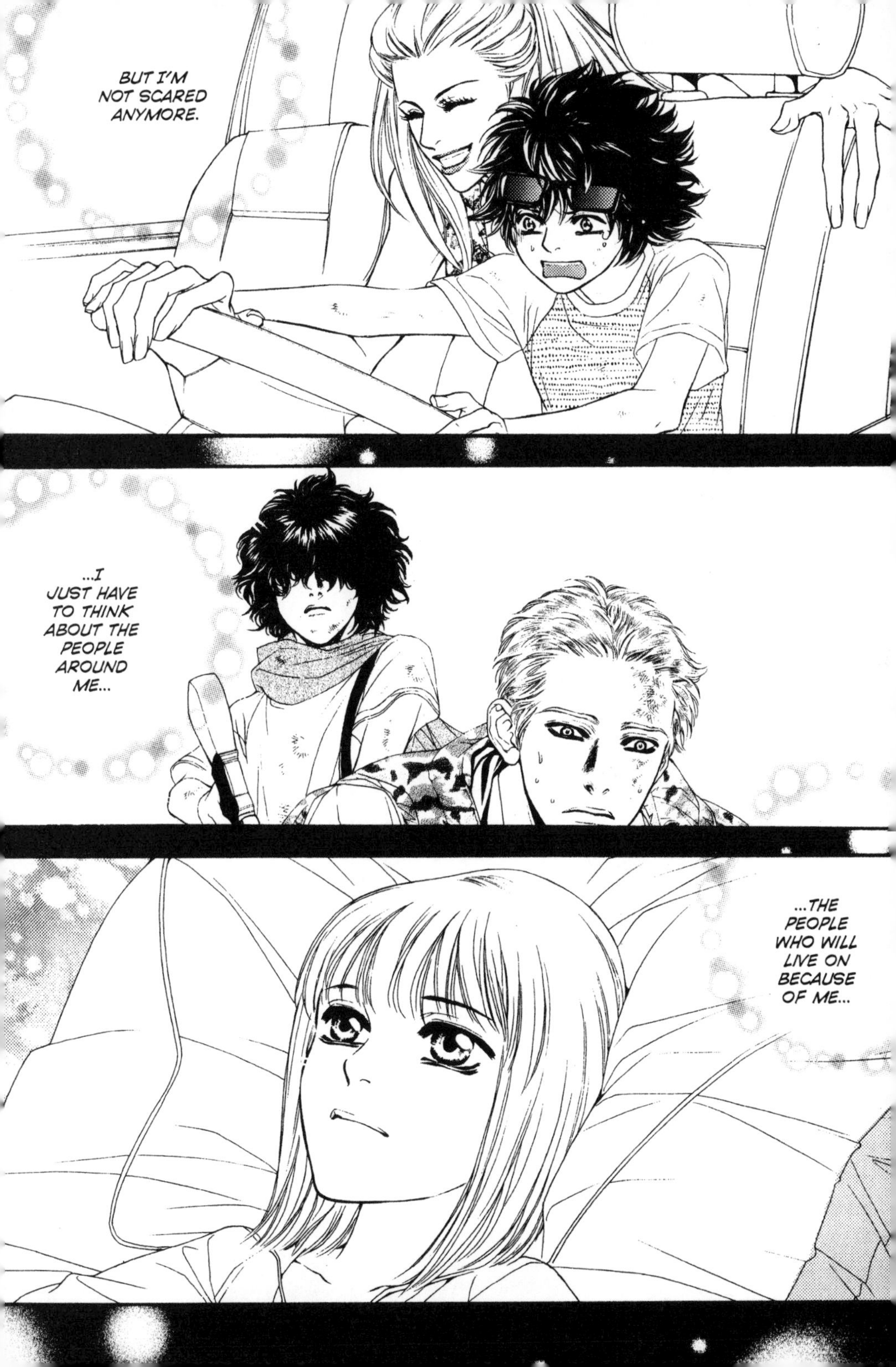
BUT I'M NOT SCARED ANYMORE.
...I JUST HAVE TO THINK ABOUT THE PEOPLE AROUND ME...
...THE PEOPLE WHO WILL LIVE ON BECAUSE OF ME...

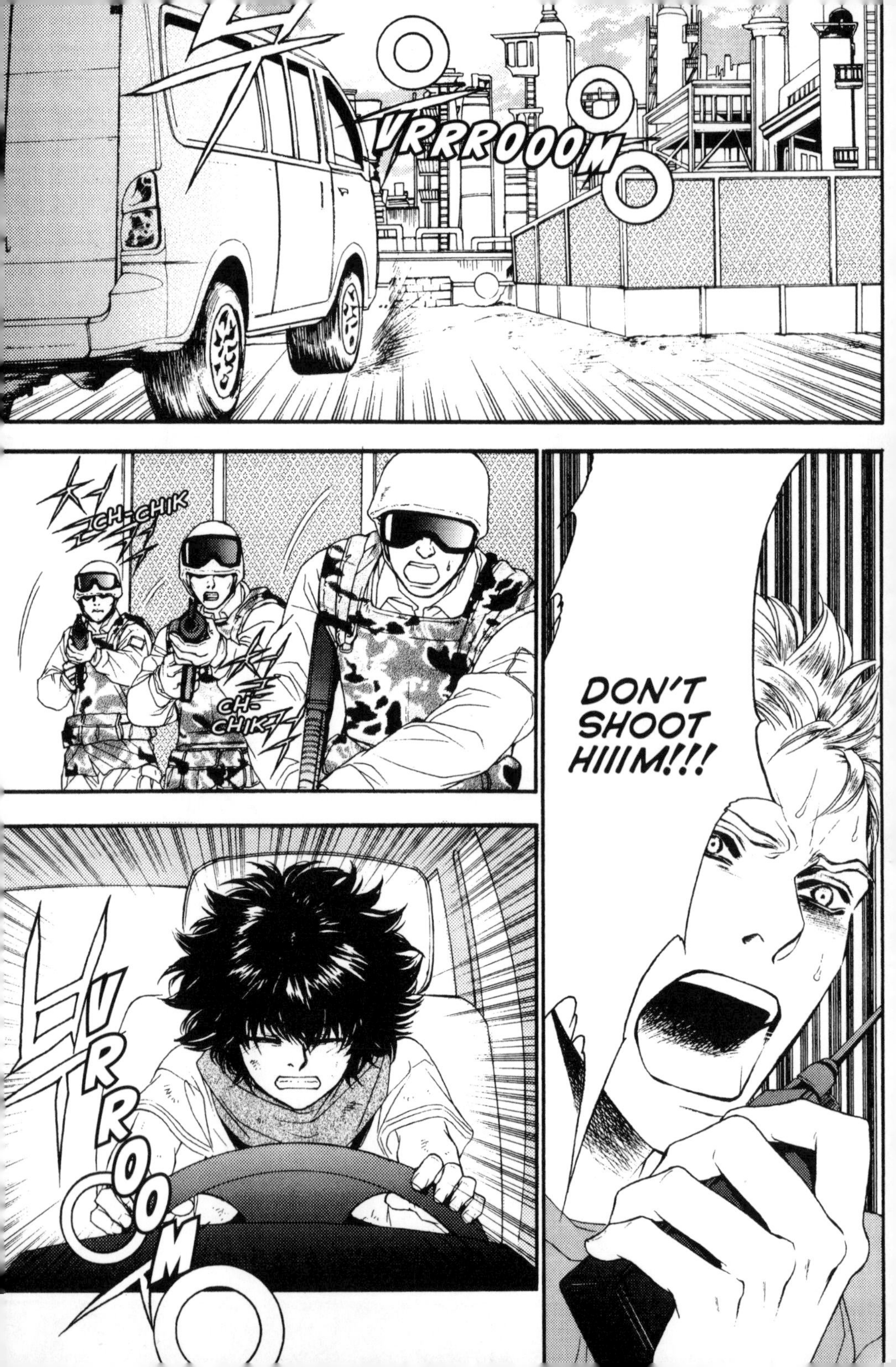
VRRROOOM
CH-CHIK
CH-CHIK
DON'T SHOOT HIIIM!!!
VRROOOM

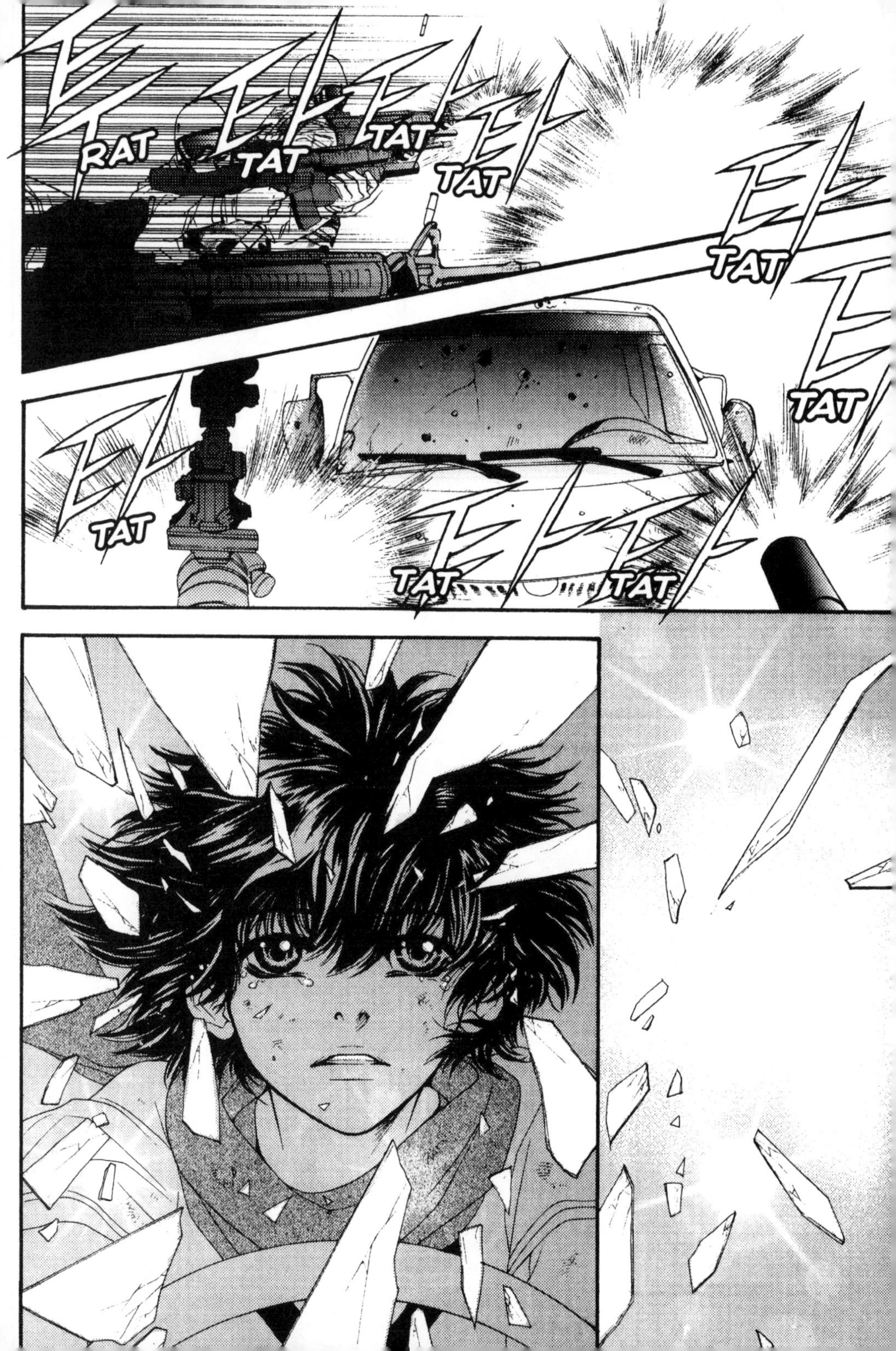
RAT
TAT
TAT
TAT
TAT
TAT
TAT
TAT
TAT

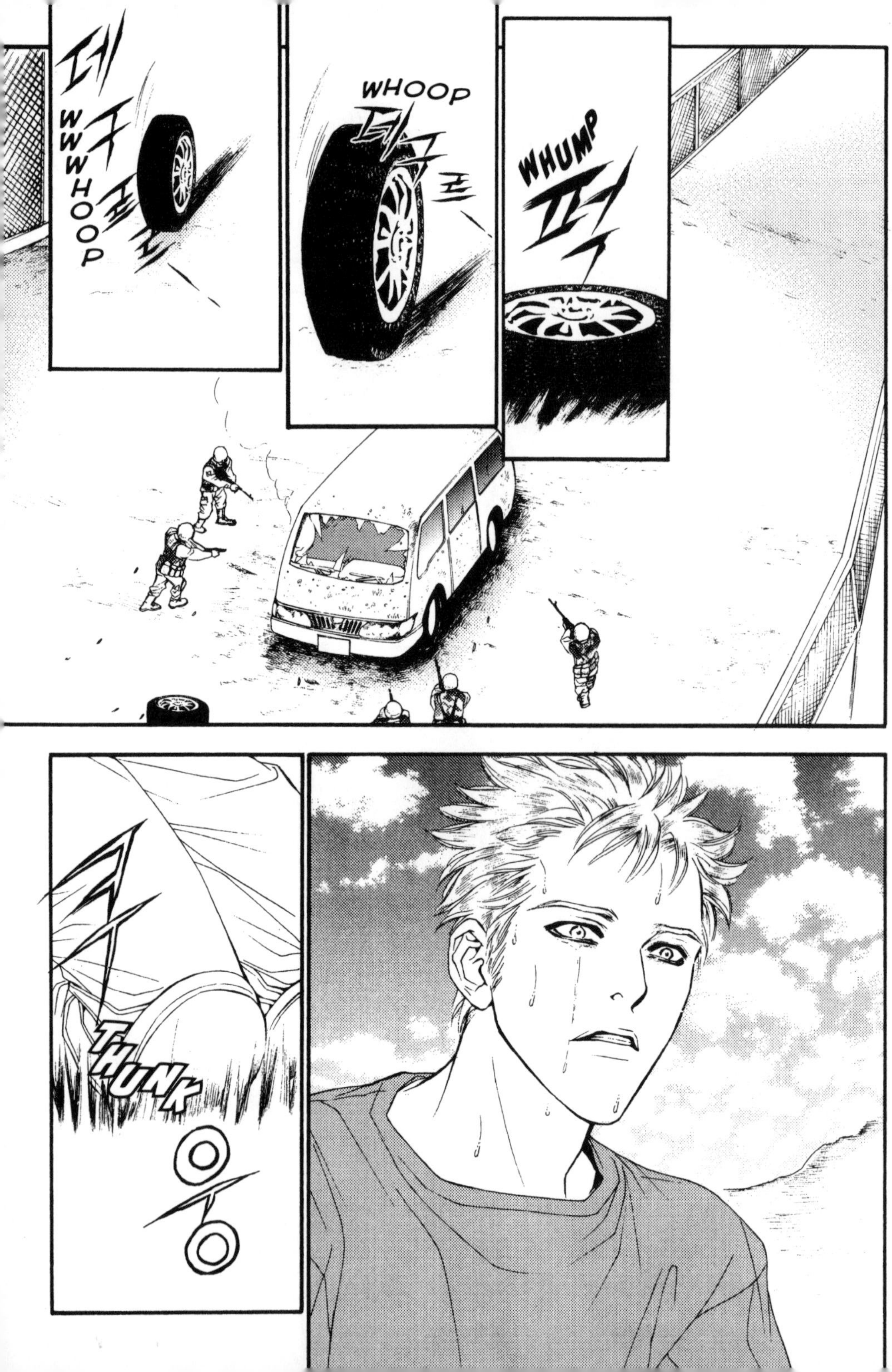
WWWHOOP
WHOOP
WHUMP
THUNK

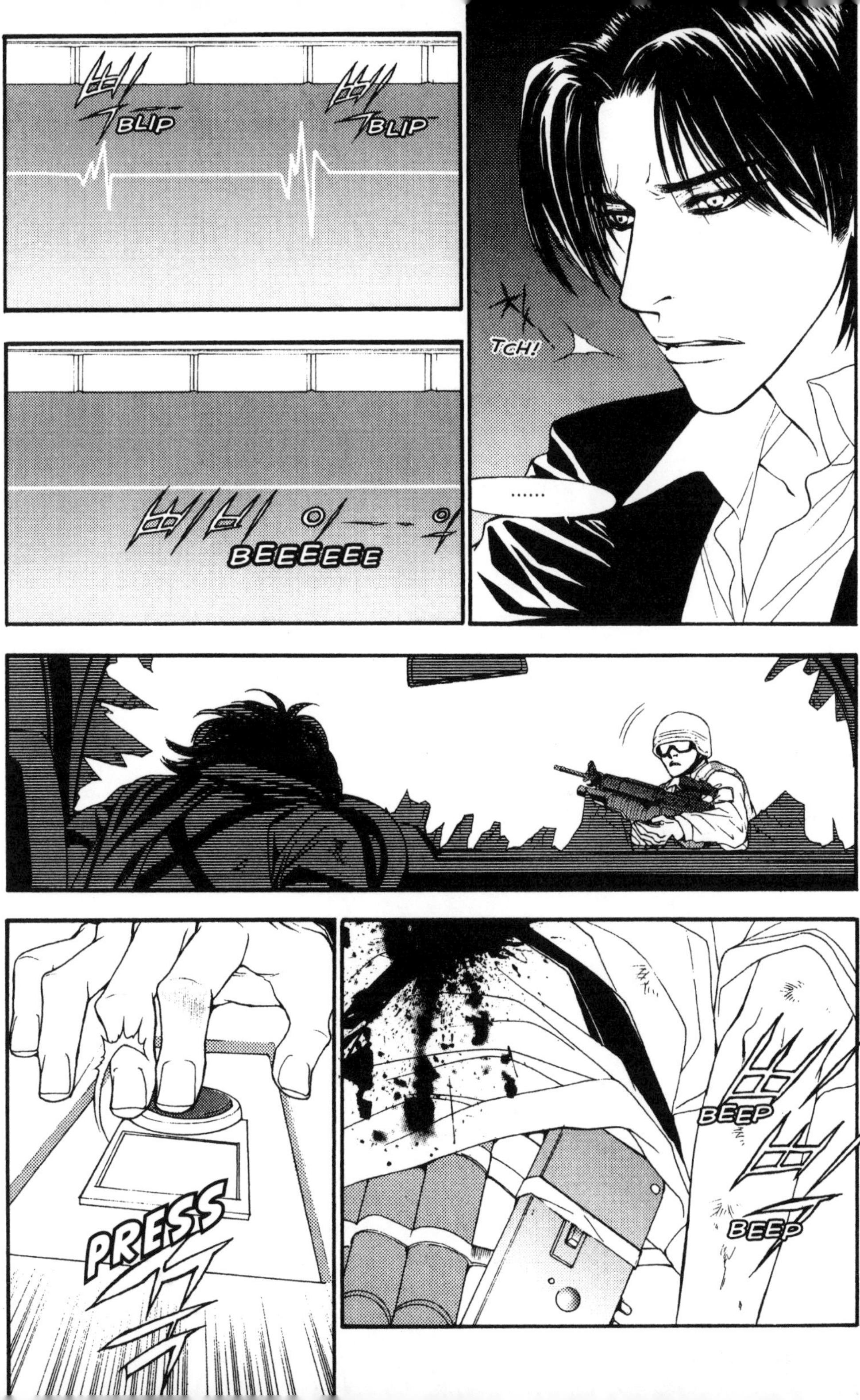

BLIP
BLIP
BEEEEEEE
TCH!
......
PRESS
BEEP
BEEP

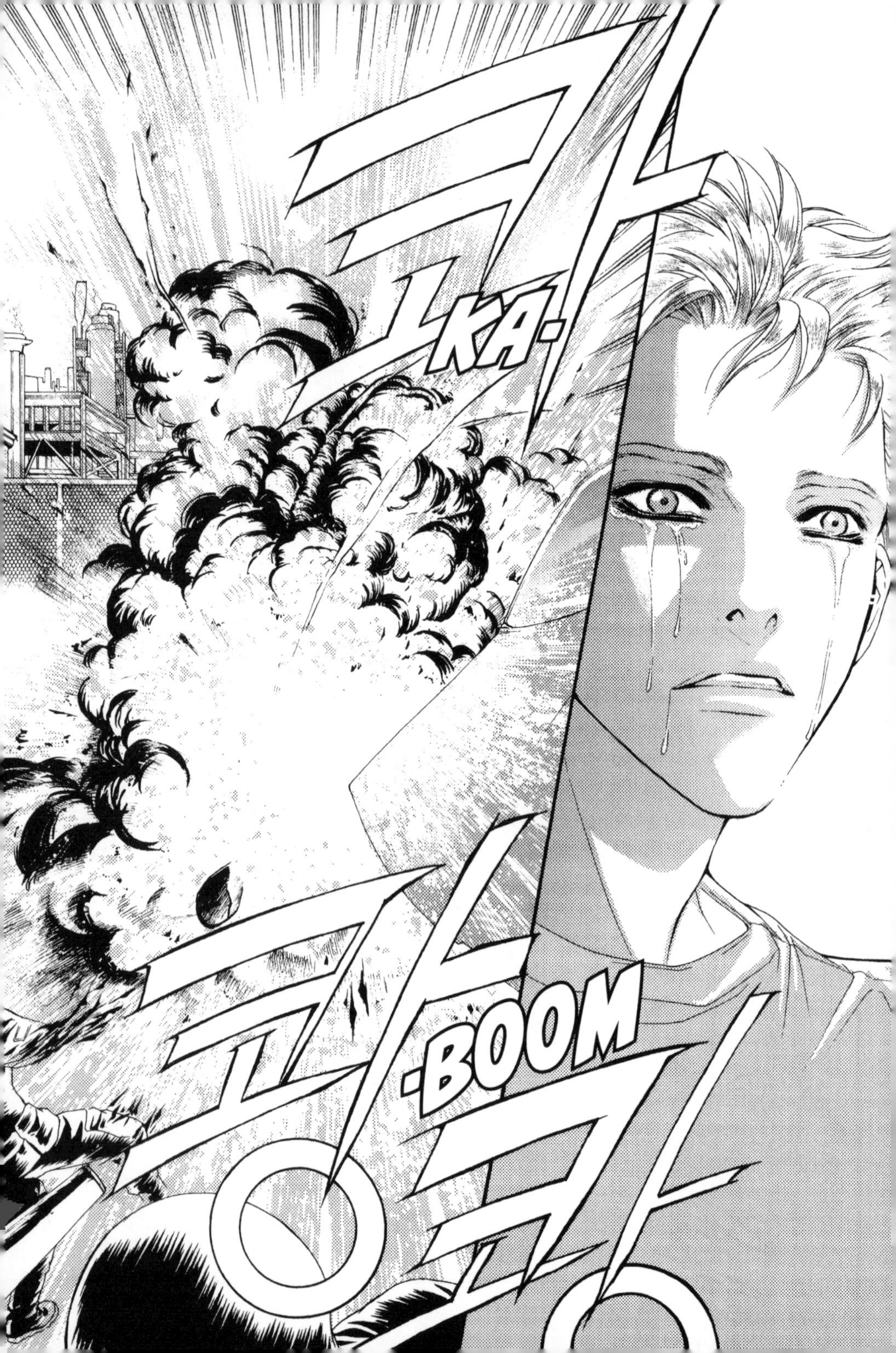
KA-
-BOOM

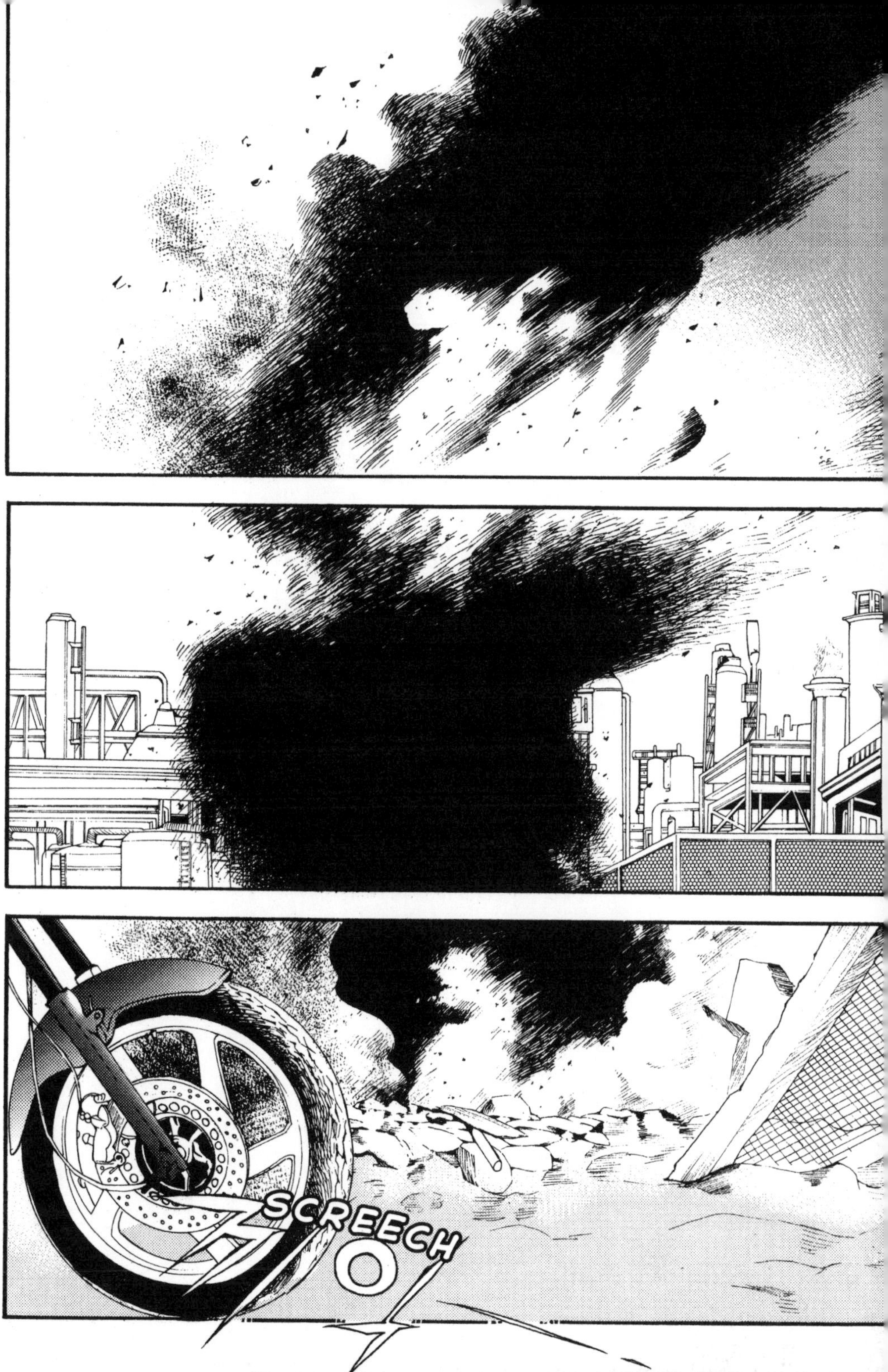
SCREECH

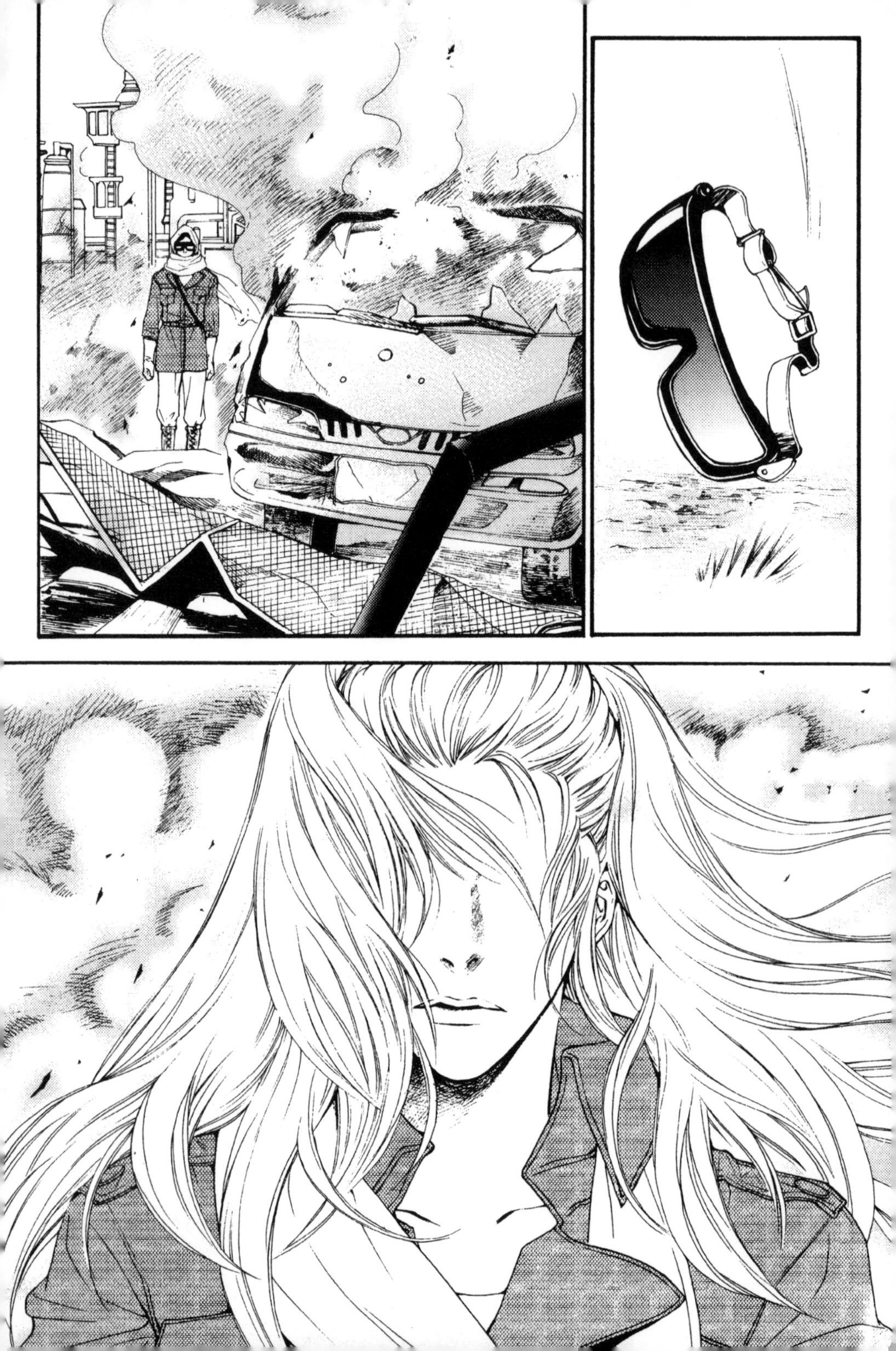

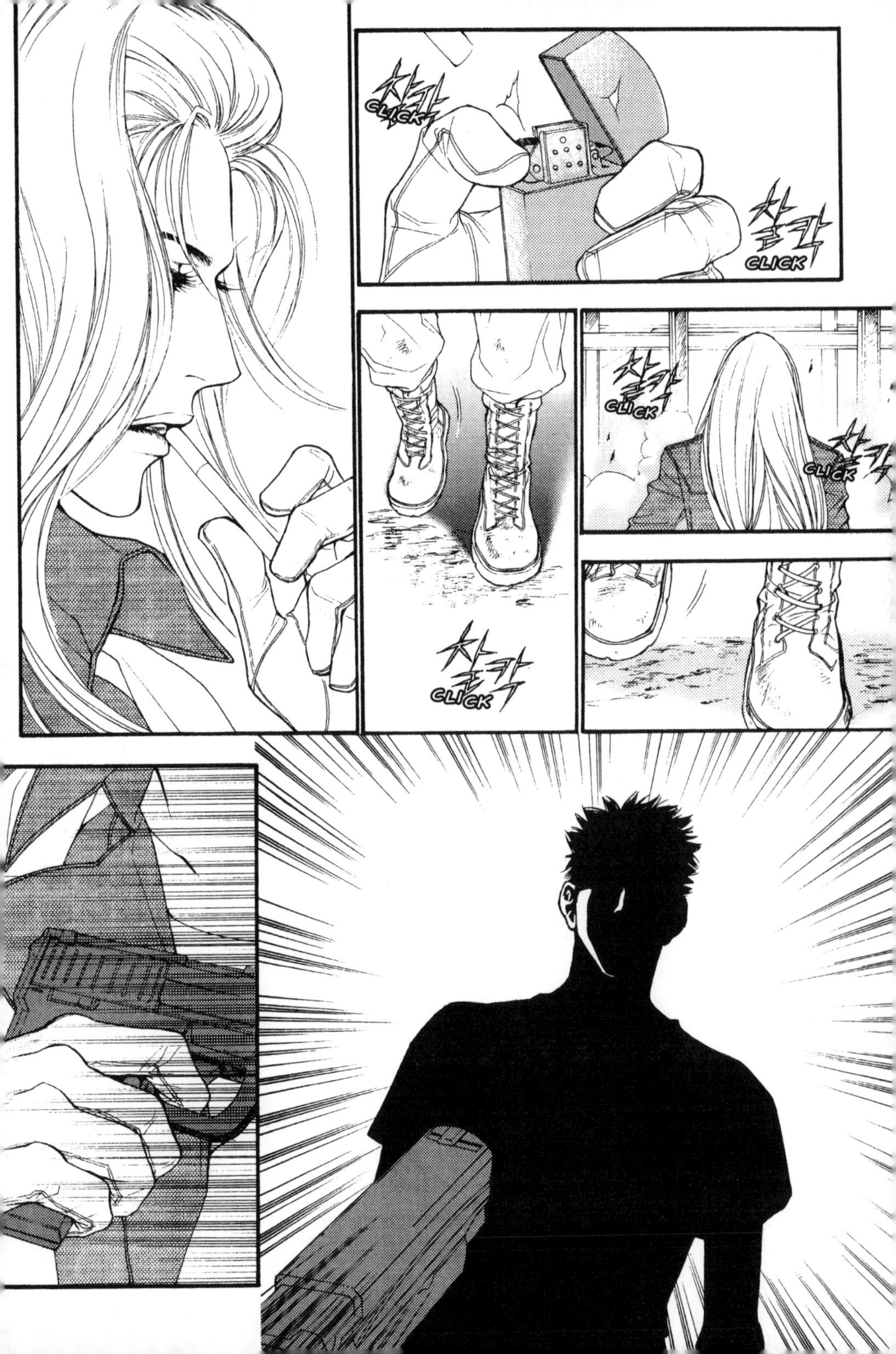

찰칵
CLICK
찰칵
CLICK
찰칵
CLICK
찰칵
CLICK
찰칵
CLICK

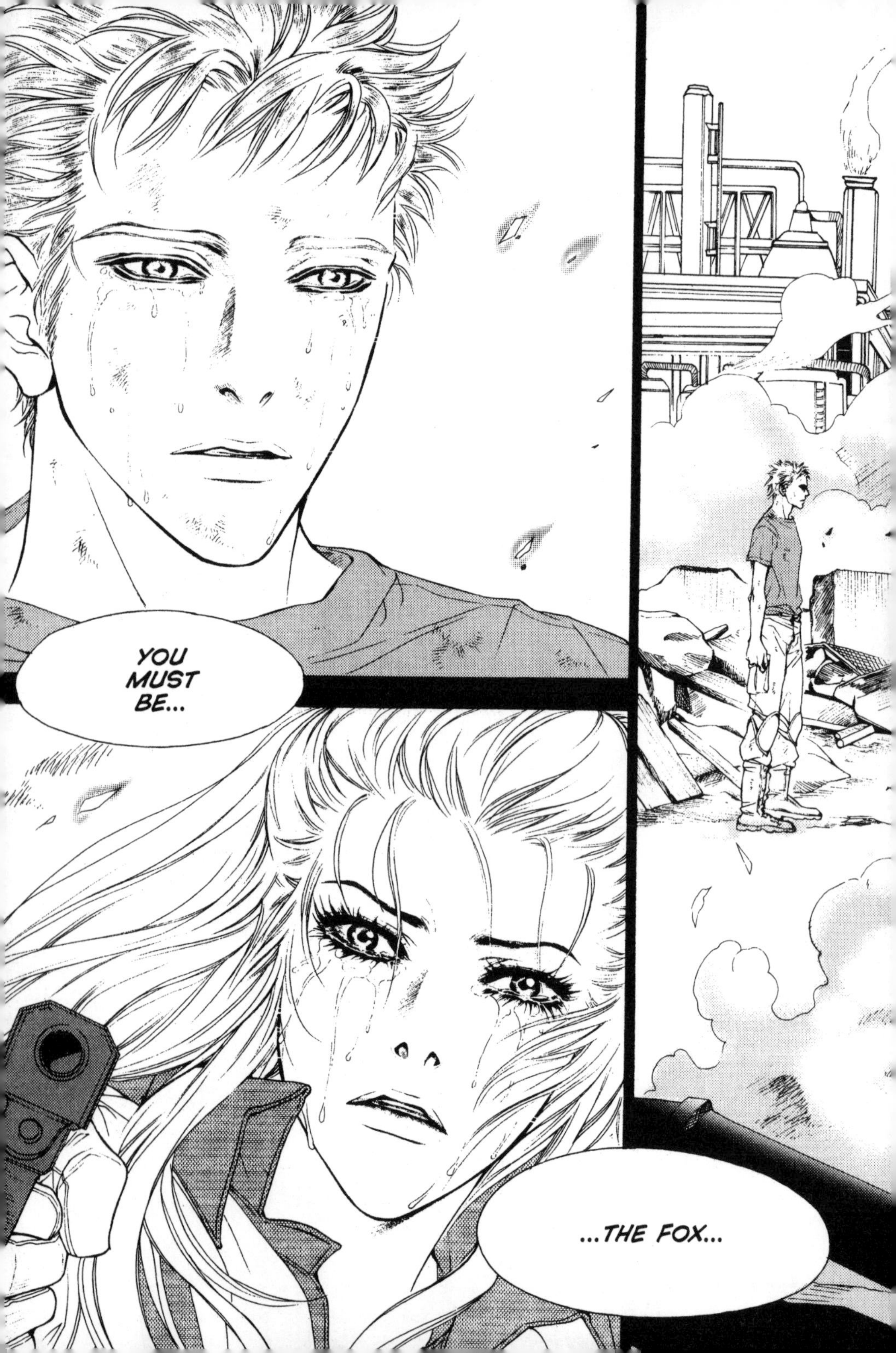
YOU MUST BE...
...THE FOX...

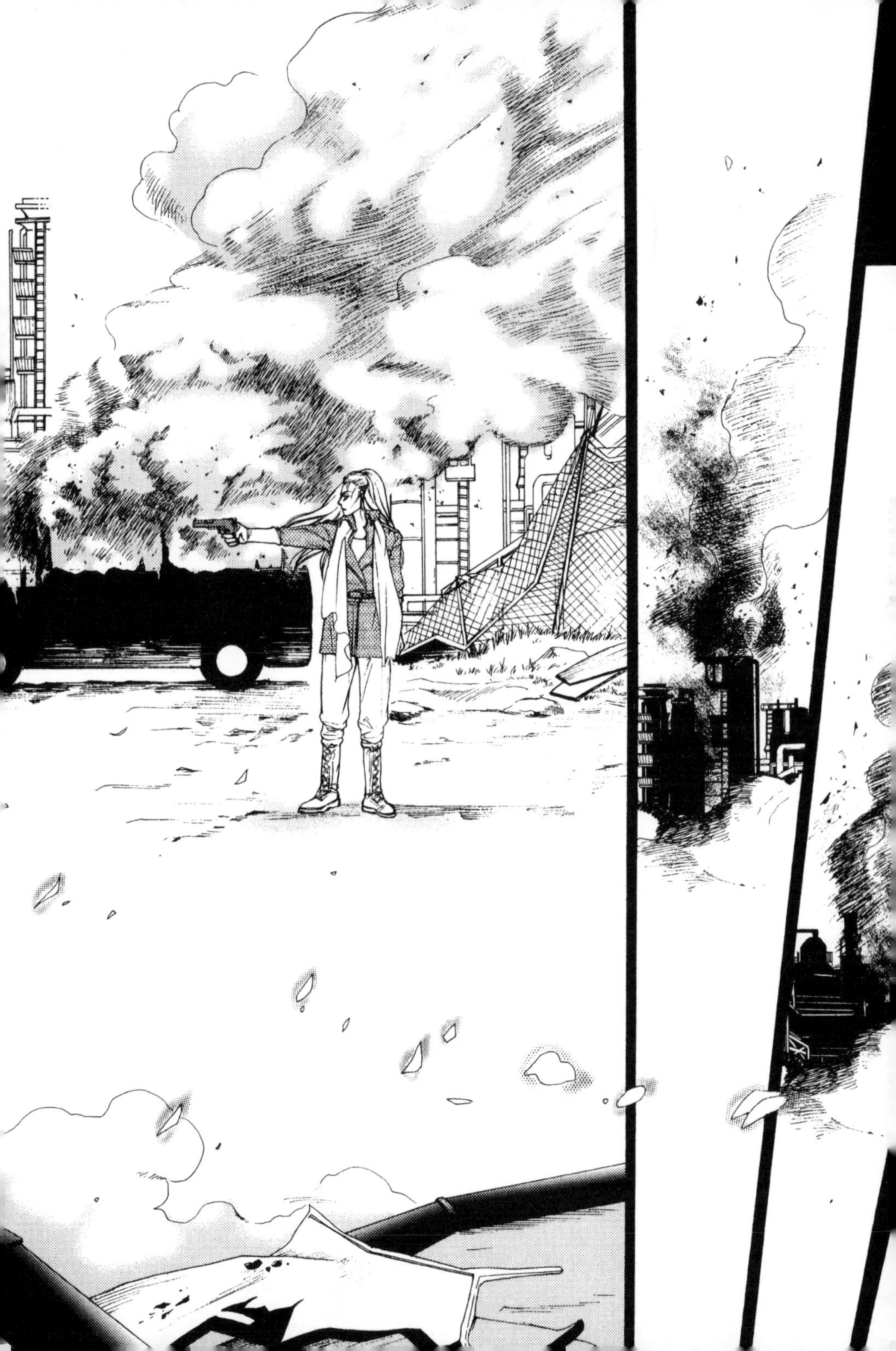

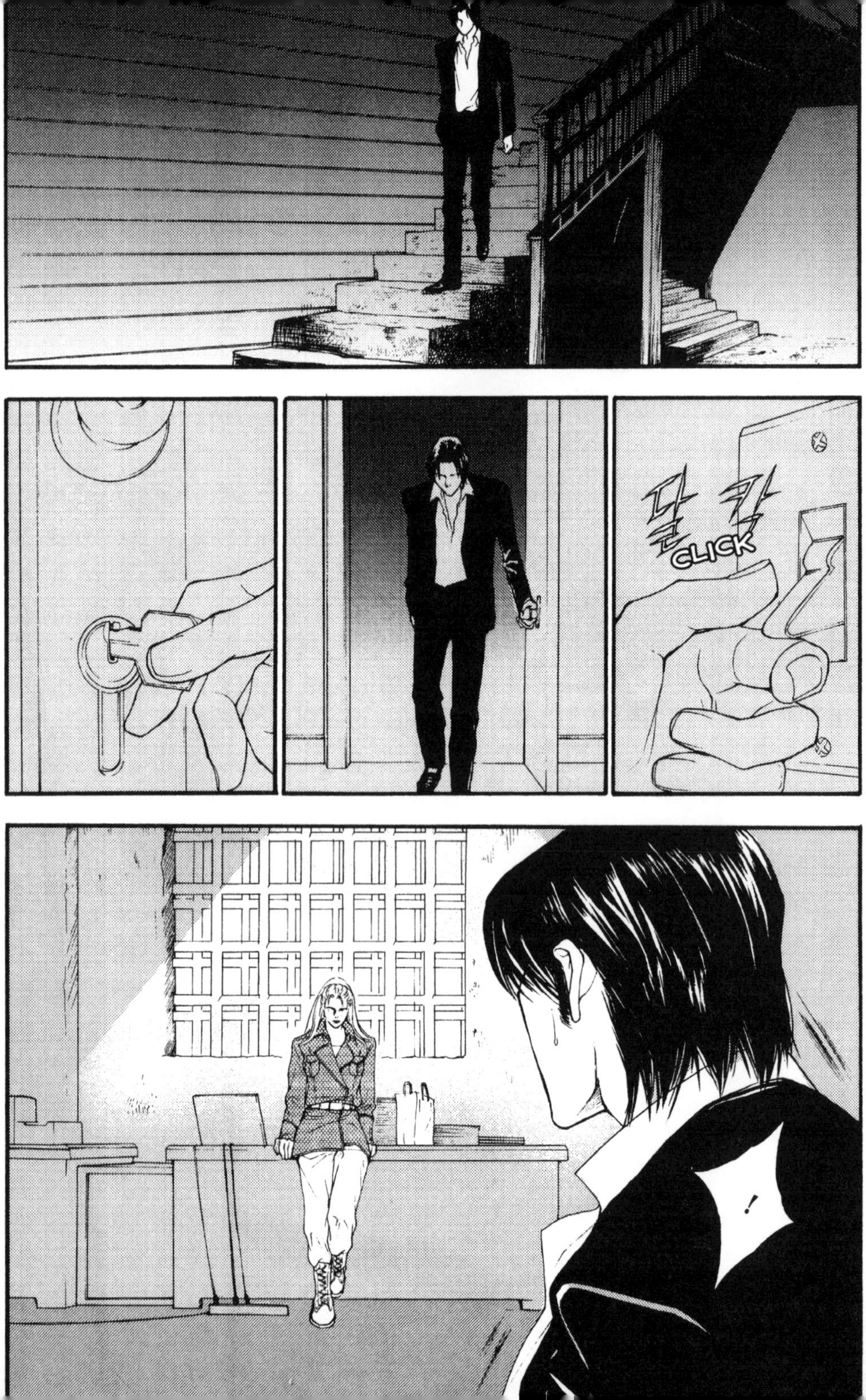
달칵
CLICK
!

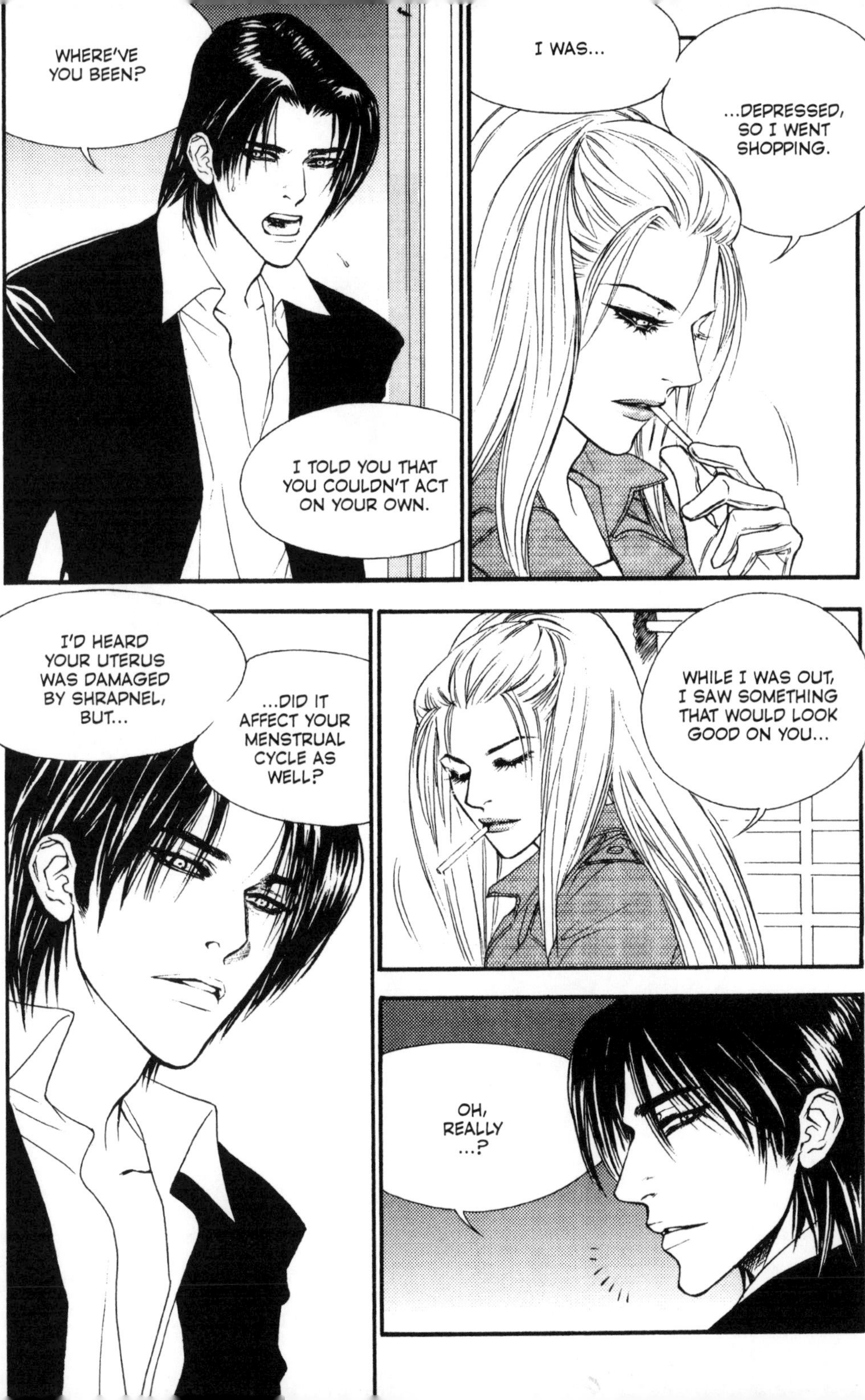
WHERE'VE YOU BEEN?
I TOLD YOU THAT YOU COULDN'T ACT ON YOUR OWN.
I WAS...
...DEPRESSED, SO I WENT SHOPPING.
I'D HEARD YOUR UTERUS WAS DAMAGED BY SHRAPNEL, BUT...
...DID IT AFFECT YOUR MENSTRUAL CYCLE AS WELL?
WHILE I WAS OUT, I SAW SOMETHING THAT WOULD LOOK GOOD ON YOU...
OH, REALLY ...?

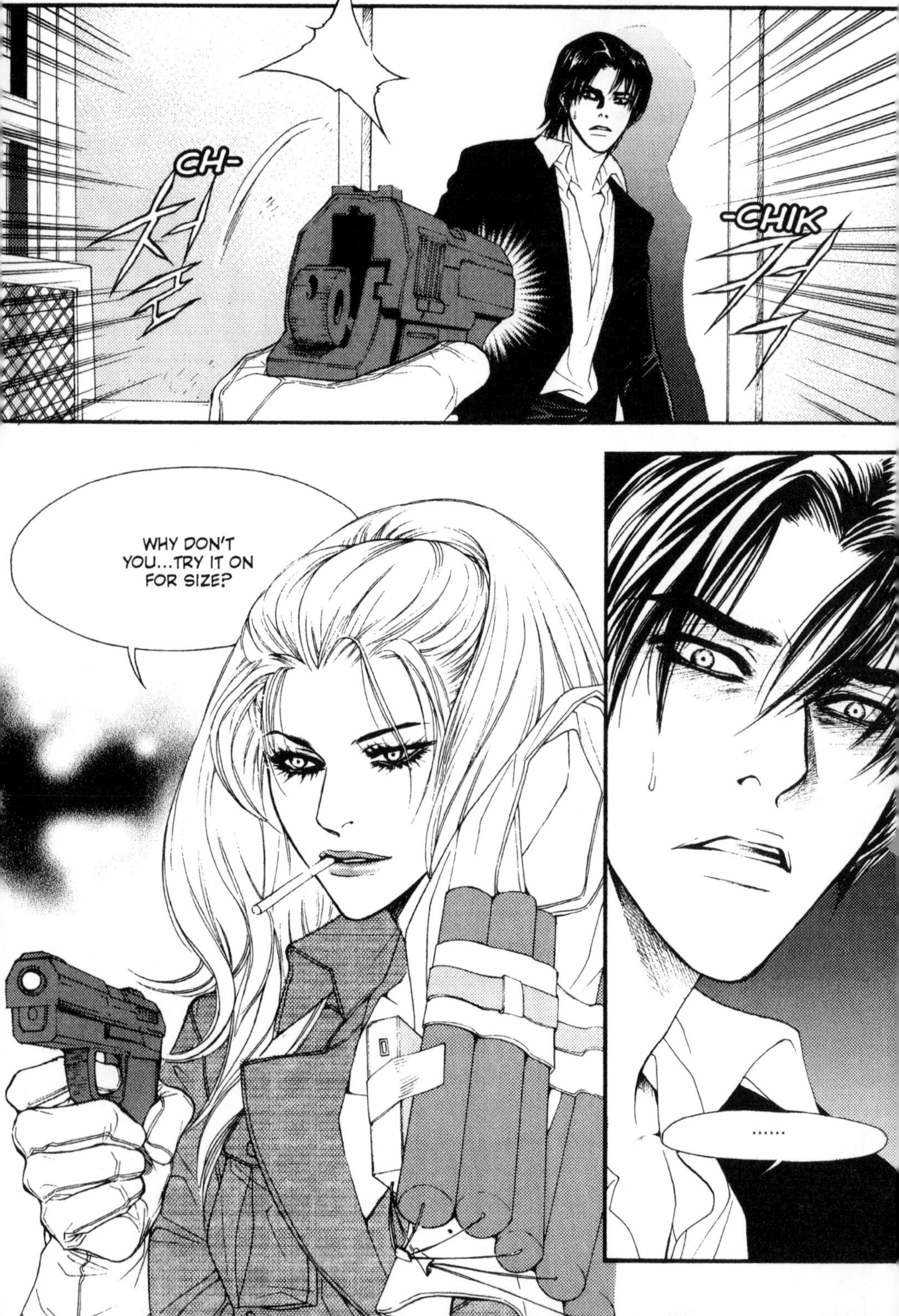
CH-
-CHIK
WHY DON'T YOU...TRY IT ON FOR SIZE?
......

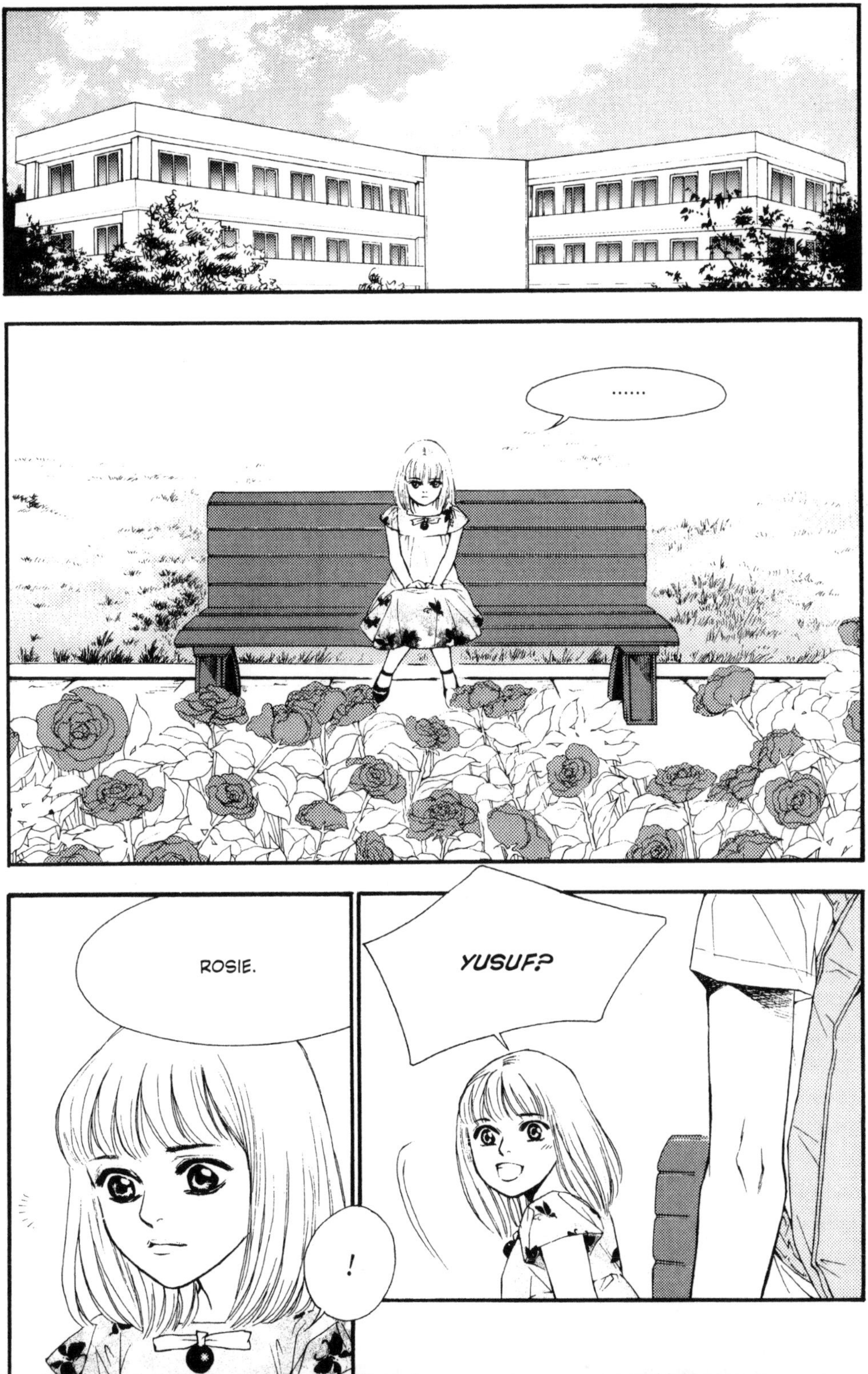

......
ROSIE.
!
YUSUF?

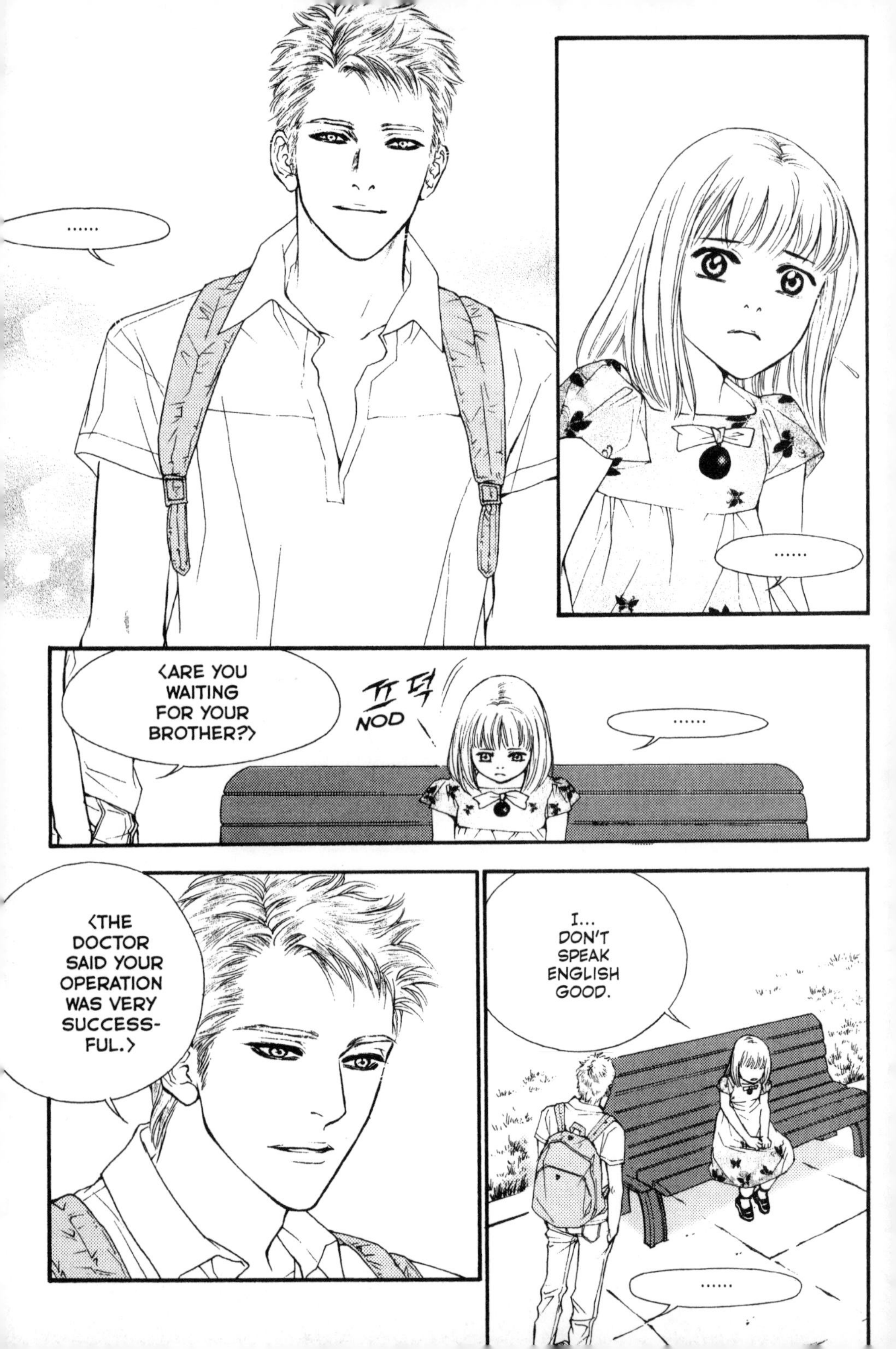
......
......
<ARE YOU WAITING FOR YOUR BROTHER?>
끄덕
NOD
......
<THE DOCTOR SAID YOUR OPERATION WAS VERY SUCCESS-FUL.>
I... DON'T SPEAK ENGLISH GOOD.
......

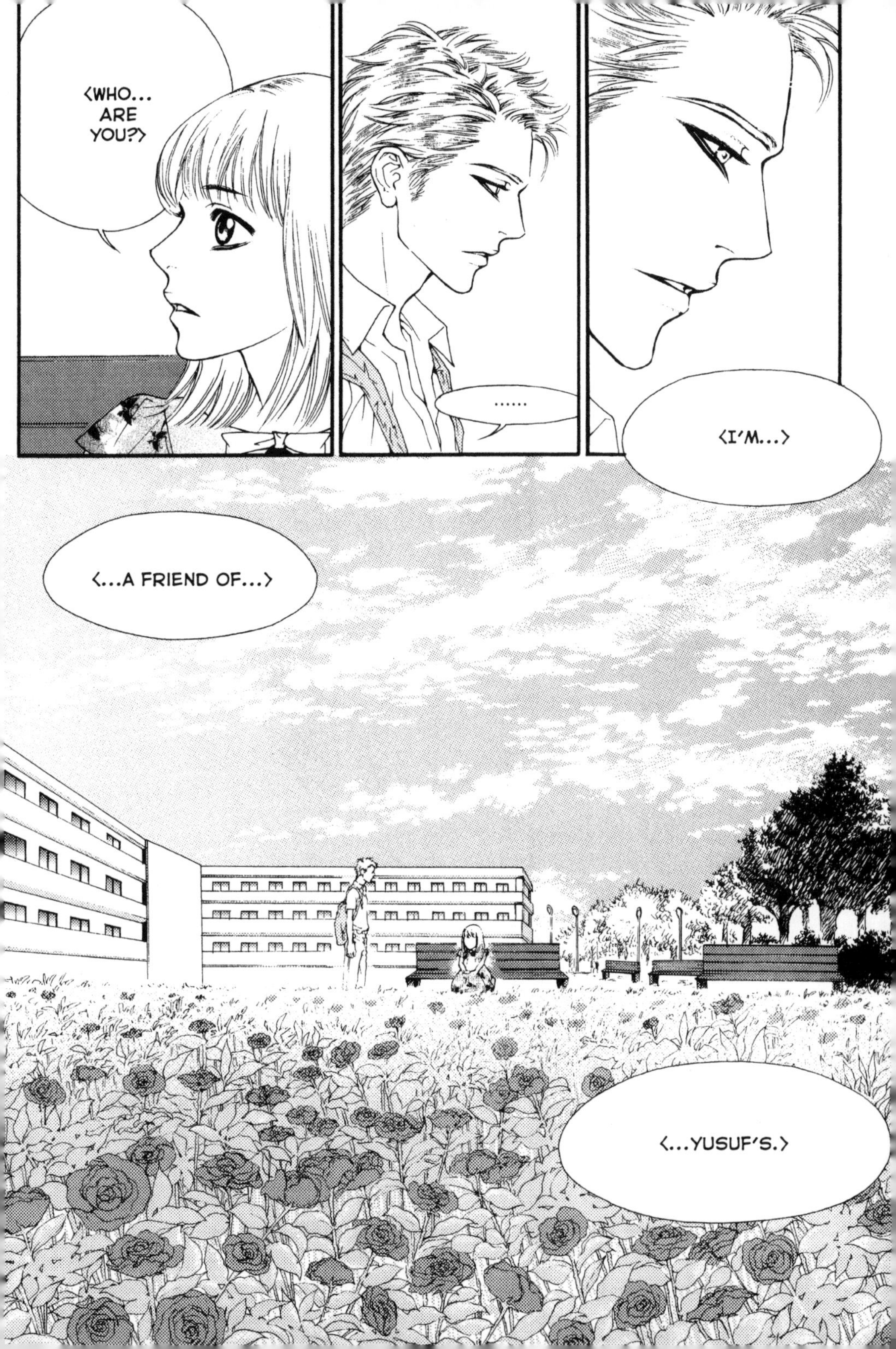
<WHO... ARE YOU?>
......
<I'M...>
<...A FRIEND OF...>
<...YUSUF'S.>

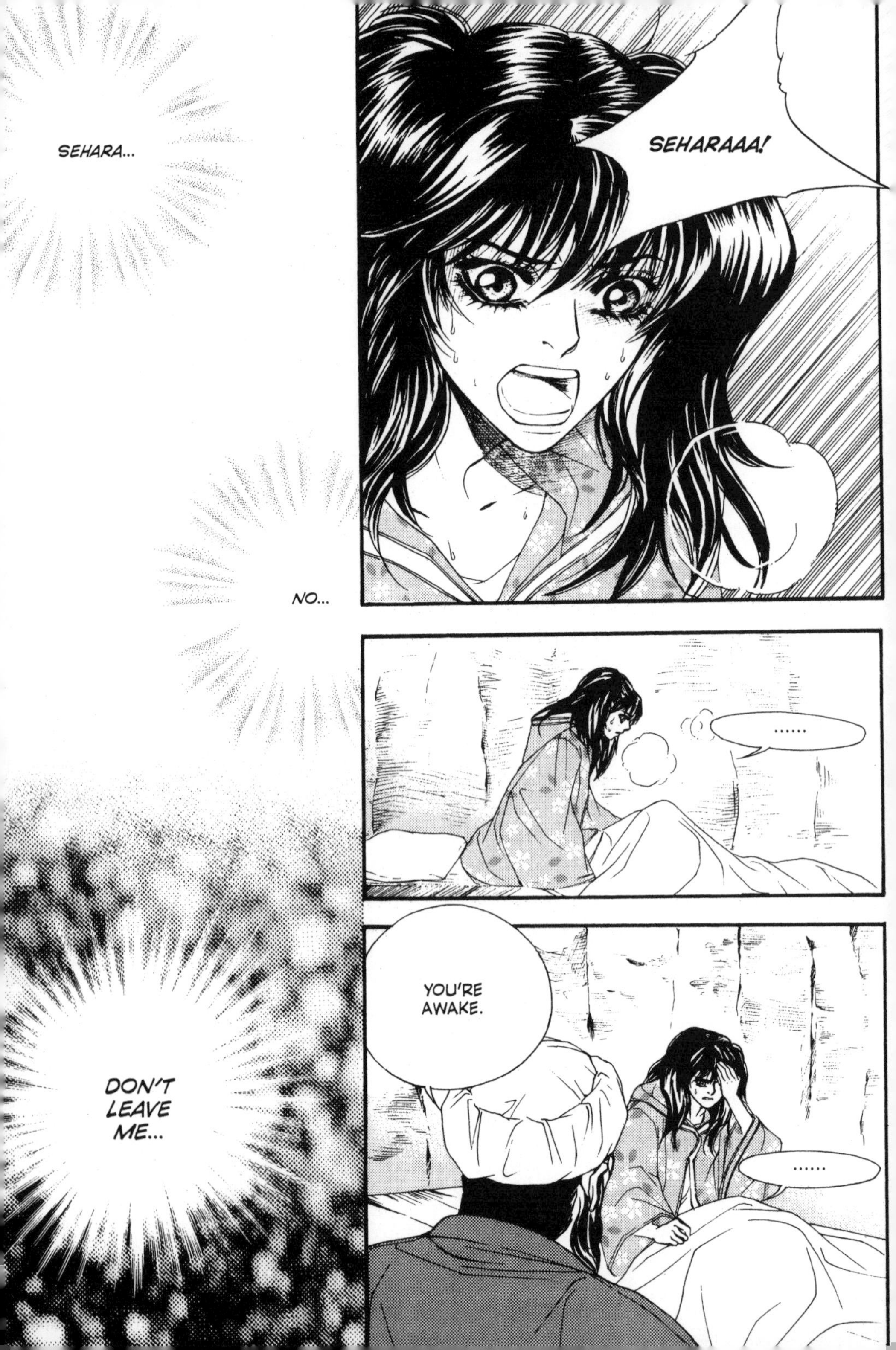
SEHARA...
NO...
DON'T LEAVE ME...
SEHARAAA!
......
YOU'RE AWAKE.
......

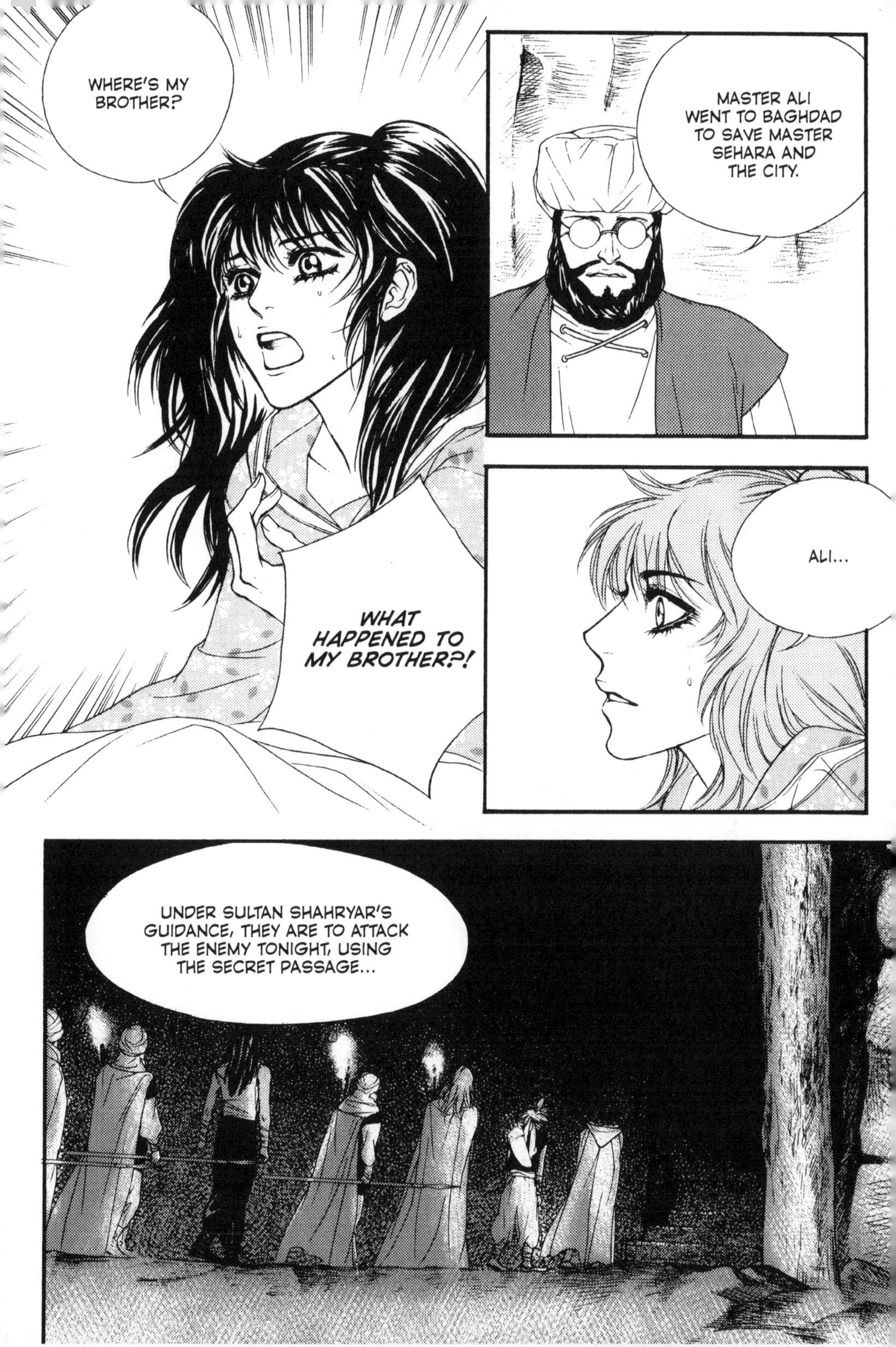
WHERE'S MY BROTHER?
WHAT HAPPENED TO MY BROTHER?!
MASTER ALI WENT TO BAGHDAD TO SAVE MASTER SEHARA AND THE CITY.
ALI...
UNDER SULTAN SHAHRYAR'S GUIDANCE, THEY ARE TO ATTACK THE ENEMY TONIGHT, USING THE SECRET PASSAGE...

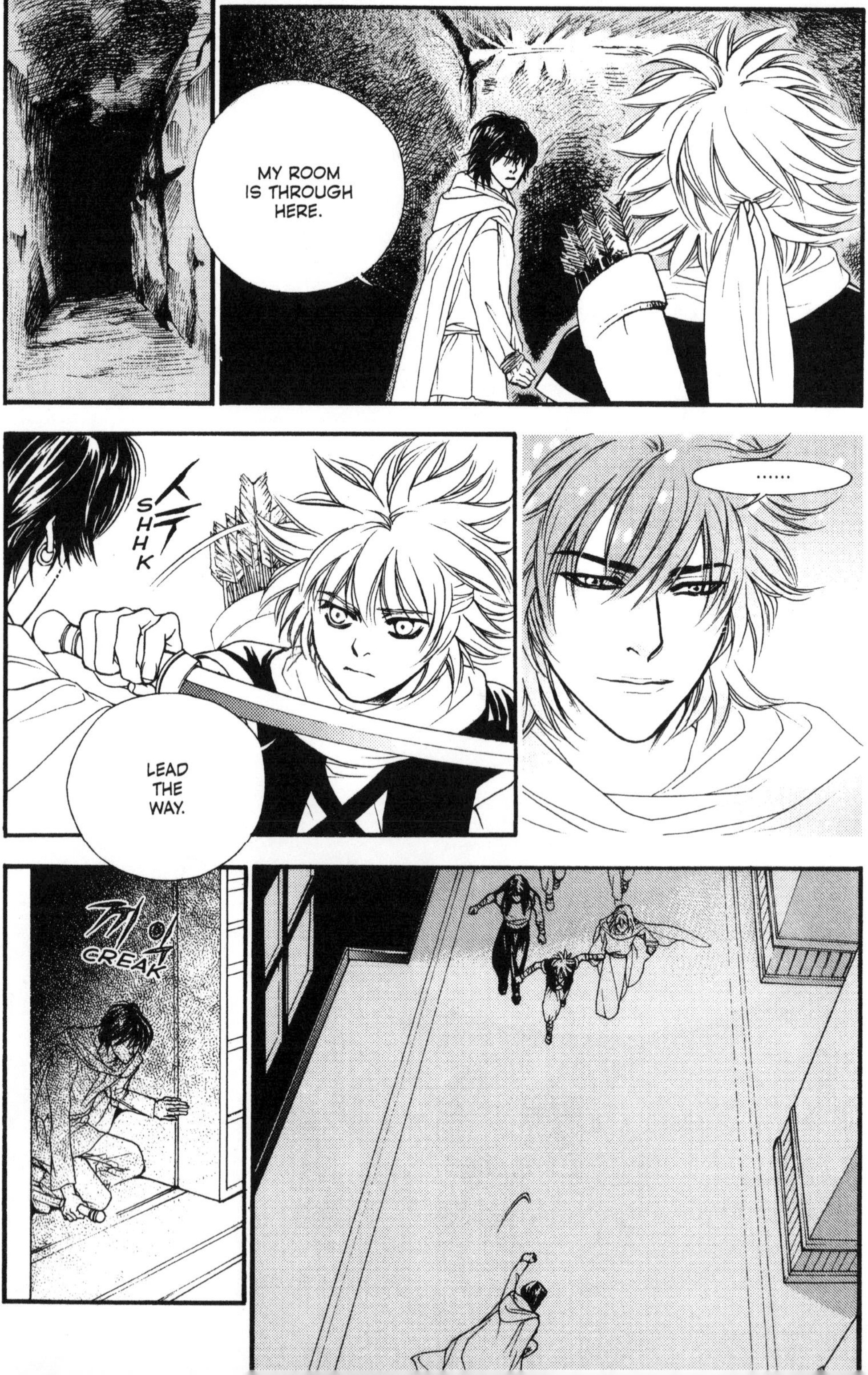
MY ROOM IS THROUGH HERE.
SHHK
LEAD THE WAY.
......
CREAK

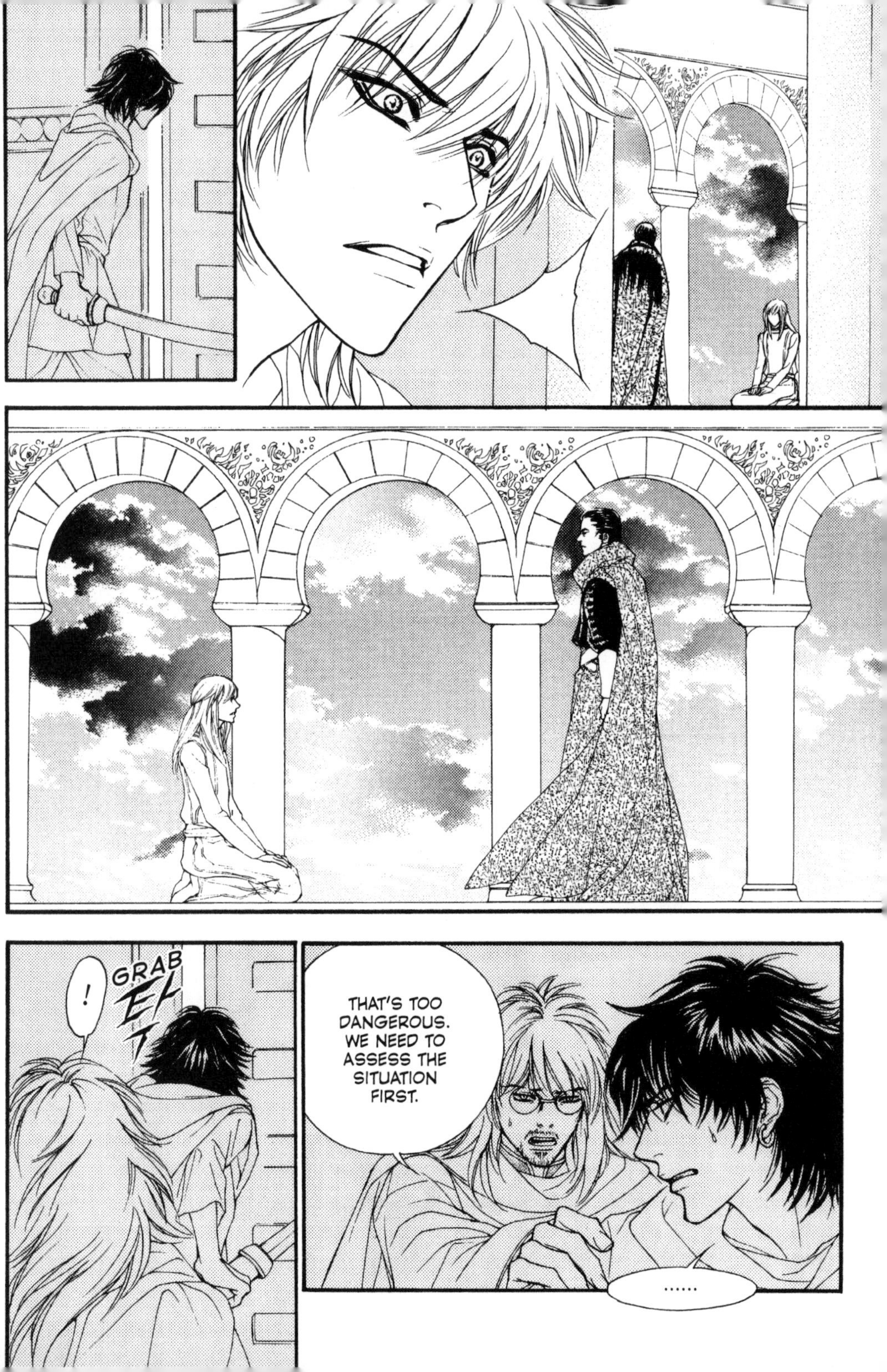
GRAB
!
THAT'S TOO DANGEROUS. WE NEED TO ASSESS THE SITUATION FIRST.
......

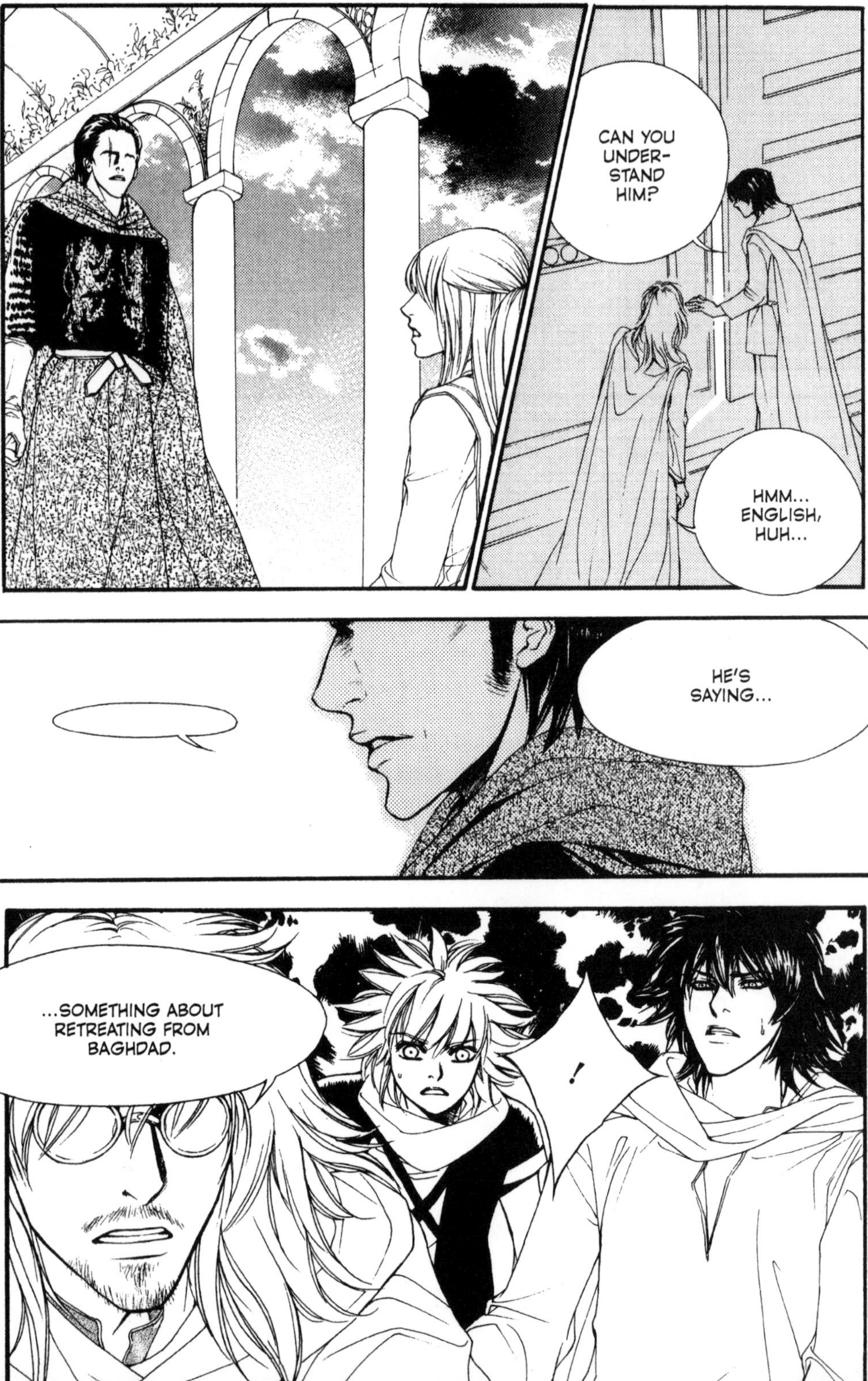
CAN YOU UNDER-STAND HIM?
HMM... ENGLISH, HUH...
HE'S SAYING...
...SOMETHING ABOUT RETREATING FROM BAGHDAD.
!

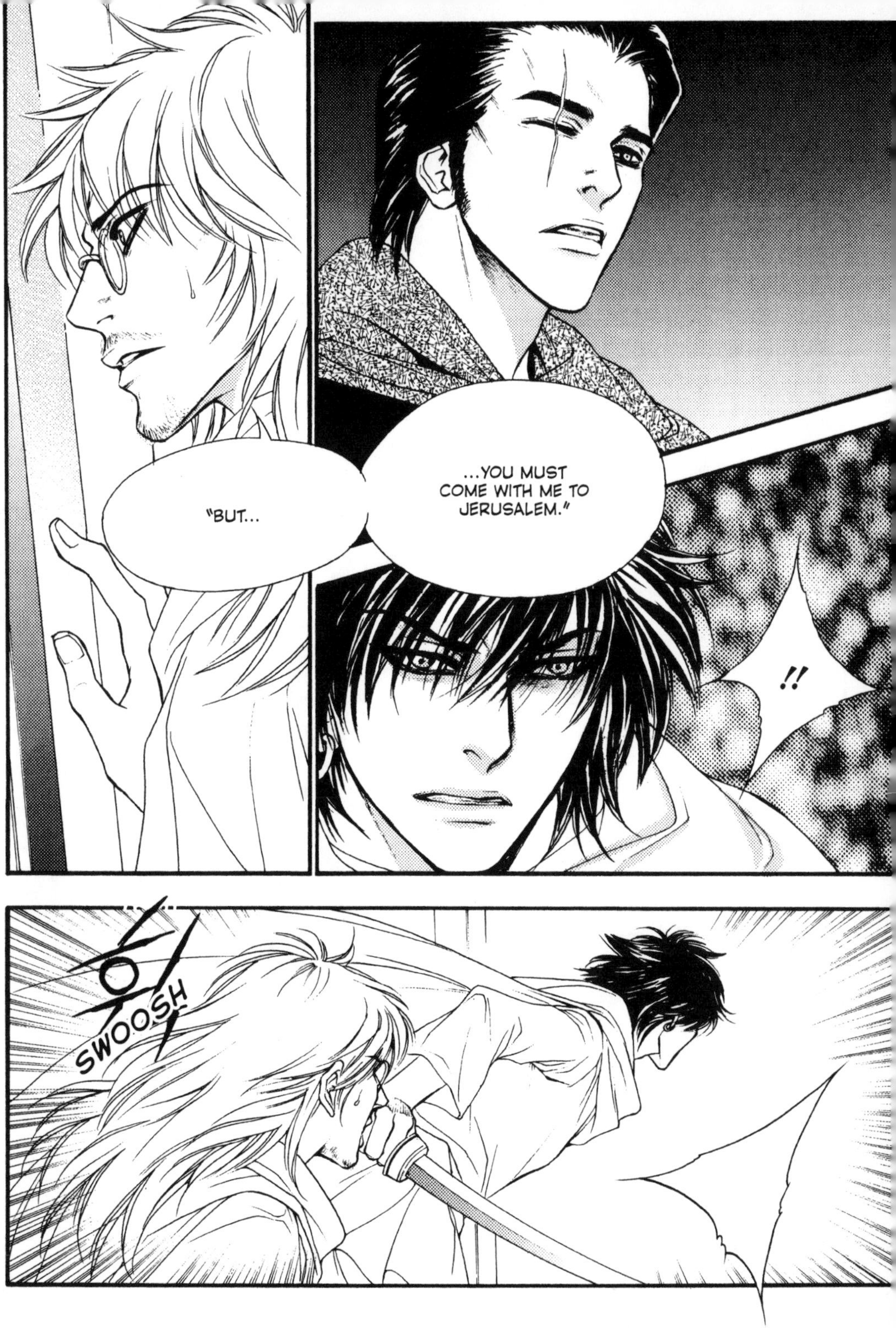
"BUT...
...YOU MUST COME WITH ME TO JERUSALEM."
!!
SWOOSH

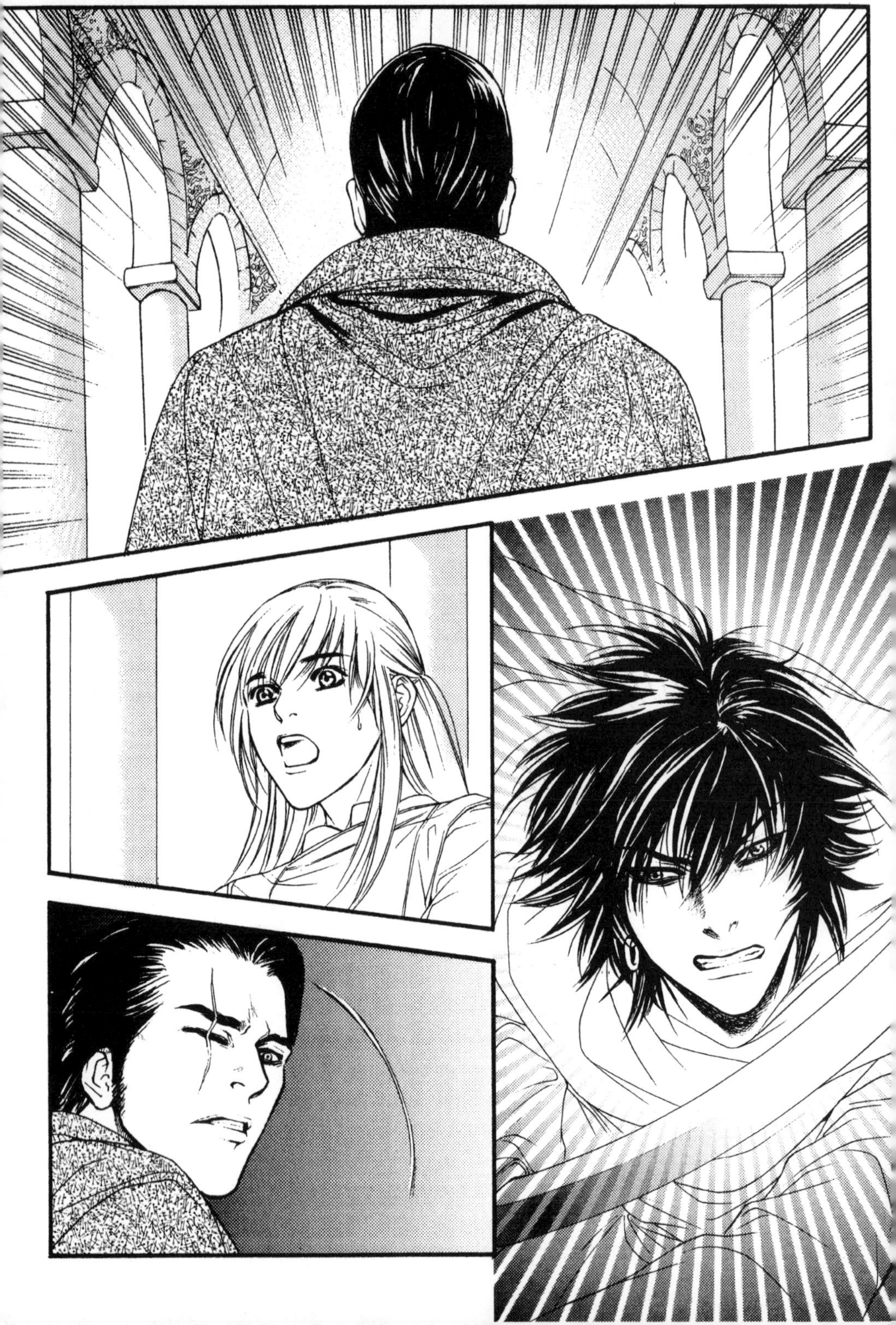

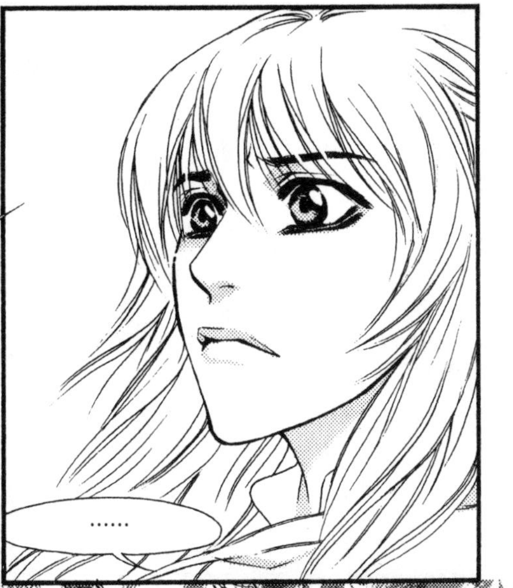
......
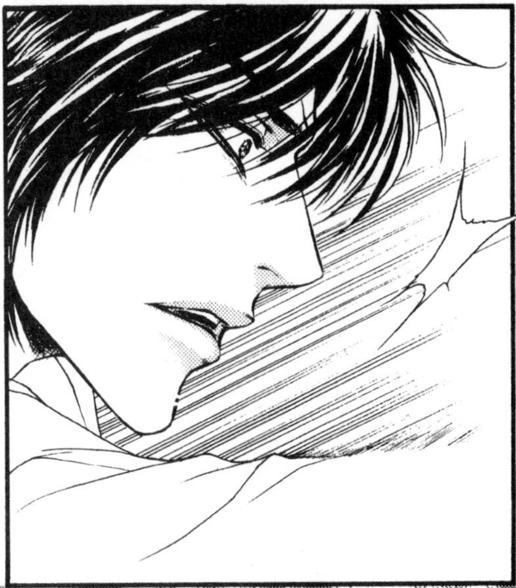
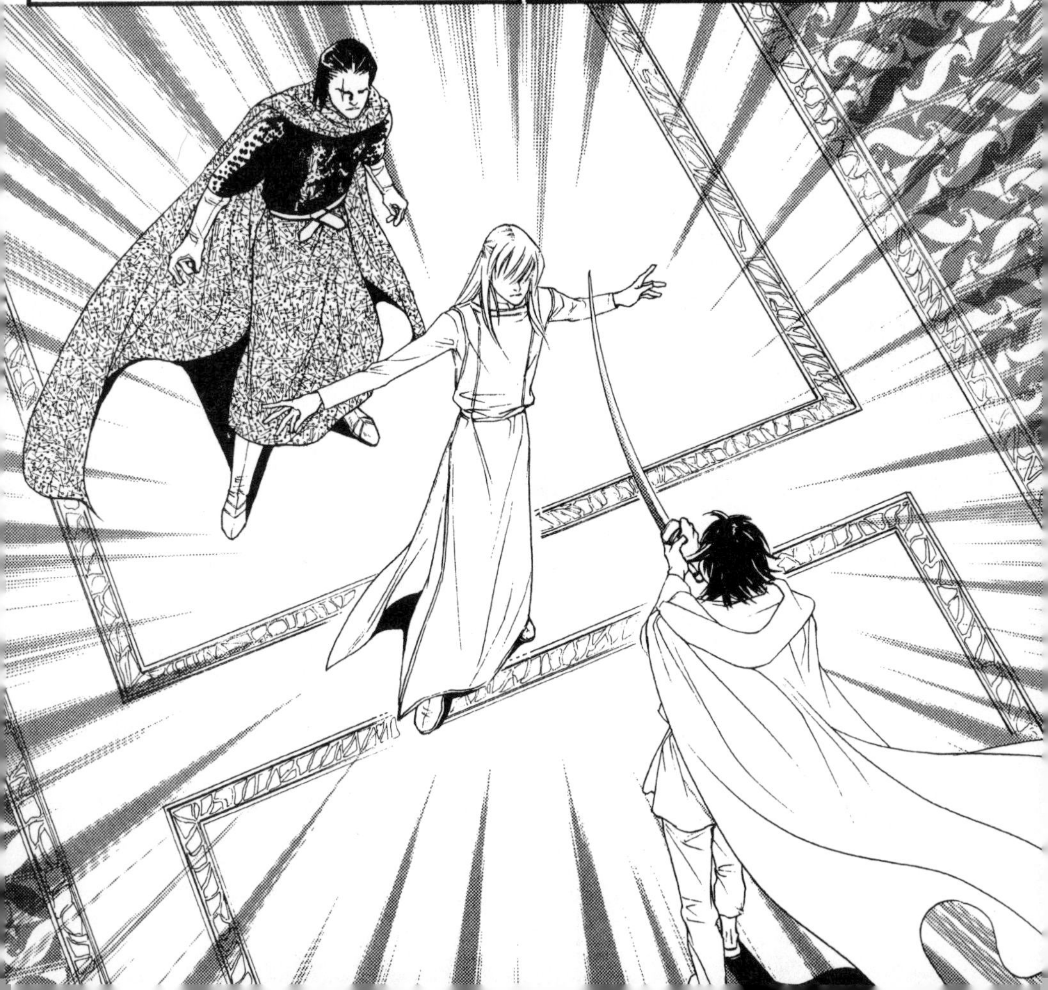

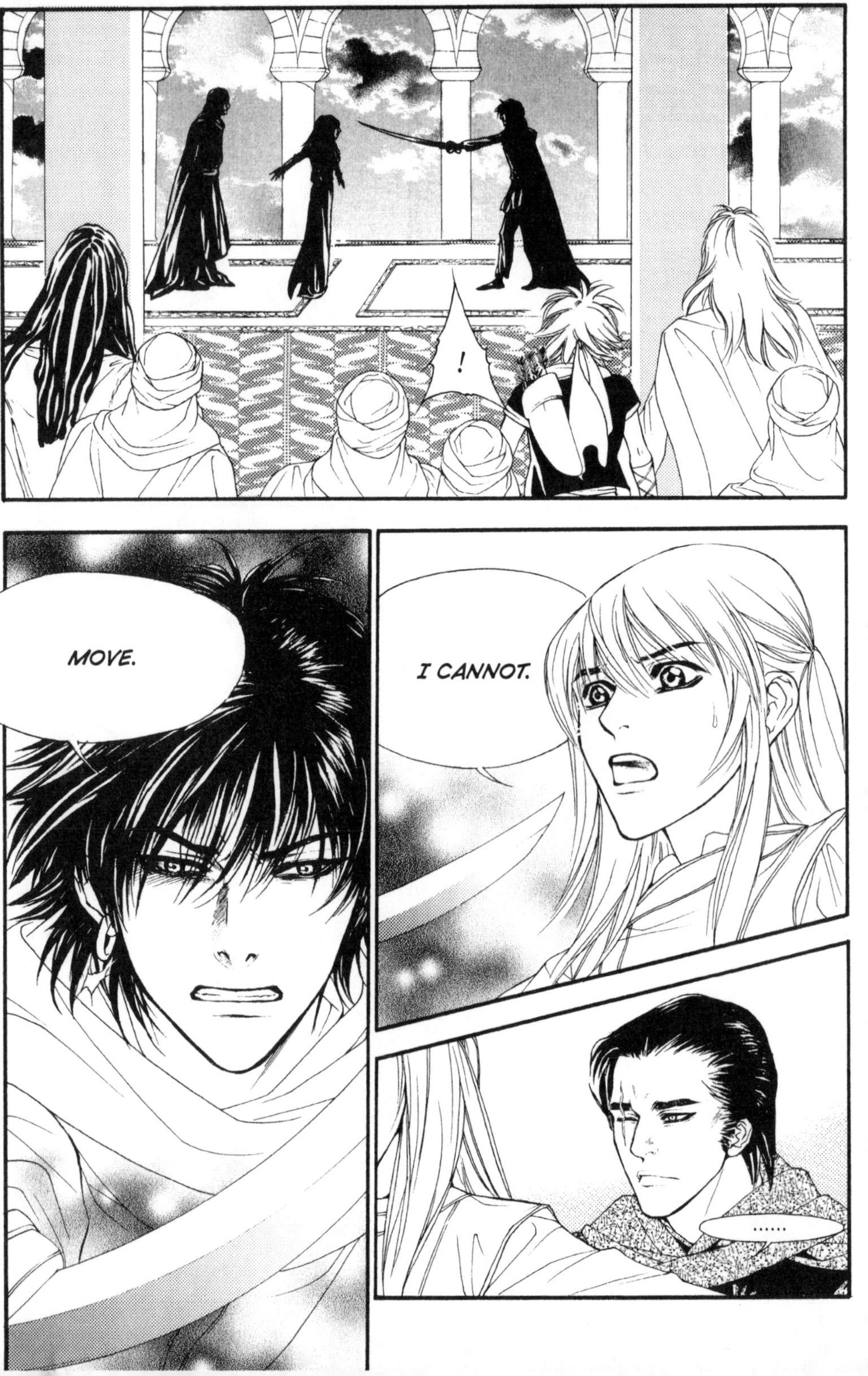
!
MOVE.
I CANNOT.
......

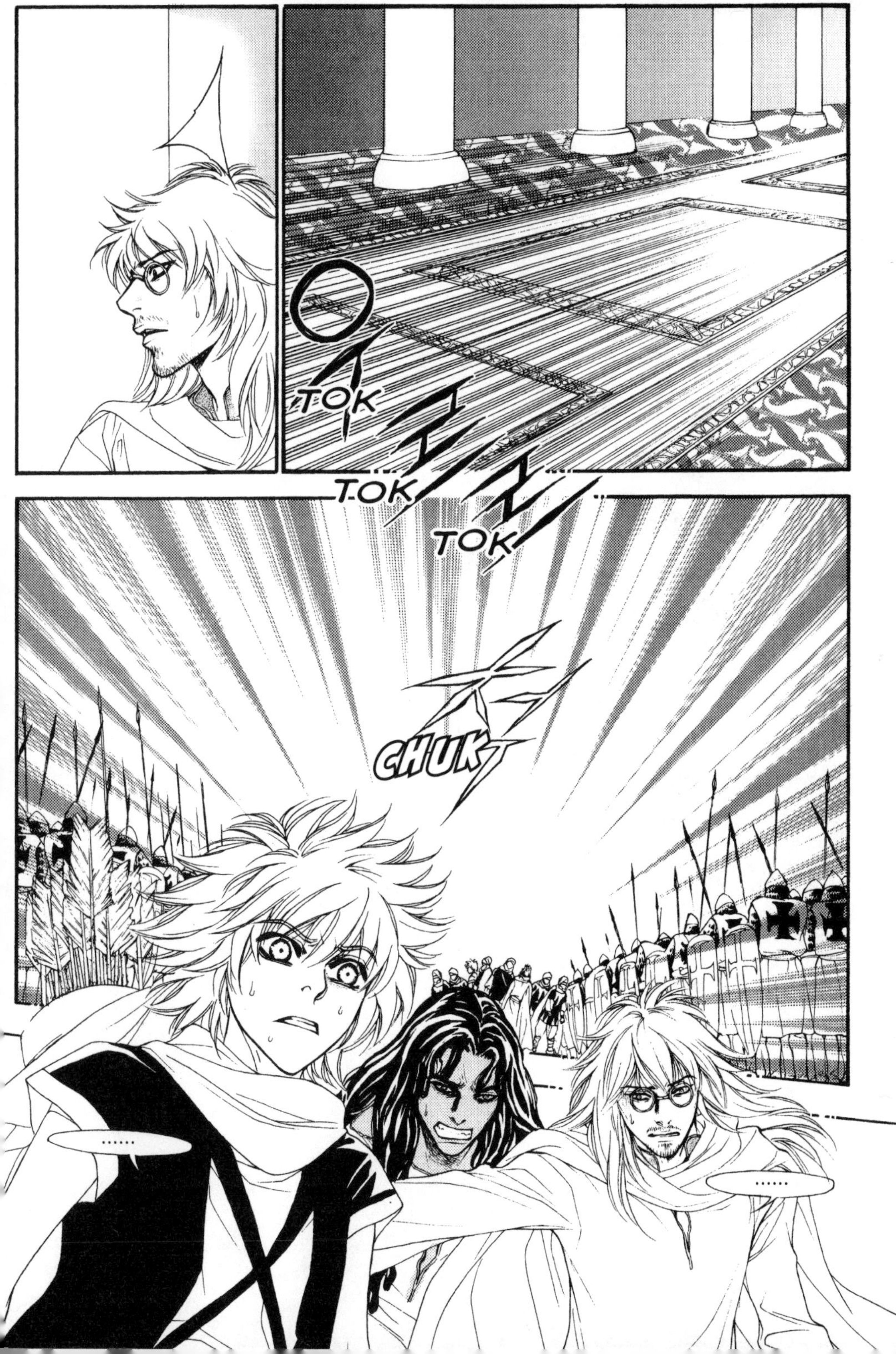
TOK
TOK
TOK
CHUK
......
......

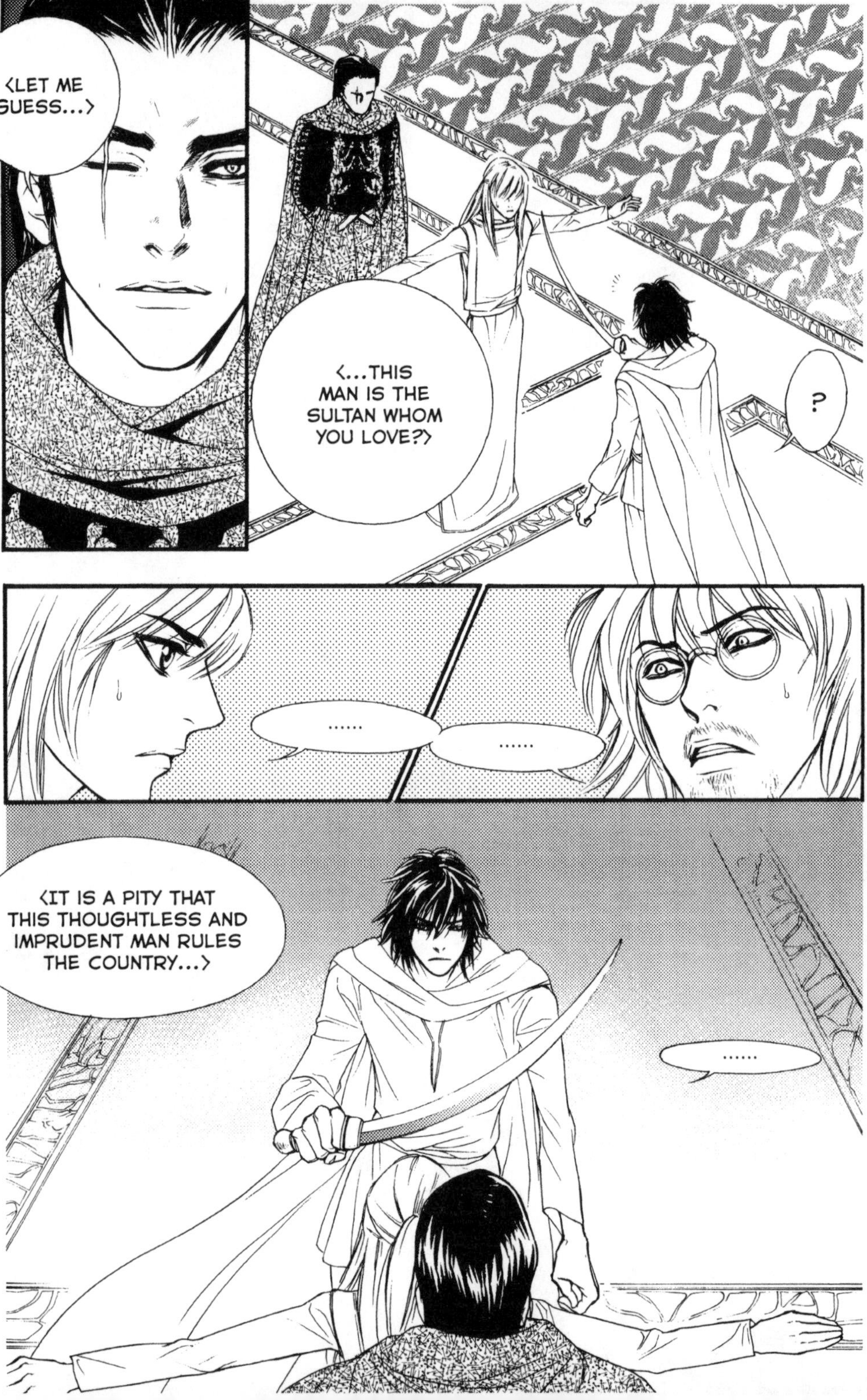
<LET ME GUESS...>
<...THIS MAN IS THE SULTAN WHOM YOU LOVE?>
?
......
......
<IT IS A PITY THAT THIS THOUGHTLESS AND IMPRUDENT MAN RULES THE COUNTRY...>
......

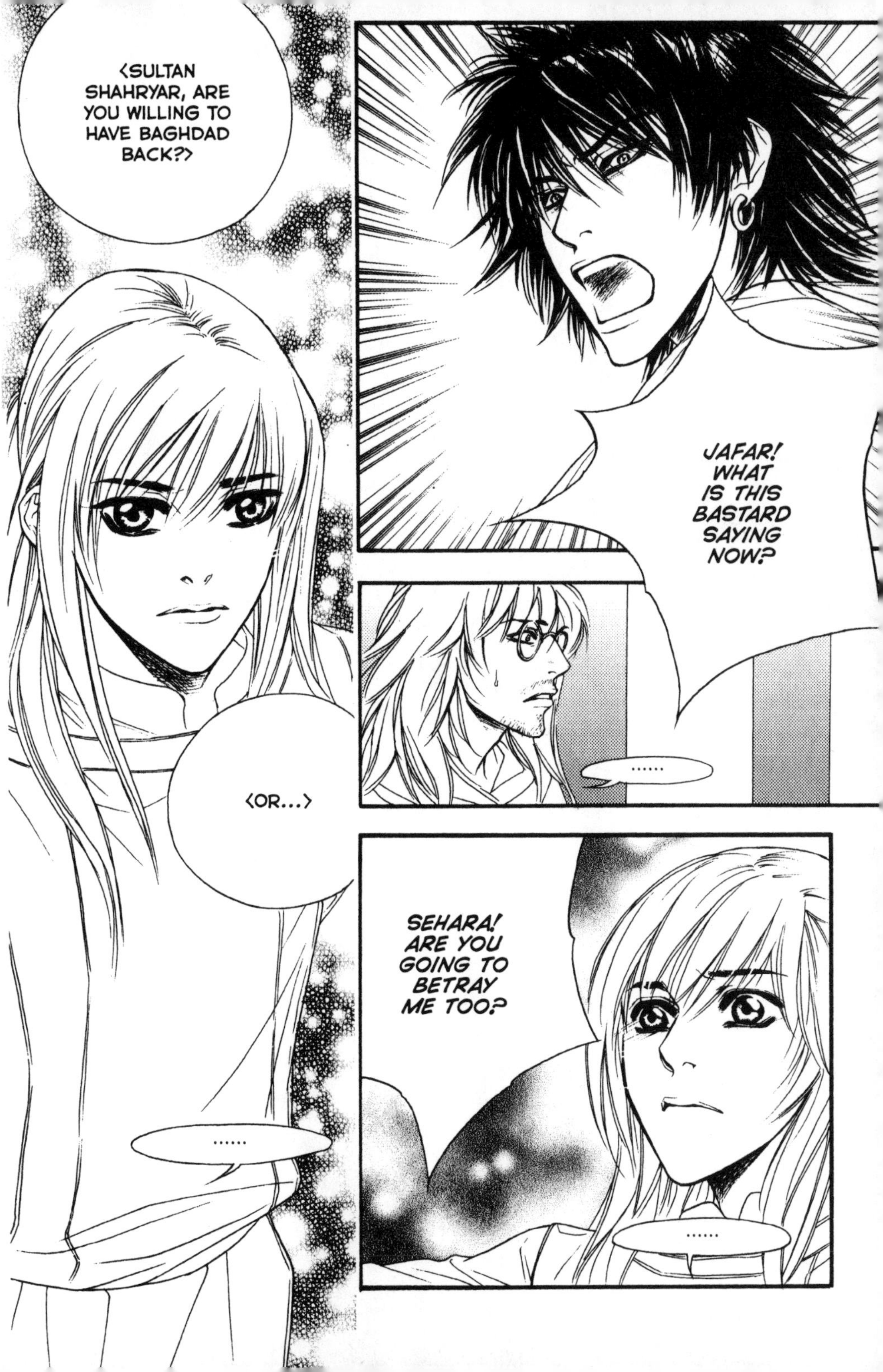
<SULTAN SHAHRYAR, ARE YOU WILLING TO HAVE BAGHDAD BACK?>
<OR...>
......
JAFAR! WHAT IS THIS BASTARD SAYING NOW?
......
SEHARA! ARE YOU GOING TO BETRAY ME TOO?
......

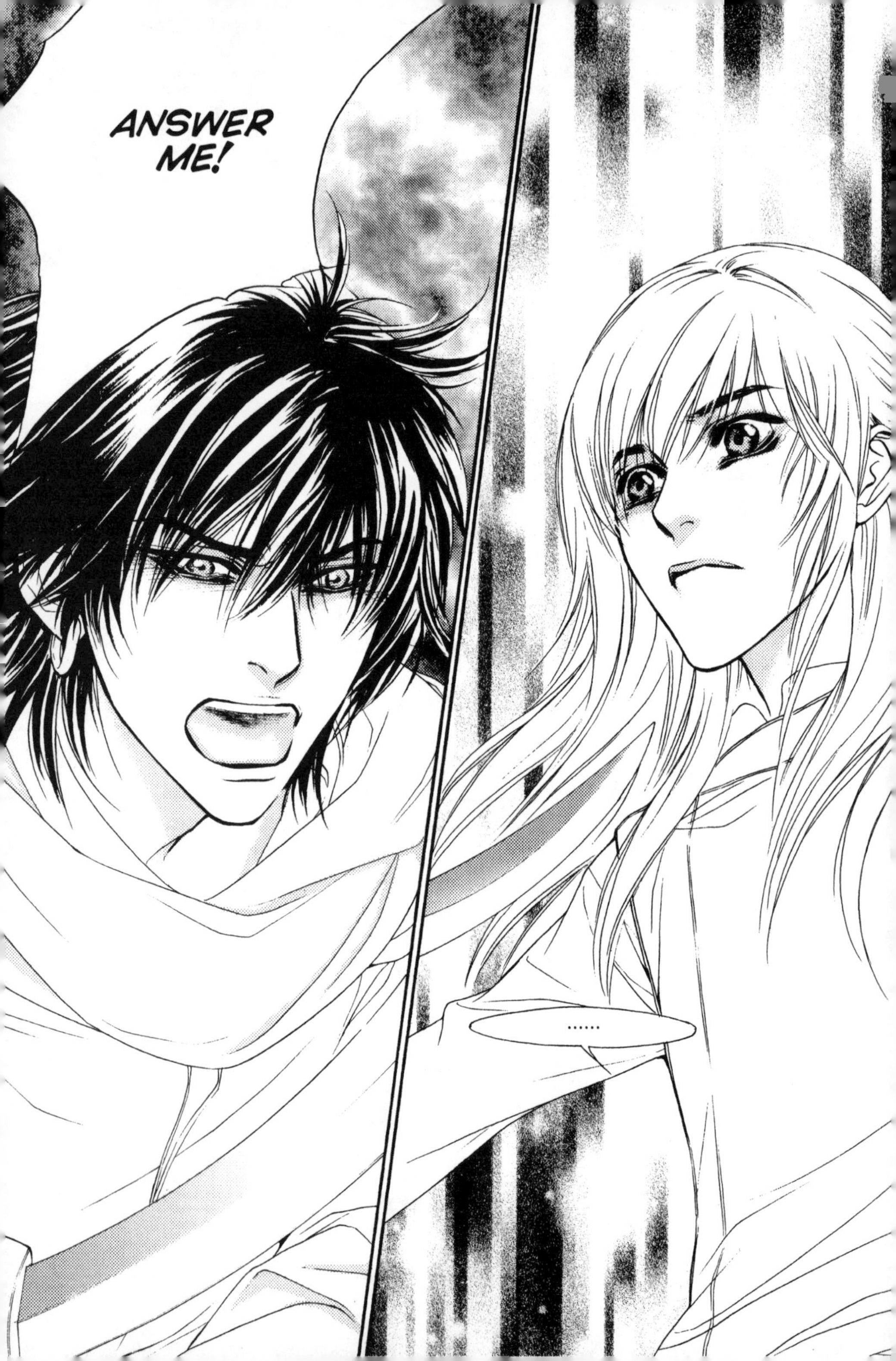
ANSWER ME!
......

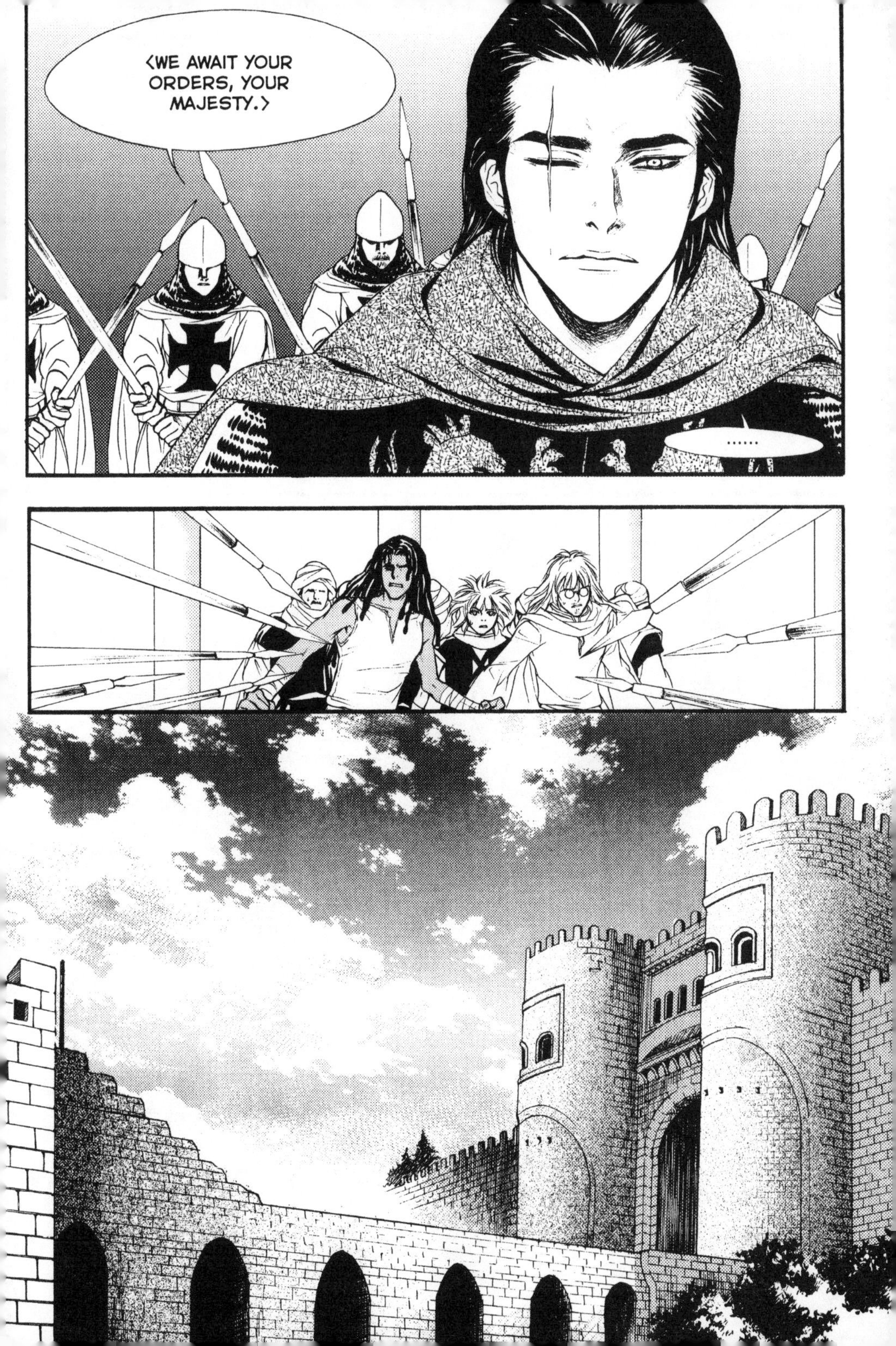
<WE AWAIT YOUR ORDERS, YOUR MAJESTY.>
......

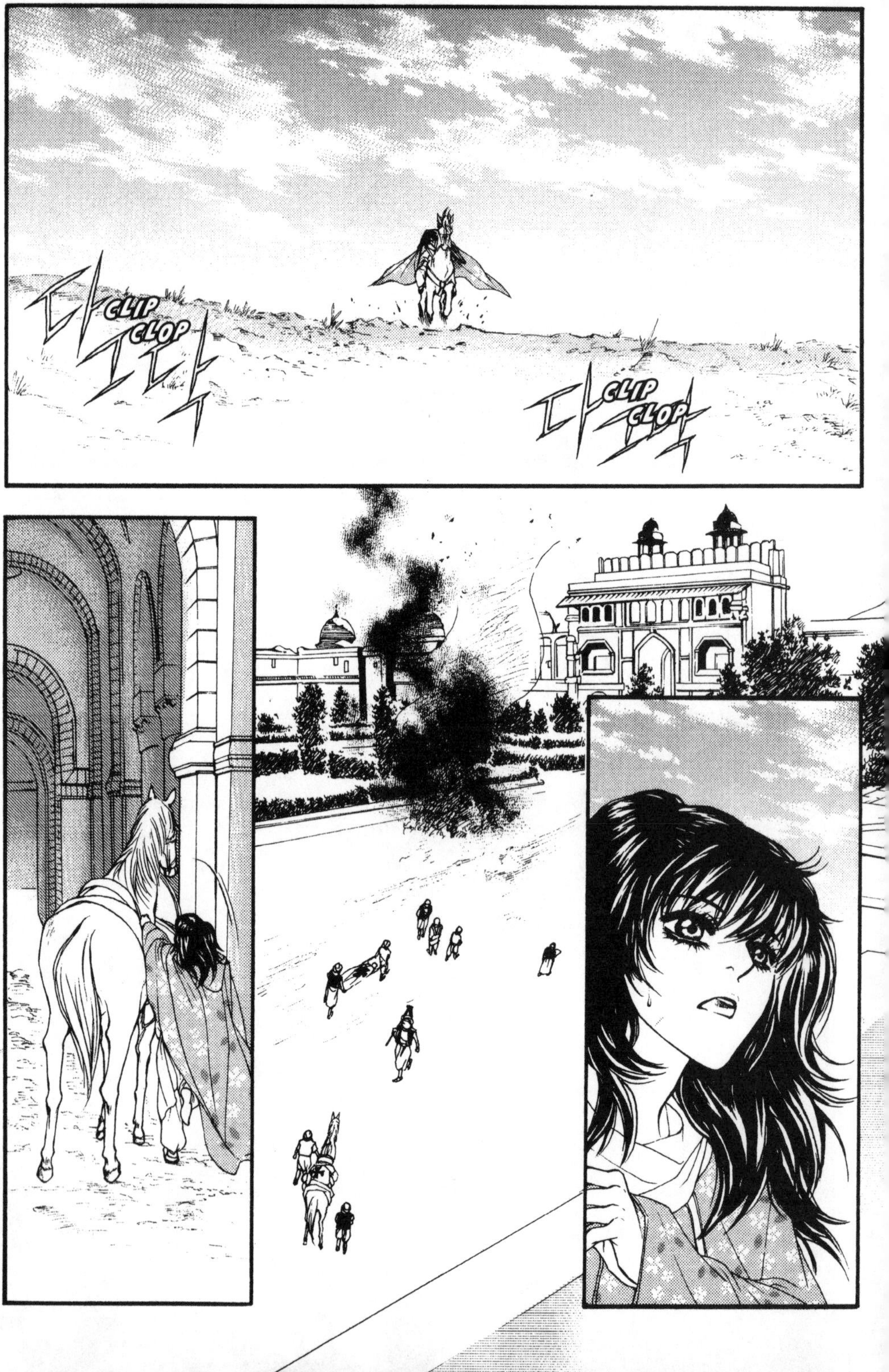
CLIP CLOP
CLIP CLOP

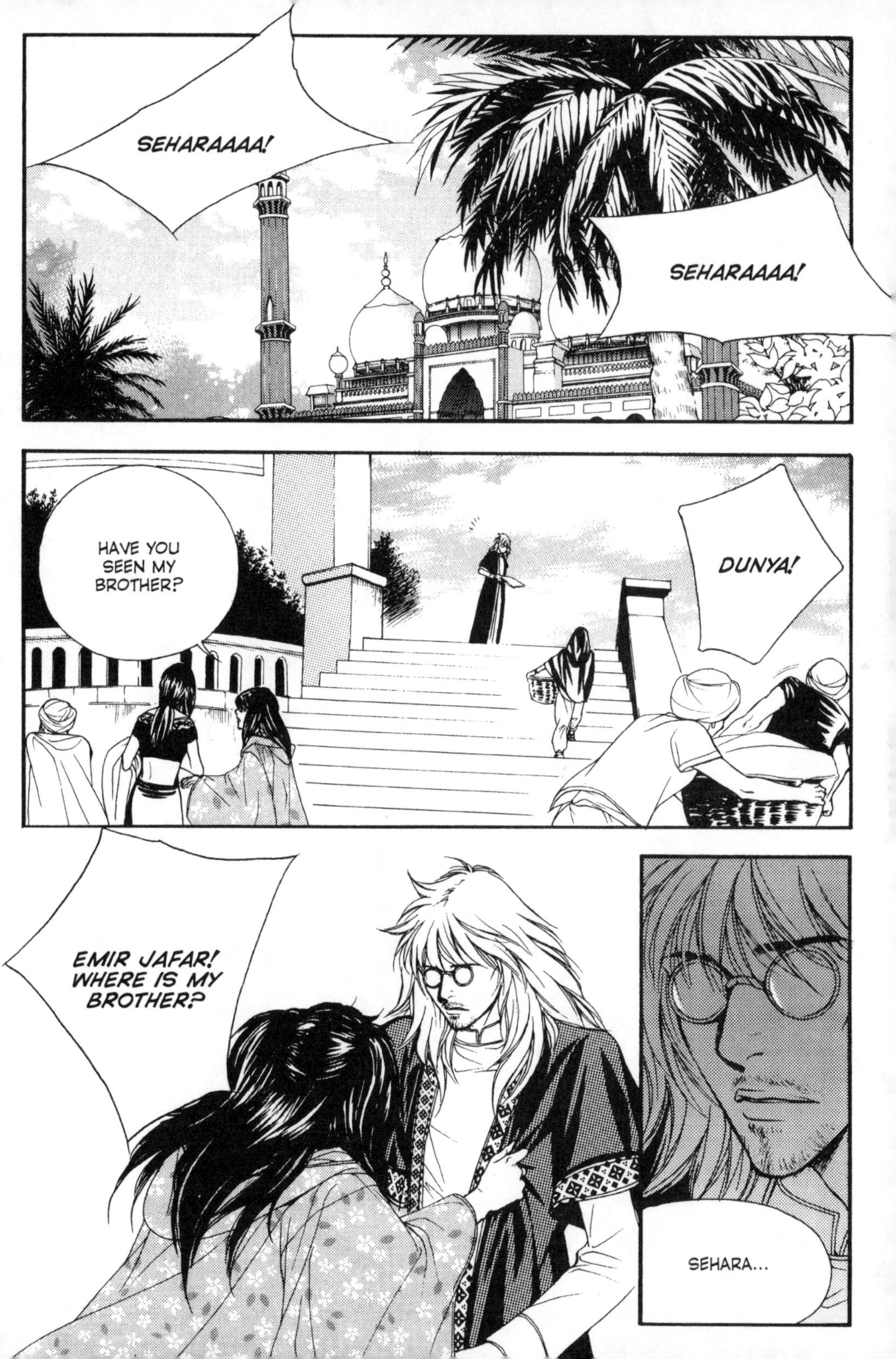
SEHARAAAA!
SEHARAAAA!
HAVE YOU SEEN MY BROTHER?
DUNYA!
EMIR JAFAR! WHERE IS MY BROTHER?
SEHARA...

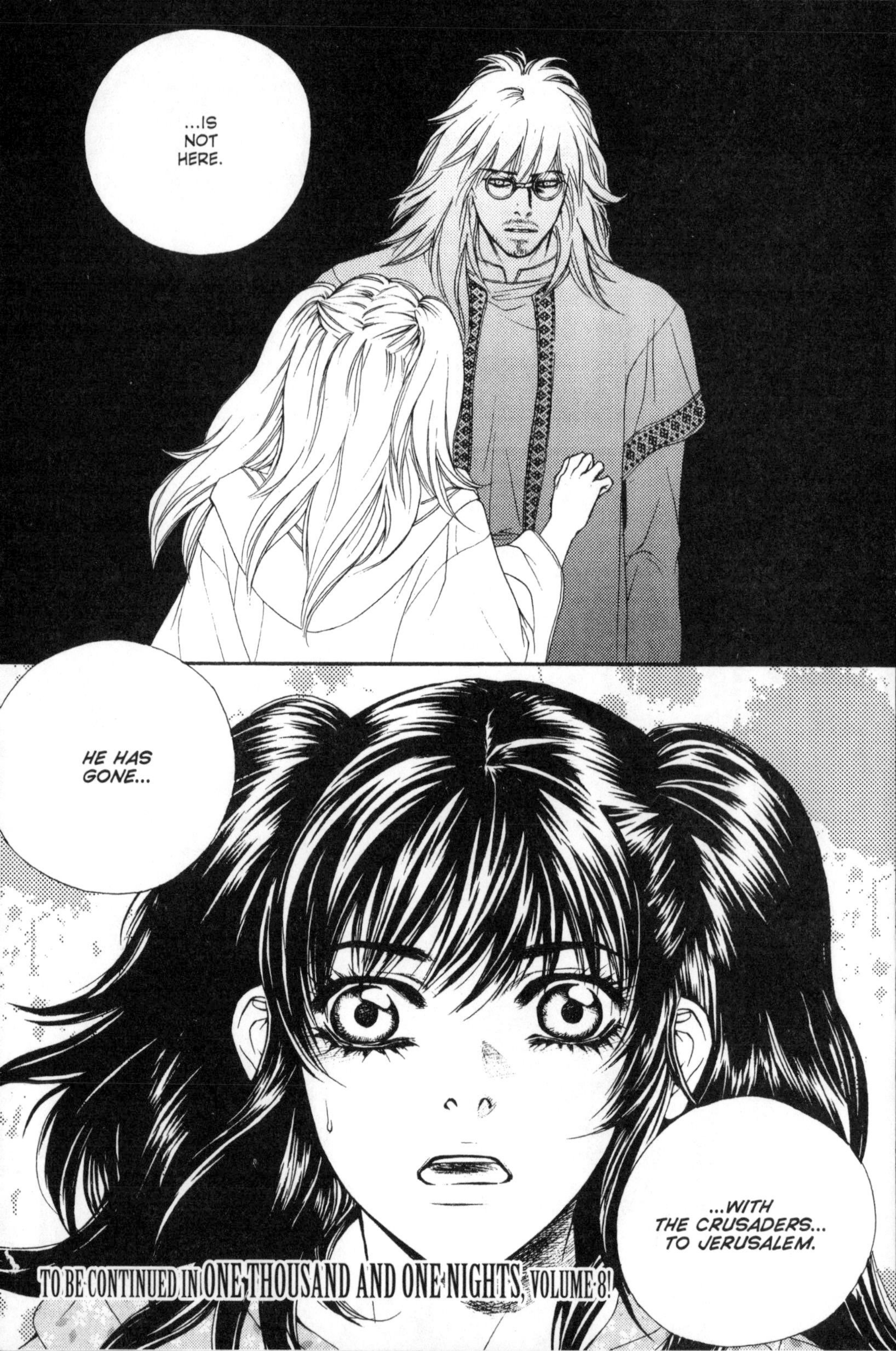
...IS NOT HERE.
HE HAS GONE...
...WITH THE CRUSADERS... TO JERUSALEM.
TO BE CONTINUED IN ONE THOUSAND AND ONE NIGHTS, VOLUME 8!

Special Commentary from the Writer JinSeok Jeon

ONE NO MATTER THE REASON, WAR IS EVIL.

LOOSE CHANGE IS ONE OF THOSE 9/11 CONSPIRACY MOVIES THAT YOU CAN FIND ALL OVER THE INTERNET. HAVE YOU SEEN IT? I DON'T KNOW HOW TRUE THIS DOCUMENTARY IS, BUT THERE HAVE ALWAYS BEEN GREEDY PEOPLE WHO HAVE PROFITED FROM WAR. THEY CREATE A REASON FOR WAR, AND THE REST OF US GO ALONG WITH IT. YOUNG AND INNOCENT LIVES ARE USELESSLY SACRIFICED. AT THE TIME OF MY WRITING THIS, KOREA HAS THE THIRD HIGHEST NUMBER OF SOLDIERS IN IRAQ, AFTER THE U.S. AND ENGLAND. WE'RE PART OF A DIRTY WAR THAT WE HAVE NO REASON TO FIGHT ANYMORE. SOME PEOPLE SAY IT'S TO THANK AND REPAY THE U.S. FOR THEIR HELP IN THE KOREAN WAR; OTHERS SAY IT'S FOR KOREA'S OWN BENEFIT. IT TOOK A THOUSAND YEARS FOR THE VATICAN TO APOLOGIZE FOR THE CRUSADES. WHEN BUSH STARTED THE WAR IN IRAQ, HE CALLED IT "THE WAR OF THE CRUSADERS."

THERE IS A GOD WHO CREATED HUMANS AND THEIR WORLD, BUT THERE DOESN'T SEEM TO BE A GOD WHO CAN STOP WARS . . . BUT I DO HOPE THERE'S A HELL WHERE SINNERS WHO DO AWFUL THINGS WITHOUT REGRET CAN END UP. I ALSO HOPE THERE EXISTS A HEAVEN FOR THE INNOCENT WHO DIE WRONGFULLY.

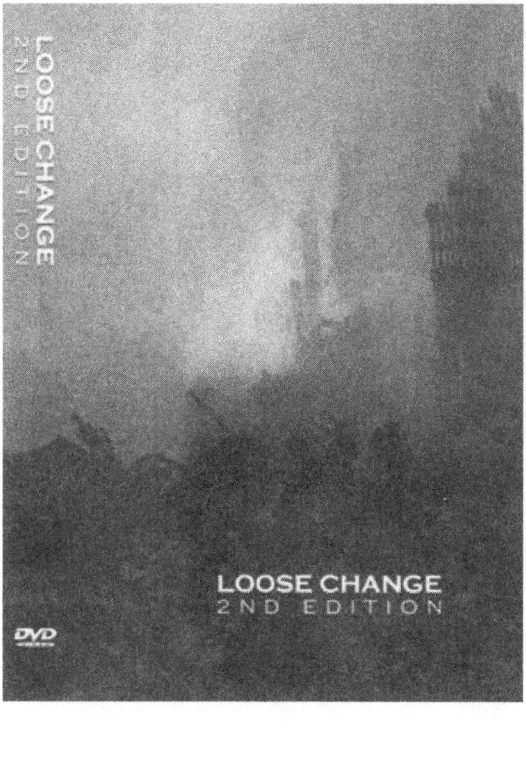

LOOSE CHANGE
2ND EDITION
LOOSE CHANGE
2ND EDITION
DVD

TWO WHILE WATCHING BOMBINGS . . .

MOST HISTORY BOOKS WILL TELL YOU THAT "THE PAST IS THE ROOT OF THE PRESENT." WE WON'T MAKE THE SAME STUPID MISTAKES IF WE LEARN FROM THE PAST. YET THE WAR IN IRAQ IS JUST LIKE THE WAR FOUGHT BY THE CRUSADERS, AND ISRAEL HAS KILLED MANY PEOPLE IN LEBANON, AS IF THEY LEARNED NOTHING FROM THE CRUSADES AND WORLD WAR II. I THINK I HEAR HITLER IN HELL SAYING, "I TOLD YOU SO." IF I WATCH *SCHINDLER'S LIST* AGAIN, MAYBE I'LL FEEL DIFFERENT THIS TIME.

- ★ MY HEAD FEELS HEAVIER THAN USUAL WHEN I TAKE A SHOWER.
- ★ SOMEONE CALLS MY NAME IN A LOW VOICE AS I'M ABOUT TO FALL ASLEEP.
- ★ WHILE WE SIT AT THE DINING ROOM TABLE, THINGS FALL FROM A SHELF ON THEIR OWN.
- ★ STRAWBERRY ( ) MAKES A HISSING SOUND AT THE SHADOWS IN THE BATHROOM.
- ★ NABI ( ) STARES OUT THE WINDOW BEHIND ME AS I'M SITTING ON THE TOILET.

...WHEN THESE THINGS HAPPEN...

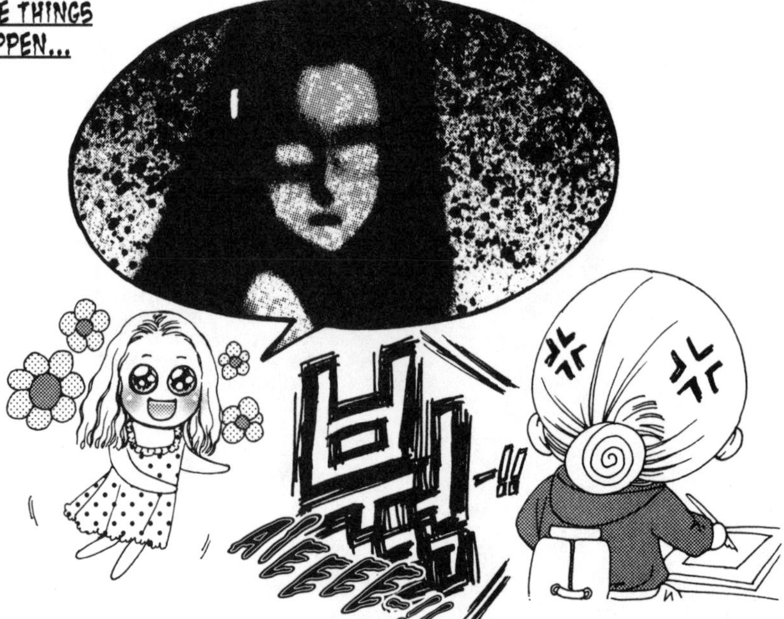
AIEEEEE!!

...KYUNG-SUN TRIES TO GET ME TO WATCH A HORROR MOVIE WITH HER. --^

One thousand
and one nights

www.yenpress.com

Becoming the princess... Isn't that every girl's dream?!

Monarchy rule ended long ago in Korea, but there are still other countries with kings, queens, princes and princesses. What if Korea had continued monarchism? What if all the beautiful palaces, which are now only historical relics, were actually filled with people? What if the glamorous royal family still maintained the palace customs? Welcome to a world where Korea still has the royal family living in their everyday lives! Only for this one high school girl, Chae-Kyung, is this a tragedy, since she has to marry the prince — who apparently is a total bastard!

THE ROYAL PALACE
Goong
vol.1~3

Park SoHee

One Thousand and One Nights vol. 7

Story by JinSeok Jeon
Art by SeungHee Han

Translation: HyeYoung Im
English Adaptation: J. Torres
Lettering: Terri Delgado

One Thousand and One Nights, Vol. 7 © 2006 SeungHee Han · JinSeok Jeon. All rights reserved.
First published in Korea in 2006 by Seoul Cultural Publishers, Inc. English translation rights arranged
by Seoul Cultural Publishers, Inc.

English translation © 2009 Hachette Book Group, Inc.

Yen Press
Hachette Book Group
237 Park Avenue, New York, NY 10017

Visit our Web sites at www.HachetteBookGroup.com and www.YenPress.com.

Yen Press is an imprint of Hachette Book Group, Inc. The Yen Press name and logo are trademarks
of Hachette Book Group, Inc.

First Yen Press Edition: April 2009

ISBN: 978-0-7595-3125-3

10 9 8 7 6 5 4 3 2 1

BVG

Printed in the United States of America